Shades of Black

RICHARD SIKLOS

Shades of Black

Conrad Black and the
World's Fastest Growing Press Empire

First published in Canada
by REED BOOKS CANADA
204 Richmond Street West, Suite 300
Toronto, Ontario M5V 1V6

Canadian Cataloguing in Publication Data

Siklos, Richard, 1965-
      Shades of Black: Conrad Black and the world's
fastest growing press empire

Includes index.
ISBN 0-433-39749-7

1. Black, Conrad.   2. Newspaper publishing –
Canada – Biography.   3. Newspaper publishing –
Biography.   4. Capitalists and financiers –
Canada – Biography.   I. Title.

PN4913.B53S45 1995   070.5'092   C95-932106-3

Printed and bound in Canada
by Tri-Graphic Printing (Ottawa) Limited

For my parents

'I sometimes think of what future historians will say of us. A single sentence will suffice for modern man: He fornicated and read the papers'

Albert Camus

Contents

Introduction

In autumn 1992, I telephoned Conrad Black's office at the *Daily Telegraph* in London. He was unavailable, so I left a message that I was contemplating writing a book about him, and wished to speak to him about it. As media reporter for the *Financial Post* in Toronto, I had been covering the affairs of Hollinger, Black's Canada-based newspaper company, and had interviewed him several times, but did not know him well.

Black's assistant called back with a polite but negative message. Black was not interested in a biography at that time. I followed up with a letter explaining to Black that what interested me was that he had only entered the newspaper business in a meaningful way seven years earlier, and I felt this was a story worth telling. As he had recently acquired control of John Fairfax, Australia's premier newspaper group, and was in the midst of bidding on New York's *Daily News*, I thought the time was right for a biography that focused on his globe-trotting newspaper deals.

I noted that anything I began at that time would not appear in print for two or three years, and that I expected, judging by what Black had been up to in recent months, that there would be much more to add by publication. (Sure enough, the next month Hollinger acquired the largest stake in Southam, Canada's counterpart to Fairfax.)

My purpose in writing to him in advance was to see if I could maintain at least the amount of access I had as a reporter, and to gauge whether Black would attempt to prevent me from talking to his friends and associates.

Black wrote back saying that if I decided to go ahead, he would agree to 'revisit the idea' of speaking to me for the book. My resolve to go ahead hardened over the next few months and I made an appointment to meet him at his Toronto headquarters late on the humid Friday afternoon of 18 June 1993.

A half-hour late (I soon found that many anecdotes about meeting him begin with this qualifier) Black strode into the small library across the hall from his office. While I attempted to stop myself sinking into a soft yellow couch, he sat in an armchair like a statesman: upright, tie straight, suit buttoned up, hands on knees, as if an official portrait were about to be taken. As we chatted about Fairfax, he told me that he had planned to attend the Australian company's board meeting the following week, but his annual black-tie fête for the good and the great, the Hollinger Dinner, was taking place in Toronto the day after the board meeting, with the President of Israel as the featured speaker. With apparent satisfaction, Black explained that because of the time difference he would attend the Fairfax board meeting by telephone while simultaneously watching, from his private box, a Toronto Blue Jays' baseball game against the New York Yankees.

By this time, Black had already decided 'by a hair's breadth' that he would publish his own autobiography that autumn, which he later said was partly motivated by the fact that others were planning books on him. In addition to my book, author Peter Newman had announced plans to update his 1982 biography which he deferred when Black published his book.

Black told me he would talk to me for my book, but first he aimed to set the record straight with his own. At times over the next few months it was admittedly odd to be researching a book on a man who was in the midst of publishing a memoir, but ultimately Black's tome, *A Life in Progress*, represented one of the hundreds of sources for this book. (I also recalled that a couple of years earlier an American journalist had written a book about the making of a film based on a book – Tom Wolfe's *Bonfire of the Vanities* – so, by comparison, my task was not unusual.) Moreover, I came to regard the publication of Black's memoir as a key episode in the personal transformation that occurred alongside his corporate reinvention.

During our first meeting, Black asked if I harboured any sort of agenda in writing my book. I did not. He asked if this was to be a 'business book', which it was. I explained that I was seeking to write an objective, dispassionate chronicle of his life, focusing on his career since taking over the *Daily Telegraph* in 1985, which I also believed to be a story of incredible change in the global newspaper industry. My role, as I saw it, was to draw on as many people and sources as possible to recreate events accurately, then to let the reader draw his or her own conclusions. 'You are the author,' Black said, perhaps finding my approach a bit idealistic. 'The book can be whatever you want it to be.'

In a sense, he was right. Every journalist strives to walk the invisible line of objectivity, but along the way countless decisions are made to gauge the prominence of events, the veracity of individual accounts, and which elements best satisfy the narrative. For this, the author takes full responsibility.

Black said he would not impede my access to anyone, and he didn't. He also never asked to see, nor was shown, prior to publication, any of what I had written. We spoke on fifteen or twenty occasions during the course of the next two years, usually on the telephone. Sometimes, he would return my call in the spare half-hour he would have while travelling in the back of his car from his office in Canary Wharf. My access to him did not extend to visiting him at home – something he has steadfastly refused all journalists over the past decade – because he believes that to allow a journalist into his home would be to appear to invite the public's attention. One preconception I had before I began this book was that for Black dealing with the media is a game. Another is that he usually wins.

'Conrad became for a while in Canada the plaything of the media, and he suffered from it,' his friend Peter White explained to me. 'What you learn from that is that you can, in effect, play with the media, and that's what he does. He toys with the media for his own purposes. He likes to say something that's shocking or titillating or whatever it might be and is bound to get him ink, and he knows that. He knows exactly what to say and what will be quoted. I think there's an argument to be made that the mere fact of being a public personality the way he is benefits his business career. And you can't do that if you're not controversial. I mean, nobody's interested in a benign, boring person. So he constantly keeps himself in the headlines when he feels that it's useful to him.'

With that in mind, one thing I attempted to do throughout the book was to strip away some of the myths about Black that had, in Canada and to a lesser degree in England and Australia, shaped him into a larger-than-life caricature. I did find, however, that even to those closest to Black, he can at times seem like a fictional character, a man whose greatest creation may be himself.

Black's remarkable relationship with the media is at the heart of this story. On any given day, he can turn up in the pages of one of his or his competitors' newspapers as the subject of an article in the business or social pages – perhaps about him suing a newspaper or writer for defamation or criticising the press generally – or he might be found as the author of an article in the comment or book review pages, or, quirkily, of a letter to the editor of one of his own publications. He even recently warranted front page coverage in the the *Globe and Mail* in Toronto for making the London *Sunday Times*'s list of Britain's 500 wealthiest people. The message: Conrad Black not only buys newspapers, he sells them.

'The history of the newspaper industry can be told only through the personalities who made it,' wrote Charles Wintour in the preface to *The Rise and Fall of Fleet Street*. This book was pursued in that spirit. If Black were not a controversial and outspoken figure, and if the newspaper business were not one which exists at the core of every nation, he would be just another wealthy financier. (He ranked sixty-eighth on the *Sunday Times* survey). His business dealings are complex chess games, usually multi-layered, rarely without conflict. As money manager and Telegraph director Stephen Jarislowsky puts it, 'I think he has a Byzantine side to him. His brain functions in a different fashion; and I guess that's in the genes.'

The way press proprietors wield power and gather influence has been the subject of fascinated debate since Gutenberg. Although such power may not be as great as is widely perceived, or exercised in ways that are more subtle than critics would believe, it does exist. The debate over the power of those who control the printed word is compounded today by the gnawing commercial question of whether buying and running newspapers is a game destined to be lost in the dawning digital age. The fact that Hollinger has so far stuck to the printed word makes it somewhat of an anachronism – much like Black, who retains an orotund, sesquipedalian manner in the era of the sound bite.

Conrad Black's irascible nature, talent for financial wizardry, and intellect combine to make him a potent player in the global newspaper realm. And he has been at it for only a decade. It was my aim that an examination of his fevered quest to assemble one of the world's top newspaper groups would also serve as a study of the media as it approaches the new millennium.

Prologue: War

'It was an orgy of self-righteous English
hypocrisy.'

It was nine months since the first salvo had been discharged, and the
situation was tense. Despite Conrad Black's public dismissiveness, the
impact of the cover price cut at Rupert Murdoch's London *Times* was
making executives at Black's *Daily Telegraph* edgy. Black all but
admitted as much on Thursday 9 June 1994 in the *Vanity Fair* ballroom of Toronto's King Edward Hotel. He was facing his shareholders at the ninth annual meeting of Hollinger Inc., the international
newspaper company which he controls and commands as chairman
and chief executive.

The *Telegraph* is the powerhouse among the more than 500
newspapers in which Hollinger has an interest, and Black warned that
he was prepared to take 'remedial action' – Blackspeak for cutting his
own cover price – against *The Times* if it were called for.

After the meeting, journalists scrummed around the press tycoon,
pressing for more details. 'Are you sticking to your previous claim that
you wouldn't cut your price to match *The Times*'s?' asked Bernard
Simon of the *Financial Times*. 'As of now,' replied Black. 'I never said
we would never do it. But I still don't see any reason to do it . . . I
mean, why cut the price?' In the same breath, Black hedged, 'The fact
is we could do it . . . We'll do it if we have to do it.'

The next day at lunch, between a morning visit to the spa in the
King Edward with his wife and a dentist appointment uptown, Black
met with a coterie of stockbrokers and institutional investors at
Toronto's National Club. In this 'off-the-record' setting, the tall, burly
man who gazes suspiciously from behind heavy eyelids could speak a
little more freely, be even more irreverent than usual.

The price war in England was the most urgent of several tricky tactical situations Black had worked his way into. In Australia, Black held tenuous control of that country's most venerable newspaper chain, John Fairfax, and had recently appeared before a bizarre senate inquiry there into a single word in his recently published autobiography. There were accusations of sleazy dealings between Black and Australian prime minister Paul Keating, and fresh rumours that Kerry Packer, a mogul of massive proportions, had designs on controlling Fairfax. Black, eager to shore up his control of the company and head off Packer or any other potential rival bidder, had enthusiastically met his accusers head on. 'That whole process down there has been, by the standards of any jurisdiction, an absolute farce,' Black growled, adding that charges that he had done anything improper 'collapsed in shards around the ears of the senators'.

The crowd was also curious to hear about Hollinger's investment in Canada's largest newspaper company, Southam Inc., where Black was mixed up with another powerful tycoon, Paul Desmarais. The problems at Southam were straightforward, Black explained. It needed to sell non-essential assets, increase efficiency and improve its products. 'They're simply not very good newspapers.' Relations with Desmarais were good, Black maintained. In fact he, Desmarais and Southam chief executive Bill Ardell had met the previous week to set performance targets for the company. 'The targets that we have set,' Black said ominously, 'are considerably more ambitious than they've seen in that place in a long time.'

Hollinger had also recently made its first major U.S. acquisition – the *Chicago Sun-Times* – and showed no sign of slowing down. How did Black respond to the growing sentiment that newspapers are a sunset business on a road to extinction known as the information highway? 'A load of cobbles! I think it is a very good business, and the more people think *that*, the easier it makes it for us to buy them.'

Black had been doing just that. In 1985, he was a forty-year-old financier with a passion for print and a string of corporate *coups* and controversies behind him in his native Canada. With military precision, and at a dizzying pace, the self-described historian set about acquiring newspapers and the influence that accompanies them.

'Conrad is the master opportunist,' says his friend and long-time business partner Peter White. 'I used to compare him to a spider sitting in the middle of a web and the spider receives messages from all the far-flung corners of the empire as to what is going on and then rushes off to see what is happening.' Black's role, he continued, is to make connections and capitalise on them. 'At any given time, probably including right now, there may be half a dozen potential deals on the horizon which he never talks about. And eventually some of them come to fruition.'

Indeed by 1995 Hollinger's more than 500 titles boasted a combined circulation of more than 4.7 million. Only Murdoch's News Corporation and the Gannett chain were larger – and both had been at the game a lot longer. 'He's a student of history,' says the Canadian publishing billionaire Ken Thomson, who sold *The Times* to Murdoch. 'But he's also a would-be participant in modern history. He likes to get involved in the world.' Now, thanks to Murdoch's price war, everything Black had worked for was under attack while the whole world watched.

In September 1993, Murdoch cut the cover price of *The Times* from 45p to 30p. The plan was simple: lure away readers from Black's *Telegraph*, the largest-selling English-language newspaper in the Western world after the *Wall Street Journal*. During 1993, the *Telegraph* sold just over one million copies a day between Monday and Saturday, at 48p each. Its nearest competitor, the *Guardian* sold about 408,000 copies, and *The Times* sold 389,000.*

Black initially brushed off *The Times*'s price cut as an 'extravagant failure' but its sales increased steadily over time. In the first three months of 1994, the *Telegraph*'s circulation had declined only slightly to 1.02 million but *The Times*'s had climbed to 454,000. As the circulation figures for the month of May became apparent, Black told the brokers at the National Club, 'It looks to me like they may have crossed 500,000.'

In fact, *The Times* had increased its sales by 35,000 since April – its largest monthly rise yet – to reach a new record of 515,000. This still left the *Telegraph* with slightly less than double *The Times*'s circulation, but crossed an important psychological barrier. Newspapers are habits, and *The Times* and *Telegraph* share very similar market

* The struggling *Independent* sold 335,000 and the *Financial Times* sold 289,000.

positioning: both are quality market Conservative broadsheets. It was said that in England when a gentleman turned forty he began to read the *Telegraph*. Clearly, this was a tradition Murdoch aimed to extinguish. Younger readers beginning to develop their newspaper habits would be inclined to go for the cheaper product, and then stick with it. 'The problem is the future,' Black conceded, 'if our chief competitor is steadily gaining from far behind us.'

At first, Black reckoned that the losses which Murdoch compounded by cutting the price of his already money-losing *Times* would force him to abandon his pricing strategy. But Murdoch had carved a career out of making brassy moves, and he was much more than the *Times*; his News Corporation was the largest media enterprise in the world controlled by an individual, with newspapers, television, film, satellite, book publishing, and advertising inserts generating annual revenues of $10 billion.*

The Times's losses looked small compared to the profits Murdoch reaped from his half-interest in BSkyB, the British satellite television service. Black's Hollinger, by contrast, was a $900 million-a-year company, with the *Daily Telegraph* and its sister paper the *Sunday Telegraph* accounting for more than half its revenues and earnings. Their strength was Black's weakness.

Nevertheless, Black's message to the Toronto investment crowd was a positive one. He dismissed the 'deeper pockets' theory that gave Murdoch an edge: So superior was the *Telegraph* franchise and cashflow that even if he matched *The Times*'s price cut, losing millions in circulation revenues, it would remain profitable; the *Daily Telegraph* was a better product – it had been named National Newspaper of the Year in the British Press Awards; plus, Hollinger was in good financial shape, having recently taken its American subsidiary public and sold 12.5 million of its *Telegraph* shares.

At the conclusion of the National Club gathering, in mocking reference to his reputation for suing journalists, Black exhorted the lunchers: 'Anyone who wants to get something off their chest should do it – *even if I sue you for it*.' No one did.

The following Tuesday, 14 June, the *Daily Telegraph* managing

---

* All figures in Canadian dollars unless specified US$, A$ for Australian dollars, or £ for pound sterling.

directors' committee held its weekly meeting at the newspaper's offices in Canary Wharf. The only items on the agenda were the latest Audit Bureau of Circulation and National Readership Survey figures. For the first time in more than four decades, they showed, the *Daily Telegraph*'s circulation had fallen below one million – another key psychological barrier – against *The Times*'s increase to over 500,000. Moreover, for the first time, readership (the amount of people who read the paper as opposed to merely buying it) had declined while *The Times* again showed gains. Black was in New York that day, and spoke by phone separately and at length with deputy managing director Stephen Grabiner, deputy chairman Frank Rogers and vice-chairman Dan Colson, all in London. Each of the executives recommended that the *Telegraph* cut its price. Black also phoned editor-in-chief Max Hastings to see what he thought. He concurred. 'I preferred to see us act from strength, and to achieve strategic surprise, rather than wait until it was widely perceived in the City and the industry that a *Telegraph* price-cut was inevitable,' Hastings recalled. 'The chairman, who is always of a combative disposition, was foremost in arguing that we could not simply remain supine while *The Times* gained ground on us.'

Black jetted home to London the following night, and met his executives over the next two days, then spent the weekend poring over reams of market research. By the next managing directors' committee meeting, on 21 June, Black was confident of his battle plan: 'We should do it and get on with it.'

Having just sold 12.5 million *Telegraph* shares to institutions from Hollinger's holdings, it was not lost on Black that he might face a public relations problem, as cutting the newspaper's price was sure to depress the stock value. But public relations problems had not stopped Black before.

That night, Black went to the Ritz where his glamorous wife Barbara Amiel was co-hosting what was described as the 'high society party of the summer'. One hundred and fifty glitterati, including Princess Diana, had gathered to celebrate Sir James Goldsmith's election to the European parliament and his wife's sixtieth birthday. It was the sort of evening that fuelled observations, like that of Lord Weidenfeld, that the Blacks 'may well prove to be the most dynamic press couple since Henry and Clare Luce of *Time Life* fame'.

Two days later, the *Telegraph* cut its cover price from 48p to 30p. 'Murdoch is a Darwinian,' Black declared. 'He wants survival of the fittest, and that's what he's going to get.'

As he saw it, the cut would cost the *Telegraph* £40 million a year in revenue, £25 million of which could be offset by reductions in marketing and an expected increase in advertising. 'If *The Times* wants to cut again they'll just make fools of themselves,' Black said. 'These papers can't suddenly become free sheets, you know.'

That day, Rupert Murdoch was in New York for a News Corporation board meeting. With very little fanfare, over a dinner, the decision was made to drop *The Times*'s price again the next day – to 20p. The result was pandemonium.

'I suppose it's really the new world being brought in to destroy the old,' said Lord Deedes, the former editor of the *Daily Telegraph*. 'I don't think this is going to do anybody any good. At the moment I really don't see how it can end. It's a game nobody can win, really. I think it's a pity to get newspapers into the detergent bracket.'

'What we are witnessing,' *Independent* editor Andreas Whittam Smith proclaimed, 'is a return to the industry's ugly past, dominated by proprietors inebriated with the power that newspaper ownership is thought to bring.'

On the London stock exchange, *Telegraph* shares plummeted from 540p to 349p. Institutions that had bought Hollinger's *Telegraph* shares at 587p on 19 May were, as expected, furious.* The broker that had handled the sale, Cazenove & Co., one of the City's blue-chip and most secretive firms, resigned from the *Telegraph* account a week later. It made the banner story in the *Financial Times*, and included an unnamed 'senior Cazenove official' saying it was 'the first time in recent memory that Cazenove had voluntarily resigned as stock-broker to a company'.

Black was enraged. 'It was an orgy of self-righteous English hypocrisy,' he later recalled. 'I mean, the fact is, I naturally had them [Cazenove] in and consulted with them the day before we cut the cover price. They didn't offer a word of dissent. You know, it's a bit rich for them to carry on the way they did. I don't think they did

---

* One attendee at the National Club earlier that month had asked Black if he sold at 587p because he did not expect the shares to increase further. Black replied that he thought 'around £6.00 was a reasonably full price'.

themselves any favours in this thing. I gave them a pretty good shot on the way out which they richly deserved.' The 'shot' Black gave was to tell the *Financial Times* that the *Telegraph* had in fact been planning to fire Cazenove, because it had mishandled the 19 May share sale in the first place. 'This famous firm just scuttled out the back door into the tall grass,' sniffed Black.

A London Stock Exchange investigation into the timing of the share sale cleared Black of any impropriety. Nonetheless analysts who followed *Telegraph* stock now declared Black would never be able to raise money in the City again. 'The credibility of the management is somewhat suspect and their reputation has been severely damaged in the eyes of the City,' said Richard Peirson, investment director at Framlington Group plc, a small but long-time *Telegraph* shareholder. Newspaper broker Hylton Philipson of Pall Mall Ltd put it more plainly: 'He has pissed off the Establishment on this one.'

The next thing Black knew, Rupert Murdoch had opened a new vein in his battle with the *Telegraph*. News Corporation bought a small stake in John Fairfax in Australia, despite the fact that News is Fairfax's chief competitor. Was it a nuisance move or was Murdoch up to something? Black's mood was sombre but stern. 'You can't make war and peace at the same time, you can't suck and blow at the same time. If you're going to regret an escalation of hostilities by an adversary who has already declared war on you, you might as well have flown up the white flag in the first place.'

Under siege, under scrutiny, unrepentant: Black had been here before. His meteoric career was defined by conflict and controversy. But rarely had so much been on the line.

To trace the path that had brought Black here, one might go within the walls of 10 Toronto Street, the former Toronto post office built in 1853 that serves as the centre of Hollinger's worldwide operations.

Walk past the grey-jacketed security men who spend their days wedged between two sets of double doors, receiving and distributing packages to couriers; pad across the elegant green and gold carpet, ignoring the nineteenth-century French paintings of the Barbizon School that hang on soothing pale yellow walls; pass the reception desk and its prim occupant and turn right into the ante-room that leads to the boardroom where directors' meetings are conducted. There, a handsome, bespectacled, grey-haired man in suit and tie sits patiently in his study, a chess set in the foreground, as if waiting for the game to begin. The man in the portrait is George Montegu Black Jr. Conrad Black called him Father.

ONE

Early Days

'That young man, judging by the shape of
his skull, is going to have a tremendous
brain' E.P. TAYLOR

Standing nearly six and a half feet tall, George Montegu Black Jr
might have cut an imposing figure to his young son Conrad. But
relations with children were one of the subtle mysteries of life the elder
Black believed he had mastered. 'Small children, dogs, fish, and
insects love me,' he once said. 'I always talk to a child as if he were
grown up, and they appreciate that. First of all, I'm a formidable-
looking creature – I must look to them as a loud voice, although I
always speak softly. I've had success with hundreds of small children
just by remaining calm and still and not making sudden loud noises or
sudden rapid movements.'

An accomplished executive and investor with the mind of a
philosophy professor, George Black could seem variously charming,
imperious, or other-worldly. A voracious reader with a passion for
history and great men, he was a droll raconteur with a grandiloquent
style. 'As Coleridge once observed of the ancient mariner, I have
strange power of speech,' he once said. Betty Black frequently advised
her husband to 'shorten things up' to which George would mutter,
'Well, for God's sake, if you're going to express something, express it.'

Betty Black doted on Conrad and his older brother Montegu. To
friends of the Black children she was a gracious hostess who took pride
in running a proper household, complete with cook, nanny, butler,
and chauffeur. Toronto, the city where the Blacks lived, was safe,
clean, predictable and controlled by people very much like themselves.

The picture of George Black as a quintessential brewery executive
of his era is summed up by a 1955 profile in *Saturday Night* magazine:

'He has tried his hand at most sports and games of skill. In his view none can compare in challenge or excitement with big business; none requires more skill or better timing. His work, which is his way of life, has only one major rival – his family: his wife, his young sons, Montegu and Conrad, and his comfortable home.'

George Black grew up in the prairie city of Winnipeg, where he was born on 3 June 1911 to George Montegu Black Sr and Gertrude Maxwell Black. The Blacks hailed from New England and lived in Halifax for a time, where George Anderson Black (George Montegu Sr's father) worked for the Hudson's Bay Company. G. A. Black had a small connection to the world of the press barons, as he was related by marriage to John F. Stairs, the Halifax businessman who gave Maxwell Aitken, later Lord Beaverbrook, one of his first jobs.

Born in 1875 and having moved to Winnipeg as a boy, the first George Montegu was engaged in a number of ventures throughout Western Canada, primarily in real estate and insurance, and was a junior partner of the original Viscount Rothermere, Harold Harmsworth. Black was not at the peak of Winnipeg 'society', but he was an extremely well connected man, garnering lengthy entries in *Who's Who*. A social highlight took place in October 1924, when his daughter Margaret, George Jr's sister, was one of four débutantes presented to the thirty-year-old Prince of Wales at a Friday night ball at the home of Sir Augustus and Lady Nanton. The following afternoon, George Sr was included in a foursome with the prince at the St Charles country club.

As the twenties progressed, many of Black Sr's ventures did not, and his main enterprise became a controlling stake in Western Breweries Ltd, a holding company he created in 1927 to amalgamate four breweries in Saskatchewan and Manitoba and a ginger ale plant. The business suffered during the Depression; Western Breweries stock nosedived from a high of $10.50 in 1930 to $2.50 in 1931, resulting in the suspension of its dividends and a main source of family income. But the family remained sufficiently liquid that George Jr wanted for little and was sent to Appleby College preparatory school in Oakville, near Toronto. This was followed by a short stint at Montreal's McGill University – the brevity due to a bout of double pneumonia which sent him home during his first year. Back in Winnipeg in 1930 he enrolled at the University of Manitoba and fell in love with Elizabeth Jean Riley (a figure-skating champion universally known as Betty), beginning a courtship he later described as lasting 'seven financially lean years'.

Black received a general arts degree from Manitoba in 1933 and his first job was with the accounting firm of Millar, Macdonald and Co., where he worked by day while attending lectures and studying for his chartered accountancy certificate by night. In 1937, his efforts began to pay off: he earned his accountant's degree, joined the family brewery as controller, and married his sweetheart in an Anglican ceremony.

The family George Black Jr married into was among Winnipeg's most prominent, possessing the stalwart, rock-solid airs of its main business, life insurance. Betty Riley's father, Conrad Stephenson Riley, traced his roots to Beverly, Yorkshire. Her great-grandfather, Thomas Riley, moved to London in the early 1850s where, with his father-in-law, he is said to have purchased a 'fractional interest' in a newly launched newspaper, the *Daily Telegraph and Courier*.

In turn-of-the-century Canada, Winnipeg, where George Black and Conrad Riley eventually settled, was going through boom times. After the completion of the Canadian Pacific Railway in 1886, and until the opening of the Panama Canal in 1914, Winnipeg was the undisputed gateway for commerce to the unexploited Canadian West. It became the biggest grain centre on the continent, and from a population of about 14,000 in 1883, when Conrad Riley arrived in Winnipeg, the city swelled to more than 165,000 by 1912.

The Riley's found their fortune in the burgeoning field of insurance. In 1895, Conrad's father Robert Riley set up the Canadian Fire Insurance Company, which he followed with Canadian Indemnity Company and Northern Trusts Company. As a young man, Conrad Riley possessed considerable athletic prowess, and his feats as a rowing champion later earned him induction to the Canadian Sports Hall of Fame. At the apex of his career, his blue-chip directorships included Royal Bank of Canada, Winnipeg Electric Company, Beaver Lumber Company, Great-West Life, and Montreal Trust. In the 1940s, a magazine profile described Riley as one of the fifty men in control of Canada's finances, which he dismissed as 'a big untrue'.

George Black Jr was grateful that during his protracted courtship of

Betty, his future father-in-law 'bore my callow unsophistication with benign indulgence'. A future in the family brewery and a stable life with Betty in one of the fine homes of Armstrong Point seemed pre-ordained for George until 1940, when Black decided to join the war effort. His first thought was to enlist in the army, but he was rejected because of failing eyesight. 'After all,' he said later, 'there's no point in having a great big tall blind man standing in a trench looking like an idiot.' The Royal Canadian Air Force, being in need of accountants as well as aces, was more welcoming. On Dominion Day, 1 July 1940, George kissed Betty goodbye and climbed aboard a Trans-Canada Airlines flight from Winnipeg to Ottawa, with orders to report to Air Force headquarters. There, he was seconded to the office of the Deputy Minister of National Defence for Air, James Duncan, who wanted him to assist in launching the British Commonwealth Air Training Plan. To avoid the discomfort of a low-ranking officer advising senior commanders, Black was removed from duty and placed in a civilian role. Displaying an air of superiority that runs through the Black line, he later described the men he served as 'a hopeless bunch of ghouls. They were totally incapable of handling anything without some assistance.'

In December 1940, Black was invited by James Duncan to an informal dinner at Ottawa's Château Laurier hotel where the guest of honour was a renowned industrialist, Edward Plunket (E. P.) Taylor. Taylor served as the civilian right hand of the minister of munitions, C. D. Howe, and the pair had recently been plucked from cold Atlantic seas after the ship on which they were steaming towards England was torpedoed by the Germans.

Taylor, born in Ottawa, the son of a smalltown banker, had built up and acquired a large swath of businesses, largely in the food and beverage industries. He was the quintessential top-hatted Canadian capitalist of the day, a cigar-chomping beer baron and race-horse owner of larger-than-life proportions. Black was impressed by this man ten years his senior who seemed the fount of an endless stream of ideas. Likewise, Taylor, who had started his empire with a small brewery owned by his grandfather, made a mental note to keep an eye on Black.

Several months later, once the training programme was off the ground, Black was recruited to help set up an aircraft propeller manufacturing operation, Canadian Propellers Ltd, in Montreal. Not long after the birth of the Blacks' first child, George Montegu III on 6 August 1940, Betty and the baby joined him in Montreal. By the war's end, Canadian Propellers had built and shipped 12,500 propellers; rising to executive vice-president, Black had directed the operations of 800 workers. When the company was wound up in the summer of 1945, it had accumulated a surplus of $5,000, which was donated to the Mechanical Engineering department at nearby McGill University. 'So if anybody says that I was a war profiteer,' Black later commented, 'they're goddamned liars.'

One day in July 1944, the industrialist E. P. Taylor was in Montreal and rang George Black, inviting him to lunch. Black had not heard from Taylor for some time, and said he would be delighted to meet him. As Black's office was far from the centre of town he arranged for Taylor to dine at the Black home on Cedar Avenue. Black's instructions to Betty, who was pregnant with their second child: 'Hold onto your hat, buy some steaks!'

After dinner, during drinks on the patio, Taylor eased into the purpose of his call. 'George, this war isn't going to last for ever . . .' What were his plans? Black hadn't really thought it through, but answered that he expected to return to the family brewing business. Taylor agreed that he should go into the brewing business, but not back in Winnipeg: 'I think you should come to Toronto and work with me.' Black later described it as a 'real bombshell' and explained that his father was counting on his return. Taylor suggested he and Betty come to Toronto for a weekend and 'look at what I've got and we'll talk about it'.

Conrad Moffat Black* was born a few weeks later on 25 August 1944, the day Paris was liberated from the Nazis. His upbringing in Montreal would be brief, due to the weekend visit to Toronto made by George and Betty in November which culminated in a job offer from Taylor in their suite at the Royal York Hotel. Nearly a year later Black reported to work at Taylor's Canadian Breweries Ltd in Toronto, as executive assistant to the president, Clive Betts, at a salary of $15,000 a year. Yet from early on it was clear that George Black's ambitions extended beyond being a mere salary man.

* The middle name, Moffat, was his paternal grandmother's maiden name.

In autumn 1945 Taylor was a driving force among a group of industrialists who decided to pool resources and create a closed-end investment holding company. Modelled after a U.S. company called Atlas Corp. (which itself took a substantial initial stake), Taylor and his cronies called their venture Argus, taking the name from the all-seeing hero of Greek mythology, reputed to have one hundred eyes. The philosophy behind Argus was that a small but dominant shareholding in a company, represented by a forceful presence on the board of directors, could have a controlling influence – particularly if that director were Taylor or, in later years, his crafty partner Bud McDougald. While many businessmen were hunkering down for another bust after the lean years of the Second World War and the Great Depression before it, Taylor and company correctly reckoned it was the dawn of an era of prosperity and growth.

The Argus plan was to acquire significant shareholdings in a small number of operating companies without controlling shareholders. Initially, five corporations, including CBL, Massey Harris Co., and Dominion Stores Ltd, accounted for nearly eighty per cent of its approximately $13.5 million of assets.

Though the extent of his holdings would not come to light until three decades later, George Black was one of Argus's original shareholders, and he continued to buy in over the years. He joined the board in 1951, and never sold his Argus shares. He later explained that he was impressed by the 'quadrumvirate' who ruled Argus: Taylor, Lt-Col Eric Phillips, Wallace McCutcheon and Bud McDougald – all business icons of their day.

From the moment he set foot in Canadian Breweries' executive offices at O'Keefe House in Toronto on 1 October 1945, Black was caught up in Taylor's expansionist plans. As a brewing executive, Black displayed an aptitude for administration and a disdain for unions. As far as the product went, he preferred spirits to beer. 'He thought of himself as an organisation man, and he felt if a company had a good organisation chart, then it should work,' says one of his contemporaries. ' "There should be a policy of delegation down the lines of the organisation chart" – and that was it. Well, delegation was fine, but you've got have competent people to delegate to.'

Black's star rose quickly when he was assigned to head a turnaround of CBL's flagging Cleveland subsidiary, Brewing Corporation of America, later to be renamed Carling Brewing Co. The company had recently moved from bottle-washing equipment to non-returnable bottles, which, along with the new cartons that carried them, were defective. 'God, there was beer and blood and broken glass all over thousands of stores,' Black recalled. 'So naturally it was a first-rate disaster. It was an imperial military fuck up, like the charge of the Light Brigade.'

By the time Black became president of Carling, new bottle-washing machines had been bought, but sales had faltered badly; the company was losing some $300,000 a month. Black fired staff to get costs in line and started building up the business again. 'I've fired so many people in my life that it's sort of an art,' Black later boasted. 'I can do it without bitterness.' Carling returned to profitability and in January 1950, six months shy of his thirty-ninth birthday, Black was named president of Canadian Breweries.

One of his next challenges was to deal with a hotel keepers' boycott, that autumn, against O'Keefe, CBL's largest unit. Black believed his arch-rival John Labatt was behind the boycott, which was a protest against price increases and was costing CBL about ten per cent of its business. 'Since I was dealing with Machiavellian opponents, I felt obliged to adopt Machiavellian tactics,' Black later recalled. Through his own intelligence network, Black knew Labatt's was going to decrease the price of its beer on the first Saturday in November by twenty-five cents per keg. He summoned his executive vice-presidents to a meeting that Saturday at nine a.m. Black's view was that if there was going to be a price war, he was going to lead it. CBL, he announced, was sending out telegrams to 2,200 hotel keepers in Ontario announcing a fifty cent decrease in its keg prices. An hour later, Labatt's telegrams went out, announcing the twenty-five cent decrease, as anticipated. The perturbed hotel owners went back to buying CBL products.

Just prior to Black's appointment as CBL's president, another of Taylor's brewing subsidiaries, Brewers and Distillers of Vancouver Ltd, offered to buy out the shareholders of Western Breweries. George Black Sr, its president and controlling shareholder, recommended that, at $31.50 per share, or a total of $8.5 million, the 600 shareholders accept.

Western Breweries was integrated into CBL in early 1950. It was one of numerous breweries Taylor would collect in Canada, the U.S. and Britain in his quest to command the world's largest brewery (and an unrealised ambition to pick up a peerage). Each year between 1946 and 1950, the company met its target of twenty-five per cent growth. The rapid expansion naturally took its toll on the CBL organisation, and in 1951 Taylor felt the company ought to be decentralised because 'too many policies and decisions were being made at head office'. Black, the new president charged with the dirty work of carrying out the reorganisation, was never one to rush decisions; he would sometimes sit for long periods at his limed-oak desk, balancing a model propeller from his Montreal days between his fingers while mulling over a situation from every angle. He took several months to formulate a decentralising plan, which was sprung on CBL's fifty top managers in November. 'I am opposed philosophically and every other way to doing complicated things in a large company in a hurry without proper consideration,' he later explained.

Not only did decentralisation work, but it suited Black's personal style. A night person, he would often arrive in the office at mid-morning or later, and rarely spent more than a dozen hours a week there. 'George *was* lazy,' ventures one former CBL executive. 'When he was president of Canadian Breweries he wasn't getting out of the house as fast as he should.' Black took delegation to the extreme and rarely attended meetings of subsidiaries under his command. His own view was that most business could be conducted over the phone and 'I find the phone works just as well at home as at the office'.

(Some aspects of George Black's routine can be seen in Conrad Black. He too is not prone to prolonged exposure to his office, can spend umpteen hours each day on the telephone – particularly in the midst of a deal – and rises late, having often stayed up until the early morning working, socialising or reading.)

George Black's eccentricities extended into his personal life as well. He enjoyed bridge and the odd round of croquet, but had quit golfing on 17 August 1937 after hitting his best round. 'He astounded himself by shooting a sixty-seven, and he thought that that was it, he had solved all the problems of golf,' says his friend and former brewery colleague, Ian Dowie. 'And the next time he played, he was in the high eighties – which of course happens to everybody. This convinced George that this was a stupid game, so he wouldn't bother with it again. That was a sort of indication of George's mental process. I did get him to play a couple of times, because I thought it was silly.'

One subject that never failed to animate Black was labour relations. His attitude towards the powerful beer unions was: 'If you can't turn around and snarl at these guys occasionally, they'll kick you to pieces.' Among his top objectives as president was the creation of an alliance with major competitors Molson and Labatt so that if the union struck against one company, they would have to strike against all three. This strategy hinged on the belief that if the breweries stood together, a beer drought·brought on by a strike would turn public sentiment against the unions.

Between 1948 and 1958, Carling sales alone increased 877 per cent to 48.7 million cases, ranking it as the fifth largest brewer in the U.S. By 1958, Carling was selling 6.5 bottles per year of its Black Label, Red Cap and Stag Beers for every person in the U.S. In the years that Black was president of Canadian Breweries, 1950–1959, it became the world's largest and most profitable brewery; it dwarfed U.S. giants Anheuser-Busch and Joseph Schlitz Brewing. CBL's sales during the period more than trebled, growing from $100.4 million to $333.8 million and net profit soared from $4.9 million to $12.4 million.

Despite the unbridled growth, there were strains in the executive suite. Tensions that led to George Black falling out with E. P. Taylor can be traced in part to Black's long-time ambition to force an industry-wide strike against a united coalition of brewers. Black realised his wish in the summer of 1959, when the brewers' union called a strike at all the breweries for seven weeks. Taylor's style was to settle right away, but Black resisted – at a cost to CBL of $100,000 a day. Taylor, in Europe at the time, conveyed his annoyance to Black. On Taylor's return to Toronto, Black argued that the strike cost Molson and Labatt plenty too, and his holding the coalition together eventually led to the unions settling for less than they had originally been offered.

Taylor did not share his protégé's view, possibly since relations between them had grown tepid even before the strike. By early 1958, Black was no longer in sync with Taylor's expansion plans. For his part, Taylor had come to feel that, whatever his personal feelings, Black had been elevated beyond his abilities. In the spring of 1959, several weeks before the strike, Taylor had suggested to Black that he recentralise the company he had decentralised eight years earlier. Black told Taylor that he was 'out of his skull', which did not go over well. On 30 October 1959, Taylor met Black and reiterated his dissatisfaction with the strike and desire to recentralise. 'Well, I did the best I could Eddie,' Black told him.

'I think it is time we had a new president of Canadian Breweries Ltd,' Taylor said.

'Well, that's fine with me, Eddie,' Black replied. 'I think your policy is nuts and I'm not going to have anything to do with it.' He shook Taylor's hand, cleaned out his desk, and never returned to the Canadian Breweries office.

Relations with Taylor remained cordial, but Black harboured some bitterness that over the years Taylor never acknowledged that Black had been right about the direction of CBL. (The company's financial health roller-coastered over the next few years, but the long-term trend was negative, and it was sold in 1968 to cigarette giant Rothmans.) Black later said that before his final exchange with Taylor as CBL's president turned ugly, Taylor had offered him a five-year contract at $150,000 a year – double his then salary – if he would stick around and do as Taylor bade. He also noted he could have swung a better pension if he'd been fired instead of quitting. But it was a matter of some pride to Black that he 'retired' at age forty-eight on his own terms.

Market investments during an era of unfettered post-war economic expansion made him a rich man, and he would never return to executive life again. 'I have all the money I'll ever need, and so have my sons, and so has my wife and so has my sister and so have her children,' he said. 'And I've made it all.'

'Certainly there was a good chance for Conrad to become a total dilettante,' says George Hayhurst, a close friend of George Black's son at grade school. 'There were plenty of guys who had equal privilege and equal access to money who went on to do absolutely nothing.' There was, however, little threat of this happening to the skinny, red-haired rebel. Black's youthful experiences in Toronto, born of material comfort but emotional isolation, were as unconventional as his later exploits on the world stage.

For their first five years in Toronto, the Blacks lived in a home in

Toronto's posh Forest Hill district. In 1951, when Conrad was six, they moved to Park Lane Circle, on what was then the outskirts of the city, but in time became one of Toronto's most exclusive areas, known as the Bridal Path. Part of a large parcel of land called Don Mills, which George Black had invested in with E. P. Taylor, but outside Argus, it was a picturesque estate. On seven and a quarter manicured acres dotted with magnificent willow trees, the home was equipped with large public rooms for entertaining and a swimming pool.

With few other young people on Park Lane Circle, Conrad was often left to his own designs. Frequent companions were his books and his father. Like his older brother Monte before him, Conrad was sent to Upper Canada College from the age of six. He would invite friends, sometimes two or three at a time, out to the Black home for weekend visits.

A favourite activity was playing the nickel slot machine George Black had provided for the playroom. Losing was never a problem since Conrad owned the key and could always open up the back for more change. Hayhurst, who sat beside Black in most classes between the ages of ten and fourteen, spent many weekends out at the Black estate. Recalls Hayhurst: 'Mostly we played with the slot machine, which was a rather fantastic thing to have in those days. Or we'd play this game called Ships and Battleships on his pool table. The red balls would be ships and the coloured balls would be battleships. Conrad was pretty good at that.'

Another preferred pastime was discussing cars, with debates over which of the latest Cadillac or Chrysler models packed the most horsepower. Sometimes they would sneak down to the garage to look at the engines or play with the newfangled automatic windows on the family cars. The centrepiece of the weekend would be Saturday lunch with Conrad and his parents in the cavernous dining hall. Meals were prepared by the cook, Thomas Dair. George Black sat at the end of the table holding forth on a range of subjects. 'His father was a bit distant and sort of looked like the great philosopher,' recalls Hayhurst. 'He sort of pontificated.'

Summers for the Black children were spent at the Riley summer compound in Kenora, Ontario. There were also winter trips to Nassau, where George Black was a member of the exclusive Porcupine Club. There, the Blacks rubbed shoulders with American dynasties such as the Mellons and the du Ponts. George Black believed in proper manners and 'putting his sons in the picture at an early age' – it was something his own father had done for him. 'I don't think it does any harm,' he once explained. 'And, furthermore, when you grow up, in later years, you can sometimes astound people by saying, "Well, of course, I once shook hands with His Royal Highness the Prince of Wales, in 1919". I did too. I was only eight years old, but I remember.'

George Black's fascination with the good and the great was not unappreciated by Conrad, who, according to a close friend, vowed early on that when he was older 'he wasn't just going to talk about people – he was going to know them'.

Conrad Black's parents were often still in bed when he rose for school. Occasionally Betty Black drove her son to school, a few miles away, but more frequently he was chauffeured by Tommy, the family's driver. Conrad was by no means the only child to enjoy limousine transport to UCC, but those few who did were duly noted by the other students.

In keeping with their parents' formality, dinner at the Black home was served at precisely the same time every day. 'To Conrad this was torment,' says another friend from school days, 'because he's notorious for being one of the most unpunctual figures imaginable.'

The brothers were in many respects different. Monte Black was a joiner. Conrad was not. Affable and athletic like many of the Riley cousins, Monte physically resembled his father and adored his mother.* Bookish and cerebral, Conrad shared his namesake grandfather Riley's build for rowing but was awkward and enjoyed sports only as a spectator. The Black boys did share an interest in boats, although Monte's taste ran to the pleasure craft that glided through the cottage-country lakes north of Toronto, Conrad's to the mighty steamships and naval juggernauts that ruled the high seas. The isolation of Park Lane Circle was enhanced by Monte's departure, when Conrad was ten, for boarding school.

Precocious, and left to create his own amusements, Conrad Black's

---

* While Conrad Black seemed to be more influenced by his father, in later life Monte seemed closest to his mother. 'He had an extraordinary affection for his mother,' said Sarah Band, who dated Monte in the early 1980s. 'The house was full of pictures of his mother, pictures of a kind-looking woman.'

capitalist urges stirred early. At age eight, he recalls that he sank his 'accumulated life savings of $60' into a single share of General Motors. 'The Korean War was on, Stalin was still in power, it was the height of the Cold War,' Black recalls. 'To buy a share of General Motors was a wise means of participating in the growth of capitalism, supporting a great institution, and casting one's vote with the side of freedom and enterprise in the worldwide struggle with the red menace which was then generally assumed to be lurking behind every bush and under every bed. It was the equivalent act to the purchase of a Victory Bond ten years before, during the Second World War.'

Black claims to have been 'filled with foreboding a few years later' when General Motors president Frederic Donner announced that the U.S. automobile industry's policy was one of 'planned obsolescence', designed to ensure that the average car would need to be replaced every few years. 'I was young and reasonably credulous,' says Black, 'but I instinctively knew that this was nonsense.'

One popular fragment of Black lore that captures the image of the young capitalist has him washing dollar bills and hanging them on a line to dry outside the Park Lane home. This tale, according to Black's first wife Joanna, was embellished and recounted by one of George Black's former colleagues, Jack Campbell, to the author Peter Newman and has since been repeated worldwide. Black had fallen in some mud and was in fact mainly engaged in the less mythical act of washing change. Campbell, says Joanna Black, 'had come to the house and Conrad was washing these coins. And he told Peter Newman many many years later that he was washing dollar bills. Conrad told me that he was doing "nothing of the sort".'

Black himself chuckles at the recollection. 'I was very young,' he says. 'I think I did actually wash mud off *one* dollar bill. But she's right – it was mainly quarters.'

A similar myth – that he spent much of his boyhood playing with toy soldiers – grew out of a 1980 Canadian Broadcasting Corporation programme that featured footage of an adult Black engaged in a toy soldier battle with his friend Hal Jackman, now lieutenant-governor of Ontario. The perpetuation of this image has always been a source of mild amusement between them. ('That's the only time we've ever played toy soldiers – for that TV show,' says Jackman, who unlike Black actually did collect soldiers. 'But I like military science, as does he; we do know the various positions of Napoleonic battles particularly. Conrad will often draw analogies to something Napoleon did in one of his battles. And that's good copy, but it's absolutely nothing to do with reality.')

Black's own youthful reminiscences include David Brinkley announcing the kills in the aerial dogfights over Korea every night, and rushing 'home early from school to watch the McCarthy hearings on television'. Though rock and roll was the rage, Black's taste ran to recordings of famous political speeches. The only contemporary disc he purchased was Elvis Presley's 'When My Blue Moon Turns to Gold Again'. A prized recording was a copy of Franklin Delano Roosevelt's speech at Madison Square Garden which he would play at loud volume over and over. 'It was an unbelievably great speech by FDR, attacking the rich, and the great rich of the Republican Party,' recalls Black's long-time friend Brian Stewart. 'His father detested FDR, and this recording would play through the house with the crowd cheering. Finally his father said, "I don't want that damn record ever played in this house again!" ' Conrad continued to play it, but behind closed doors, at hushed volume, in the wing that served as his apartment.

Much of Conrad's time was spent in what was intended to be a vast playroom, but as he grew older, became more of a library. Says Stewart: 'At seventeen or eighteen, he had his own library of military encyclopaedias and military books, probably not much less than a thousand books in all. Then he had his father's library on top of that.'

Norman Elder, who lived next door to the Blacks for eleven years and would grow up to be an explorer and author of some renown, would occasionally come over and thumb through *Who's Who* with Conrad, the boys measuring the achievements of people their parents knew. Even for Toronto in the 1950s, this was not most adolescents' idea of a good time.

Two interests which George Black shared with his younger son were chess and Napoleon, with the elder Black lending the younger numerous volumes on the latter. Also in common was a remarkable capacity for retaining facts and figures.

'His father had an outstanding memory, and I think trained Conrad from early childhood to work on it, kind of like a muscle in the brain,' said Stewart. 'His father would read encyclopaedias and remember eighty-five, ninety per cent of them. Pretty astonishing. I used to pepper him with the most obscure trivia questions, like "Who was the world's greatest bullfighter?" And he would agonise and think, and strain his brain and sure enough he'd give the right answer.'

One day, when Conrad was quite young, Taylor came over to the Blacks' house after a trip to North Carolina. Little Conrad turned up and Taylor asked him, 'Where do you think North Carolina comes into the line-up of the states as to population?' Without blinking an eye, Conrad replied, 'Fourteenth.' 'Conrad,' Taylor said, 'if you're right on that, I'll give you a quarter.' Conrad trooped upstairs and shortly returned with a gazetteer (which he had recently been studying), verifying the figure. Taylor later told George Black, 'You know, that young man, judging by the shape of his skull, is going to have a tremendous brain.'

By the age of twelve, Conrad Black's feats of memory reputedly included the length, breadth and armament of every fighting ship on the seas, the length and tonnage of the greatest steamships, leaders of obscure countries, whole cabinets of former Canadian governments, and endless statistics from professional hockey and baseball. 'You always had to be careful what you said to Conrad,' a long-time friend recalled. 'If you have a discussion with him, he's apt to quote back verbatim some foolish remark you made fifteen years ago.'

Conrad Black's long memory is always razor-sharp when it comes to recalling the eight years he spent at Upper Canada College. Culminating in his dramatic expulsion at age fourteen, Black unenthusiastically pursued his studies, nurtured a smouldering distaste for authority and can be said to have earned extra credits in corporal punishment techniques of the 1950s.

His friends attribute his self-described feelings of rebellion to a sense of imprisonment Conrad felt in his childhood. 'I know he rarely, if ever, did any work,' says George Hayhurst. 'In grade nine, he would have certainly been in the bottom ten per cent of the class. He would occasionally do some work in the limousine on the way to class, but I think he felt he didn't have to do any work – and he probably didn't.

'He was a little distant. He didn't come out and scrimmage with us at recess when we played hockey or football, but he was certainly not ostracised by any stretch – nor did he ostracise people.'

Whatever oppression Black felt was institutional, rather than personal. Even at a tender age, he derided his prep masters (from afar) as 'gauleiters'. One day in 1954, Black told his chum John Fraser, who later in life would work for him as editor of *Saturday Night* magazine, 'This place is a concentration camp, but most of the inmates are oblivious to the fact.' The schoolboy had a way of warming to his subject. 'Our pig-stupid colleagues think of this place as the universe. E. P. Taylor could buy up this land and forty more parcels like it without blinking. These jerks that control our lives are pure flotsam.'

In his book *Telling Tales*, Fraser recalls time spent with Black served as a valuable English tutorial – Fraser didn't know what flotsam meant – for even at age ten Black talked with 'big words and strong statements'. Conrad, his friend maintains, 'set himself against the imposed establishment right from the beginning and always resented the power others, like masters or prefects, had over him. In addition, he had a terribly sharp tongue, which is not appreciated in the young.'

Another student recalls Black as the most 'ostentatiously rich' student in his class, once showing off a wallet bulging with $80 – a large sum for the late 1950s. He is remembered as someone who would enquire of his classmates how many servants they had, and one classmate recalled the brusque manner in which Black treated his nanny. Although Black didn't have many friends and was not among the school's leaders, he was likeable, had panache, and his contemptuous tirades were rarely taken at face value. 'I was impressed by him because he was an aggressive, brassy kind of guy,' says one friend from Upper Canada who has not seen Black since. 'He'd act tough and belligerent but he wasn't. It was his adopted mode. He was very much a Machiavellian kind of guy. His favourite book was *Napoleon and his Marshals* and he used to love to read about how they all schemed.' Sometimes Black would defy the school edict that no one was to leave the grounds at lunch by having the limousine wait just beyond the drive, where select classmates would be invited to sit with him and read comic books.

More than three decades after his explusion, Black's venom toward UCC is undiminished – although he admits some of his canings were not undeserved. Nonetheless, in his memoir, *A Life In Progress*, he wrote, 'All those who, by their docility or obsequiousness, legitimised the excesses of the school's penal system, the several sadists and few aggressively fondling homosexuals on the faculty, and the more numerous swaggering boobies who had obviously failed in the real world and retreated to Lilliput where they could maintain their exalted status by constant threat of battery: all gradually produced in me a profound revulsion.'

The result, at age fourteen, was 'a systematic campaign of harassment and clerical sabotage against the regime'. Black's antics began with breaking into an office to remove himself from the school's battalion and alter the files of schoolmates he disliked. He also poached his records from the athletics director as a way of avoiding sports activities.

Then Black's mischiefs took a cataclysmic turn. As grade nine year-end approached, amid the disarray of major building renovations, Black and three accomplices, John Hornbeck, Gerry Hazelton, and Bill Koerner, stole the cache of final exams from the school office. Black then proceeded to offer them for sale on a sliding scale – based on the fact that he already knew how well most of the students in the Upper School were doing in their studies, having previously pinched their academic records. The sale netted $1,400 – 'a lot of money for a fourteen-year-old in 1959,' Black admits.

To some of his contemporaries, the episode seemed more the schemings of someone craving attention and the approbation of his peers than an act of sabotage. One of his co-conspirators in the exam heist dismisses the idea that Black was rebelling. 'I can't imagine anything more ridiculous as a justification,' he says. 'I don't say I know what his motive was.' This person claims his own motive was to get the exam for his own use, and that he was not aware Black was selling them until it was too late. 'Conrad takes the goddamn papers and the only reason it ever came to light is because he's selling the damn things to upper-classmen,' he says. Black's version differs. 'I was not seeking attention,' claims Black. 'What happened was one of my colleagues was a little indiscreet and indicated to one of his classmates that he could help him. And then people started coming to me. I didn't set out to sell these things.'

On 9 June 1959, one of Black's customers was apprehended and ratted on Black. Conrad and his cohort were expelled, but not before George Black had tried to make the case to principal Cedric Sowby that his son was merely showing strong entrepreneurial instincts. The principal announced two days later that all the boys would write new exams. 'Those who had been among the most eager to purchase were suddenly transformed into the Knights of New Jerusalem,' recalls John Fraser. 'Overnight [Conrad] became a pariah and a number of boys even burned him in effigy on his father's front lawn.'

In his memoir, Black apologised to his accomplices in the caper. 'I am neither proud nor ashamed of what happened,' Black wrote. 'It was an awful system whose odiousness was compounded by banality and pretension, but I was becoming somewhat fiendish and in the end inconvenienced hundreds of unoffending people, students and faculty.'

Although the episode is an important piece of Black legend – revealing an early tendency to mischief, rebellion and a flair for the spectacular – Black eschews any psychoanalysis of it. When asked thirty-three years later by an Australian television reporter whether the exam caper was a formative event which fuelled his adult ambitions, Black demurred. 'I was fourteen years old at the time,' he said sternly. 'I suppose the temptation must reside in the mind of a journalist to read some extrapolating significance into it. But I really don't think that the incidents that you refer to have any significance today.'

Black's next academic foray was as a boarder at Trinity College School in Port Hope, where his brother had studied. The disciplinary problems persisted, and his stay lasted less than a year. By this time Conrad Black was a heavy-smoking teenager with few friends and plenty of notoriety. His last chance was Thornton Hall in Toronto – 'a bit of a cram school,' says Brian Stewart, whom he met there – from which Black managed to graduate.

Armed with mediocre grades and a chequered record, Black was accepted at Carleton University in Ottawa where he enrolled in journalism, switching to history after a semester. 'I concluded the courses were more interesting if I took general arts because I was more interested in history and political science than I was in the *techniques* of journalism.'

Being 'not much of a joiner', he moved into a basement flat in the Savoy hotel, some distance from campus. Black quickly established a regimen that included playing cards with various senators and back-benchers who also lived at the hotel, familiarising himself with the taverns across the Ottawa River in Hull, Quebec, and attending sessions of the House of Commons. Studies took a backseat.

'[Prime Minister John] Diefenbaker's government was in a minority position at this point and its status became more tenuous throughout the fall and into the new year, 1963,' Black recalls. 'My progress as a freshman followed a roughly parallel course.'

As he careered towards another educational disaster, his first-year history professor, Naomi Griffiths, sent Black a note telling him, in effect, to get his act together or else. For a change, Black did, and the two struck up a friendship, exemplified by Black's tendency to submit voluminous essays running a considerable length over what was required. 'He's extraordinarily hard working and an extremely shy person,' Griffiths reminisced in 1979. 'He's one of those people who looks warily at others and says: "Well I wonder what category you fit into?" '

From the Savoy, Black moved into a two-bedroom apartment in the Juliana, one of the finer buildings in Ottawa at the time.

One night in his second year, Conrad met a cousin from Montreal, Jeremy Riley, at a Chinese restaurant. There he was introduced to a keen and worldly young parliamentary assistant named Peter White.

Through White was six years older than Black, they struck up a fast friendship based on a shared fascination with things political. Born in Sao Paolo, Brazil, where his Canadian father was Latin American sales manager for Sperry Gyroscope, White grew up in Montreal, but had lived briefly in the south of France and Majorca, and studied for two years in Switzerland. He had graduated from Laval University with a law degree in 1963 (one of his classmates and closer friends was Brian Mulroney, the future prime minister) but had no interest in practising law. Instead, he took a job as special assistant to Maurice Sauve, minister of forestry and rural development in the government of Lester Pearson.

Though he worked for Sauve, a Liberal, White was an active young Progressive Conservative. Black was a Liberal who would entertain friends with hilarious imitations of prominent parliamentarians they met, particularly Jack Pickersgill and Paul Martin Sr. 'Paul Martin was very very ponderous and extremely circumlocutory and loquacious and would take five minutes to answer a question and was very careful during those five minutes to say absolutely nothing,' says

White. 'So Conrad got very good at giving a Paul Martin-type answer to a question in the House of Commons.'

Several months after they met, out of his lease and in need of a place to stay for six months, White readily accepted when Black offered his spare bedroom in the Juliana. As a young professional with a job, White couldn't always partake in the after-hours carousing his student room-mate frequently indulged in. Late one night White was rudely awakened when Black and some giggling accomplices entered his room and dumped a door from Conrad's large convertible on his bed. (It turned out one of the passengers had opened the door while Black was backing the car into his underground spot, striking a pillar.)

One nocturnal rite of Black's that caught White's attention in less dramatic fashion was his late-night phone conversations with George Black. By this time George Black had been retired for some five years, and had grown increasingly reclusive. He was occasionally melancholic, but whatever demons afflicted him mentally were amplified by severe cataracts in both his eyes and painful, debilitating arthritis in his legs.

Says White: 'Conrad was the apple of his father's eye. I think he saw the genius in Conrad. George was a recluse at that point in his life, living in that lovely mansion, and he would stay up till three or four in the morning. What he loved to do most of all was watch the Marx Brothers, or W. C. Fields movies, things like that, on late late TV with some very stiff drink beside him the whole evening.

'When finally the television channels all shut down and he'd had his last drink and he couldn't think of anything else to do, he would telephone Conrad. This would happen religiously every night. Conrad had the dilemma: "Do I go to sleep or stay up?" More often than not, he chose the latter.

'The phone would ring at three or four in the morning. They'd talk mainly about the day's events, but a great deal about history also. George would always ask Conrad what he was reading, and what were his professors saying. Roosevelt, De Gaulle, Churchill, Napoleon – they both had very serious interests in a lot of things, sort of a salon-type of conversation. And it would go on for an hour and sometimes two hours.'

Another favourite topic was investment, and White recalls an animated Conrad explaining to him the share structure and interne-cine intrigues of Argus Corporation.

The aimlessness that characterised Black's youth continued through his undergraduate years. From his military, historical and political interests sprang a natural fascination with world affairs, which would be heightened by trips to Europe in the summers of 1963 and 1965. Travelling with his brother in '63, Black met his friend Brian Stewart, who was then starting a career as a cub newspaper reporter in England and Spain. He and Black spent night after night in sidewalk cafés, sipping cognac and drinking coffee, 'discussing the world, where Rommel went wrong in the desert, MacArthur's greatest battles, forever listing the ten greatest this and the ten greatest that'.

Black had never displayed more than a passing interest in the media, save for his flirtation with the journalism faculty. Stewart was surprised one day in Madrid to hear that his companion had added William Randolph Hearst to his roster of heroes.

'He had just read the book *Citizen Hearst*, and it struck me as a very unusual person for Conrad to be fascinated by,' says Stewart. 'He'd go on about Hearst and quote him endlessly. I could never understand what is the interest in this guy; I mean, *a mere publisher?*'

Stewart noticed similar references to Beaverbrook and Northcliffe creeping into his friend's lexicon. During their travels, Black began to do a curious thing. Like most people on the road, most days they would buy a newspaper. But where Stewart's inclination was to peruse the front page or sports pages, Black would turn immediately to the masthead, or comment on the amount of advertising.

Through Peter White, Black and Stewart – at this point a scribe at the Oshawa *Times* – obtained tickets to the 1964 Democratic convention in Atlantic City, to see the coronation of their hero, Lyndon Johnson. 'Conrad clearly had a mystical love of America which is very strong to this day,' says Stewart, going so far as to portray young Black driving to Atlantic City in Kerouac terms. 'Very hard to picture now, but he loved driving, he loved the road, the highway, the movement, the bigness of America.'

On the drive down, they pulled over in Pittsburgh, where the rivers Ohio, Allegheny, and Monongahela converge, and Black waxed about the might of America. The convention did not diminish his adulation. Thirty-five thousand Democrats crammed into the Atlantic City hall. One night there was a birthday party for LBJ and Black stood among the sea of people while fireworks went off and placards waved. He was in his element. Says Stewart, 'Conrad has always been impressed by the impressive – in the sense that he likes political figures to look impressive, be regal, authoritative in appearance. That's why he likes De Gaulle. He likes the grandeur of these figures, and LBJ had it then. People won't believe it now, but he sure had it in 1964.'

Johnson won a decisive victory over Barry Goldwater that autumn, but it was the beginning of the end for the great Democratic machine. Perhaps it was on the drive back to Canada that Black's ideological leanings, rooted in liberalism, began to shift towards the right. He and Stewart had observed the first scattering of anti-Vietnam protesters at the convention, and driving back through Philadelphia they came face to face with the first major race riots of that long hot summer. In the coming liberal years of flower children, free love and radical student protest, Black went in the opposite direction. He was a forthright proponent of the Vietnam War, contemptuous of the anti-war movement.

'Social unrest had become severe in most Western countries by the late 1960s,' says Black. 'By that time, our society, as the ultimate product of tensions between left and right, had subjected itself to the crowning indignity of the so-called counterculture. There were frenzied attacks on supposed bourgeois slavishness, insipid middle-class sex practices, and the routinisation of life. I was amazed at the time – and I spent some years enrolled in universities that saw a good deal of agitation of this sort – at the counterculture's ludicrous combination of nihilism and sentimentality.

'In the fifteen years from 1953, when I bought my share in General Motors, to 1968, with the riot-torn fiasco of the Democratic Party in Chicago, much of society had forgotten the unprecedented achievements of capitalism and of its bourgeois practitioners.'

Black's grandiose ideas did not immediately translate into personal success. In autumn 1964, with his Bachelor's degree from Carleton in hand, Black enrolled at Osgoode Hall Law School in Toronto; he flunked out after one year.

Another trip to Europe in the summer of 1965 was a good way to weigh his diminishing options. Stewart suggested a carefree interlude of living in London for a year, working as a bus conductor, maybe selling ties at Harrods. Black sniffed that he felt he could do better. 'He was really wondering what he would do with his life at that stage,' says Stewart. 'There was a sense of his parents being fed up. In the early '60s, right through to the '70s, there was a sliver of Conrad that was slightly Bohemian. Had he not ended up a rich businessman, he would have ended up a polemicist, or a writer on the Left Bank or something.' White disagrees, and says Black's uncertainty was not the typical student dilemma of what to do with the rest of his life. 'It was more like, "What do I do between now and when my destiny is fulfilled?" '

With few immediate options, Black thought he might move to Quebec, where White was now working. When White heard from his friend, he suggested Black might like to come to rural Quebec to edit a tiny weekly newspaper he owned. It was several hours away by car, but a million miles from the weight of his parents' disappointment. Black accepted, gathered some belongings, and headed off for self-imposed exile in a place called Brome County.

TWO

Coming of Age

'We didn't suddenly sit down one day
and decide we would become media
tycoons'

There were two prominent features on the front page of the 24 November 1966 edition of the *Eastern Townships Advertiser*. One was the article about the tenth anniversary of the Stage House Restaurant, 'an event of great social as well as commercial significance'. The other was the letter to readers about the 'new and promising era' for the *Advertiser* under the direction of Mr C. M. Black.

Among the enthusiastic plans outlined in his letter Peter White, as President of The Eastern Townships Publishing Co. Ltd, announced an impending revamp of the paper's format and a new distribution scheme that would quintuple circulation, taking it to some 2,100 copies. Black had already been penning editorials at the paper for about a month, and White commented that, 'Readers of this and succeeding issues will notice an improvement in the *Advertiser*'s news coverage and literary merit.'

Sixty miles from Montreal, Black's new home, Knowlton, cradled the shore of Brome Lake, a three-by-five-mile holiday watering hole popular with English-speaking Montrealers. During the summer, the populace of Knowlton swelled to about 3,000, double its winter level. White's grandfather had bought a house there in 1920, and Peter spent summers there with his parents. In the late 1950s he purchased the paper and its assets from its founder – a journalism student whose parents had a place in nearby Bondville – for $1.

Black's arrangement with White included another paper White owned in nearby Farnham, the French-language *L'Avenir de Brome-Missisquoi*. With a free circulation of about 15,000, *L'Avenir* was a much larger and more profitable paper than the *Advertiser*. White sold Black his interests in the papers for a percentage of profits, amounting to something under $500.

At the time Black took over the paper, White's mother was living in the house in Knowlton. Black moved into her flimsily insulated shack of a boat house, the former residence of a Catholic priest. It was a long way from Park Lane Circle, and Black would glare enviously across the lake at the manor home of John Bassett, owner of the *Sherbrooke Record*. The Whites' boat house had minimal heating and insulation, and the fierce Quebec winter sometimes induced Black to pry open a window to the main house in the middle of the night in order to sleep.

At the *Advertiser*, Black handled virtually every aspect of the paper: editorial, lay-out, circulation and marketing. He also penned a rather academic column, called 'Commerce', in which he enlightened the rural Quebec readership with *Wall Street Journal* detail about investing, industry and financial markets.

Friends would occasionally help him out. Once, Black ran a page from the telephone book instead of an editorial (with little complaint from readers). Filling in as editor one week, Brian Stewart remembers scribbling out a barely legible cartoon to fill a last-minute hole.

The only other employee at the *Advertiser*, two days a week, was managing editor Maureen Johnston-Main. She recalls Conrad Black as a lone and somewhat incongruous figure in what he later described as a 'bucolic redoubt'.

'He was a young kid who drove too quickly,' Johnston-Main recalls. 'He could be quite friendly, but most of the time he was quite serious. He seemed to look down his nose at folks around here.'

Black made the job interesting by waging war on the local town council through heavily worded editorials, and by enmeshing himself in the political machinery of the region. Stewart noticed that, in his new capacity as publisher, Black had acquired the tendency endlessly to poll strangers for their opinions. He'd ask the barber whether MacArthur should have stopped at the thirtieth parallel. The petrol pump attendant was queried about the Diefenbaker legacy. 'Conrad, what the hell do you care what all these people think about all these obscure topics?' Stewart finally asked. 'They all have very reasonable views,' Black replied. 'They don't often put them very well, but their views are important. Their passions are important to know.'

Peter White remembers that Black was equally eager to know

people's impressions of him. Says White, 'He was always very curious and anxious to know what people thought of him. Whenever he met anybody that he looked up to or that he was impressed by, he always wanted to know what they thought of him. He doesn't do that much any more, but he used to do that all the time.'

Generally, says White, the colourful, intelligent young man made a favourable impression. '[Brian] Mulroney always had the same anxiety,' he says. 'I'm not a psychologist but it's a sort of need for appreciation and recognition that I think Conrad and Mulroney and a lot of other people share.'

In 1967, Canada's centenary, great political change was afoot. The Maple Leaf, Canada's new flag, had just been introduced, but nationalist sentiments were countered by growing uneasiness fuelled by a flourishing sovereignty movement in Quebec. The Vietnam War raged. Black immersed himself further in the French experience by enrolling at the French-language university, Laval, in Quebec City. Black was only one of about a dozen anglo students among the 600-member law faculty. His boat-house days behind him, he selected a spacious apartment overlooking the St Lawrence River, forsaking the student ghetto where the rest of the anglo clique lived.

At Laval, despite the extra burden of learning to speak French, Black now excelled at his studies. His chum White ran working at the nearby Quebec parliament as an aide to premier Daniel Johnson, and through him Black became acquainted with the premier and his entourage. Black's closest friends at Laval were Jonathan Birk, scion of the Montreal jewellery retailing family, and Daniel Colson, son of a Montreal police detective. 'We used to regularly have long boozy dinners,' recalls Colson, 'and invariably we'd end up screaming and arguing about something or other, but it was always good-natured. Conrad usually won the argument because he knew more about the historical background of virtually anything than any of us, plus he was that much more articulate than we were. So the odds were stacked.'

'What I do remember vividly,' he continues, 'is that Conrad has always had this great fascination with power. Newspapers – quality newspapers, big newspapers – are obviously closely associated with power and influence. The fact that he ultimately became interested in and involved with newspapers to that extent doesn't surprise me in the least.'

Through Peter White, Black met David Radler, who would complete their newspaper-buying partnership. The son of a New York-born restaurateur, the short, scrappy Radler was born and raised in middle-class post-war Jewish Montreal environs, where fond reminiscences include watching Chuck Connors – who played The Rifleman in the television series – play first base for the Montreal Royals, and hustling subscriptions to *Liberty* magazine in order to further his baseball card collection. Franklin David Radler attended McGill and took his MBA at Queen's in Kingston, Ontario. He was by no means short of confidence and ambition and in his early twenties he worked as a business consultant on Native reserves in Ontario and Northern Quebec, helping residents start businesses ranging from handicraft production to grocery stores. Radler's father ran a French restaurant in Montreal called Au Lutin Qui Bouffe (the elf who gorges himself). Quite apart from the establishment's culinary merits, it featured a concession where customers could have their photos snapped with live piglets. Au Lutin was somewhat of a Union Nationale hangout, and it was at a party function there in 1968 that Radler was introduced to Black by their mutual acquaintance, White. Radler was as blunt and street-wise as Black was erudite and aristocratic. Both were unsentimental and intensely ambitious. It was the beginning of an association that would continue for an eventful quarter-century.

Black's and White's early successes at *L'Avenir* led them to set their sights on bigger game: the nearby *Sherbrooke Record*. Early approaches by White to the *Record*'s long-time owner, John Bassett, were brusquely rebuffed, but by spring 1969 the paper was in a precarious financial state, no longer owned by Bassett, and very much available.

The *Record* had undergone a painful strike and Bassett had become an absentee owner. He sold the *Record* to Ivan Saunders, the newspaper's long-time general manager, essentially allowing him to give the paper a go in return for assumption of debts. Saunders had arranged to buy a new press from Goss, but the paper was rapidly heading towards insolvency. With losses mounting – $180,000 in less than two years – Saunders was more than willing to sell out, again for nothing more than assumption of debts and the payroll. White suggested to Black that they bring in Radler as a partner in the venture, and over lunch one day they worked out the details. The three young men put up $20,000 most of it borrowed from banks. The paper had no assets, save the goodwill of its name and a circulation of about 8,000.

Radler and Black shared a room at Sherbrooke's L'Hermitage hotel the night before they assumed ownership on 1 July. White opted for a cheaper room in a fleabag hotel, the Royal, which was across the street from the *Record* offices at CPR Terrace. The fact that Black had inherited at least $200,000 from his grandparents might have dulled the risk of taking over the paper. But the confidence of being a rich young man was not in evidence as they nervously awaited the dawn of their new venture, says Radler. 'Conrad,' he recalls, 'was crapping in his pants. So was I. Don't get me wrong – I may have been worse.'

When businesses, and newspapers in particular, pass between owners, there are usually two versions of what transpired. Those whose careers were disrupted or terminated by the incoming managers invariably deride the new owners, lamenting the decline in the quality of the product, the demise of tradition and the most intangible journalistic quality of all, 'community service'. Those brought on by the new owners after the house is put in an order to their liking, however, tend to be more sympathetic to their new employers. The *Sherbrooke Record* in the summer of '69 was no exception.

Under the new owners, White was president and Black was publisher, while Radler ran day-to-day operations. White and Black were more or less responsible for editorial matters (although an editor was in charge), while Radler handled advertising, administration and circulation. Black was somewhat of a roving proprietor, always involving himself in key decisions. All three would, at one time or another, sell ads, help design pages, and even deliver papers.

Because they did not buy the new press as part of their deal, one of the first tasks was finding a new printing arrangement. Radler found the best deal with a printer some thirty miles away in Newport, Vermont, which meant that, for a time, the *Record* laid claim to being the only daily newspaper in the world to be printed in another country. The lack of a press notwithstanding, the paper's biggest problem, it was quickly determined, was that its payroll was padded beyond necessity. Former owner Saunders was simply too close to his

long-time employees to put them out of work, but without considerable rationalisation it would not be long before the paper ceased
operation altogether. The new owners merely kept firing people until
they reached the threshold under which it was apparent the paper
would cease to function in decent form. It was a ruthless exercise, and
the staff of forty-eight was soon pared in half.

Crosbie Cotton, now an editor at the *Calgary Herald,* began his
career at the *Record* in the early 1970s by winning his job in a chess
game with Peter White. He describes White and his colleagues as
'great mentors for somebody who was starting out in the business at
that time. The training that they gave to young reporters was
exceptional.' This included everything from reporting to delivering
papers, and being subject to a rather arbitrary variable remuneration
system, under which Black and Radler would take it upon themselves
at each week's end to decide how much money individual reporters
deserved. On the rare occasions when raises were granted, Black
assured the recipient with mock seriousness that pay cuts could just as
easily be imposed – 'downward payroll adjustment' he called it – if
performance tapered.

Cotton recalls that he never saw the upside of the variable
remuneration system. 'One day, I delivered papers in the morning,
covered something in the afternoon, then I covered school board that
night, taking my own pictures. I got back to the office around eleven
o'clock, wrote my stories, developed my pictures, and left there at
three a.m.' The next morning, Cotton was fined $25 – out of a weekly
paycheck of $82 – 'because I missed the North Hatley Ladies
Auxiliary Garden Tour at eight a.m. I'll never forget that.'

Lew Harris, another young reporter, who worked on the *Record* for
two years from 1971, recalls Black as a formal though good-humoured
person seeming far older than his twenty-seven years, but with 'a
certain playfulness' and always keen to discuss baseball. 'They weren't
the original blunt instrument,' he insists, noting that Black preferred
to employ terms like 'phase-in' and 'phase-out' when talking about
getting rid of excess employees. 'At one point, Black said to one of the
reporters, "We're phasing you out, Bernie." I thought that was a
funny choice of words, and sure enough six months later he wasn't
working there.'

Black's legendary vocabulary was already well honed. 'I used to go get a dictionary,' recalls Cotton. 'I'd get three words a day – I would find the most startling words, words that I could not fathom – and I would ask him to define what they meant. He never lost.' Indeed, there were few twenty-seven-year-olds in rural Quebec who could bandy about, as Black did, such terms as 'scutcheon', 'tenebrous', 'dolorous', and 'calumniate'.

Radler, meanwhile, seemed to exist solely on hot dogs while gleefully paring costs wherever he could. Whenever accounts payable came into the newspaper, Radler would methodically write out a cheque, date it, then put both the cheque and the bill in his desk drawer. Then he would wait until the supplier's demand for payment reached near-violent proportions, and calmly produce the cheque. By 1971, the paper was producing annual profits of more than $150,000.

The owners rarely interfered in editorial matters, but one former reporter recalls an intervention by Radler over the *Record*'s coverage of protests by students from the two local universities against the U.S. military testing of atomic bombs underground in Alaska. 'Why aren't these same people complaining when China does nuclear testing?' Radler demanded. The *Record* was one of the few papers to come out noticeably in favour of the testing, in spite of the local protest angle.

A more notorious episode was White's ill-fated candidacy in the 1970 Quebec provincial election. Even though White ran for the Union Nationale in Brome, largely outside the *Record*'s readership area, Radler insisted on prominent coverage of White's bid. The partisanship may not have had the desired effect, but it could hardly be blamed for White's loss – the Union Nationale was soundly defeated by the Liberals throughout the province. Still, the *Record*'s present-day editor, Charles Bury, contends that on account of the episode there are residents of Sherbrooke who to this day refuse to read the paper.

Black played the part of publisher eagerly, dressed in three-piece suits, his Cadillac Eldorado – with rare front-wheel drive – parked prominently in front of the *Record* office. But he also found time to submit the occasional article, most notably the opus that ran on his twenty-fifth birthday, 25 August 1969. 'A year after Chicago: Homage to LBJ' was a page-and-a-half canonisation of Lyndon Baines Johnson, printed seven months after he left office, ostensibly in honour of Johnson's forthcoming sixty-fifth birthday. Under a stern photo of the former president, a caption declared him 'A great man much reviled'. Beyond its sheer length, the invective-laden tirade is notable for the contrariant view Black took. Rather than the contemptible tyrant LBJ's critics portrayed him as in his waning days, Black viewed LBJ as a misunderstood man of compassion and vision. 'A less patient and dedicated man,' Black noted, 'when taunted incessantly with the chant "Hey, hey, LBJ, how many kids have you killed today?" might have been tempted to reply: "None, unfortunately." '

The story was sent to Johnson by the American consul in Montreal, and read into the congressional record by congressman Jake J. Pickle, a crony of Johnson's from Texas who held his old seat in the House of Representatives. Betty Black proudly framed the personal note sent to her son from the former president thanking him for his editorial.

These contacts came in handy the following year when Black decided to travel to Southeast Asia and asked Pickle if he could help him get through official channels in Saigon. On arrival, 'I announced myself to the marine guard in the lobby of the U.S. embassy, and his jaw dropped, he picked up the phone and said, "Mr Black is here." It was like the arrival of Stanley and Livingstone. They had a telegram from Secretary of State William Rogers claiming that I was a friend of LBJ – which was taking considerable liberty with the facts. So they gave me quite a tour. I met everybody who was over there.'

The high point was a hard-to-come-by interview with Vietnamese President Nguyen Van Thieu, arranged by the U.S. embassy in Saigon. The resultant story, which Black wrote that day, was picked up around the world, including in the following day's *New York Times*. Black describes it as 'the highlight of my sporadic career as a journalist' and it was no doubt a major *coup* for the deservedly obscure *Sherbrooke Record*. But there were a few townsfolk, recalls Bury, who looked askance at a gallivanting publisher running exclusives from Vietnam while local coverage declined. Black, White and Radler may have saved the paper and made themselves a small fortune in the process, but Bury – who at the time was editing a local monthly – says it was at the expense of 'less coverage, more wires, and when one of them didn't feel like writing an editorial they ran an editorial from the *Winnipeg Free Press* of all places'.

Whatever criticisms may have been levelled at Black by rivals, only a few months into his ownership of the *Record* his own views of the trade were already well honed. He penned a precocious submission to the Senate Committee on Mass Media headed by Keith Davey, stating, 'My experience with journalists authorises me to record that a very large number of them are ignorant, lazy, opinionated, intellectually dishonest, and inadequately supervised. The so-called "profession" is heavily cluttered with abrasive youngsters who substitute what they call "commitment" for insight, and, to a lesser extent, with aged hacks toiling through a miasma of mounting decrepitude. Alcoholism is endemic in both groups.'

The attack, Black later claimed, was based largely on his observation that English-language journalists disposed towards the separatist cause in Quebec were engaging in 'supercilious partisanship' within such institutions as the Canadian Broadcasting Corporation, *Montreal Star* and Montreal *Gazette*. For the next two decades, the passage would be widely regurgitated as an indictment of Black's suitability as a press owner. In latter years, as his relationship with the media has grown into an ever more complex web, Black has publicly played down the passage, pointing out the limited context for which he says it was intended. 'Of course, the personal lives of journalists were never any of my business,' he says, 'and when I wrote those words it was not entirely without admiration.'

Black's next move in his ascent through the Quebec intelligentsia was to author a voluminous biography of Maurice Duplessis, the imperious former premier of Quebec who ruled the province from 1936 until just prior to his death in 1959.

In what, after five years of dedication, would become the exhaustive volume entitled *Duplessis*, Black was willing to forgive Duplessis' less appealing characteristics, while building an argument for his subject's greatness.

The tome weighed in at 743 pages, and has come to be regarded as the definitive work on the Quebecer's life and career. 'Like an all-seeing father, severe but benign, Maurice Duplessis rewarded the deserving, punished the unworthy, and ruled vigilantly over his brood,' Black wrote.

Author and subject seemed to have much in common. As a blossoming young conservative, a fascination with the consummate right-wing Quebec statesman was a reasonable avenue for Black. But there was more. Both enjoyed and excelled at debate, both possessed a stupendous memory, both had an aversion to sporting contests beyond the occasional round of croquet. Like Black, Duplessis is depicted as 'an avid devourer of bulky legal and theological tomes and political biographies'. And there was a familiar ring to Duplessis' belief that ' a gentleman could allow himself almost no informality, that all manner of bygone proprieties had always to be maintained'. A conclusion that perhaps no one but Black could have drawn was that much of what Duplessis' critics 'decried as dictatorship and corruption was really a puckish love of farce'.

Once he had embarked on the project, Black decided to integrate his research with a part-time Master's degree thesis, for which he attended McGill University in Montreal. By now Black had taken a sparsely furnished apartment in the Port-Royal on Sherbrooke Street in Montreal, where he wrote into the night after tending to business interests during the day. Says Dan Colson, 'I can remember vividly going to visit Conrad many times and his apartment would be filled to the ceiling with cardboard boxes of documents and letters and research.' Broadcaster Laurier LaPierre, who as a McGill history professor advised Black on his thesis, recalls him being 'pleasant' but 'socially inept' – he rarely mixed with the other students and never seemed to have girlfriends (an observation Black disputes). He was guarded, though a skilled raconteur, and almost always dressed in suit and tie. 'He would come to the country,' where LaPierre and his wife had a home, 'and we would say, "Remove your tie Conrad, for God's sake." '

Despite his obvious regard for Duplessis, Black did not gloss over his imperfections in his book. 'It would be unjust to omit all reference to Duplessis' personal manner of government. He drank very heavily, was frequently intoxicated, abusive and belligerent at public ceremonies of secondary importance.'

Nor did he spare the odd personal detail, such as the revelation that while Duplessis lay on his deathbed suffering from a cerebral haemorrhage, a doctor's attempt at urinalysis proved difficult as the premier suffered from 'hypospatias, a condition in which the urethral aperture is at some remove from the end of the phallus, in this case about an inch'. Parenthetically, Black added: 'Without attempting a psychoanalysis, this condition can have psychological consequences, and may have influenced Duplessis' social life.'

Duplessis was published in late 1976, receiving for the most part respectful coverage for the contribution it made to the historiography of Quebec. 'Unevenly written and overwritten; idiosyncratic and at times bombastic, the book itself is nevertheless one of the most revealing, indiscreet, and fascinating accounts ever written of a Canadian public figure and his times,' wrote a reviewer at the Montreal *Gazette*.

There were exceptions, most notably Professor Ramsay Cook of York University, whose review ran in the *Globe and Mail* just before the book's publication. The verdict was not kind, to say the least: 'Verbally inflated . . . badly organised . . . unjustifiably long . . . a ramshackle volume', were among Cook's findings.

Cook had been an outside examiner on Black's MA thesis, and had written a highly critical opinion of it, which Black considered 'gratuitously insulting and provoking'. There is even an endnote in *Duplessis* referring to the 'churlish flippancies of Ramsay Cook'. On reading the review, Black stormed over to the home of the publisher of the *Globe* in order personally to present his letter of response. It called Cook 'a slanted, supercilious little twit' and he later added on television that Cook had 'the professional ethics of a cockroach'.

For his part, Cook was nonplussed by Black's ire, maintaining that (despite what Black believed) he had never requested to review the book. 'I have no idea why he's so upset about my review,' Cook said at the time. 'He seems to be obsessed with it.' A friend of Black's, journalist Brian McKenna, recalled Black telling him, 'Remember those old games with the Montreal Canadiens where you'd have seventeen seconds left and a bench-clearing brawl? Well, I want a bench-clearing brawl with Ramsay Cook.'

It would be two decades before Black would write another book – this time about himself – but during those years Black would present hundreds of copies of *Duplessis* to friends and those he wished to befriend, a calling card that said its bearer was about more than commercial matters. Douglas Creighton, the co-founder and long-time chairman of the *Toronto Sun* newspaper chain, recalls Black bringing him an autographed copy. Creighton accepted tentatively. 'You know, Conrad, I appreciate this very much, but it's over 1,000 pages, and I haven't had much interest in Duplessis.' (Creighton's achievements include introducing tabloids to major Canadian cities, and the term 'Sunshine Girl' – for the page three cheesecake photo – into everyday parlance.) 'Give it back to me,' Black replied. That same day, the book arrived back at Creighton's office, this time with a note explaining how to read it and milk the value out of the book by reading only a key 110 pages or so.

During the same five years that Black toiled on *Duplessis*, he and his partners pursued the newspaper business with equal zeal. They made enquiries into buying the *Toronto Telegram* when it folded in 1971, but the paper's subscription lists and presses had been sold. Before long Black and his cohorts were calling their venture the Sterling Newspapers chain, after adding several other small papers including the *Granby Leader Mail* and, in Sept Iles, *L'Avenir de Sept Iles Journal*. By 1976 Sterling owned nine dailies and nine weeklies. 'We didn't suddenly sit down one day and decide we would become media tycoons,' Black contends, although later on it would certainly appear that way. 'But after we bought the *Record*, we just asked ourselves: "Where has this business been all our lives?"'

Black and Radler rang small-town publishers from coast to coast to see if they were open to bids. Ontario was the most desirable location, but they found that someone else already owned most of the choice properties – Thomson Newspapers, the monolith that had grown out of the small-town chain of Roy Thomson, the first Lord Thomson. Western Canada, however, was an unexploited frontier of family operations whose owners were not averse to retirement. Black admired Thomson's legendary profit margins and sought to emulate its success wherever he could. Black and Radler toured the West and began buying papers.

At the same time, the dwindling English poplace of rural Quebec – and the political mood – convinced them to begin selling their earlier acquisitions. In early 1973, staff announced to Robert Fleury, publisher of *L'Avenir de Sept Iles*, that they were seeking union accreditation. Fleury immediately called Montreal. 'He [Black] said, "Don't touch anything. Don't do anything. I'll handle it,"' recalls Fleury. Black drove all night, and when he arrived 'he did fire a couple of guys and he gave promotions to a couple of people' in an attempt to thwart the union drive. The firings landed Black before a labour tribunal – he claims the firings had nothing to do with the union – and the paper ended up paying higher severance than it would have otherwise, but kept the union at bay until after the paper was sold. *L'Avenir* and other Quebec papers were sold in short order; the last to go, in 1977, was the *Sherbrooke Record*. Montreal lawyer George MacLaren paid $865,000, a fortune considering the Sterling partners' initial $20,000 and that its profits had been used to fuel other purchases.

With the focus now on the West, Radler and his new wife Rona moved in 1972 to Prince Rupert to oversee operations. Within a few months, the Sterling stable consisted of several papers including the *Alaska Highway News* in Fort St John, the *Terrace Daily Herald*, the *Trail Daily Times* and the *Alberni Valley Times*. If Radler's 'division' was Western Canada, Black's was the East, and here he negotiated the purchase of the *Summerside Journal-Pioneer* in Prince Edward Island after St Clair Balfour, the president of newspaper giant Southam, suggested to him that the owners wanted to sell out and preferred a non-Thomson buyer.

The financial approach to each acquisition was virtually identical. For example, with the *Alaska Highway News* the purchase price was $240,000. Sterling agreed to pay half up front and half 'on the come' – over time. Says Radler, 'We used to tell the bank that we were doing a deal for $240,000 and we needed $120,000 from them. And they'd say, "How do you propose to handle the balance?" And we'd say, "We'll take care of it" – which we did. They didn't necessarily know how we were doing it.' In other words, Black and his colleagues rarely put money into their ventures.

Once in charge, hammering at the paper's cost structure was a priority, but profits were also generated by buying weekly papers in monopoly markets and turning them into dailies. Before long, operating profit margins reached between fifteen and eighteen per cent, levels usually surpassed only by Thomson. In 1979, a particularly rich year, a twenty-five per cent margin was achieved at Sterling, with operating profit of $4.6 million on revenue of $18.5 million.

The editorial quality of Sterling newspapers has always been suspected of being something less than sterling, an accusation that grates on Radler and his managers but which has some merit. Author Peter Newman notes that when a Pacific Western Airlines jet crashed at Cranbrook, B.C. in early 1978, coverage at the *Daily Townsman*, a Sterling paper, relied heavily on wire stories from the Canadian Press news agency. Even this would not have been possible when, several years later, sterling withdrew from CP in favour of its own in-house news agency. 'There's a lot of things about them that anybody in the field of journalism wouldn't be too thrilled about,' charges William Saunders, secretary of Communications Workers of America Local 226 in Vancouver, which represents several Sterling locations. 'One is that they don't put too much weight on editorial. They think editorial is the absolute minimum that's required to get the advertising out.'

Radler, who once (partly in jest) suggested that his contribution to journalism was the 'three-man newsroom', with two of the occupants selling advertising, might well agree. He makes no pretence of being in journalism for social or intellectual reasons, and simply believes that newspapers should focus on making serious money first, and quality will follow. The 1981 Canadian Royal Commission on Newspapers noted in its report that it was difficult to infer what weight Sterling 'gives to the objective of service' in its newspapers. 'Radler told us he wrote some editorials for the Sterling papers,' the report's puzzled author noted. 'When asked if he was a newspaperman, he responded: "I am a businessman." '

In July 1974, Black returned to Toronto, having been away for eight years, at last able to hold his head up proudly. He had gained a law degree, built a chain of newspapers, and his book was nearing completion. He knew important people and at times referred to himself as a historian.* Black was also making a name for himself as a political commentator. For a short time he became a regular on CBC's English-language Montreal radio, where he and Laurier LaPierre engaged in animated discourse on political matters, Black arguing from the right and LaPierre from the left.

Black ascribed his move to the increasing intolerance in Quebec of the English, institutionalised by the government through laws subverting English education and language. On the day he departed

---

* Black's fascination with power had led him to Quebec's Cardinal Paul-Emile Leger, whom Black got to know and nominated for the 1973 Nobel Peace Prize, obtaining the signatures of many luminaries including former prime ministers Lester Pearson and John Diefenbaker. (The prize went to Henry Kissinger and Le Duc Tho.)

for Toronto, 26 July 1974, Black delivered a radio soliloquy slamming the Quebec government of the day as 'the most financially and intellectually corrupt in the history of the province'. His invective skills by now well developed, Black would not go quietly into the night. 'The English community here, still deluding itself with the illusion of Montreal as an incomparably fine place to live, is leaderless and irrelevant, except as the hostage of a dishonest government.

'Last month one of the most moderate ministers, Guy Saint-Pierre, told an English businessman's group, "If you don't like Quebec, you can leave it." With sadness but with certitude, I accept that choice.'

Black rented an office for Sterling Newspapers in the Bank of Commerce building and set about reingratiating himself into the Toronto scene. He was a frequent attender at the Toronto Club, the exclusive enclave to which Argus Corp. chairman Bud McDougald had presented Black with membership on his twenty-first birthday. And he was no stranger at 10 Toronto Street, where Argus maintained its headquarters. For several years, Black's elder brother Montegu had been toiling in the securities industry, although not as a mere employee, the Blacks and their father having purchased twenty-five per cent of a mid-sized brokerage firm, Draper, Dobie & Co., for $250,000.

The private dining room at Draper's Adelaide Street office provided a venue for weekly roast beef lunches, where the brothers entertained the local financial and political heavyweights in the finest Old Toronto WASP never-too-early-for-a-stiff-cocktail tradition. Monte, a very large man with thick glasses and a linebacker's neck, provided a friendly and humorous foil for his erudite younger brother. Whereas Conrad was now in possession of three university degrees, easy-going Monte boasted 'no degrees, but several attempts'.

Conrad Black became more involved in the affairs of Ravelston Corp., the private company which controlled powerful Argus Corp. and of which the Black family company, Western Dominion, owned 22.4 per cent. George Black intended his sons to take over his interests in Ravelston, and had been quietly transferring his Western Dominion shares to them throughout the 1970s in order to avoid estate taxes. But Conrad Black's first noticeable presence in Argus came in 1975, when Paul Desmarais made an unwelcome bid for control. Desmarais, who rose from stewardship of his family's obscure Sudbury school-bus company to build one of Canada's most potent empires, Power Corporation, had been encouraged by Argus co-founder E.P. Taylor. Now living in the Bahamas and with little interest in Argus affairs, Taylor believed the ageing partners who ruled Argus would happily sell out for the right price. What Desmarais did not take into account was that Ravelston, which beneficially owned sixty-one per cent of Argus, was set up six years earlier specifically to wrest power away from Taylor and towards his successor as chairman, McDougald.

The son of a well-to-do Toronto financier, John A. 'Bud' McDougald, like Black, did not take to Upper Canada College – he flunked out at age sixteen. His father helped him get a job at Dominion Securities, where Bud was syndicate manager by the age of twenty. The family lost its fortune during the Depression, but Bud more than reversed that through his Argus investment and his presidency of Crown Trust Co. His pride was his collection of vintage cars, which he kept in the chandeliered garage at his estate, Oriole Farm.

In rallying the defence against what he portrayed publicly as an undesirable francophone interloper, McDougald sought and found in George Black's young son an articulate and spirited ally. (This despite the fact that George Black, like Taylor, actually endorsed the idea of liquidating Argus.) Given a public platform, Conrad Black was unambiguously behind McDougald. 'The fact is,' he told one interviewer, 'the key to Argus's success – and it is now surely recognised by everyone as a great and successful company – is that it has had three chairmen only, and they're all three, I can authenticate this fact, they're all three great men. Lt-Col Eric Phillips, Mr Taylor and Mr McDougald. This quality – that's consistent, continuous quality. It's a quality operation.' And Desmarais? 'This kamikaze raid that just came out of the blue from Montreal was an absurd development.'

Though of retirement age, McDougald was not the sort to slow down. He had no children, and amid the threat of Argus falling into Demarais' grasp the murmuring began around Toronto that the heir apparent to Argus was none other than Conrad Black.

By 1976 George and Betty Black were rarely seen outside their Park

Lane Circle home. Conrad Black attributes this largely to their failing health, particularly the condition of his sixty-five-year-old father. In the evenings, his mother would go to sleep early, but his father would stay up, sometimes all night. 'He was happy enough to have people visit him in his home,' says Black. 'He wasn't a recluse in the sense of not wanting to see anybody, and he wasn't a recluse in the sense of not staying in touch. He read the paper and he watched television, so he knew what was going on. If you visited him, he was well dressed, clean-shaven, alert and well aware of what was going on in the world. But his problem was that his eyes failed and his legs failed, so he just wasn't very mobile.'

A stiff drink was never far from George Black's side, and one person close to the family isn't sure if health was the only factor. 'He retired at the age of forty-eight,' the friend notes. 'Now most people who would be able to retire at forty-eight would either have gone on to a second career or just spent their life travelling, on the golf course, writing books, whatever their interests were. But he sat there in his house and didn't go anywhere.'

George and Betty Black died ten days apart in June 1976. Betty succumbed to cancer on 19 June, which left George despondent and Conrad charged with trying to console him. Black recounts in his memoir, *A Life in Progress*, how they spent their last evening together. At a critical juncture, George Black began to walk up the circular stairs in the front hall, and moments later 'came the unnerving crack of straining and breaking wood, followed by the descent of my father backwards through and over the banister to the floor about ten feet below'. An ambulance was called and when his father came to he 'spoke of having lost his balance on the stairs and having no desire to live'. He was taken to Scarborough General Hospital, where he told Conrad he was 'a good son'. Conrad did not know it would be their final exchange. 'He was getting a bit incoherent and I didn't particularly want to stay around for that,' he recalled. 'So I came home on the understanding that they would call me if there were any developments.' Several hours later, the hospital called and told Black his father had died.

When Peter Newman recounted George Black's death in his 1982 biography of Conrad Black, *The Establishment Man*, a picture of a more embittered father is presented. Newman quotes George Black telling his son that 'Life is hell, most people are bastards, and everything is bullshit' before his fateful walk upstairs. Conrad Black contends those words were never said. 'I never heard him say that,' Black explained one afternoon almost two decades after George Black's death. 'Certainly in his latter days he would have said things sort of approaching that, but not as bad as that.' Black recalls his father's death as nothing more than a tragic accident, noting that 'He was melancholy, but he wasn't depressive.'

Others close to Conrad Black saw it as more of a slow suicide, which frightened Black, who had personally, most acutely in the early 1970s, suffered from anxiety attacks during which he would begin gasping and sweating, or feeling nauseous. At one point, he carried around a sick bag. Black underwent psychoanalysis, and even took courses towards becoming a psychoanalyst. 'The physical symptoms were reminiscent of descriptions of historic death throes like those of Henry VIII or Alexander VI (Borgia),' Black wrote in his autobiography of his most serious attack, adding that it was 'far more terrifying than anything else I have known'. According to one person who was close to Black after his father's death, Black feared that depression might overtake him, that at some point he might lose control and give up on life as his father had. 'It's a wonderful fear, because if you're frightened of [suicide], you're probably never going to do it,' says the person. 'But it leaves a big hole. It asks big questions.' Black's anxiety episodes lasted sporadically into the mid-1980s, but he says psychoanalysis unearthed the root cause of the attacks – which he declines to reveal – and he has not had a problem since.

THREE

Boy Wonder

'He's just getting rich'
STEPHEN JARISLOWSKY

Although Conrad Black worked mainly out of his Sterling Newspapers office in the Bank of Commerce building in 1976, his telephone would ring through to the offices of Draper, Dobie, the brokerage house run by his older brother, Monte, on nearby Adelaide Street. The instructions for the Draper, Dobie secretaries were simple: If the Sterling phone rang between nine and eleven a.m., they were to explain that Mr Black was in a 'meeting'; between eleven and two he was at 'lunch', and from two to five he was 'unavailable'.

En route to lunch or a chat with his brother, Conrad Black would stroll through the Draper, Dobie office in vice-regal manner, often leaving the secretaries in a fluster as his renown grew. One recalls taking down a message for him and, not knowing Black, asking one of her co-workers to deliver it to him. When Black was given the message, from around a corner the secretary who took it could hear him declare, 'Doesn't she *know* who I am?' How arrogant! the secretary thought, but then Black came around and introduced himself and was actually quite pleasant.

The next time this particular secretary encountered the younger Black brother, she was asked to type up a letter from Conrad to Newell Lusby, the president of Diner's Club. Black was incensed over a scandalous incident during which he was denied credit. Once again, the acid tone of 'Don't you know who I am?' was struck.

Black showed up at her desk soon after. 'How did you like my letter to Newell Lusby?' he enquired with a mischievous smile. 'Didn't you think it was funny?' Suddenly the secretary, Shirley Walters, saw Conrad Black in a different light – sure, there was arrogance, but his tongue was planted firmly in his cheek, and a self-deprecating wit lurked behind the bluster.

Soon after, Black's permanent office moved into Draper, Dobie. He and Walters struck up a fast friendship, with Black saying to her things like, 'Now that my mother's dead, you'll have to tell me when I need a haircut.' With brown hair and light eyes, Walters was bright, cheerful, down-to-earth and as straightforward as Black was guarded. She hailed from well outside the society circles in which Black was frequently sighted. At night, as she prepared to go home, Walters would find herself, coat on, leaning against the wall in Conrad's office, fascinated by the tales of history and personalities he would recount. When *Duplessis* was published in late 1976, she was flattered to find her name among the acknowledgements (one of three singled out as 'conspicuously kind and efficient'), which she later realised was 'just his way of telling me he likes me'. Black did indeed take a growing interest in Walters, six years his junior. At one point she mentioned that her marriage was breaking up and she needed to find a lawyer. The next thing she knew an attorney was on the line, saying he had been referred by Conrad Black.

At this point, Black was squiring a voluptuous Brazilian-born woman, Anna Maria Marston, about Toronto. Shirley was protective towards Black, because people were making snide comments about the relationship behind his back.

In the 1960s and 1970s few young women's dream date was a fleshy man in a three-piece pin-stripe suit ruminating on Napoleon or Disraeli. Certainly, throughout his teens and twenties, Black was awkward around women. But the era of free love worked for him as it did for others and Black had what he calls 'ample experience'.

Even in his twenties, noted Black's thesis adviser and radio partner Laurier LaPierre, he seemed to walk 'as if he is encased in cement.' By his early thirties, Black moved even more stiffly, as if his burly shoulders were held tautly in an invisible vice. Writer Philip Marchand, now literary editor of the *Toronto Star*, noted on meeting him in 1977, 'The curious sense he projects [is] of someone alone, of someone who has, almost in an unconscious way, renounced certain desirable aspects of human existence – it is impossible to imagine him passionately in love, for example, or even fully giving himself over to the joys of cameraderie, of having fun with the boys.'

One day, Black phoned Walters at the office from home. 'Would you work late tonight?' Black asked, explaining he had some pressing work which needed attending to. He added, 'I'll take you out to dinner.' This gentle approach would become their first date. On the way to the restaurant they circled the block as they listened on the radio in Black's car to Quebec premier René Levesque delivering a speech in New York.

Before long, the friendship became something more. Walters could see beyond Black's exterior, and found an appealing vulnerability. In early 1977, Walters became pregnant with Black's child. This was complicated by two factors: first, although she was legally separated, Walters was not yet divorced; second, she was not sure she wanted to continue a relationship with Black, let alone marry him. Black, she says, impressed upon her that if they didn't get married they would never know if they were meant to be together. Shirley, who changed her name to Joanna in 1990, agreed to continue the relationship and soon they decided to marry.

The pregnancy presented other complications for Black. He wanted to keep it quiet, for fear the press would find out. And when their son Jonathan Black was born in November 1977, his father's name was purposely left off the registration. Until the child was roughly a year old, several months after their marriage, Jonathan's existence remained a well-guarded secret – even some close friends and relatives did not know about him until two weeks before the wedding. Neither parent felt they had done anything to be ashamed of, but to Shirley it seemed that her husband was concerned that the less liberally minded likes of Bud McDougald might look down on him if they knew.

If only, Shirley hoped during this strange interlude, the media would also stop characterising the father of her child as 'Canada's most eligible bachelor'.

On George Black's death, McDougald invited the Black brothers to Oriole Farm, where in addition to collecting cars he bred fine horses and miniature poodles. Conrad and Monte had inherited their father's 22.4 per cent interest in Ravelston, and were worried that the holding company's other shareholders, led by McDougald, might force them out. Those fears proved unfounded, as McDougald made good on a pledge to their father and invited the Black brothers to share the positions, save that of vice-president of Argus, that their father had held in the group. Monte filled slots on the boards of Dominion Stores and Standard Broadcasting, while Conrad took the more critical seats on the boards of Argus and Ravelston. McDougald also helped Conrad realise his ambition of becoming a director of a major Canadian bank by arranging for him to join the board of the Canadian Imperial Bank of Commerce, where George Black had also served as a director. Monte joined the board of the Toronto-Dominion Bank.

On the ides of March, 15 March 1978, McDougald died in Palm Beach. It was his seventieth birthday. At home that day, in Toronto, Conrad Black was clearly distracted by news of his mentor's death: he sliced his hand while carving a turkey. Until then, Black was an up-and-coming author and historian who also owned part of a small-town newspaper chain. The death of Argus's chairman presented the opportunity for Black to leap onto the national and, potentially, international stage.

McDougald's talent, which made Argus, was to exercise control from a minority position through sheer force of personality and, when called upon, intimidation. McDougald's personal interest in Ravelston* was 23.6 per cent, but a similar interest was owned by the estate of his late brother-in-law, Lt-Col Eric Phillips, whose widow Doris was the sister of McDougald's wife Maude. McDougald reinforced his control over the Phillips estate through his roles at Crown Trust Co., which was the corporate trustee of the Phillips estate.

Without McDougald, the Argus mystique would soon expire. Massey-Ferguson in particular, though Canada's largest multinational, was in increasingly dismal financial health. Conrad Black later reflected that the all-powerful corporate octopus had, by the time of McDougald's death, become 'a tired group of entries: Indifferently managed companies in mature industries'.† The whole point of

---

* Ravelston was named after McDougald's grandfather's house in Scotland.

† Argus's main assets were twenty nine per cent of Hollinger Mines Ltd, sixteen per cent of Massey-Ferguson Ltd, seventeen per cent of Domtar Ltd, twenty-six per cent of Dominion Stores Ltd, and forty-eight per cent of Standard Broadcasting. Through Hollinger, the company also owned sixty-one per cent of Labrador Mining, twelve per cent of Iron Ore Co. of Canada, and ten per cent of Noranda.

Argus, Black concluded, was that 'for fifteen years after the war, E. P. Taylor and his partners bustled around Canada buying things for their own account and then peddling them into the Argus group at handsome profits, in an era before capital gains taxes and self-dealing rules'. It was not much more, said Black, than 'a rather elegant confidence trick'.

Hal Jackman, whose family interests owned nine per cent of Argus and who joined its board in 1975, described a typical executive committee meeting. 'Argus didn't do anything in the years I was around,' he says. 'McDougald would tell stories about 1929, 1916, when they used to get drunk before putting in their bids for the latest Canadian National Railway franchise, usually some off-colour story. And everybody would just sit around and listen.'

Still, there were some $4 billion in assets under Argus control, and through its ownership of sixty-one per cent of the company's voting common shares – which represented only ten per cent of Argus's overall equity – Ravelston maintained firm control. Five groups owned Ravelston: the Blacks held 22.4 per cent through their Western Dominion Investment Co. Ltd; McDougald and Phillips had their 23.6 per cent each; Canadian General Investments and an associated trust company, both headed by Colonel Maxwell Meighen, the elderly son of former prime minister Arthur Meighen, held 26.5 per cent; and 3.9 per cent was owned by General A. Bruce Matthews, then the executive vice-president of Argus.

The day after McDougald's death, Conrad and Montegu met Alex Barron, president of Canadian General Investments. It was a long-standing dinner engagement at Park Lane Circle, the Blacks' late parents' house, where Conrad was now living. Conrad Black told Barron he aspired to become a vice-president of Argus and to have Monte elected to the board. Black contends that Barron left him with the impression he would support their elevation, while Barron later said he sympathised with the Blacks but could not commit to anything.

The following week, on 22 March 1978, the Argus executive committee met to appoint the post-McDougald executive officers. Black, caught in a traffic jam on the Don Valley Parkway, arrived four minutes late and found the nominations closed – and he and Monte shut out. It would probably have made no difference if Black had spent the previous night in the boardroom. The triumvirate of Meighen, Barron and Matthews had no intention of inviting him into the Argus inner sanctum just yet. Meighen took the chairman's office, Matthews became president, and Barron was named executive vice-president. As Meighen later recalled, McDougald's instructions regarding Black were to 'bring him along exceedingly slowly. He's too precipitious [*sic*]. We have to educate him.' Black, of course, had a different view. He expected to be an Argus executive, which would have sent a clear signal that he was a potential successor to head the group. 'We were happy to co-operate with this new triumvirate and we were prepared to live with almost any arrangement provided we got a little recognition, just a *crumb* of recognition.'

Recognition was not a concept readily embraced by the self-anointed rulers of Argus. Jackman, who was at the board table that day, didn't understand the significance of Black becoming an Argus vice-president or whatever – after all, it didn't pay much, if anything. 'Look, there's been a lot of speculation in the press about me,' Jackman recalls Black telling the stony-faced Argus elders. 'I'm one of the heirs apparent. If I'm not an officer it will look bad, the press will read something into it.' Meighen quickly replied, 'We are running this company, not the press.'

Beyond the older Argus partners' lack of interest in publicity in general and Black's public image in particular, they didn't take him terribly seriously – an attitude which McDougald had cultivated behind Black's back. Accepting McDougald's portrayal of Black would prove to be Black's opponents' most critical mistake. 'McDougald was a real divide-and-conquer kind of guy,' says Jackman. 'He would encourage Conrad while he was talking to him, then he would belittle Conrad to the others.'

Had Black been given a nominal vice-presidency at Argus – like his father before him – the company's future might have turned out very differently. Instead, Meighen patronised this man less than half his age, telling Black sternly (in equestrian terms), 'You're rushing your fences.' He later claimed that he added, motioning to his ageing accomplices, 'Just take a look around, you won't have to wait long.' (Black contends this was never said.)

'Well, in the interest of this company and its affiliates,' Black coolly replied, 'I am not going to rock the boat at this time. But I want to tell you that we're not satisfied.'

Black's pledge not to 'rock the boat' proved short-lived. What happened next suggests the execution of a military master plan, but Black preferred to give the impression that he was simply responding to outside forces. That too was probably part of the strategy.

The Black brothers plotted in their offices at Dominion Securities, where Monte ran the brokerage's equity operations.* As it happened, they were not the only ones unhappy with the manner in which Meighen, Barron and Matthews had carved up Argus's executive authority – so were Bud McDougald's widow, Maude, seventy-five, and her sister Doris Phillips, seventy-eight. When the widows approached the Blacks about joining forces against the others, recalls Monte, 'Well, I need hardly tell you that was music to our ears.'

The executors of the Phillips estate were also on the Blacks' side, in particular Dixon Chant. A chartered accountant who had been a close associate of Phillips for many years, Chant felt swindled out of a promised executive post at Argus. Chant had suffered a heart attack the previous year, and Black had visited him in hospital. Black later told Peter White that visiting Chant and joining the board of the Bank of Commerce were two 'absolutely crucial' elements of his successful Argus take-over.

The first phase of Black's strategy was to acquire control of Crown Trust Co., which was the corporate trustee of the Phillips and McDougald estates. 'Knowing something of the propensity of elderly ladies to change their minds,' Black later explained, they bought Crown 'to ensure as much stability as possible for whatever course we embarked upon together.'

Black also secured the willing support of multimillionaire Nelson Davis, Bud McDougald's best friend and an old friend of the Black family. Anticipating difficulties, Conrad and Montegu had sought Davis's counsel shortly after McDougald's death. 'Bide your time, bite your lips and these guys will dig their own graves,' Davis advised.

In a strange side-show, Black was the coy but willing target of a

* Draper, Dobie had been sold to Dominion Securities in 1977 and Monte became a Dominion vice-president.

Canadian Broadcasting Corporation television crew charged with filming seven one-hour documentaries based on Peter Newman's *The Canadian Establishment,* a who's who of the country's rich and powerful. The effect of that show and the subsequent Newman biography of Black which focused on the Argus take-over was the transformation of this peculiar young hybrid of businessman and intellectual into the personification of Canadian capitalism. In short order, thirty-three-year-old Black would be plastered all over Canada's television screens, as well as its business pages.

'To meet Black in those halcyon days before his ascendancy was to be kept waiting only forty-five minutes on a mid-winter's evening,' recalled Ron Graham, then a CBC television producer. 'He glided down the corridor of Dominion Securities in Toronto, tendered an apology, extended his hand low enough that an involuntary bow was required to grasp it, and said hello with an *ennui* that contradicted his quizzical gaze. The petitioner was ushered graciously into an unkempt cubicle where, surrounded by unpacked boxes, a photograph of Joe Clark, a sheaf of pink phone messages, and a stack of his biography of Maurice Duplessis, Black entertained for several hours with droll verbiage, slanderous insights and a hilarious piece of French vitriol he had just dispatched to the editor of *Le Devoir.* One laughed at his jokes, admired his intelligence, deferred to his position, and came away with the promise of an interview.'

With the necessary supports in place – not least of which was an increasingly intrigued public – Black's plan moved to overdrive. On 15 May 1978, Maude McDougald and Doris Phillips agreed to vote their Ravelston interests with the Blacks, creating a shareholder bloc just shy of seventy per cent. More importantly, the Blacks became sole owners of the right to invoke the obscure 'compulsory transfer' provision in the original 1969 Ravelston shareholders' agreement. This curious provision had been included to ensure that a majority of the partners could get rid of any other partner who had grown senile or just undesirable.

The Blacks wasted little time. Two days after signing the agreement with the widows, Conrad Black and Dixon Chant served Colonel Meighen with a notice of compulsory sale of his 26.5 per cent of Ravelston. It was, Black later recounted, at the 'enthusiastic urging of the ladies'. The old guard was ambushed from within. 'There have been no policy differences,' a bewildered Alex Barron told *Maclean's* magazine. 'Relations were excellent.' In fact, he added, Black had voted in favour of Meighen's appointment and had voiced no opposition.

Black was quickly establishing a habit of extending the battlefield to the black and white realm of the press. Barron's assertion, Black replied in the same article, is 'not in accord with demonstrable facts. There were substantial policy differences. Unless Alex has succumbed to a massive attack of amnesia, he should be able to recall some of them.' Indeed, Barron should have recognised the most obvious policy difference of all: the effrontery to suggest that Conrad Black was not yet ready for the exalted offices of Argus.

All was running smoothly until 13 June when Ian Anderson, a reporter at the *Montreal Gazette*, decided to phone Maude McDougald (who was known as 'Jim') and Doris Phillips for their side of the story. When asked if she had empowered Black to acquire Meighen's Ravelston interests, McDougald replied, 'I don't think I did, but I suppose I must have.' she added, 'I have a bird brain about business and I don't know anything about it.' Phillips, who had just returned to Toronto from a long vacation in Palm Springs, was equally perturbed. 'I've signed hundreds of documents since my husband died,' she told Anderson. 'You know more about it than I do.'

As Black later recounted acidly, 'When the inevitable publicity ensued, the ladies confected an entertaining fiction on an arsenic and old lace theme and painted me as a rapacious young man.' The widows did this, he contends, because they did not want to admit publicly what they felt privately – that Meighen was a threat to their joint position as the dominant shareholders in Ravelston, and the firebrand Black would be their agent to ensure that Meighen didn't trouble them again. Now they were suggesting that Black was the proverbial camel let within the tent, using their shareholdings, the late great Bud's affections, and his legal savvy to sew up control of Argus for himself. Black's view was soon supported publicly by Nelson Davis – 'I agree with everything that the Black boys have done' – and the widows' lawyer, Louis Guolla: 'There is no doubt that these ladies were aware of the consequences when they signed the document, but they have been quite upset by all the publicity.'

Whatever their original motive had been the widows' reaction to the attention resulted in their attempting an end run on the Blacks. Repudiating their 15 May agreement with the Blacks, they set out to purchase General Bruce Matthews's four per cent, which would have given them fifty-one per cent and left the Blacks out in the cold. Only a week earlier, the widows, knowing him to be an admirer of Napoleon, had given Conrad Black a wooden statue of Bonaparte that had belonged to Lt-Col Phillips. But now they were egged on in their about-face by a third sister, Cecil Hedstrom, and by John Prusac, a wealthy real estate developer. Prusac hailed from far outside the accepted Establishment circles but had been courting the sisters, harbouring barely suppressed designs of his own on Argus.

Black's key ally turned out to be Chant. The Phillips estate trustee met Prusac with the widows and General Matthews one afternoon in late June and immediately distrusted him. Chant was even less impressed when Prusac produced documents to purchase fifty-one per cent of the Ravelston shares from those present (the widows' forty-seven per cent and Matthews's four). Chant wanted to read the papers through, but Prusac kept insisting he sign, that it was what 'the girls' wanted. Chant refused and grew irritated. 'If Bud McDougald were here,' he growled, 'he would have you thrown out the front door.'

'You can't talk to me like that,' snapped Prusac.

On hearing that the Argus prize might be snatched out of his grasp, Black consulted his lawyer, Igor Kaplan of Aird & Berlis. 'On the day that Conrad heard about the ladies' ploy,' Kaplan recalled, 'he phoned me at home to tell me, eleven o'clock at night. I stayed awake thinking the thing through and went into the office at four in the morning. More lawyers gathered, five of us maybe, and we began to talk through the options.' With Black, they decided on two courses of action. One was to threaten to invoke the compulsory transfer and buy the ladies' shares. It was a tactic of questionable legality, but it was a good show of force. Step two: Peter Atkinson, Aird & Berlis's head of litigation, drafted a strongly worded writ suing the ladies for violating the 15 May agreement and the original Ravelston agreement. Kaplan phoned up their lawyers and warned them, 'If it came to a crisis, we'd issue it.'

The next day, Tuesday 27 June, during a break at a Massey-Ferguson board meeting, Black walked over and served a compulsory transfer notice on General Matthews. Unlike the one served on

Meighen, this notice did not contain the widows' signatures; Kaplan's legal opinion was that they were not required. The widows were overwhelmed by the Blacks' aggressive stance. On 4 July their lawyers arrived at the Black estate on Park Lane Circle to capitulate; they proposed that the Blacks buy out the McDougald-Phillips stock – a striking change of heart from their initial goal of using the Blacks to preserve Argus in Bud's spirit.

The widows asked for $10 million each for their respective 23.6 per cent stakes. The Blacks offered $8 million, and a price of $9.2 million each was agreed on. The entire amount was borrowed; half from the Bank of Commerce, half from the Toronto-Dominion Bank.

With the widows out of the way, questions about the Blacks' conduct would linger; but most people wanted to know what they would do with Argus and its $4 billion in slumbering assets. Now perched atop a many-tentacled giant with interests in natural resources, chemicals, farm equipment manufacturing, grocery retailing, and broadcasting, Conrad Black would be the most celebrated Canadian tycoon of his generation. With considerable satisfaction, Black, not yet thirty-four years old, took the keys to 10 Toronto Street. 'We're talking about business,' says Hal Jackman. 'It's not a moral issue. There's no right and wrong in this. The prizes go to the stronger, and Conrad was the stronger.'

Alongside Conrad Black's signature on the crucial compulsory transfer document presented to Max Meighen in June was that of Shirley Gail Walters, who had become the corporate secretary at Western Dominion, the Black family company. And in the midst of the Argus imbroglio, on 14 July, she and Conrad Black were married.

The Anglican ceremony was conducted by Reverend John Erb at Grace Church on the Hill, where the funeral service for George Black had been held two years earlier. Monte Black and Leigh Beauchamp, Brian Stewart's girlfriend, were witnesses. After the wedding, Shirley deposited her bouquet of white roses with pink edges at George's and Betty Black's graves in Mount Pleasant Cemetery. They returned to the Blacks' home where about twenty guests drank Dom Perignon and dined on crown roast of lamb catered by Winston's, the Establishment restaurant where Black frequently power-dined.

Black's personal and professional orbits were never too far from one another, and the event alternated between marital celebration and business banquet, with much Argus strategy discussed by the pool. Throughout the evening, Black frequently conferred with his brother, White, Radler and Kaplan. The groom, with white carnation in the lapel of his blue suit, kept apologising for talking business. 'I'm sorry I have to keep bringing this up but I have to keep everything straight in my mind.' While the Blacks' guests and Shirley revelled into the night, the exhausted groom turned in early, alone.

Despite his professed desire to keep things quiet, a gaggle of reporters had gathered by the gate at Black's estate earlier that day, and four days later a large colour photo of the newly-weds graced the *Toronto Star*. ('Wall of privacy surrounds tycoon and four-day bride'.) Reporters were frustrated by their inability to unearth much about the new Mrs Black, except that she had been married for about two years previously with no children, hailed from Montreal, was the daughter of an accountant for the Canadian Imperial Bank of Commerce, and grandniece of Robert Stanley Weir, the judge who wrote the English words to the national anthem, 'O Canada'.

Attempts to elicit interviews at the Black doorstep generated only a brief comment that she didn't want to be seen as a spouse in the Margaret Trudeau vein, and that she didn't want people to think 'Conrad married his secretary'. The *Star* did get hold of Margaret Barker, a normally timid friend of Shirley's, who shockingly revealed that 'the new Mrs Black has never entertained on a large scale but is "very competent in the kitchen", tending towards pork chops, mixed grills and chicken dishes'. (The *Star* did not uncover Black's affinity for chocolate mousse and banana cream pie.)

More seriously, Black's efforts to keep the existence of their infant son under wraps were briefly threatened when a writer for the *Globe and Mail* phoned his new mother-in-law to enquire about the rumours of a child. She didn't speak to him, but quickly called Shirley. Black says that his only reason for keeping Jonathan's existence quiet was for his son's protection. 'When they phoned my mother-in-law she phoned my wife and my wife raised it with me,' recalls Black, 'and I spoke to [*Globe* editor-in-chief] Dick Doyle. And he said, "That's fine, quite right, what do we want to get into that for?" '

Certainly the press soon had plenty of other Black-mania to fill their pages. There was no shortage of super-confident, chin-forward photos of Black, many of them featuring him regally thumbing through an ever-present copy of *Duplessis*. Conrad Black was the *Globe and Mail*'s *Report on Business* Man of the Year for 1978, the *Toronto Star*'s 'Prince of Tycoons' and *Fortune* magazine's 'Boy Wonder of Canadian Business'. Rod McQueen, writing for *Maclean's* magazine, tried to discover what motivated Black during an encounter in his office. But Black was proving to be as enigmatic as he was accessible. 'I'm a man of the people,' Black offered drolly. 'I'm a retired pensioner living on my investments.' Then he tried a more serious tack. 'Avocationally, I'm a historian and a publisher. Fundamentally, I'm an ideologist.' The slight smile never quite departed Black's lips as he searched for the right words: 'I'm motivated by . . .' An uncharacteristic lapse but, as always, Black dug deep and salvaged the thought at the last possible moment. 'It's difficult. One doesn't want to sound pretentious or superficial. I am perplexed at the erosion of conviction and the gradual descent of our society into a moral torpor. There is a great deal of hand-wringing going on; I'm reduced to reading Spengler. His theme is that the decline of civilisation is as likely as the turning of autumn leaves. I have this semi-romantic notion about ideological questions. I guess there's a bit of the missionary in all of us.'

Things were a little more straightforward for the elder Black brother. Monte was happy to let his younger brother bask in the spotlight. With Conrad on a honeymoon, both literal and metaphorical, Monte, by now married more than a dozen years and with children of his own, found the Argus grab a cause of some marital discord. 'We had a very difficult time,' recalled Mariellen Black, who separated from Monte in 1981 and whose divorce was finalised in 1988. 'There were some very serious security concerns about the children. We had guards on the children. There had been vandalism at the house. Our life had been severely affected by all of the fame and notoriety.'

During one drive back to Toronto from their cottage in Muskoka, an exasperated Mariellen said to Monte, 'I really don't understand what all of this is about. What is it worth? We live in the same house. The kids have always gone to private school. What's the benefit?'

'Well,' Monte replied, 'it's a monopoly game. It's a lot of fun.'

Up to this point, Monte Black had always had difficulty living within his means. In the 1970s he had borrowed more than $300,000 from his parents and at a particularly low point in 1973 was given money monthly by his father to get by.

Monte would not soon forget his wife's reaction on 5 July 1978, when he informed her that he and his brother had just borrowed $18.4 million to buy out Maude McDougald's and Doris Phillips's interests in Ravelston. Mariellen, he later recalled, 'was startled that this amount of money had been borrowed and wondered how I was going to pay it back – a question I had a hard time answering at the time'.

On a purely superficial level, the $30 million that the Blacks ended up paying for all of Ravelston seemed a small price for control of assets worth $4 billion. But any knowledgeable investor knows that there is often little relation between the value of the assets of a company on its balance sheet and the value investments in that company will fetch if sold. (Hal Jackman, for one, believes Black paid a hefty price for Argus, relative to the underlying share values, although this is a tough point to prove since Argus common shares rarely traded.) But this was all part of the illusion of Argus influence that Black knew – although perhaps not to the degree that he would soon discover – was in marked decline.

What possessed them to gamble on Argus? Conrad Black had helped create Sterling Newspapers, through which he could boast that he made it on his own, without family money. Monte had a comfortable career in the investment industry as a vice-president of Dominion Securities. They also owned a malting business, and stood to inherit a further $4.2 million from their father's estate. They could also have simply sold their Ravelston stock and, based on what they paid the widows, have walked away with some $9 million more.

The most obvious explanation is that Ravelston was their largest asset, and since they were 'seriously disquieted about its deteriorating condition' they had to do whatever they could to protect it. Second, the Blacks believed that among the factions within Ravelston only they could reverse Argus's decline by pursuing a strategy of unsentimentally disposing of assets, which in Conrad Black parlance was known as an 'asset upgrade'. Perhaps the most revealing insight into Black's motivation is his statement that 'my brother and I had known Argus all our lives, and while we always liked and admired Mr Taylor and Mr McDougald, both of whom our father had loyally served as a junior partner, we thought, in some indefinable way, that it was justly our turn.' Indeed, George Black went to his grave convinced, with some justification, that Taylor had made a mistake by replacing him as Canadian Breweries' president in 1958. 'I was slightly miffed at the way I thought the old Argus quadrumvirate used him, and then set him aside for a while,' Conrad Black says of his father. 'In any case, to the extent I was miffed I more than compensated for that when we took over Argus.'

With Conrad as president of Argus and Monte as president of Ravelston, the Blacks spent much of the summer of 1978 putting in place a new group of investors for forty-nine per cent of Ravelston, culled from the ranks of Toronto's ruling classes. Nelson Davis, Argus's new chairman, and Hal Jackman each took sixteen per cent of Ravelston, and department store scion Fredrik Eaton bought four per cent. John Finlay, Douglas Bassett and Dixon Chant bought one per cent apiece, and ten per cent went to the Blacks' cousin Ron Riley.

The Blacks were also wary that the Argus structure was susceptible to aggressors, most notably Paul Desmarais, who owned more of its equity but less of its votes after his ill-fated 1975 take-over attempt. If Desmarais were suddenly to decide to acquire a major interest in one of the underlying Argus companies that were ostensibly controlled through shareholdings ranging from ten to twenty-five per cent, Argus lacked the financial muscle to counter him. One of Black's first moves once in charge was to cosy up to Desmarais and buy his Argus shares for about $80 million – $65 million in cash borrowed from the Commerce and Toronto-Dominion banks and a promissory note – taking him out at his price, 'The price was a price that he said,' recalls Monte Black, 'and we didn't wish to argue.'

This move brought Ravelston's voting interest in Argus up to eighty-seven per cent, and a further purchase of Jackman's nine per cent interest brought it to ninety-six per cent. In December 1978, the Blacks sold Argus's eleven per cent stake in Domtar to Macmillan Bloedel for about $70 million. As Monte explained, Domtar did not want them on the board, and the Blacks began a series of reorganisations aimed at shoring up their positions in cash-rich

Hollinger Mines* and Dominion Stores. 'We had to . . . eliminate those companies where we didn't have any influence and beef up and strengthen those companies where we did have an influence so we could get to a controlling position and not have to worry about being raided or being outvoted by a majority of the shareholders.' Once control was achieved, he and his brother could do with the companies as they pleased. And they did; ultimately selling off the whole lot.

In 1979, Massey-Ferguson was the Blacks' most urgent business. With a 140-year history and annual sales of $3 billion, venerable Massey was the largest farm-machinery company in the world. It would be the first proving ground for Conrad Black's as yet unseen operational abilities.

Bud McDougald and his Argus cronies had attained much of their grandeur through their Massey ownership. The Duke of Wellington and other luminaries sat on the board of directors, and important trips abroad were a mainstay of the agenda. For Black, one of the perks of Massey control was the increased opportunities it presented for him to indulge his fascination with meeting and knowing important international bigwigs. In 1980, Massey sponsored a conference at the Four Seasons Hotel in Toronto which featured Henry Kissinger and *Economist* editor Andrew Knight as speakers. Another attendee, former British ambassador to the U.S. Peter Jay, recalled that as he and Kissinger were walking together, Black muscled him out of the way to get alongside the former U.S. secretary of state. Jay commented, 'It was a revealing encounter to me of the technique of Conrad.' (Black dismisses the account as 'a wild bowdlerisation'.)

There is little doubt Massey was neglected under the latter McDougald years, when Argus focused on achieving a steady flow of dividends, its only income, at the expense of Massey using its cash flow internally. Between 1978, when the Blacks acquired control of Argus, and 1980, external events accelerated Massey's downward spiral: farm markets did not recover as had been predicted in the wake of the energy crisis; rising interest rates pushed the company into default on its interest payments and debt covenants. In the year ended 31 October 1978, Massey had logged the largest loss in Canadian corporate history, $257 million.

* Hollinger Mines was renamed Hollinger Argus.

With 40,000 shareholders, 45,000 employees and 250 bankers in the balance, turning the company around was an epic challenge. Enter, against this backdrop, Conrad Black. He moved into the boardroom-sized chairman's office at Massey-Ferguson, vacant since Lt-Col Eric Phillips's death fifteen years earlier. By Black's own account, by late 1978 he was spending about two-thirds of his time on Massey-Ferguson business (although his newly appointed president at Massey, Victor Rice, later pegged the workload ratio at eighty-five to fifteen in favour of Argus, and it was pointed out elsewhere that the Argus offices were being redecorated at the time of Black's relocation). Before long, Massey's public relations department enquired whether Black would like any assistance. No thank you, he assured them, he was more than capable of handling the press personally, a stance he has maintained through his career.

'There is mounting evidence the company is turning around,' Black assured the *Globe and Mail* at the end of 1978. 'The bedrock business of Massey-Ferguson is fundamentally sound. When the flood of bad news rolls, that fact encourages me. I remember the thought that institutions, like people, are strengthened through adversity.'

At the same time as he cultivated the notion that he was able and determined to salvage Massey, Black made a point of distancing himself from the deterioration and noting he was not responsible for its decline before he took over. But even as Massey's financial situation went from bad to worse, Black hoped he could restore the company – elevating its new chairman in the process – to greatness. As he wrote in a letter to Robert Anderson, president and chief executive officer of Hanna Mining Co. on 28 April 1980: 'The fact that ill-considered management decisions and bad luck led it to the brink of insolvency must not obscure the enormous opportunity presented by this company, whose acute state of under-capitalisation has made it possible for us to buy real and absolute control of it so comparatively inexpensively, while being hailed as saviours as we do so.'

Under Black's eye and president Victor Rice's stewardship, the company did make fast progress. Rice slashed its international work-force by almost one-third, sold off unprofitable assets (resulting in write-downs of $600 million) and eked out a small operating profit in 1979. But the turnaround was shortlived. Burdened by a debt load of

$1.7 billion, soaring interest rates and a precipitous downturn in the North American farm-machinery market, Massey could not meet conditions imposed by its lenders for the second year in a row. Unless terms were renegotiated by 1 November 1980 – and this meant a new equity issue – Massey would be bankrupt.

Black was willing to put more Argus money, perhaps $100 million, into Massey. But the company needed much more, and without guarantees from the Ontario and Federal governments investors were leery of becoming more deeply involved. 'I am amazed by the number of so-called financial experts who are luxuriating in the view that I am some sort of a punch-drunk prize-fighter on the ropes,' Black said to a journalist from *Maclean's* magazine. 'Well, screw them.'*

Effectively, Black slowly receded from the Massey fray throughout 1980. In May, he relinquished the posts of chairman and chief executive to Rice, but retained the powerful post of chairman of the board's executive committee. Argus's investment in Massey was written down to nothing on its books. But he continued to push for government assistance, meeting and corresponding with industry minister Herb Gray, a move that did not sit well with his critics. As Dixon Chant, then Argus's executive vice-president and a director of Massey recalls, 'Herb Gray's remark to us was that as long as those fat cats at 10 Toronto St weren't going to put any money in, the Federal government wasn't going to put any money in. So we knew we had to do something and stir them up. So then they didn't have any fat cat to criticise and they eventually had to put up money. Strange how those things happen sometimes.'

What Black did took just about everyone by surprise. Chant recalls that Black lumbered down the hall on the second floor of 10 Toronto Street on the afternoon of 1 October 1980, and declared that he had decided to give Argus's sixteen per cent interest in Massey – worth

---

* Black's bluster could sometimes be too much even for himself. In the same article, Black declared: 'I am a historian by vocation, and by that bar I will be judged.' More than a decade later, he recalls, 'I thought to myself as soon as I said it: "That is a terribly pompous thing to say. What does history care about this?" ' Black was reminded of the statement while observing a parliamentary debate in the British House of Commons. 'One of the members of the government said, "History will judge something or other," and another MP, Peter Tapsell said, "I think history will have other things to do." And that's exactly how I felt at the time but I didn't put it to myself as well as that.'

nearly $30 million – to Massey's pension funds. This would no longer create a barrier to government assistance, and Black would (publicly, at least) continue to profess his desire for Argus to participate in Massey's resurrection. As he later explained, 'I was not prepared to tolerate for one more day the allegation that I was attempting to be bailed out.'*

In his 1981 book, *Massey at the Brink*, journalist Peter Cook calls Black's decision to walk away from Massey 'as surprising and controversial as any business decision ever made in Canada'. Black's view was that by withdrawing Argus from Massey, he cleared the way for the government to move forward with their plans. Yet Federal officials later said they were working all along on the premise that Argus would be involved in some sort of solution. And with Argus's withdrawal, Massey's already jittery banks became even more agitated.

Wrote Cook: 'For a self-appointed spokesman for free enterprise like Black to withdraw from Massey was to admit that something very fundamental had gone wrong. He was, after all, declaring that a great Canadian company – with 133 years of history behind it – would be better served by putting itself in the hands of governments and banks than by enjoying the continued participation of its largest private shareholder. Tactically, he may have acted in the best interests of himself and his friends who ran Hollinger Argus. But the precedent of admitting defeat, and leaving the problems to be solved by others, was hardly a helpful one.'

Black's withdrawal was derided by harsh editorials in the *Toronto Star* and *Toronto Sun*. In the media's fickle glare, overnight boy wonder became *enfant terrible*. The liberal *Star*, under the headline 'Black left Massey in lurch', called the stock giveaway 'the sort of irresponsible, self-serving action that has no place in the top echelons of the Canadian marketplace'. Black replied swiftly in a letter to the editor. 'I worked at Massey-Ferguson for nearly two years for no pay and played a modest role in the greatest year-to-year improvement of results in Canadian history. Argus's presence as holder of a modest but traditionally strategic share position was being used as a pretext for governments to do nothing for Massey-Ferguson, while Argus was

---

* It also allowed Black to claim a capital tax loss of $39 million.

being accused of seeking a bail-out to which we were, in fact, opposed . . .

'What then possessed the editors of the *Star* to produce this gratuitous drivel about my "morality and social responsibility"? My associates and I acted as we did because it was the right thing to do. The *Star*'s editorial performance, on the same subject, consisted of misinformed comment from a familiar source, uttered with the conviction that self-righteous ignorance can alone impart.'

The *Toronto Sun* erroneously suggested – and corrected – that by giving away Argus's Massey shares, Black has got rid of some $2 billion in debts. Black wrote to the *Sun*: 'For the record (not that the *Sun* is a newspaper of record for anyone who doesn't suffer from lip-strain after ten seconds of silent reading), the *Sun*'s theory that we should mortgage all the assets of our other companies, which are all prospering and have hundreds of thousands of other shareholders, to bail Massey out of a mess that none of us had any hand in creating, is too asinine to merit further reply.'

Conrad and Monte Black later reflected that the Massey episode was something of which neither was particularly proud. 'We were sitting there worrying about Massey – Massey, Massey, Massey, that's all we did,' recalls one Black insider. 'The actual investment, in the final analysis, was peanuts, but I guess it was the prestige company.' And, once free of its Argus ties, Victor Rice did soon arrange a refinancing of Massey and led it back to health, reinvented as an auto parts company and renamed Varity Corp.

Shortly after buying into Argus, Conrad Black almost exited the newspaper business. In autumn 1978, he and his partners agreed to sell Sterling Newspapers to media group Maclean Hunter Ltd. Sterling, by this time with nine regional dailies and nine weeklies (all, except for the paper in Summerside, Prince Edward Island, in British Columbia), was put up for sale as a means of raising much-needed cash to finance the Ravelston buy-out.* Maclean Hunter agreed to pay $14 million, subject to due diligence, and Black later asserted that its chairman Donald Campbell tried to 'chisel $1.5 million off the purchase price' at the eleventh hour. Campbell claimed the price was

---

* Other steps included the sale by the Blacks of Crown Trust.

based on a multiple of earnings formula, but Sterling's audited results for the year ended 30 June 1978 'did not produce' the expected result. David Radler, who was handling the sale, says merely that the idea of selling was a 'mistake' and that he was relieved it fell apart. To Radler, this string of unspectactular newspapers was and remains 'the base'.

In 1980, Sterling was folded into Western Dominion Investments after a committee of independent (that is, non-Black) directors at Ravelston, in a rare show of dissent, rejected a proposal to buy it.* In addition to providing cash flow to help finance Black's holdings in Ravelston, the amalgamation of Sterling into WDI brought his newspapering partners, Peter White and David Radler, into the Argus adventure as full partners.†

Black might have sold Sterling to an outside buyer but he had by no means lost interest in newspapers. Indeed, Black had his sights on bigger prey: FP Publications Ltd, a federation of eight old family newspapers including Toronto's *Globe and Mail*, Canada's Establishment journal. The chain also included the *Times* and *Colonist* papers in Victoria, the *Winnipeg Free Press* (from which the FP name was derived), the *Ottawa Journal*, and a well-regarded news service. Its *Montreal Star* had recently been closed after failing to recover from a lengthy strike, and a few of the five family blocs controlling the company were ready to sell out. John Bassett and George Gardiner, president of investment firm Gardiner Watson Ltd, invited Black to join them in a bid for the chain. Having just taken over the helm at Argus did not diminish Black's interest in print. 'You've got to take these opportunities when they come and sort it out later,' Black explained afterwards, 'as long as you're not over-extending yourself financially.'

In late November 1979, Black found himself sitting beside *Globe* publisher Roy Megarry at a luncheon for Alberta premier Peter Lougheed given by lawyer (and future prime minister) John Turner. Rumours of his bid were already about, and Megarry greeted him

---

* Monte himself later noted, 'The major item on the balance sheet of Sterling Newspapers was goodwill and goodwill is air and wind.'

† The Blacks' fifty-one per cent interest in Ravelston was held through Western Dominion Investments. About sixty-five per cent of WDI was owned by Warspite Corp., the Black brothers' joint investment company. As a result of the Sterling deal, Radler owned about 13.5 per cent of WDI, White about 12.5 per cent, and Conrad Black held another nine per cent.

with, 'I understand you're negotiating with FP. I think that's great.' After lunch, Megarry offered Cardinal Emmett Carter, head of Toronto's Archdiocese, the use of his car, and Black gave Megarry a lift to the *Globe*. As Black recalls it, they parked in front of the *Globe* on Front Street and 'chatted' for about ten minutes.

The publisher came away from the chat convinced that Black was dead set against his plan to transform the *Globe* into a national newspaper. Black says he only said that while he didn't object to the idea, he thought the *Globe* should ensure it maintained its position in Toronto. According to Black, Megarry's parting words were, 'Well, I'm not against this. It is not a negative thing and it could be really a good thing for us. I'm not against it.' Black replied, 'We'll be in touch.'

Black later felt Megarry was 'extremely disingenuous' when he proceeded to confer with the *Globe*'s editor, Dick Doyle, telling him: 'We will have to do something about this.' Whatever impression Megarry might have given Black, the idea of his group assuming ownership of the *Globe* was received with something less than warmth, although most of the opposition was directed towards Bassett, who, as publisher of the *Toronto Telegram*, had adopted a hands-on and in-your-face style. Some at the *Globe* had either left the *Telegram* under Bassett or had lost their jobs when the paper folded in 1971, and had no desire to work for him again.

The uneasy *Globe* staff were gathered in the newsroom by Megarry. He announced that he couldn't substantiate the rumours of a bid by Black and his group, but rallied support for an employee buy-out. Despite the spirited financial pledges of the journalists, by January FP was sold to billionaire Kenneth Thomson for $165 million. The Black-Gardiner-Bassett group had dropped out of the running some $40 million earlier, but not before Black had delivered a scathing letter for publication – something he was developing quite a penchant for – in the *Globe*, accusing Megarry of being 'indiscreet and amateurish', adding that 'we are not the ravaging dragon trying to defile the virgin *Globe and Mail*'.

Although the *Globe* is one which got away from him, Black had plenty of other things with which to keep himself occupied. His hallmark quickly became shuffling the companies in the Argus group. Between 1978, when he and his brother took over Argus, and 1984, the holdings within the group were reorganised no less than eight times.

To fans, Black was a grand-master moving his pieces around the board or a general orchestrating a battle. To critics, it had the appearance of an elaborate shell game. 'He's just getting rich,' Montreal investment counseller Stephen Jarislowsky told the *Financial Post*. 'If you look at it, he buys in cheap, at a discount, then he liquidates the assets at a higher value. It's very simple. But he's not doing anything for shareholders in the meantime.'

A 1984 report by analyst David Ramsay at Wood Gundy Inc. in Toronto cited a 'Black Factor' that depressed the value of some of the companies' stocks by an estimated ten per cent. Unfazed, Black responded with his own theory that the so-called factor worked to his advantage, because he could buy back shares and do more reorganisations at attractive prices, freeing value out of Argus's moribund companies.

When called upon to explain his actions, Conrad Black is capable of sending forth large armadas of military metaphors and analogies.

He often cites 'Napoleon's famous maxim that force equals mass times velocity. As the Argus group was a collection of passive minority shareholdings in rather tired companies and the only cash flow was dividends, there was no mass, in Napoleonic terms. So our only strength came from velocity, as in Napoleon's first famous campaign, in Italy in 1796 and 1797. On that occasion he marched and counter-marched 30,000 untrained ragged conscripts around with such skill that he bundled the much superior Austrians right out of Italy, while rarely actually giving battle. I hope it is not too self-indulgent to consider our activities at Argus in our first six or seven years a pallid adaptation of those tactics. We had to conduct a war of manoeuvre because we had no financial divisions with which to fight a pitched battle.'

Black explained that he and his associates wanted to sell most of Argus's assets, and use the proceeds to shore up control over those businesses they wanted to keep, and 'reposition ourselves in businesses we were better suited to. We didn't know our exact destination or a precise map towards it, but we did know, generally, how to get there.'

So complex did Black's dealings become during this period that Jack Boultbee, his private accountant, plotted organisation charts of the Black empire on wallet-sized cards so that he could see which company owned what at any particular moment. Where Argus was headed was unclear. But it also seemed that the more the organisation chart shifted, the greater Black's ambitions grew.

FOUR

Blacklash

'I'm willing to take up the cudgels for
those less able to defend themselves
than I'

During the late morning on 27 June, 1980, Conrad Black materialised in the doorway of George Humphrey Jr's office on the twenty-sixth floor Cleveland, Ohio headquarters of the Hanna Mining Co. In addition to being a descendant of Hanna's founder and a member of its largest group of shareholders, Humphrey was also Hanna's vice-president of sales. Among the myriad corporate interests Black and his brother Montegu controlled through their Argus group was a 10.5 per cent interest in the Iron Ore Company of Canada, and Conrad Black served as a director.*

Hanna, in turn, owned 26.5 per cent of Iron Ore and managed it under agreement. Black was in the building to attend the Iron Ore board meeting that day. The association between Hanna and Argus was long standing, and Black had taken an active interest in the American company's affairs since getting to know former Hanna chairman George M. 'Bud' Humphrey Sr through board meetings at Massey-Furguson and at Labrador Mining (of which Hanna owned twenty per cent).

Bud's son George did not know the visitor in his doorway well, but Black seemed to know much about him. The Hanna board had appointed its first non-family chief executive, Bob Anderson, after Bud's death the previous year, and Black asked Humphrey how he felt about his family being 'shunted out of the mainstream' of Hanna's management. Black's instincts were correct; Humphrey was not

---

* The interest in Iron Ore was held 7.5 per cent by Hollinger Argus, formerly Hollinger Mines, and three per cent by Labrador Mining and Exploration. Hollinger Argus owned sixty-seven per cent of Labrador.

happy about it. 'He was extremely embittered at what he felt to be the unfair treatment by the incumbent Hanna management of his family and himself,' Black recalled, 'and he was severe in his criticism of the management and very troubled because he was part of the management and his family was still heavily invested in the company stock and he was in a very serious quandary about what to do.'

Black's advice was cautious. He said that from his vantage point, as an Iron Ore shareholder, Hanna seemed to be in very capable hands under Anderson. At the same time Black could relate to George's dissatisfaction, having made his own name in the wake of the death of another Bud. He told Humphrey that his situation 'was to me a little reminiscent of some of the treatment my brother and I received for a time after the death of the former chairman of our company, who was not personally related but a man we knew very well, and that I could sympathise with him but I thought patience would be rewarded'.

Naturally, when Black said he had some ideas about collaborating with the Humphrey family on the ownership of Hanna, Humphrey told his visitor he would be open to discussing it further. Several weeks later, Black joined Humphrey and his wife for dinner at their home in Gates Hills, Ohio. The conversation was the same, but at considerably greater length, with Humphrey reiterating his disgruntlement, and Black mentioning that Hanna looked like an 'interesting vehicle' for expansion into the United States because of the long-standing corporate association with Argus. Humphrey mentioned that he would like to run Hanna someday. Black emphasised that he was not trying to 'exploit any factionalism' within Hanna and that his potential involvement was 'one of conciliation'. Black continued to praise Hanna and its management, and said that if George or any member of his family objected to Black's becoming involved with Hanna on a friendly basis, he would not proceed. Both men agreed to mull over their respective positions.

Black was enamoured not just of Hanna but of the notion of expanding in the U.S. and into the resource sector in particular. In late 1979, Black had begun to add Norcen Energy Resources, a Calgary-based oil and gas producer with no dominant shareholder, to the ever-shifting Argus stable. Through Labrador Mining, where he was vice-chairman, Black began to buy ten per cent of Norcen on 12 December of that year. The next day he phoned Norcen chief executive Edward Bovey, with whom he enjoyed friendly relations. Bovey asked Black his intentions, and he said Labrador might wish to buy more shares at some point, but did not aspire to more than fifty per cent and 'did not wish to relegate Norcen to the role of subsidiary'.

Subsidiary or not, around mid-January, 1980, Black decided to bring his interest in Norcen up to thirty-six per cent and effective control. Bovey soon retired, and Black became vice-chairman and later chairman. Edward Battle, a Texas-born petroleum engineer who had been with Norcen since 1957 and president since 1975, was named chief executive. Once in control at Norcen, the Black brothers' aim was to assemble a powerful resource group which could take maximum advantage of tax shelters available to oil and gas exploration at the time, to shelter the earnings they generated through Hollinger Mines. As Montegu Black said: 'In the companies that we had in Argus Corporation, the one with the money and horsepower was always Hollinger.'

That horsepower was derived largely from its interest in Iron Ore. Hollinger earned most of its cash flow from royalties on Iron Ore's sales of up to 16 million tons of iron pellets per year to U.S. steel companies. Labrador received a sales commission of five per cent, which could amount to as much as $50 million annually.* Under its management agreement, Hanna's appointed CEO of Iron Ore was labour lawyer Brian Mulroney, whose political aspirations were well known, and who, like Black, studied law at Laval University. Mulroney and Black were both directors of the Canadian Imperial Bank of Commerce, as was Norcen's Bovey.†

Hanna seemed to fit Black's criteria for expansion. Founded in 1853 by Mark Hanna, Hanna Mining's iron ore fields in Minnesota and northern Michigan fuelled a powerful financial and political machine. Mark Hanna virtually ruled the Republican Party in the late 1800s and is credited with engineering the election of William McKinley as president in 1896. (It was a minor irony that Conrad Black should target a pillar of the corporate world in Cleveland for it was the same city where his father had made his name as a young brewery executive more than three decades earlier.)

* See diagram 'The Black Companies in 1981' on p.83.
† Mulroney also sat on the board of Black-controlled Standard Broadcasting Co.

The Black Companies in 1981

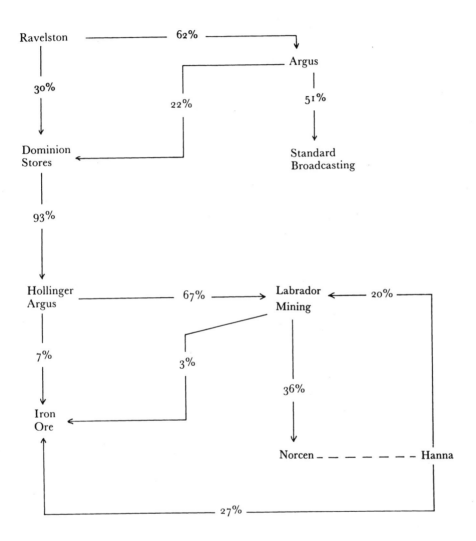

What seemed especially appealing to Black was the big league prestige that Hanna represented. Certainly Black was a big fish in Canada, but his disenchantment was growing both with his public image there and the general business climate. He was impressed by the course the U.S. economy was taking, and became more so when Ronald Reagan was elected in 1980. Since 1978, the year he took control of Argus, Black had spent his winters in Palm Beach, the bastion of dynastic opulence on Florida's Atlantic coast. To winter there was not only to follow in the footsteps of former Argus head Bud McDougald, but to rub shoulders with the cream of American tycoonery. 'Palm Beach isn't everyone's cup of tea,' Black told writer Peter Newman. 'Some people are offended by the extreme opulence, but I find it sort of entertaining.'

Wintering among them was one thing, but to tangle head on with the big boys in the U.S. was a achievement uncommon even among the first rank of Canadian tycoons. In Hanna Black found a venerable company, without any controlling shareholder, that was feeling the brunt of recession and a crisis among its main customers, the U.S. steel industry. Hanna generated profits of US$44 million on sales of US$290 million in the year ended 31 December 1981. The Humphreys, Mark Hanna's heirs, held a cumulative interest in Hanna Mining estimated at twenty per cent, amplified by connections and shareholdings with such American dynasties as the Mellons, Bechtels and Graces.

Black would later recall the Hanna episode as 'a fierce litigious and regulatory firefight which entertained the financial press and its devotees for almost a year'. But for Black himself it was more: After the rise of his corporate star in Canada, the move on Hanna was chief among a string of controversies which would add a darker shade to Black's reputation. The Hanna battle and its aftermath led him to question institutions and friendships he had valued in a country where he had risen to a prominent position, and for others to judge Black more harshly.

The next Humphrey family member to encounter Conrad Black was George Humphrey's mother, Louise 'Lulu' Humphrey, Bud's bejewelled widow. The backdrop was a white-tie tribute to Canada at New York's Lincoln Center Metropolitan Opera house on 4 April 1981, almost ten months after Black's encounter with George. There, about sixty Canadians, led by Prime Minister Pierre Trudeau and his date, Texas model and socialite Lacey Neuhaus, were entertained. Lulu, one of the opera's patrons, knew Black was an acquaintance of her son and of her daughter who lived in Toronto, and arranged for him to be seated beside her, at table ten. They spoke at length, and at one point the Humphrey matriarch criticised Hanna management and told Black she was concerned about her sons' careers. She asked Black to keep in touch and, as he recalled, 'I floated very gingerly with her the idea of whether, if we bought some shares, whether that would be regarded as a friendly or an unfriendly thing by her family. She replied, "No, not at all," that in fact they would be "delighted if we bought some shares".'

As Hanna's representative, George Humphrey arrived in Toronto the next month for Labrador's annual meeting; afterwards Conrad and Monte invited him to meet them privately at their offices at 10 Toronto Street. Conrad Black again raised the possibility of an investment in Hanna, on a friendly basis – then asked that Humphrey keep their conversations private. Next, he spoke to Brian Mulroney, who assured Black he would 'diplomatically present that case' to his masters at Hanna when called upon.

In August 1981, a full year after his dinner at George Humphrey's home, Black and Norcen president Battle laid plans to buy up to 4.9 per cent of Hanna's outstanding stock on the open market – any more would have to be disclosed to the U.S. Securities and Exchange Commission. On Saturday 15 August at around seven p.m., Black phoned Humphrey at his holiday home in Maine and said he was now contemplating buying into Hanna on an 'imminent basis'. He reiterated that he wanted only to proceed on friendly terms, and that he would be willing to buy shares from the Humphreys if they had any they were willing to sell. Humphrey did not react as Black expected. The 'situation had changed completely', he told Black. For one thing, Humphrey had recently been elected to the Hanna board of directors, which gave him more security about his family's interests; he was now fully committed to working with Hanna management. 'This was around the dinner hour and I didn't want to spend all night on the phone with Conrad Black,' he later recalled.

Undeterred by Humphrey's brush-off, the next Monday Norcen began making open market purchases of Hanna stock through Michael Biscotti, the chief trader at Dominion Securities Ames Ltd. Three days later, Battle arranged for a $20 million line of credit from the Canadian Imperial Bank of Commerce to purchase up to 4.9 per cent of Hanna's stock. The account was outside Norcen's normal operating lines of credit, was assigned a secret account number, and bank officers were under orders not to deliver statements to Norcen's offices.

By 9 September, Norcen had accumulated 58,000 shares, about two per cent of the company. That day, the executive committee of Norcen's board met in Calgary and discussed the Hanna investment. The minutes for the meeting included the entry, 'U.S. Acquisition: Mr Battle stated that the Company, subsequent to telephone contact with the members of the executive committee, had initiated through stock market transactions the acquisition of a 4.9 per cent stock interest in a U.S. company listed on the New York stock exchange with the ultimate purpose of acquiring a fifty-one per cent position at a later date.' This would later prove to be a contentious statement.

By the end of October, Norcen owned 4.9 per cent of Hanna. Black planned to contact Hanna management at this point, but the strategy changed when Black received an unsolicited phone call from James 'Jimmy' Connacher, who was the head of Gordon Securities Ltd, in Toronto.

Connacher offered Black a huge block of Hanna stock, about 575,000 shares. Although it represented a departure from Black's previous plan of staying below the public disclosure threshold until approaching management, and the shares were several dollars above the market price at $37, Black accepted after speaking to his brother and Battle. He later claimed in court – where this escapade would soon be headed – that Connacher gave no indication he was aware Black was buying Hanna shares, nor how Gordon had accumulated the block. 'He did not tell me,' said Black, 'and I did not ask.'

At three thirty p.m. on 28 October 1981, Carl Nickels, Hanna's executive vice-president, was on the phone with Mulroney speculating about who was buying all the shares in Hanna. Although Mulroney must have surmised it was Black, he apparently did not say so. According to Nickels's intelligence, there was an open purchase order for the shares at Gordon. Meanwhile Black had tried to contact Anderson but he was away in Brazil. In the midst of his chat with Mulroney, Nickels's secretary brought him a note saying that Conrad Black was on the other line.

Nickels finished his conversation with Mulroney, and, putting two and two together, picked up the phone and barked, 'What the hell are you doing, Conrad?' Even Black might have been startled by such a reception, but he quickly told Nickels that Norcen had acquired an 8.8 per cent stake in Hanna 'for investment purposes', and that they had no ulterior motive – they were fans of Hanna's management and looking to find a way to diversify into the United States because of disenchantment with the business climate in Canada. 'We like Hanna very much, and we like what they are doing, and we would like to increase our investment,' Nickels recalled Black saying.

Black told Nickels he and Norcen were 'absolutely friendly buyers, and had no sinister motives, and there was a range of alternatives that we could talk about'. Black gave his word not to buy any more shares until he met Anderson. He and Norcen's chief executive, Edward Battle, would fly to Cleveland as soon as possible.

That night, Black phoned Mulroney and asked him to make good on his pledge to assure his Hanna masters 'that I didn't have cloven feet and wear horns'. His objective, 'in the best of all possible worlds', he told Mulroney, was a stake in Hanna around twenty per cent – about the size of Hanna's investment in Labrador.

The next day, Black left a message with George Humphrey, who phoned back and told Black his purchases had caused consternation among management. 'He used a football metaphor with which I was not altogether familiar,' recalled Black. 'He said that he welcomed it "as long as we are not blind-sided, and I am sure we won't be", and I am afraid my knowledge of football is such that I was uncertain of what he meant.'

On 4 November, Conrad Black and Edward Battle met Robert Anderson and Carl Nickels in a first-floor conference room at the Sheraton Hopkins Hotel near Cleveland's Hopkins Airport. Anderson kicked off the meeting by telling Black in no uncertain terms that he wanted Norcen to 'peel off' its shares – to sell them, but slowly so as to attract little attention.

Black had been warned that Anderson possessed a somewhat volatile personality. Black did not know that Nickels, after their telephone conversation, had phoned investment banker Goldman Sachs and ordered a full report on Black. Goldman delivered a stinging indictment of the man, compiled largely from Canadian press reports, portraying him as a shuffler of assets. The report was presented at a Hanna board meeting convened on 3 November. After recounting his conversation with Black to the board, Nickels had talked about the 'problem areas' he foresaw with Black's investment. One, Nickels later explained, was 'the general overall impact that Conrad Black – that a Conrad Black – would have on the type of partnership arrangements that we have, where we have really a very close fiduciary relationship, where you would never expect a man sitting next to you as a partner to turn around and start buying you without talking to you'.

The Hanna board voted unanimously to oppose Black as an investor. At one point during the meeting near Cleveland airport the next day, Nickels told Black he considered him a 'paper shuffler'. Black took umbrage, and pointed out that he and his brother had rationalised companies which had been run in 'a somewhat anachronistic manner'. Pointing to his pocket, Black claimed that along the way he and Monte had increased the equity of Ravelston, the private company atop the Argus group in which they had their investment, by some $200 million.

The meeting lasted ninety minutes. Before they parted, Black said to Anderson, 'Could you give us any incentive to sell our shares?' Anderson steadfastly refused to consider any of the ideas Black threw out, including a trade of Norcen's Hanna shares for Hanna's Labrador Mining shares, or a standstill agreement. As they returned to Toronto on their plane, Black and Battle surveyed the wreckage of their planned 'amicable arrangement' with Hanna. They now had 8.8 per cent of the company but no workable plan.

The next day Black ran into Mulroney at a directors' meeting. Mulroney reported that he had tried to ease the way with Hanna, as Black had asked, but the reception was so cold he thought Norcen had no serious option but to do as Anderson said and sell its shares. Mulroney said he was beginning to feel like the 'jam in the sandwich'.

On 9 November 1981, Norcen filed its required schedule 13-D with the Securities and Exchange Commission. Under the heading 'Purpose of the Transaction', the document stated that the purpose 'was to acquire an investment position in Hanna', and that Norcen would review its position 'from time to time' and may seek to acquire further shares or sell them. There was no mention of the resolution cited in the minutes of the Norcen executive committee two months earlier: that the ultimate purpose was to acquire fifty-one per cent of

Hanna. On the advice of Norcen's U.S. counsel, Black instructed that the SEC filing should be 'as short and antiseptic as possible'.

Later that month, William Kilbourne, Norcen's chief legal officer and the man responsible for keeping minutes of board and executive committee meetings, asked high-powered New York law firm Cravath, Swaine & Moore to prepare research about state and federal laws that applied to buying control of Hanna. Kilbourne later said he was merely 'preparing for all possible contingencies'.

Around the same time, Black decided once again to approach the Humphrey family. On the Thanksgiving weekend, Black called Lulu Humphrey at her home in Tallahassee, Florida, and explained that he had bought shares but was now immobilised and wondering what to do with them. The matriarch deferred the matter to her son and principal financial adviser, Gilbert Watts Humphrey, known as Watts. Black told Watts how he was 'somewhat flabbergasted at the militancy of Mr Anderson's request' not to buy any more shares and added that 'we didn't want to rock the boat and we just sincerely didn't know what do to'. Watts agreed that a meeting might be useful.

On 21 December, Conrad Black, Monte Black and Edward Battle visited Watts Humphrey, younger brother of George, at his home in Sewickley, Pennsylvania. Black summarised the evolution of the Argus relationship with Hanna. Black again said he was interested in getting involved with those who had significant interests in Hanna, specifically the Mellons, Bechtels and Graces, using terms such as 'those are very good people to be associated with' and 'they are substantial and their interests are broad-ranging'. Black asked if Watts could foresee 'any useful collaboration' between himself and the family, with the proviso that it could not be perceived to be hostile towards management. Humphrey appeared interested, and said he would consult other family members and Paul Mellon, a significant Hanna shareholder and his neighbour. After the meeting, an encouraged Battle instructed Kilbourne to have prepared two draft tender offers for Hanna stock. These included a stock purchase agreement with members of the Humphrey clan, described in the drafts only as 'Z family'.

On Friday 5 February 1982, a second meeting was held with Watts Humphrey, Monte Black and Edward Battle, over lunch at Sewickley's Edgewood Club. Soon into the lunch, Battle said Norcen was 'ready to go' with a tender offer. This surprised Watts. He had already decided he didn't want to pursue an alliance with the Norcen people, but did not say so. Battle said Norcen was willing to give the Humphreys an option to purchase a percentage of the stock acquired under the offer. The meeting ended with no commitments, and that night Watts called his brother George, and learned of the talks his brother had held with the Blacks earlier. Watts thought over the situation all weekend, then called Monte Black and explained that he had problems with Norcen's approach and had decided not to go along with them. He sensed disappointment on the other end of the line during the ten-minute phone call. Norcen's designs on a partnership with the Humphrey clan were quickly evaporating.

The Blacks' efforts to woo the Humphreys did have a positive effect: word of the meetings with Watts reached Hanna chief executive Robert Anderson. Accompanied by Nickels and George Humphrey, Anderson travelled to 10 Toronto Street to meet the Blacks and Battle. This was much more to Conrad's liking. Anderson said he now might consider the Blacks' earlier idea of swapping Hanna's Labrador shares for Norcen's Hanna shares. Black was interested, while Battle, seeing no obvious benefit in that for Norcen, pressed the idea of Norcen achieving a twenty-five to thirty per cent stake in Hanna and entering into a standstill agreement under which it would agree to buy no more shares for a period of time.*

Anderson and Nickels flew to Palm Beach for a follow-up meeting with Black and Battle at Conrad Black's winter home. There, they presented a one-page swap agreement, which included an commitment from Black not to buy Hanna shares for ten years. Black now concurred with Battle that there was nothing in such a deal for Norcen and continued to press the idea of a twenty per cent investment, which included buying Hanna shares out of its treasury. Anderson replied that he was not authorised by his board to discuss anything but the swap proposal. Nothing would be resolved that night. Black took his guests outside for a drink, then back to the airport.

Determined to bring the episode to a conclusion, a dozen days later

---

* Norcen wanted to own at least twenty per cent of Hanna because under Canadian accounting rules it could then incorporate Hanna's earnings into its own profit and loss statements, rather than merely account for its shareholding as an investment.

Conrad and Montegu Black assembled their legal and banking advisers at Conrad's Florida *pied-à-terre* and developed a strategy for a possible tender offer. A climactic meeting with Anderson was set for four thirty p.m. on Friday 2 April 1982, again in the first-floor conference room of Cleveland's Sheraton Hopkins Hotel. Anderson and Nickels were surprised when Battle and Monte Black arrived sans Conrad. In Palm Beach, wife Shirley was seven months pregnant with their second child and feeling ill, and Black did not want to leave her, even for a day. The Hanna executives were even more surprised when Battle kicked off the proceedings with, 'I am here today to tell you, number one, that on Monday morning the board of directors of Norcen has authorised me to go for a tender offer for fifty-one per cent of the Hanna Mining stock.'

Battle added that Norcen had retained Lehman Brothers and renowned New York take-over lawyer Joe Flom of the firm Scadden Arps.* The hostile bid could only be avoided, Battle continued, if Hanna accepted a standstill agreement which gave Norcen the ability to buy thirty per cent of its shares, but no more for the next five years. Most of the shares would be bought from Hanna's treasury, which would give it needed capital. But in return, Norcen wanted board representation and a say in how Hanna could spend the $70 million or so Norcen proposed to invest in the company. Norcen considered the condition a reasonable means of protecting its investment; to Anderson and his team, it was nothing but a clever tactic for locking up control. Leaving the Hanna executives to consider the proposal, Battle added that he and Black had a private plane departing Hopkins Airport at seven fifteen p.m. If they did not hear from Hanna by then, they would launch the take-over offer. If, however, Hanna was willing to negotiate a standstill, Battle would stay through the weekend to finalise the details. One way or another, Black's two-year-long ambition to become a major shareholder in Hanna would be achieved.

After taking a break for about twenty minutes, Anderson concluded Norcen had put Hanna 'in an awful box and put a gun to our head'. He said he would consider the proposal and another meeting

---

* Norcen had already arranged another special line in credit with the Bank of Commerce for $400 million – approved at a board meeting when Mulroney happened to be absent.

was arranged for Sunday morning at the offices of Hanna's Cleveland law firm, Jones, Day, Reavis & Pogue. Anderson telephoned Conrad and asked him to attend, but Black did not make the trip to Cleveland. Privately, Black thought that it would appear to his brother and to Battle that he lacked faith in their abilities if he were to re-enter the negotiations now. At the Sunday meeting, Anderson counter-offered to allow Norcen a twenty per cent interest, a ten-year (rather than five-year) standstill clause, and no control over board decisions. After a half-hour break, Battle re-entered the room and threw copies of Hanna's proposal on the conference room table, declaring, 'I'm not even going to bother with these agreements because they are completely unacceptable. They are not what we want.' 'You have moved so far from our position that there is nothing here to negotiate,' Monte Black added. This incensed the Hanna executives, who felt they had in fact come a very long way – from wanting Norcen to own no Hanna shares to allowing the Blacks and their associates the twenty per cent they had claimed was their ambition all along. Apparently long-forgotten as well were Conrad Black's early assurances that he did not wish to rock the boat. The meeting ended and the Canadian executives boarded their jet.

Anderson again telephoned Conrad Black and asked him to intervene. But Black says he did not want to overrule Battle and particularly Monte by getting directly involved in trying to salvage the negotiations. 'Our thought was that we had a real good shot to negotiate something,' Black later recalled. 'So I thought that they might not negotiate all the way through it on Sunday and I could come in later. But then the whole thing collapsed. That was not what we were expecting.'

Nevertheless, on Monday morning, Norcen followed through on its threat and launched its tender offer at US$45 a share. Hanna stock, which had been trading in the US$26–27 range, had risen to almost US$32 on rumours of a bid.

Hanna had been waiting. Barely an hour after the bid was announced, Hanna filed a fraud and racketeering suit in the United States District Court for the Northern District of Ohio, Eastern Division, against Norcen, Conrad Black, Montegu Black, Edward Battle, and Lehman Brothers Kuhn Loeb Inc. Hanna claimed that Norcen had made false disclosures to the Securities and Exchange

Commission about their intentions in order to depress Hanna stock, and a temporary restraining order against the bid was issued that day by the court. No fewer than thirty-seven lawyers from Jones, Day, Reavis & Pogue, Hanna's firm, were dispatched across the continent to put together the case against Norcen. Black and his lawyers, equally versed in corporate warfare, prepared an aggressive defence for the case set to be heard in Cleveland ten days later.

On 10 April, the day before Easter, two lawyers from Jones, Day, descended on Black in Palm Beach to take his deposition.* The Hanna counsel questioned Black for nearly twelve combative hours. Black knew the entire affair had begun badly, and would later reflect on the court challenge with more than his usual metaphoric vigour. 'It was the adventures of King Pyrrhus, rather than MacArthur and Napoleon,' he later reflected. 'That was a real fifteen-round main event we had going for a while there.'

In gathering evidence, the Hanna lawyers believed they had unearthed indisputable proof of Norcen's illegal behaviour – and the document bore Conrad Black's signature. The key piece of evidence was the 9 September minute of the Norcen executive committee, prepared by Kilbourne and signed by Black, which authorised the initial purchase of 4.9 per cent of Hanna, 'with the ultimate purpose of acquiring a fifty-one per cent position at a later date'.

Although it was standard procedure for him to review the minutes and sign them, Black said he did not sign the minutes in question until some two months after the 9 September meeting. The minutes were disclosed in an amended 13-D filing by Norcen to the SEC on 9 April, with the explanation that the notion of fifty-one per cent was intended by Battle as a 'corporate goal consistent with Norcen's long-range planning to be achieved by Norcen over a period in excess of five years'. Norcen's defence would also reveal in embarrassing detail the extent of George Humphrey's disgruntlement with Anderson before being made a director, and attempt to show that Black had in fact been encouraged in his Hanna forays by members of the Humphrey family.

In Palm Beach, Hanna lawyer John Straugh pressed Black on the

---

* Black was joined by Norcen vice-president William Kilbourne, three Cravath Swaine lawyers representing him, and, elsewhere in his house, his friend Emmett Cardinal Carter, Archbishop of Toronto.

9 September meeting, and Black explained the fifty-one per cent idea came up only when Battle 'tossed it off as an ultimate possibility'. Black proved to be a smug and rambunctious deponent.

'Now you are leading the witness,' he told Straugh during one exchange.

'I'm what?'

'You are leading the witness a little tendentiously.'

'Let me explain to you,' Straugh countered, 'that is permitted under cross-examination in our country.'

'I'm not suggesting it isn't permitted, I'm suggesting I would rephrase in my own words what I'm saying, if I may.'

Black argued that it wasn't a big deal what the minutes said; that the idea they represented an intent to take over Hanna was a 'misleading conclusion'.

The minutes, Straugh pressed, suggest 'that the initiation of the stock market transactions referred to were undertaken with the ultimate purpose of acquring a fifty-one per cent position at a later date, doesn't it?'

'It would be entirely possible to derive that erroneous impression, yes,' Black replied.

Straugh asked if Battle ever used the term 'investment purpose' – which eventually appeared on the SEC filing – during the executive committee meeting.

'No,' said Black, 'it is not a phrase that leaps to the tongue very readily.'

'I wasn't asking you about the extent to which the phrase leaps or doesn't leap to the tongue or anywhere else,' Straugh snapped. 'Did anyone else, including yourself, describe this stock acquisition programme as one for "investment purposes"?'

'I don't recall anyone doing so. It was just . . . that could be taken as tautology in the use of the word investment, however.'

'Could be taken as what?'

'Tautology: self-evidently true.'

'I understand the meaning of that word and others in the English language.'

As the day wore on, tension grew between Straugh and Black's lead lawyer, Paul Saunders, over such minutiae as whether there had been a lunch break. 'We have been sitting at this deposition since nine o'clock this morning,' Saunders complained at one point. 'We didn't take lunch. We didn't . . .'

'Let me interrupt,' Straugh interjected.

'Don't interrupt!'

'Don't shout at me, pal,' Straugh glowered. 'I offered you lunch and you refused it.'

'Sit down.'

'Don't make a speech for the record . . .'

'John, don't interrupt me,' Saunders warned.

'. . about not having had lunch.'

'Sit down. Don't mention . . .'

Finally, Black chimed in, 'Nobody mentioned lunch.'

The case came to trial before Judge John Manos on 15 April in Cleveland's U.S. district court-house. 'The defendants' repeated misrepresentations concerning their plan to gain control of Hanna were not the result of inadvertence or indecision,' Patrick McCartan of Jones, Day told Manos in his opening statement, 'but, instead, were part of a carefully constructed plan to accomplish their objective in a market they intended to deceive and to manipulate in order to acquire control of Hanna at the lowest possible price.'

For two of the hearing's several days, Conrad Black took the stand. Manos granted Hanna's request for a preliminary injunction against Norcen on 11 June, calling Norcen's construction of the record 'strained and unpersuasive'. Contrary to the defendants' contention that Norcen's intent to make a tender offer for Hanna was formulated on the eve of the bid, Manos found the evidence 'established conclusively' that Norcen contemplated the action as early as 9 November 1981, if not earlier; yet Norcen described its intent as 'investment' in the 13-D filing it made that day and on three other occasions. Black and Norcen immediately appealed against the decision to the U.S. Court of Appeals in Cincinatti, receiving approval for an expedited appeal.

In late June, the SEC withdrew charges that Black and Norcen had made false and misleading statements when Black and Norcen signed a 'consent decree'. (A fairly standard wrist-slap under which neither guilt nor innocence is established.) They admitted no previous wrongdoing, but promised to refrain from future securities law infractions.

The spectacle came to a sudden end in early July when Black negotiated a $90 million truce with Hanna that saw Norcen achieve a deal much like earlier, rejected proposals: Norcen purchased 1.25 million treasury shares at US$45 – the tender offer price – which, added to its 8.8 per cent, brought it up to twenty per cent. Norcen agreed to an eight-year standstill; the two Black brothers and Battle were added to the Hanna board, with Conrad Black joining the executive committee. Norcen also purchased Hanna's twenty per cent interest in Labrador Mining & Exploration and its forty per cent stake in another subsidiary, Hollinger North Shore Exploration, doubling its share of the royalties of Iron Ore Company in the process. From then on Black was welcomed on the Hanna board, the hostilities quickly forgotten.

'I never had any fears how it was going to end up,' Black declared at the time. 'It's all atmospherics in the United States. They never believed a goddamn word of all that bunk about racketeering. But some of our more credulous and Boy-Scoutish locals sure believed it.'

In private, Black was considerably less self-assured, says Peter White. Indeed, as far as White could tell, his long-time friend and business partner was 'paranoid' about the legal challenges mounted against him. 'Conrad was astounded, I think, at the strength and the force and the viciousness of the response' from Hanna, says White. 'He certainly didn't expect to be accused of racketeering for what he did.' White recalls walking down the second-floor hall at 10 Toronto Street one day in the midst of the episode and finding Black pacing around his office.

'Peter, they are out to get me,' Black announced. 'But they won't.'

The truce with Hanna, however, was far from the end of the matter. It was just Act One in what Black came to call an 'Orwellian Drama' – with himself cast in the lead role.

At some point after Black's corporate ascent some four years earlier, the Metropolitan Toronto Police Department's fraud squad opened an active file on his activities, spurred by the private criticisms of stockbrokers who knew members of the squad. Those who followed Black's moves drew analogies to Robert Vesco, an American financier who looted millions from investors through a pyramid of mutual fund companies and fled to a life of grandeur in Central

America. The more the police watched Black's byzantine transactions, the ultimate result of which was Black's private holding company, Ravelston, getting richer, the more suspicious they grew. No complaints were made by minority shareholders to the police or the Ontario Securities Commission, despite whispers that these moves were oppressive to them.

'He had the argument in every instance that there was a valid corporate purpose for what he was doing,' says one person who had access to the police file. 'But the consequence was undeniable, that his private holding company – which had nothing [beyond its ownership in Ravelston] to begin with – kept getting richer and richer. And it was that money that he eventually used when he essentially left Canada and went over and bought into the newspaper business in England.'

Obviously, the notion that Black increased his wealth through his actions is not one with which he would disagree. The suggestion that his asset-stripping was in some way illegal, however, was a far more serious matter. The manoeuvre the Toronto police zeroed in on during the Hanna proceedings was a decision taken by the Norcen board of directors in Calgary on 16 October 1981 – at the same directors' meeting where the board ratified the executive committee's decision to buy up to 4.9 per cent of Hanna – to buy up to 4.99 per cent of its own shares, a fairly common practice by companies who believe their shares are undervalued by the market. In order to buy back the Norcen stock, the directors approved a draft of a notice that was to be sent to all shareholders. This notice, or 'issuer bid circular', invited shareholders to sell their shares and, as prescribed by Ontario securities law, disclosed any material changes the company had planned. 'Norcen has no present plans or proposals for material changes in its affairs,' stated the material sent to shareholders on 28 and 29 October 1981.

The purpose of material change disclosure is to ensure that the market is fully informed when making decisions: Had it been disclosed that Norcen was planning a major acquisition, the value of its shares might have increased or decreased.

The police also believed that the stock buy-back was a step towards firming up Black's control over Norcen. Before the buy-back, Black held thirty-six per cent of Norcen indirectly through Labrador Mining & Exploration. As a result of cancelling 4.99 per cent of

Norcen's shares, Black's interest would increase slightly – not a great difference, but one that would cost Norcen $33.7 million and Labrador nothing. The police believed that Black was taking steps to protect against Hanna responding to his unwanted advances with a counter-attack: a take-over bid for smaller Norcen.

As tenuous as the police's hypothesising might have sounded to Black, to them it was as plausible as the official explanation, that buy-backs increase the value of the remaining shares.*

The Toronto police suspected that the issuer bid may have been a 'forgery' as defined by the criminal code of Canada: a false document on which other people might rely. They felt confident enough of their suspicions to act. Robert Barbour and Robert Greig, both sergeants with the fraud squad, drew up three search warrants with the help of crown attorney Brian Johnston. The warrants listed forgery and uttering as the suspected offences.

On 13 May 1982 – while Judge Manos's judgement on the Norcen bid for Hanna was being awaited in Cleveland – the police search warrants seeking documents related to the take-over were executed against three Toronto law firms. Black said he felt the police had every right to investigate him or anybody else, but also claimed his phones were being illegally tapped by the police. Black was particularly incensed that warrants were served on Hanna's Canadian lawyers, Outerbridge Barristers & Solicitors and Davies, Ward and Beck. Serving Hanna's lawyers meant the Toronto police investigation was drawn to the attention of Judge Manos, then in the midst of his deliberations.

The same day that warrants were served, an angry Black phoned Roy McMurtry, Ontario's attorney general. So did Fred Huycke, a lawyer at Osler Hoskin which was representing Norcen, who was a long-time acquaintance of McMurtry's. An urgent meeting was requested by both men, on the grounds that someone within McMurtry's ministry was interfering with a U.S. legal action.

Late that Thursday afternoon Black, Huycke and Paul Saunders, the Cravath, Swaine lawyer who was in town counselling Black on the Hanna case, strode into McMurtry's eighteenth floor office just

---

* Moreover, the interest paid on money borrowed to buy back shares is a tax-deductible expense.

around the corner from 10 Toronto Street. There, McMurtry was joined by the head of his department's civil section, Blenus Wright, and deputy minister Rendall Dick. The attorney general was surprised by Black's allegations that the U.S. case was being improperly influenced by the police investigation in Canada; he was unaware of any Canadian criminal investigation into Black. He later claimed that had he known he would never have granted the meeting. Nonetheless, McMurtry sat and listened as Black protested his innocence and railed against the smear job he felt was being mounted against him. McMurtry's surprise grew when Black also claimed Johnston had phoned Judge Manos in Cleveland in the midst of his deliberations on the Hanna case, and that Manos had been forwarded a copy of one of the Canadian search warrants. Indeed, the heart of Black's charge was that Hanna had been feeding the Toronto police information with the hopes that news of the investigation would reach the Cleveland court. It was all done, Black growled, 'in such a way as to make it look like we're routinely regarded as criminals in our home jurisdiction and this is terribly damaging to us'.

McMurtry later said he had rarely heard anything as conspiratorial in his seven and a half years as attorney general. Crown attorney Johnston later denied that he had called Manos, and said instead that a member of Manos's staff had contacted him. As for Black's assertion that serving Hanna's lawyers with search warrants was unnecessary and designed to influence the Cleveland proceedings, the crown attorney and police claimed that they believed that swift access to Hanna's case files was critical. If Hanna and Norcen reached a friendly settlement out of court – which indeed happened several weeks later – key documents could be harder to obtain. Johnston says he considered that by serving Hanna with a warrant he would give Anderson and his colleagues more public relations ammunition to use against Black but would not be influenced by 'partisan' considerations.

Black was also convinced that Brian Mulroney, in trying to serve his most powerful masters – Hanna – had played a role in this. Black learned that Sam Wakim, an old undergraduate room-mate of Mulroney's, and a lawyer who represented Hanna and Iron Ore, was an acquaintance of Johnston's. While Black and Mulroney were always friendly, and Mulroney continued to phone Black to offer his assistance and even played a role in the settlement between Hanna and Norcen, Black was suspicious of the future prime minister's true motives. 'I have always got along well with him, and, in general, we like each other,' Black wrote in his autobiography. 'But his protestations of helpfulness and innocence on this and a few other occasions were hard to endure, not so much for their smarminess as by their implicit presumption of cavernous naïveté on my part.'

For his part, Mulroney dismisses Black's assertions. 'I can guarantee you,' he says, 'that any suggestion that my conduct was anything other than friendly, constructive, and fully ethical at all times, is improper and unacceptable. That's for sure.'*

In their discussions on 13 May, McMurtry did express doubts to Black that the stock buy-back at issue was a criminal act. He ordered his officials to review whether there was an offence, and, if so, whether it fell under the purview of the criminal code or securities legislation. (If it were the criminal offence of forgery, as the police were suggesting, the accused could face prison terms; a securities conviction frequently resulted in a small fine, and rarely in a jail sentence.)

After Black's meeting with McMurtry, crown attorney Johnston was pulled from the case. Although Black says he made it clear that he was in no way attempting to get the attorney general to curb the investigation – and McMurtry later confirmed this – the meeting and Johnston's subsequent removal were magnets for speculation. And Black did not stop with McMurtry: he also complained in person to Metropolitan Toronto chairman and police commissioner Paul Godfrey, and to metropolitan Toronto police chief Jack Ackroyd. Black became the object of media suspicion that he was a fat cat using his personal power and contacts to influence the judicial system. Ironically, Black maintained that his only motive in petitioning high-ranking officials was altruism: he was standing up for the little guy who found himself similarly persecuted but lacked his or Norcen's means. 'I'm willing to take up the cudgels for those less able to defend themselves than I.' Even after Norcen and Hanna had reached friendly terms and the SEC had been satisfied, the Toronto police

---

* In any case, whatever animosity Black felt was well suppressed; he supported Mulroney's campaign to become prime minister and in 1990 Black was awarded the Order of Canada.

investigation plodded on for some eighteen months. And Black was clearly the target.

On 19 July 1982, Black sent a letter to McMurtry, which he also released to select members of the press, explaining his public protests of outrage. 'I must emphasise that I do feel a legitimate grievance about the earlier phase of this investigation, and my directors and I are extremely disquieted about its indefinite continuation. The widely publicised fact that our company is the subject of a criminal investigation is extremely embarrassing and has now become an unnecessary inconvenience.' Black went on to say he regretted 'any inconvenience to you resulting from misrepresentations of what I have said in the press', reiterated his desire to co-operate with investigators to expedite the matter and asked McMurtry to 'encourage your investigators to produce their recommendations as quickly as possible', especially considering he and Norcen had settled the matter with the SEC in the U.S. some two weeks earlier. McMurtry thought the letter 'fairly aggressive'.

Someone else in Black's uncomfortable position might have opted for a low profile. But as the investigation dragged on, his impatience and indignation grew. In the months after Black's initial meeting with McMurtry, Norcen co-operated fully, with Black and Norcen's directors sitting through hours of police questioning; there was no need for search warrants to be served on them. But when the investigators tried to widen their probe to look at the affairs of other companies in the Black orbit during the previous three years, Black expressed his view that this was nothing but a witch hunt. 'Have you ever heard such a bizarre case as this?,' he asked *Maclean's* magazine writer Linda McQuaig. 'Doesn't it strike you as a little odd what's going on here?

'There is nothing here. All they've got is that one ambiguously worded minute from September 9. All the supporting evidence, as all the testimony shows, is only a hypothetical long-range possibility in the single unauthoritative opinion of Mr Battle, at that time. It is absolutely not any kind of corporate intent in the terms of the securities act. The whole thing is just a fabrication.'

Normally, the Christmas Day editions of Toronto newspapers are light on hard news and local controversy. But the 25 December 1982 edition of the *Globe and Mail* included an unusual piece by reporter

Jock Ferguson. 'Early yesterday a reporter was jolted awake by a call from Mr Black, best known for his acquisitive habits of buying and reshuffling corporations,' Ferguson wrote, 'who complained for an hour about the way his corporate and personal reputation were being harmed by what he called "a spectacle of public cowardice".' Black was incensed by an earlier article Ferguson had written about a provincial committee hearing, at which McMurtry had testified that Johnston had been pulled from the Norcen file because he was not a specialist in securities law, rather than (as Black said McMurtry had told him) because he had committed improprieties. McMurtry also disparaged Black's continuing public commentary on the case. McMurtry might have concluded that by doing so he would invite only more of the increasingly familiar invective.

Since their 13 May meeting, Black told Ferguson, he had run into McMurtry at an Ontario government luncheon for former U.S. secretary of state Alexander Haig and had challenged him to lay charges or wind up the investigation. But according to Black, although McMurtry had said the investigation 'stank', he had also said that he could do nothing as 'a lot of police were going round saying I'm in your pocket'.

'It's a capricious investigation that's damaging innocent people's reputations,' Black thundered. Black subsequently heard from another journalist that McMurtry had been disquieted by Black's comments, and his wife Maria said publication of the story had 'certainly spoiled Christmas morning'.

'Isn't that *tragic*,' Black aped. 'Poor Maria!'

The attorney general denied that he had said that the case stank as well as the comment about being in the pocket of the police. He responded publicly by wondering what fuelled the Black imagination. 'Maybe we should all try it,' McMurtry mused in *Maclean's*, 'because obviously his imagination has produced some degree of financial success.'

Less facetiously, he added: 'I find this not only highly unusual, bizarre, peculiar – I find it absolutely inexplicable that a man in his position would not deal with any concerns he had through normal channels as opposed to debating the issue through the media.'

Some of Black's friends also wondered if Black's comments were goading the attorney general and police to come and get him. 'If you're the attorney general of the province, you say to yourself, "that guy's going to get it with both barrels",' is Hal Jackman's assessment of what happened. 'And that's exactly what happened. And so [Conrad] brought the whole bloody thing on himself.'

John Fraser, Black's friend from his Upper Canada College days, recalls Black inviting him to lunch at Winston's restaurant in Toronto during this tense period. 'Winston's,' says Fraser, then an entertainment writer for the *Globe and Mail*, 'was then the leading noshery for the movers and shakers of Toronto's business community and was run by the alarming Johnny Arena, a man who gave unctuousness its inner meaning. Winston's main dining room was heavy with "mahogany" panelling, self-importance, art nouveau decor, sycophantic waiters, and immoderately priced entrées of varying quality.' Fraser was aware of the police investigation – indeed there had been 'some gleeful speculative analysis' in the press that very morning – but the matter was hardly discussed during the lunch. In the middle of the meal, Black was talking when Fraser noticed a large cockroach emerging from the wood panelling behind his companion's head. 'Nice place you brought me to,' Fraser said, pointing out the insect.

He recalls, 'Conrad turned his head and then, in quick succession, without any pause, he started snapping his fingers and bellowed out a summons like General de Gaulle at a staff meeting:

' "Mr Arena!" he shouted at the hapless manager across the room. Everyone stopped talking. Johnny Arena lumbered across his dining room with two liveried garçons in tow.

' "Yes, Mr Black. What is the problem?"

' "Mr Arena," barked Black, pointing to the cockroach and making sure everybody was hanging on to each word, "I told you if you ever let *Roy* into this restaurant, I would never come back. Eliminate him." ' As Fraser tells it, friends and enemies alike broke into spontaneous laughter and applause.

Although determined to convey a defiant and serene exterior to the Winston's crowd, these were not easy times for Black. For eighteen months, he endured visions of the police descending on his office, or worse yet his home, with television crews in tow to chronicle the spectacle of corporate Canada's *enfant terrible* being handcuffed and led away. More was at stake here than just Black's carefully cultivated public image.

'He was as wounded over that whole affair as anyone could possibly be,' recalls his friend and lawyer Peter Atkinson. 'I know because I lived with it virtually every day. He would constantly call, usually in the evening, from his home, when the anxiety of it all would get to him. Just the concern, "Could these police officers really be so stupid as to lay charges? Am I going to face a search warrant? Are they suddenly going to show up at my door and cuff me and walk me off to the station?" From time to time we'd have those kinds of discussions. I don't think it had anything to do with profile, I think it had everything to do with a complete loss of faith in Canadian institutions. I think it was as hurtful and upsetting a thing as he's ever been through in his life.' At home, when Black was feeling particularly anxious about the investigation, his wife would assure him that his reaction was normal, that if in fact he were not upset about being under investigation she would be worried about him.

Eleven months after the warrants were served, on Wednesday 14 April, the Ontario Securities Commission announced that it had concluded its investigation into Black and Norcen and would not lay charges. But two weeks later, the cover of *Maclean's* featured a story by writers Linda McQuaig and Ian Austen on the Black investigation, centring on a leaked 138-page internal Ontario Securities Commission report into the Norcen affair.

The report called for twenty-six charges of misrepresentation and other violations of the Ontario Securities Act to be laid in connection with the Hanna bid. Nine of the proposed charges were against Black himself, with nine directed at Battle and eight at Norcen. The recommendations were not only made by the OSC's investigators, Gary Curran and David Knight, but were backed by Roy McMurtry as well. Yet the commission unanimously, and on more than one occasion, decided not to proceed with the charges. Its release said in part that there were 'not sufficient grounds to support a recommendation to prosecute or to institute any other proceedings against Norcen or any of its officers or directors under the Securities Act'. The OSC chairman, Peter Dey, was dismayed that the report was made public, and said it was 'not unusual at all' for the commission to reject the recommendations of its staff. Nonetheless, the article pointed out that charges under the Securities Act were strongly recommended by

McMurtry himself, via two of his crown attorneys most experienced in securities matters. When the *Maclean's* journalists phoned McMurtry's office for an interview, he, through a spokesman, declined to comment, citing again 'the ongoing criminal investigation'. Black was outraged: 'We have been completely exonerated by the most authoritative body on the matter,' Black told the magazine, 'and the fact is that the attorney general and the police have a great deal of explaining to do about what they've been doing for the past eleven months.'

In the end, no explanation was forthcoming, no charges were laid, and McMurtry, after an internal investigation, said that there was 'no evidence' to support Black's original claim that Hanna's lawyers had been manipulating the Canadian justice system for their own gain in a Cleveland court. Black fumed over the *Maclean's* article's insinuation that he or members of Norcen's eminent board of businessmen and lawyers had somehow conspired to pay off the entire Ontario Securities Commission.

One outcome of the episode was the Black, his faith in Canada's legal system shaken, acquired through his private company, Ravelston, a large security company, giving him a veritable army of blue-blazered security guards (described by his wife as 'rent-a-meatballs') and more seasoned experts who could sweep 10 Toronto Street for bugs and wiretaps. 'I suppose I overreacted a bit, but it's very tiresome, you know, picking up the phone and having it tapped,' Black says now. 'I mean, once they get their whole bungling bureaucratic intimidation monitoring apparatus fixed on somebody, it is a terrible nuisance. As if I am some common criminal or something! And if I'd actually done anything wrong I would have taken it in better spirit than I did.

'You can at certain times get the impression that the police are no thundering prize, you know. The whole thing was a farce, it was a fraud. The real fraud was the investigation. And yet I had to put up with this crap for a whole year, reading every week or every other week that this criminal investigation into me was continuing, as if there was a real "nip and tuck chance" – as Foster Hewitt used to say – that I would be . . . packed off to the Harold Ballard *salle* at Beaver Correctional.'

Evident less and less through Argus's various corporate reorganisations, divestitures and controversies, was Monte Black. Under the fraternal division of labours, Monte was chairman of Dominion Stores and Standard Broadcasting. His forte, from his career in the stockbroking business, was his grasp of numbers and investment strategies. Conrad's big brother was jovial and known for his appreciation of things big – big cars, a big Muskoka cottage with big magogany boats filling its seventeen-slip boathouse, big cigars, big three-pieced pin-striped suits. It was Monte who arranged for a local sculptor to create the Black logo of an eagle eating a snake, which he had replicated as hood ornaments for their cars, and had emblazoned on the tail of their Canadair Challenger jet. 'He's not keen on the spotlight, but he loves the big life,' says Sarah Band, a Toronto businesswoman who was involved with Monte for three years in the early 1980s, after he separated from his wife. Compared with his younger brother, Monte 'is a much more easy-going, caring individual, almost to a fault. But intensely loyal. The people who work for him have worked for him for ever. He's extraordinarily generous.'

An image of good-natured excess was one that seemed to typify Dominion's performance. With some 25,000 employees and more than 370 stores around the time the Blacks took it over, Dominion Stores' slogan was 'It's Mainly Because of the Meat', and one might have imagined its chairman tucking into one of its sirloins. One person close to the Blacks said Monte had 'hedonistic fun' on the job but critical management issues had not been addressed at Dominion for years. Monte 'went to all the food shows, he was photographed with Charlie's Angels and flying around on the plane and he spent time redecorating it', says the friend.

'Monte was no worker', agrees another executive who knows both Blacks. 'Say what you want about Conrad, he manages to get into the office at an odd hour and manages to stay until he has to.' 'Monte is an extraordinarily capable person with numbers and stuff, but has never really been challenged,' says Band. 'And Conrad's just way ahead of him, in terms of tactical moves.'

The role Monte Black's personal style played in the decline of Dominion is debatable. Whatever their talents at murky financial engineering, the Blacks remained largely unproven as builders of businesses. In the year ended March 1981, Dominion earned a modest

$28 million on sales of $2.772 billion. The following year profits slipped to $16.7 million, a level they roughly remained at between 1982 and 1984 while sales slowly diminished to $2.208 billion in fiscal year 1984. In the six months ended 30 September 1984, the company reported a loss of about $24 million, its worst performance in its sixty-six-year corporate history. As far as Conrad Black was concerned, Dominion was 'already in steep decline' when he and Monte aquired Argus in 1978. Yet it was one of the first companies over which the Blacks shored up their control, and was a frequent fixture in their various corporate reshufflings. What began as a food retailer when the Blacks took it over in 1978 was by 1984 also a holding company for their resource holdings and their fifty per cent interest in Standard Broadcasting.

'Everyone thought that Dominion was doing well,' says a Black insider. 'Remember, those were the great inflation years. I remember saying at times to Monte: "Dominion Stores had $300 million worth of inventory. At the end of the year, your inventory is worth $337 million, instead of $300. That's basically the whole profit." '

In 1980 Dominion had 376 stores, many of them ramshackle, small and losing money. An analysis of each store was conducted, and a wave of sell-offs and closures ensued. In 1981 Dominion sold eighty-six Quebec stores to Montreal retailer Provigo Inc. for $95 million, and two years after that its remaining six Western Canadian stores were sold to Canada Safeway Ltd. Management shut nearly one hundred stores in Ontario, of which thirty-eight were converted into franchised Mr Grocer stores, which were lower-cost because they avoided hiring from the ranks of the Retail, Wholesale and Department Store Union.*

For two of the critical years under Black control, 1982 to 1984, veteran grocer John Toma was president. Toma had started with Dominion in 1951 as a produce clerk and worked his way up. The Blacks were initially very bullish about Toma and his abilities, but ended up firing him just before Christmas 1984, making acrimonious

---

* According to a Wood Gundy report, the return on equity in Dominion's core food business declined from a respectable 16.9 per cent in 1979–80 to 5.4 per cent in 1982–83. Operating profit margins dropped from 3.2 per cent to 2.8 per cent, but so tight are the margins in the food business that each 0.1 per cent reduced operating profit by more than $2 million.

allegations. Toma was forced to sue over his severance, and it took five years to reach an out-of-court settlement. Toma was replaced by Argus axeman David Radler, which left 'Argusologists' (as the analysts who followed Black were called), with few illusions as to the company's fate.

Within two months of Radler's arrival, Dominion had sold ninety-three of its 133 Ontario stores, two distribution centres, its head office and its very name to the Great Atlantic and Pacific Co. Ltd for more than $145 million. The once ubiquitous Dominion, later renamed Domgroup, was left with some forty stores and a grab-bag of related assets including a dairy, bakeries, real estate and a food distribution subsidiary – which were all eventually sold off. 'It was a dry rot that had gotten into that company,' says Dixon Chant, who was on the board and played a senior role at Dominion. 'I guess we grew up a little bit.'

There was, predictably, little kudos for the Blacks in the aftermath. 'As other chains tried new ways of marketing, Dominion lost touch with what its customers wanted and where the food business was going,' said consultant John Winter, who traced the origin of Dominion's decline in market share to 1975.

Erivan Haub, the West German grocery tycoon who controlled A&P and more than 4,000 grocery stores in Europe and North America, agreed. On a stop in Toronto not long after the acquisition, he ventured that in the previous five to ten years Dominion had 'become a relatively soft competitor' and its former owners had 'neglected their chain for some time'. Richard Currie, the president of Galen Weston's Loblaw Companies Ltd, gloated to shareholders at that grocery chain's 1985 annual meeting that 'your company represents the basic cause of Dominion's decline'. A notable voice among the critics was that of Black biographer Peter Newman. By the time Dominion was being dismantled, Newman was no longer impressed. He wrote in *Maclean's* that the sell-off 'raises pertinent questions about Conrad Black's willingness and ability to hang in and operate functioning companies instead of merely trading corporate blocks and shucking ventures that no longer meet his high profit expectations'.

In concluding, Newman wrote: 'Conrad Black has created nothing. In his fortieth year he finds himself comfortable and rich, but surrounded by a rising chorus of voices questioning his future course and asking why he refuses to fulfil the potential for corporate greatness he once inspired among his peers.'

'We had all kinds of people who lost their jobs because of the efforts of Conrad Black, people in their fifties, who had no opportunity of getting another job,' remarked Don Collins, head of the union that represented some Dominion Stores workers. 'He never did anything for them other than what he was required to do by law and even then we had to fight in order to get that much.'

As Black later presented it in a column he wrote for *Report On Business* magazine, blame for Dominion's downward spiral lay not with the controlling shareholders to whom the business was ultimately accountable, but with history and incumbent management. Dominion, he wrote, 'was run by an inbred, furtive, overconfident and, in some cases, disingenuous management. It had never made more than one cent on a dollar's sales. Dominion could not possibly repay the huge investments that would have been necessary to reverse that decline.' Black could not resist a parting shot at Dominion's more successful rivals: 'The domestic competitors were chronically addicted to the decline of Dominion Stores like a group of junkies sharing a joint.' In any case, it is doubtful Black embraced the role of Produce King. For his efforts in selling off Dominion and other assets, the *Globe and Mail*'s *Report on Business* magazine sarcastically bestowed Black with an award for 'the self-inflicted corporate enema of the year'. Black later responded drolly: 'In commerce, as in matters of mundane physiology and probably journalism too, enemas are sometimes necessary and often invigorating.'

In the province of Ontario, forty-nine companies withdrew some $187 million of surplus cash from pension plans in the twelve months ended 31 March 1986. Among them was the rapidly diminishing Dominion Stores, which in November 1985 applied to and, in early 1986, received permission from the Ontario Pension Commission to remove cash surpluses totalling about $62 million. The removal of surplus monies was a long-established practice, and Dominion had similarly withdrawn $16.5 million in 1983. Such actions were based on the principle that employers must honour their commitment to pay pensions when times are bad, and conversely should have access to the upside when times are good – so long as pensions are paid and liabilities covered. The principle is that when an employer 'overfunds' a pension, he is entitled to take back the surplus. Overfunding was the order of the day in the mid-1980s. Whereas in the late 1970s pension funds averaged annual returns of nine and ten per cent, by 1986 returns were consistently exceeding twenty per cent, leading to a quantum increase in surplus withdrawals.

At Dominion Stores, the withdrawal was greeted by a sceptical, if not hostile, work-force; already hundreds had lost their jobs. Present and former employees, many of whom were given no severance when they were let go, were predictably very wary of what the Black-controlled company was up to. They had received no notice either from Dominion or the pension commission which gave its blessing to Dominion to withdraw the funds. The transaction, however, was no secret. It came to light in the 22 November 1985 interim statement of Hollinger Inc. Chairman and chief executive Conrad Black concluded his report by explaining that wholly owned subsidiary Dominion had applied that month for approval to withdraw surplus pension funds that could total up to $75 million. What particularly rankled with some Dominion employees was Black's boast that the surplus recovery was 'expected to be offset very significantly by costs related to the winding-down and rationalisation of Dominion's ongoing activities' including 'employee termination costs'. In other words, the surplus derived from the fund whose primary purpose was to assist in the retirement of employees, would ironically be used to help finance the forced retirement of those very same workers.

Six Dominion employees and their union took Dominion and the Pension Commission of Ontario to court over a portion of the withdrawal – $38 million – challenging the commission's authority in approving the withdrawal and demanding the monies' return. In August 1986, the Ontario Supreme Court ruled in the workers' favour.

The decision, penned by Justice Robert Reid and signed by two other justices, noted that 'Dominion's managers saw the pension funds as a source of succour.' Fault was found not with Dominion, let alone Black, but with the pension commission for allowing the withdrawal to go through. And since the commission declined to file an affidavit in its defence in the suit, its justification for giving

Dominion access to the funds was never explained. 'In my opinion, the commission failed in its duty of fairness and its decision should not be allowed to stand,' the judge wrote.

Bob Rae, leader of Ontario province's socialist New Democratic Party seized on the opportunity to argue that surplus withdrawals constitute 'legalised theft from pension plan members'. Rae rose in the Ontario legislature and declared: 'I have a question for the Premier, who I am sure will be aware that the most symbolic representative of bloated capitalism at its worst, Conrad Black, the owner of Dominion Stores, skimmed off $62 million from the pension fund under the open eyes and ears of the government's pension commission.

'At the same time, Dominion Stores is refusing to pay severance pay to the 400 employees who were laid off as a result of a decision by Dominion Stores to shut down several stores. What does the Premier intend to do about that to assure the workers of this province that there is some industrial justice in Ontario in 1986?'

Black quickly responded to Rae's attack, calling the New Democrat leader 'a symbol of swinish, socialist demagoguery'. Each man may have underestimated the other's staying power. 'He is a dishonourable politician facing an involuntary change of career at the next election,' Black thundered (Rae was elected the province's first socialist premier in 1990). 'Long after Mr Black is embalmed somewhere in the British House of Lords, I'll still be in politics,' Rae taunted, referring to a recent investment Black made in London's *Daily Telegraph*.

Rae, said Black, was a 'coward and a liar' hiding behind parliamentary immunity and trying to 'foist upon this society the utter, defamatory falsehood that I have been enjoying blowing workers out the door while stealing their pensions'.

'I never said that anything that Mr Black has done was illegal. I said it should be illegal,' Rae told reporters. 'This goes beyond the question of Mr Black's ego to the question of what's morally right.'

Having a socialist call his morals into question may have been too much for Black. In an interview with the *Globe and Mail*, he pointed out that unscrupulous Dominion Stores employees were stealing millions of dollars of food from the chain each year. 'We had $30 million in produce stolen by employees every year,' Black stormed. Losing a job 'is a sad thing,' he told the *Globe*, 'but it's sometimes difficult for me to work myself into an absolute lachrymose fit about a work-force that steals on that scale.

'I'm sorry for honest people who are out of work, I honestly am. And to the degree that we can, we have helped them. But on the other hand, we are not running a welfare agency for corrupt union leaders and a slovenly work-force.'

About a week later, Dominion issued a three-paragraph statement that said it regretted that 'certain recent statements made to the media' about the closure of several stores had been 'in some cases misconstrued'. The statement said of the loss of inventory through theft at Dominion stores: 'While some employees obviously abused their position in a very serious way, the majority of Dominion Stores employees carried out their duties in an honest and responsible manner.'

Black personally never recanted his statement, although he claimed in his *Report On Business* magazine column that the *Globe*'s headlining of this aside was 'somewhat irresponsible'. It did not seem to matter to anyone whether Black's comments on theft were valid or not. There is little ambiguity about Black's feelings towards the grocery chain and its work-force. Recalling the latter days of his ownership of Dominion in his autobiography, Black writes: 'I recommended that a scythe be taken through the ranks of the low-lives at the warehouse, and it was.'

The dispute was settled in 1987 with Domgroup retaining about half the $62 million it withdrew, and giving the rest back to the unions. Pension laws were subsequently changed and the Pension Commission of Ontario was overhauled that year. 'The overhaul really should have been done two years ago,' John Kruger, premier David Peterson's special adviser who oversaw the reforms, commented in the *Financial Post*. 'But now, everything at the commission is dated BC or AD – Before Conrad or After Dominion.'

The personalising of the Dominion pension issue was contested by Black through a series of defamation suits against journalists and news organisations which persisted in the erroneous suggestions that Black had personally taken the pension money, or that its removal had been illegal. Ann Finlayson, who wrote a 1988 book on pensions, noted that some journalists and politicians had begun treating Black and Dominion as 'virtually synonymous', and that the result was often provocative but erroneous headlines such as the *Toronto Star's* on 3 February 1987: 'Black can keep $30 million pension cash in union deal.'

All the suits resulted in apologies, some with cash settlements; none went to trial. Despite her passing defence of Black, Finlayson herself was sued by him over a passage in her book. Two years after the book came out, the publishers and author agreed to a settlement which included an advertisement in the *Globe and Mail* apologising to Black and announcing that all remaining unsold copies of the book's hardcover edition (some 6,200 copies) would be destroyed. The offending reference had been changed 'as a courtesy' in the paperback edition, which Finlayson's publisher, Penguin Books Canada, touted in a news release as having 'already brought on a lawsuit by one of Canada's best-known business personalities'. Penguin's associate publisher Jeff Boloten told the *Globe and Mail* that the lawsuit had provoked considerable interest in the book, which might otherwise have petered out.

Another legacy of the Dominion Stores controversy is Black's venom towards Bob Rae, who went on to become Ontario's premier from 1990 to 1995. After Rae's election, Black routinely lambasted him in speeches – calling his government a 'kleptocracy', or worse – and even moved Hollinger's head office out of Ontario to British Columbia (although ostensibly for tax savings) after he came into power. Rae is perturbed by Black's enduring antagonism towards him, once mentioning it to Black's friend Hal Jackman, whom Rae frequently sees in his capacity as Ontario's lieutentant-governor. 'You know,' Rae said to Jackman, shaking his head in disbelief, 'I think I've only met him once in my life.'

FIVE

The House Black Bought

'Good man, Conrad Ritblat'
LORD HARTWELL

On New Year's Eve, 1984, Conrad and Shirley Black stayed at home. Forgoing the glitzy party circuit in Palm Beach, they spent a quiet evening with Peter Atkinson and his wife Stephanie. It was a warm clear, picturesque Florida night, and the Atkinsons volunteered to cook a dinner of scallops, washed down with a few bottles of Puligny-Montrachet.

An interruption to the occasion was a telephone call from Brian Mulroney, who was spending his first New Year's Eve as Prime Minister of Canada shmoozing prominent people like Black, who had helped elevate him to that office four months earlier.

Not long after midnight, Shirley and Stephanie said good-night. Black hoped Peter would stay up with him, and he did. They strolled along the beach running adjacent to The Breakers, the posh resort not far from Black's house, occasionally catching the wafting voices of New Year's revellers. Later, the lawyer and his client sat outside the house with drinks and talked some more.

New Year is typically a time for reflection and resolution, but Black was in a particularly philosophical mood. He had certainly survived some low moments over the past couple of years. And as his lawyer through trying times, Atkinson was one of the few with whom Black could share his private thoughts.

Black had now spent seven years engaged in complex restructurings at Argus. While they made him a richer man – a $100 million man, by his own count – Black had paid a price in headaches and controversies. At the age of forty he was rapidly becoming the caricature of the corporate fat cat, and he knew it. This was a man, his critics charged, who built nothing but his own ego and private fortune. The media spotlight that had heralded Black as corporate hero now held him in a sceptical glare. 'I am just trying to do my job,' he complained. 'I know that sounds terribly humdrum but I am consistently astounded by the facile typecasting that has gone on. I don't regard myself as a source of entertainment.'

As much as Black considered himself a patriotic Canadian, he was beginning to feel disenchanted with his native country, and the indications were that the feeling was mutual. Moreover, during his tenure at Argus, Black had discovered that he had a limited appetite for most of the businesses he was in.

But Black did not dwell too long on his problems. Like the generals he admired, Black was well advanced on a strategy to move himself into a more appealing sphere of operations and influence. That night with Atkinson, he explained exactly what he wanted to achieve over the next year or eighteen months, including the terms under which he would dispose of what remained of Dominion and other assets. Black knew that the money he raised would enable him to move into a new phase in his career, to buy out most of the partners who had supported him through the Argus adventure, including his brother, and then, as his own man, there was no telling what might come up. . . .

'It was showtime, I think, in his mind,' Atkinson recalls. 'I remember about two years later I would remind him of this discussion, and we would both shake our heads and marvel at how well it had gone for him. From that point on he just went from strength to strength, as they say. It's been an amazing story when you think that in 1984–85, except for the Sterling group of newspapers, he just wasn't in that business.'

It was a sign of things to come that his brother Monte was less and less publicly visible through the sale of Dominion's assets and the subsequent pension controversy. 'The end of the line was coming,' Monte later recalled. 'The company didn't have much left, and there wasn't really room for both of us. So he was the logical one to carry on, and I was very happy to move on.' As Monte recalled it, the decision to split took place over lunch in the dining room at 10 Toronto Street during February 1985, at which point Dominion was selling off its assets and plans to sell Standard Broadcasting were in the wings. 'Quite clearly there wasn't enough work to go around,' says Monte, 'and it was at that lunch that I said to Conrad: "Well, why don't you buy me out?" And so he and I retired to my office which was across the hall.'

Black had also decided that he wanted to buy out most of the remaining Ravelston shareholders, some of whom were grumbling that they had not received dividends for most of their time as investors. Dixon Chant, the Blacks' surrogate father, and Conrad's long time partners Peter White and David Radler would remain as Ravelston shareholders. Ravelston's main asset, in turn, became its roughly fifty per cent interest in a new company. In one last corporate restructuring, Black amalgamated companies Hollinger Argus, Labmin Resources (as the holding company for Norcen and Labrador was now known) and Arcgen Holdings (the latest depository for Dominion). Black selected the name Hollinger for his new flagship.

Conrad agreed to pay Monte $22.4 million for his approximately seventeen per cent interest in Ravelston, an amount that valued the company at roughly three times what the Blacks had paid to gain control of Argus seven years earlier. Although he did not formally buy out his brother and the rest of the investors until the autumn, from February onwards Monte did not attend meetings unless his brother asked him to. 'As far as I was concerned the thing was over,' said Monte, 'and after that was tidying up.' The parting of ways, according to some Black friends, was also motivated by the fact that Monte was in the midst of an acrimonious and costly divorce battle, raising the spectre that his wife Mariellen might end up as a significant Ravelston shareholder as part of a divorce court decision.

Conrad Black was and remains intensely loyal to his brother. Some say he was loyal to a fault at Argus, but on the other hand Conrad could not have done what he did without Monte's backing. And there was little doubt to associates of both Blacks that it was trying for Monte continually to hear about his 'smarter' younger brother. Monte would pursue his own investments and later join Hollinger's board, and the brothers would remain linked through their family foundation, which Monte described thus: 'Conrad and I put in money each year and we sit around and throw it away. It is terrific. Some of the best humour of the year.'

Some business people, when they need a break from the action, go golfing or broil themselves on secluded beaches. When Conrad Black isn't concocting elaborate financial schemes, one of his preferred pastimes is the discussion of weighty political and economic issues with prominent international 'thinkers'.

It was in this context that Black found himself in Arrowwood, New York, on the weekend of 10–12 May 1985, at the annual Bilderberg meeting. Black had been a member since 1981 of Bilderberg, a group which takes its name from a Dutch resort where its first meetings were held in the 1950s. The composition of the 120-odd attendees of Bilderberg meetings closely resemble that of NATO, with Americans representing the largest contingent.

With so many giants of business and statesmanship gathered and the inclusion of spouses frowned upon, some of the best networking takes place outside the regular programme. Such was the case when Black chatted with Andrew Knight one evening and suggested they have 'one more fiery little armagnac'. As editor of *The Economist* since 1974, Knight was one of Britain's most esteemed journalists. Five years Black's senior, he is a slim, handsome man with a cool, distant bearing, which is amplified by piercing grey eyes. Knight had first met the Canadian at a Massey-Ferguson-sponsored conference in Toronto in 1980 where Henry Kissinger had spoken. They had kept in touch, especially after Black joined Bilderberg and its prestigious steering committee, and occasionally lunched or supped together when Black was in London. Once, with their wives, they had attended the musical *Evita*, although Knight was slightly unhappy that the best seats he could come up with on short notice for his visitors were at the back of the house.

In Arrowwood, as the night wore on and one fiery armagnac became became two, then three, and the conversation turned to newspapers, Black told Knight about how he had attempted to buy the *Globe and Mail* newspaper in Toronto several years earlier, but had been outbid by the Thomson group, and how he had a nascent interest in Southam, Canada's largest newspaper chain. Black expounded on his plan to buy out most of his partners and how in fact the two people with whom he was continuing were the ones with whom he had started in the newspaper business nearly two decades earlier. Naturally, he and Knight talked of the possibility of his one day owning a UK newspaper.

'As it happens', Knight said, 'the *Daily Telegraph* looks somewhat unstable.' It was spending a large amount of money on a new printing plant, and its owners the Berry brothers were both septuagenarians with no clear successors.

This immediately drew Black's attention; the *Telegraph* was the British paper he read and appreciated the most. Indeed, Black was an unabashed fan of Margaret Thatcher and her right-wing policies, and the *Telegraph* was the traditional organ of Conservative middle-England. He did not dwell on the matter; it was a friendly conversation not unlike dozens Black regularly had.

On arriving at Heathrow airport a few days later, Knight picked up a copy of *The Times*. He was intrigued to see an article by City columnist Kenneth Fleet about how the *Telegraph* had been trying to raise money but its investment banker, N. M. Rothschild & Sons Ltd, and broker, Cazenove & Co., were having difficulty drumming up investors.

Knight quickly rang Evelyn de Rothschild, chairman of the namesake firm and also chairman of *The Economist*. De Rothschild confirmed the story – the pressure was on, institutions were willing to invest £20 million, but another £10 million had yet to be found. Knight said he could think of at least two people who might be interested in putting up the extra money. (His first candidate was Black, but he also had in mind Katharine Graham of the *Washington Post*, who had been a close friend of *Telegraph* chairman Lord Hartwell's late wife.)

Knight asked for a copy of the private placement document, and, after perusing its contents, decided he should call Black straight away. Finding him proved to be difficult, but through Donald Macdonald (another Bilderberg alumnus who later became Canadian High Commissioner in London), Knight secured Black's unlisted home phone number.

It was lunchtime in London, Monday 20 May. Knight misjudged the time difference and overlooked the fact that it was a holiday, Victoria Day, in Canada – although in any case, the chances of Black being awake at seven a.m. were not great. When destiny called, Black couldn't face it and asked if Knight would ring back in a couple of hours.

When he did, Knight told him about the offering memorandum

and that he had spoken to de Rothschild, who had also met Black through Bilderberg. Knight asked Black if he wanted him to send the document by courier. 'They are indeed having some difficulty, and the position is quite strategic.'

'Sure,' said Black. 'Send me the stuff.'

The first edition of the *Daily Telegraph and Courier* was published on 29 June 1855. It was around this time that Conrad Black's great-great-grandfather, Thomas Riley, moved to London and was said to have purchased a 'fractional interest' in the paper.* The notion of Black investing in the paper was not quite the young Bolingbroke reclaiming his family's estates, but the ancestral link added the dimension of destiny that seems to surround the affairs of Black.

The *Telegraph*'s founder, Arthur Burroughes Sleigh, a recently retired colonel, began the venture as a vehicle for a vendetta (the details of which are long forgotten) he had against the Duke of Cambridge continuing as the Crimean War's nominal commander. Like many papers of its day, the early *Telegraph* ran to a scant four pages, but the Colonel had trouble from the outset covering his printing bills. If Riley was in fact an original investor in the paper, it was not a shrewd move. Joseph Moses Levy, a printer and for a short time owner of the *Sunday Times*, agreed to print the *Telegraph and Courier* with the proviso that if the bills were not paid the paper would become his – a scenario which materialised within a matter of weeks.

A year after Levy took over the words '*and Courier*' were dropped from the title and Levy set out to build 'the Largest, Best and Cheapest newspaper in the world'. Growth was spearheaded by Levy's son Edward, who changed his surname to Lawson and later became Lord Burnham. Within six years the paper's circulation was almost equal to that of all other London papers put together.

One aspect of the paper's appeal was its wide-reaching coverage: By the end of 1857 it included a weekly letter from Toronto. By 1876, the paper boasted the largest daily circulation in the world. It had ups and downs over the next four decades, and by early 1928 circulation had slipped to 84,000 from 240,000 in the 1880s.

* Thomas Riley did go on to invest in other publishing ventures, including papers called the *Maritime Gazette* and the *Tower Hamlets Gazette*.

It was then that the paper changed hands again, for £1.2 million. The buyers were Sir William Berry, Gomer Berry and Sir Edward Iliffe. The Berry brothers were originally from the town of Merthyr Tydfil in the mountains of South Wales, where their father was the estate agent of Gwaelodygarth.

Along with Iliffe, they were well-known publishers and the *Telegraph* was their first foray into quality papers. Over the years the empire they founded embraced the *Daily Telegraph, Sunday Times, Financial Times, Comic Cuts, School Friend, Advertising World, Boxing,* and some hundred other publications.

When Duff Hart-Davis described the take-over of the *Daily Telegraph* in January 1928 for his book, *The House the Berrys Built*, he might well have been writing about 1985 and transposed Conrad Black's name for William Berry's:

'The paper William Berry and his two partners bought was thoroughly run-down. Its premises were decrepit, its presses out-of-date, its staff old and eccentric, its readers both elderly and dwindling in numbers.'

Berry, who became the first Lord Camrose, rose to be one of the most successful, if least mythologised, proprietors on Fleet Street, with a personal style that formed the basis for Lord Copper of Evelyn Waugh's 1938 satirical novel *Scoop*. Camrose, along with his brother, who became Lord Kemsley, re-equipped the plant and revived the paper. In the 1930s the trio split their interests, with Kemsley taking the *Sunday Times* and Camrose focusing his attentions on the *Telegraph*.

Thanks to Camrose's unstinting emphasis on hard news, by 1939 the *Telegraph* was selling 700,000 copies daily and was the dominant national quality daily, a position it would not relinquish over the next half-century. In 1954, control of the paper passed from Lord Camrose to his two sons, Michael and Seymour, Lord Hartwell and the second Lord Camrose respectively, with the younger Hartwell as chairman and editor-in-chief and Camrose as deputy chairman.

Some of this information was covered in the obligatory company history section of the 24 April 1985 private placement memorandum which Black was sent from London. But those sections pertaining to the present day told a more cautionary tale.

As he read, Black was struck by the huge risks Hartwell had exposed the company to by commissioning new printing plants at a

cost of £130 million without arranging financing or having agreements in advance from the powerful Fleet Street unions on job
reductions which would justify the expense. 'It appeared very odd,'
Black later commented, 'that a man who had operated so conserva-
tively for so long had embarked on such a hazardous course.'

Perhaps the simplest explanation for the path taken could be found
on page thirteen of the prospectus, under the description of directors
and senior management: Lord Hartwell, chairman and editor-in-
chief, aged seventy-three; Lord Camrose, deputy chairman since
1948, seventy-five; H. M. Stephen, managing director since 1963,
sixty-nine, and R. J. Holland – 'the baby of the group' in the words of
one board member – financial director, sixty-six. Indeed, with an
ageing executive team and a business adrift, it was not hard to draw
comparisons between the *Telegraph* and the old Argus.

Whatever the *Telegraph* had become, good and bad, it owed to
Hartwell. His life was his newspapers. After studying at Eton and
Oxford he became editor of the *Glasgow Sunday Mail* by the age of
twenty-three and managing editor of the *Financial Times* a few years
later. After serving in the war, he gradually took command of the
Telegraph. By 1985 he was a remnant of a bygone era, the last of the
'personal proprietors'. Although the *Telegraph* was as much a staple of
English life as the BBC or *The Times*, the average Briton did not know
of Lord Hartwell the way they knew of Beaverbrook or Northcliffe,
Thomson or Murdoch, Maxwell or even Eddie Shah. When he was
spoken of, Hartwell was invariably described in terms such as 'decent'
and 'ethical'. Rightly or wrongly, Lord Hartwell regarded himself as
the custodian of a venerable institution.

Hartwell is a shy man with a stammer, but through the efforts of his
glamorous wife Lady Pamela, theirs had been one of London's
liveliest salons. After her death in 1982, Hartwell had become even
more remote and singularly devoted to overseeing the daily content of
his newspapers. Six full days a week he installed himself at the office,
Saturday being the day on which he would don a tweed suit so ancient
it had leather patches not only at the elbows but at the knees. A profile
in the *Observer* described the proprietor's typical arrival at 135 Fleet
Street:

'His first endeavour is to sidle into the lift without attracting the
attentions of the bemedalled commissionaires. Old and sometimes

crippled through they may be, they are usually too quick for him. Salutes are given, buttons pressed, and Lord Hartwell is escorted to the lift. His next terror is that someone else will be ascending with him. To meet this conversational emergency, he has devised a question, "What do you think of the canteen?", which can happily be batted to and fro even, if necessary, until the lift reaches his pine-panelled suite on the fifth floor.'

Once inside, Hartwell would rarely emerge from the private apartment, complete with butler and gardener (an avid horticultural-ist, Hartwell maintained a small fifth-floor garden adjacent to his office). He communicated with staff primarily via an ancient intercom on his desk that would later evoke comparisons from Conrad Black to the systems in World War II battleships. But Hartwell's eccentric, outdated trappings were well-earned: the *Daily Telegraph* remained the undisputed leader in arguably the fiercest newspaper market in the world. Between October 1984 and March 1985 daily circulation averaged 1,226,359 – more than the *Guardian, Times* and *Financial Times* combined.

But it was in a worrisome decline. In the previous five years it had lost 300,000 readers while *The Times* and *Guardian* shared gains of almost exactly the same sum. Even less encouraging were the figures for the *Sunday Telegraph*, which Hartwell had launched in 1961 and considered his crowning achievement; its circulation, at 695,056, achieved third place behind the *Observer* (754,986) and the powerful *Sunday Times* (1,271,393).

Internal marketing surveys at the *Telegraph* showed that much of the slippage was attributable to a dislike among younger readers of the *Telegraph*'s staid, old-fashioned layout and approach. Only twenty per cent of the *Daily Telegraph*'s readers were under thirty-five; the paper had the most elderly readership profile in Fleet Street, but also one of the wealthiest.

Another key measure of a newspaper's attractiveness to advertisers is the average number of readers per copy. In this respect, the *Daily Telegraph* had declined over the past decade from 3.6 to 2.8, and the profile of its readers had also grown steadily older. New presses would allow colour, more flexibility, and the ability to produce papers of more than forty pages. (The limited length of the paper often led the *Telegraph* to refer advertisers to competitors because it could not accommodate their business.)* Thirty million pounds had already been spent on the printing operations in Trafford Park, Manchester, and West Ferry Road on the Isle of Dogs in East London before the refinancing difficulties became critical. A jittery banking syndicate composed of Security Pacific International Leasing (Europe) Inc., Wardley London Ltd and National Westminster Bank plc agreed to provide £80 million in loan financing for the facilities, subject to the private placement raising new equity of £30.1 million.

At this time, 96.9 per cent of the paper was owned by the Telegraph Newspaper Trust, set up by Hartwell and Camrose in 1978, with the balance held by Hartwell's Cowley Charitable Trust. At the conclusion of the proposed private placement, the Berry trusts would own 59.8 per cent, and new shareholders 40.2 per cent. Another sentence on page thirteen of the prospectus noted that 'it is hoped that the eventual successor to Lord Hartwell will be a member of the Berry family'. Camrose had no children (although he was involved with and subsequently married the mother of the Aga Khan) so this was clearly a reference to Hartwell's sons Adrian, forty-seven, and Nicholas, forty-two. Neither had been involved in *Telegraph* management, although Nicholas had been a City writer before becoming a book publishing executive, and Adrian, whose career had included a stint at *Time* magazine, was a science writer at the paper.

Black discussed the situation in a series of phone calls with Knight throughout the week of 20 May. Obviously he didn't see much point in investing in the paper for a mere minority interest. Perhaps, they hypothesised, some kind of option on future share issues could be arranged, which might potentially lead to control down the road, particularly if the company's projections turned out to be as over-optimistic as they appeared. . . .

Black quickly arranged a lunch in Toronto with John Tory, vice-chairman of Thomson Corp. The late Roy Thomson had owned *The Times* of London and *Sunday Times* for more than two decades,† but his son Kenneth had sold them to Rupert Murdoch in 1981,

* The strict work practices of the unions limited the number of pages to thirty-six in any case.
† Roy Thomson bought the *Sunday Times* in 1961 from Lord Kemsley, to the shock and dismay of Lord Hartwell, who thought he and Kemsley held informal first rights to each other's papers. Soon after, Hartwell launched the *Sunday Telegraph*.

having produced nothing but losses for two decades. It was not surprising, then, that Tory told Black that he felt negative towards investments in British national newspapers – particularly minority investments. 'I told him,' recalled Tory, 'to stay away from it.'

Black is not one to let his heart rule his head, and Tory's warning served to firm up Black's resolve only to cut a deal that made economic sense. When de Rothschild phoned to ask if he would come to meet Lord Hartwell, Black said he would be happy to, but not on such short notice. He didn't say so, but Black didn't see why he should drop everything to fly to London over what he considered to be a 'casual investment'.

When de Rothschild quickly suggested New York as an alternative, Black agreed. 'I would have had to be fairly unobservant not to notice that they were under some pressure,' he recalled later. 'I didn't try to exploit that.'

Word was conveyed to Lord Hartwell that an investor may have been found, and Hartwell's first reaction was that he hoped it wasn't the flamboyant financier James Goldsmith, a man he detests. He was reassured that it was in fact a Canadian, a Mr Conrad Black. 'I've never heard of him,' said a satisfied Hartwell.

On Saturday 25 May Black phoned Rupert Hambro at his country home and asked if he would help out. Hambro, the debonair chairman of London's Hambros Bank, had met Black while working in Canada in the early 1970s. Both young men had been invited one weekend to the farm of Dodie Dale-Harris, daughter of the film star Leslie Howard, and her husband. ('They were making hay or something,' recalls Hambro. 'I don't think Conrad spent much time helping make hay.') Over the following years, they would get together whenever Hambro visited Canada and 'always had a laugh'. Hambro was happy to assist, but admitted he knew little about the *Telegraph* or its predicament. It was the start of a bank holiday weekend, but Hambro managed to get hold of Michael Richardson, a senior Rothschild partner, who sent over a package of documents.

The earliest Black was able to meet in New York was Tuesday, 28 May and arrangements were made for Hartwell and his group to arrive that morning by Concorde. A suite was reserved at the JFK Airport Hilton. Hartwell, managing director H. M. Stephen, deputy managing director Hugh Lawson, and Patrick Docherty, a junior

Rothschild representative, prepared for the day trip. Holland, the finance director, was unable to attend because he couldn't obtain a U.S. visa on the Bank Holiday Monday.

Separately, Rupert Hambro made his way to the British Airways VIP lounge at Heathrow, and ended up on the aircraft sitting beside a man he quickly realised, although they had never met, was Lord Hartwell.

'The trouble was I introduced myself but I had his deaf ear,' recalls Hambro. 'He was on the window and I was on the aisle. And the Concorde makes a filthy noise anyway. So he couldn't hear me anyway. He read every single word of that day's *Daily Telegraph* – the lot.'

Some four hours later, by nine a.m. New York time, the group settled into the hotel suite to await Black. Black flew from Toronto on his corporate Challenger jet, a flying cocoon of mahogany and leather, its tail emblazoned with the Black/Argus logo of an eagle devouring a snake.

Until Black arrived alone a short while later, no one among the *Telegraph* contingent knew what to expect. Very little was known about him save that he was fairly young and some sort of financier. It was later suggested that the Holiday Monday in England inhibited routine enquiries about Black – an astonishing comment on the British work ethos at the time and in particular on the managerial sclerosis at the *Telegraph*.

Black's flight was delayed, and he arrived about nine forty-five. The meeting was informal and relaxed, in the sitting room of a nondescript suite where the windows vibrated each time a plane flew over. The only heated moments took place in negotiations with room service over the difficulty of procuring some coffee.

Hartwell dominated the conversation, talking to Black about completing the issue that would finance the plants which would ensure the *Telegraph*'s prosperity. To Black, the *Telegraph* chairman seemed a fairly charming and elegant figure, although he was clearly wrestling with problems he wasn't equipped to handle and was deflecting detailed questions to his team. Stephen seemed a steady but mainly technical man, and his deputy, Lawson, while quite a bit younger than his superiors at fifty-three, struck Black as an implausible executive.

As he listened to the obese and monocled fellow's occasional piping interjections, which seemed principally to consist of 'Hear hear', or 'I say' or 'Rather', and his laugh punctuated with snorting noises, Black was not filled with confidence in the next generation of management.

Nevertheless, after more general discussion about the finances, trades unions and position of the paper, Black got down to negotiations. Nothing he had heard at the meeting altered his approach to the situation. 'Look,' he said to Hartwell, 'I've read the prospectus and, subject to a little more investigation which could be done very quickly, I suspect I can make the investment to top up the equity part.'

This is what Hartwell wanted to hear. But, added Black, he would have to have a pre-emptive right on any issue of new *Telegraph* shares, or any sale of the Berrys' shares. Any prudent person in his position would have to make the same condition, given the speculative nature of the investment.

Lord Hartwell replied without hesitation. 'I don't think we can resist that.'

Hartwell had not anticipated Black's terms, but he didn't see the harm in them and didn't want the search for equity to come up dry again. The Canadian seemed to fit the bill – at one point he told Hartwell of his $200 million in cash flow, and 'all he had to worry about was which pocket it was coming from'.

It had not dawned on Hartwell, as it had on Black and Knight, that the *Telegraph* might need more money at some later stage. After all, up to this point the company had not issued shares in nearly six decades of Berry ownership. 'I didn't think it meant very much,' Hartwell said much later.

Shortly after the key exchange, Black and Hambro went for a walk outside to discuss the situation. Black's share would be £10 million, or about $17 million, for fourteen per cent. As airplanes roared overhead, they deduced that in the worst-case scenario Black might lose half his money. In the best case, he might make five times his money, and with his pre-emptive rights might even achieve control in five years.

When they returned to the room, both sides reconfirmed the deal, shook hands, and went their separate ways. No papers were drawn up or exchanged, and Black announced that Hambro would deal with

Rothschild & Sons and his solicitor would handle the legal side. A waiting car hired by Black drove the British group to the terminal, then swung back to whisk him to his plane. He was back in Toronto in time for a late lunch.

Before they parted, Black asked Hambro to retain on his behalf the services of Daniel Colson, a partner in the London office of the Canadian law firm Stikeman, Elliot. The son of an Irish Montreal police detective, Dan Colson had met Black in Quebec City during the late 1960s, where both studied law at Laval University. Although his law career had since taken him from Montreal to Hong Kong and then to London, Colson and Black had remained close: Colson is godfather to Black's children. When Black called his friend a couple of days later to tell him he planned to invest in the *Daily Telegraph*, Colson replied, 'Lie down until the feeling passes.'

Through the summer and into autumn, an uneasy peace prevailed among the new and old shareholders of the *Daily Telegraph*. On 11 June, a small item appeared in the *Telegraph* announcing 'Mr Conrad Black of Toronto' as a fourteen per cent shareholder and director through Ravelston Corporation, but gave no whiff of the side agreements. Those were to be revealed two days later in a *Wall Street Journal* article quoting unnamed sources, but the *Telegraph* maintained that Black's investment was 'purely passive'. The unease within the *Telegraph* was not alleviated when one of the staff thought he heard Lord Hartwell say, 'Good man, Conrad Ritblat.'

A carefully worded memorandum of agreement was drawn up under Colson's supervision and signed, at a meeting which commenced a five thirty p.m. on 14 June, by the principals of the 140 Trustee Company which controlled the Telegraph Newspaper Trust. the Right Honourable William Michael, Baron Hartwell of Peterborough Court of Fleet Street in the city of London and his brother, the Right Honourable John Seymour Thomas, Viscount Camrose of Hackwood Park of Basingstoke in the County of Hants, signed on the bottom line.

Meanwhile, emotions were running high within the Berry clan. Both of Hartwell's sons, Nicholas and Adrian, had recently joined the *Telegraph* board, but neither had been apprised of Black's controversial agreement with their father. Nicky Berry was not pleased to learn about it in the *Wall Street Journal.*

Back in Canada, Black's investment in the *Telegraph* was viewed as a curious development for a conglomerateur on the wane.

Black was deluged by requests for interviews from British and Canadian publications. Usually a ready source of florid comment, he maintained a cool silence. For one thing, it wasn't clear to him how things were going to work out with the *Telegraph*. For another, as Black reflected in his spacious *Telegraph* chairman's office in the Isle of Dogs almost nine years later, 'I'd gone all through that instant baptism with the media in Canada and I didn't want to go through it again. I'd do it if it was going to serve my interests but it wasn't going to.

'My impression is that in things like that, observers . . . tend to resent and be suspicious of people who suddenly emerge and get a great deal of publicity and appear to be enjoying it. I had been through that, and I didn't think it was in my interest to go through it again. I never have. I never have had much publicity here.'

In a similar vein, it seemed curious to some that Black was in no hurry to fly to London to see at first hand the business he had invested in. But plant tours and glad-handing employees had never been of particular interest to Black. Rupert Hambro, his representative on the *Telegraph* board, was in constant touch. As was Colson, whose work drafting the key agreements between Black and Hartwell was becoming more relevant daily as the *Telegraph*'s finances deteriorated.

Befuddled *Telegraph* employees resented that they were learning more about Black's investment from rival newspapers, and were puzzled that Lord Hartwell had not fulfilled his pledge to write a leader* introducing his new partner.

Black was moved to risk his low profile in the British media, however, in response to an article about Ronald Reagan in the 20 July 1985 issue of the literary weekly, the *Spectator*. Under the headline 'Living with a Dying President', writer Christopher Hitchens had argued that Ronald Reagan's recent cancer treatment belied a greater illness and that Reagan ought to resign. Even if Black's published letter to the magazine was not intended as a taste of what Fleet Street might expect from its newest entrant, that was the message received.

---

* In North American terms, a leader is an editorial.

'I have generally been disappointed by the lack of integrity and serious analysis in British (and most foreign) reporting of American affairs,' Black wrote. 'This was one of the lesser reasons why I recently purchased a sizeable interest in the *Telegraph*, as it is . . . one of the few British publications whose reports on the United States are not habitually snobbish, envious and simplistic.

'There is ample room for debate over Mr Reagan's performance as president, but no one in his right mind could dispute that he has been an effective statesman and as a cancer patient, he deserves better than Hitchens' nasty, macabre, vulgar, and insolent claptrap.'

Black flew to London twice in autumn 1985, the first trip over three days in late September. Now he could see at first-hand the time-warp environs of 135 Fleet Street. On 24 September, Hartwell hosted a post-board meeting dinner in Black's honour at his home on Cowley Street, a cordial but somewhat sombre event. A more portentous gathering took place two nights later in the dining room atop *The Economist* building in St James's.

In the four months since Black had taken his stake in the *Telegraph*, he and Knight had spoken frequently. Knight had made it known that after more than a decade as editor of *The Economist*, he thought he should begin looking for new challenges. Should Black take a greater role in the *Telegraph*, Knight said he would like to get involved.

The son of an air force officer, Andrew Knight worked at merchant bank J. Henry Schroder Wagg after graduation from Balliol College, Oxford. After two years there he spent two more as a scribe at *Investors Chronicle*, before joining *The Economist* in 1966. He spent time in the Washington office, became assistant editor in 1970 and editor in 1974.

Whatever was to happen, he thought that Black might benefit from a meeting with Frank Rogers. One of British publishing's elder statesmen, sixty-five-years-old at the time he joined Black and Knight for supper, Rogers was chairman of magazine, newspaper and printing group East Midland Allied Press. His had been an impressive career spanning almost five decades, including, at one period, running the Daily Mirror Group.

The politically astute Knight thought Black could benefit from having in his corner someone like Rogers, who knew his way around Fleet Street. Rogers had been predicting the financial collapse of the *Telegraph* as a consequence of its outdated printing arrangements since the mid-1960s, and he and Black got along from the start. Towards the end of the dinner Rogers said, 'This most convivial occasion brings together a potential proprietor of the *Daily Telegraph*, a potential managing director of the *Daily Telegraph* and a potential director of the *Daily Telegraph*. Let us delete the word "potential" and decide what *we* are going to do with *our* newspapers.'

Rogers joined the *Telegraph* board in October, filling the second seat granted to Black under his shareholder agreement. When Hartwell commanded the *Telegraph*, he didn't believe in having directors from outside the company, but as part of the June private placement, two other new board members – in addition to Black and Hartwell's sons – were added to satisfy the institutions: Lord Rawlinson, a former attorney general, and merchant banker David Montagu, a former chairman of Orion Bank and, at the time, deputy chairman of J. Rothschild Holdings.

By the time Black attended his first board meeting in late September, it was brutally obvious that the rosy financial projections presented to investors during the June private placement would not be realised. Before the meeting, Black, David Montagu and Lord Rawlinson lunched at Rupert Hambro's office. The men agreed that the *Telegraph* needed a new chief executive. Knight was discussed as a candidate, as was Ian Irvine, who had recently stepped down as chief executive of Express Newspapers.

As chairman of a newly formed audit committee, Montagu (who later became Lord Swaything) now subjected the *Telegraph*'s accounts to unprecedented scrutiny. Horror stories of non-existent, let alone archaic, accounting systems surfaced daily while advertising revenues slipped away – in part due to the recent imposition of a value-added tax on ads – and the rising cost of the new plants. No one felt the books were deliberately doctored, simply that they didn't have the right information, and senior managers had not liked to burden the proprietor with bad news.

In October, auditors Saffery Champness were dismissed and replaced by Coopers & Lybrand. From then on, the company faced one monetary crisis after another. 'A nickel and dime store in Parry Sound is run better than this place,' Black was heard to say, sending puzzled Fleet Street journalists to their atlases in search of the reference (a small town in Ontario). After the first board meeting he attended, just to see how a potential customer would be treated, Black telephoned the classified advertising department at the *Telegraph*. 'I was told I could wait for several weeks and I was referred to *The Times*,' he later recounted, 'and actually given the telephone number of the *Guardian*.'

When, at Montagu's urging, he returned to London for the October board meeting – a twenty-four-hour round trip on Concorde – the situation was grave. Hartwell agreed quite readily when Montagu and Black suggested a new chief executive would send a positive signal to the banks, and the board decided Hartwell would offer the post to Knight.

The onset of the grey London winter was a cheery contrast to the mood within the *Telegraph*. The board was informed by Coopers that unaudited results for the six months ended 30 September showed a loss of £14.4 million against a projected profit of £5.5 million. Dan Colson was now working virtually full-time on *Telegraph* business, and was in daily contact with Black, usually phoning him late at night London time, and several times on weekends.

A new game was afoot, and one of its main features was plenty of finger-pointing. Nicholas Berry wanted to know how this 'predator' Black had persuaded his father into giving away the Berry birthright, and why Rothschild & Sons had allowed it. The institutions and banks wanted to know how Rothschild & Sons could have underwritten a rights issue not five months earlier that was based on inaccurate information. Lord Hartwell was confounded that the situation was grim so soon again. He enlisted the help of a willing Nicholas to try to find a new friendly investor who would buy out Black and salvage the situation.

Rupert Hambro recalls: 'Many of us felt we should sue [Rothschild & Sons] actually, because it had been such a faulty prospectus. But in the end it was Conrad's call, not our call. And Conrad said, "Well, fine. What am I going to achieve? I bought into this business. I like the business. We're going to make it work. I sue Rothschild and I get a bit of money that's not going to help me very much. We'll just make sure they do an awful lot of work for not very much fee for a long time to come." '

Rothschild countered the criticism by laying the blame on the auditors and *Telegraph* management, and pointed out that it was brought in at rather a late stage to help Hartwell out of the urgent financial bind he had got his papers into.

If anything, Black was excited to find that the scenario he had envisioned perhaps two to five years down the road was becoming reality mere months later. Certainly there was the sense that in Rothschild's view the best outcome was the passing of the paper to Black. And the fact was, to Nicholas Berry's growing dismay, Rothschild had been hired to represent the interests of the *Telegraph*, not Hartwell personally. 'I didn't get the advice,' Hartwell later lamented. 'Perhaps I should have asked for it. I should have known more about whether we would ever require more money, but I was told it was going to be all right. I didn't ever reject any advice; it's advice I didn't get which I regret not having.'

Indeed, as far as David Montagu could tell, Rothschild had 'handed the Berry family's balls to Conrad Black on a silver salver'.

The disarray of the previous six months was just a warm-up for the chaotic tragi-comedy that was to unfold in the four weeks starting in mid-November. The *Daily Telegraph* was now technically in default on its bank financing and Black's options were the key to keeping the company out of the clutches of receivership. While few people seemed initially to grasp the import of Black's rights, Nicholas Berry actively sought a way to keep the paper in family hands, or at least out of Black's.

Amid Berry's growing hostility towards Black, Rupert Hambro visited him to explain that the Canadian was not to blame for what had occurred. 'Conrad actually is not trying to steal the newspaper,' Hambro explained. 'He is not actually against the Berry family.' Berry was polite, but his attitude towards Black did not change.

Speaking with Colson on the telephone from Toronto on Thursday 14 November, Black specified his position: He would inject up to £20 million more into the *Daily Telegraph*, but would insist on at least fifty-one per cent of its shares. Given the parlous financial state of the paper, the stock would have to be sold at considerably less than the 140 per share Black had paid in May for his fourteen per cent stake.

Montagu told Colson the new shares would likely be priced at no more than 50p, given the high risk involved and the likelihood the company would produce no dividends for at least three years.

On the other hand, if Hartwell wanted to find another buyer for the company, that was fine with Black – under his agreement, he could either match any offer or sell. Nicholas Berry was still searching. He arranged a dinner at the swish Boodles club with executives from Australia's John Fairfax Group, chief executive Greg Gardiner and general manager Fred Brenchley, who were already in Europe on other business. In what would prove in retrospect to be a wildly ironic comment, Hartwell explained to Andrew Knight that as opposed to Black, the Fairfaxes, as newspaper folk, were more 'our kind of people'.

Hartwell proposed to Gardiner that Fairfax and the Berrys together buy the company and hold it fifty-fifty. Hartwell would run the editorial side and Fairfax the business end. When Gardiner asked Hartwell what it might take to buy out Black, Hartwell figured somewhere in the range of 200p to 250p per share, a 'decent' premium over the 140p Black had paid in May. But once it became obvious that Fairfax would have to buy out the institutions as well as Black, the Australians lost interest.

At another point, Lord Hanson, one of England's wealthiest industrialists, approached Rothschild with the intention of making a bid, but he too demurred after perusing Black's 14 June shareholder agreement. The crucial article of the agreement read: 'In the event the Company proposes to issue further shares of any class, the Trustee hereby agrees that if possible under the terms of the issue, Ravelston shall have the right, but not the obligation, to subscribe and purchase any or all the shares being offered by the company to the Trustee (or its nominee) in addition to any shares which Ravelston may be entitled to subscribe for and purchase in proportion to its own shareholding.'

On Friday 15 November Colson relayed Black's position to Hartwell. Black would insist on control, but diplomatically hoped Hartwell would stay as a minority shareholder and editor-in-chief, and Nicky Berry would remain on the board. Hartwell responded by saying he didn't seem to have much time to find another buyer, and expressed concern that the low price of the planned rights issue would appear as a 'rescue'. The affable Colson decided not to point out that this was precisely what it was.

For his part, Montagu, sensitive to the growing split in the Berry family, suggested that Black might put in the money but increase his minority position to a controlling one over time, instead of straight away. Over the next few weeks, Knight also proposed similar structures of shared control, raising suspicions in Black's and Colson's minds that having no clear owner suited Knight's own ambitions – Knight having enjoyed similar autonomy at *The Economist*.

On 18 November, Black received a copy of Rothshild's 'proposed strategy' for the rights issue. A £20 million investment by Black at 50p per share would be structured to give Black thirty-nine per cent of equity and multiple voting rights to exercise control, including an option to buy further shares until April 1989 at 100p to bring him over fifty per cent of the equity.

When the directors met again on 21 November, Coopers delivered another shock with its latest figures. Revised forecasts for the next three years now showed a meagre *aggregate* profit of £300,000, as opposed to £55 million at the time of the May private placement and £22 million at the time of an audit committee meeting several weeks earlier. Projected cash flow to March 1988 now showed a £10.2 million deterioration, meaning the banks might have to be asked for an additional £10 million in working capital financing, or the crucial printing plants might have to be scaled back.

The banks rang Montagu to tell him they would not be making a £4 million payment due on the West Ferry Road plant at the end of the month. Hartwell was still quibbling with Knight over the level of stock options he would receive as the new chief executive. Colson heard through Coopers that a senior executive of NatWest, the *Telegraph* long-time clearing bank, had called the accounting firm to see if it could act as receiver.

On another front, Coopers' frenzied auditors had discovered about 300 extra staff working in production at the papers than the *Telegraph* accounts had indicated. That might have been a bizarre joke if it didn't mean than £10 million more would have to be found for redundancy payments.

On three separate occasions, Hartwell dipped into his family trusts to produce emergency loans totalling more than £4 million so that his newspapers could avoid receivership.

Colson accompanied Montagu on endless rounds of meetings with the banks to make sure they knew there was a shareholder ready to stabilise the situation by putting in the necessary equity. All that was needed was a little time and pressure on Hartwell to firm up the details. At one particularly grim session with officials from the Security Pacific and NatWest banks, Montagu rang up the Governor of the Bank of England Robin Leigh-Pemberton to discuss how bad it would be for the City were this 'national institution' to fall into bankruptcy. The banks caught Montagu's unsubtle drift and a reprieve was granted.

As they left the meeting, Montagu explained to Colson how the Governor had not been available and he had in fact been speaking to an underling as if he were the Governor. 'I told the then-Governor afterwards,' recalls Montagu. 'He roared with laughter.'

Back in Toronto, Black was not laughing when the 23 November issue of the *Spectator* hit the stands in London. In it, Canadian author John Ralston Saul wrote an article that presented to the British audience the harshest views of Black in his native country.

'He has the abstract talents to make money out of paper, the animal talents to take over other people's companies with or without their co-operation and the intellectual qualities to engage in aggressive public debate on almost any subject at an extremely high level. He has also written a 700-page political biography,' Saul wrote.

'There is only one disappointing side to his achievement. While Mr Black personally grows ever richer, some of his companies seem to grow ever poorer.'

The article ran through Black's 1978 take-over of Argus and its aftermath, focusing first on Black's controversial extrication from Argus of control of Massey-Ferguson, and more recent sales of chunks of Dominion Stores. It skimmed over the Ontario Securities Commission investigation into his affairs ('In the end no action was taken') and then described Black's state of affairs at the time he bought into the *Telegraph* in June 1985:

'With nothing left to reorganise, he turned on his partners – including his own brother – and restructured them out, leaving only himself, a solitary, rich young man with his reputation severely undermined in Canada.'

In concluding, Saul observed that 'one searches for the spirit of sacrifice in Mr Black's career and finds self-help. Nevertheless, the driving force of his personality and his brilliant sense of applied historical perspective will impress all who meet him. Only with time may they feel that the driving force deforms the perspective so that his masterful conclusions are often wrong.'

For the second time in four months, Black penned a letter to the *Spectator*, printed in its 7 December issue. He did so with Frank Rogers's and Dan Colson's encouragement but against the advice of Andrew Knight, who was not yet fully familiar with Black's talent for verbal dust-ups.

Black wrote that Saul's article, 'which purported to be about me, contains several assertions that were so dishonest and malicious that they should not be allowed to pass without comment. An absolute majority of the sentences in the piece were false and a detailed refutation would require a more extensive exposé than is deserved by so crude and transparent a smear.'

Black defended his roles at Massey and Dominion, and noted that 'in his perfervid search for a "non-failure" in my commercial career, Mr Saul omits any reference to Norcen (the oil and gas concern that Black still retained), which, he pointed out, was generating more annual cash flow than Massey and Dominion 'ever produced together in any three years. That, essentially, is what I am in business for.

'The suggestion that my associates retired from their partnership with me on any basis other than complete amicability and great profit to themselves is a shameful untruth.'

In conclusion, Black delivered what would come to be recognised as one of his better-known *coups de grâce* of invective: 'Those who would retain his services should confine him to subjects better suited than this one was to his sniggering, puerile, defamatory and cruelly limited talents.'

The matter continued the following week, when Saul replied in the magazine that 'the enduring impression' of Black's rebuttal 'remains that of a maddened corgi yapping at one's heels'.

Saul retracted nothing and concluded that, 'in short, it is difficult to imagine how the odours of what has been cooked in Canada can be prevented from wafting across the waters to England'.

Others in Fleet Street took up the anti-Black cause, including *The Times* in an article by Kenneth Fleet which described him as 'Genghis Khan' and the *Daily Mail* in a piece which noted, 'In the somewhat suffocating provinciality of Toronto, he is no doubt a large fish in a very small pond.'

The literary skirmish with Saul was of course a mere side-show to the main event. Of greater concern to Black was Colson's growing sense of impending disaster at the *Telegraph*.

At the *Telegraph* board meeting on 28 November, Colson was relieved to hear Hartwell announce, in the presence of his son Adrian and brother Camrose, that he had agreed in principle to the new proposal from Rothschild. Control would be ceded to Conrad Black.

But within a matter of minutes Hartwell's visage had changed from relatively sanguine to decidedly unwell. The elderly peer collapsed and fell sideways from his chair. Shock and alarm spread through the boardroom – Lord Hartwell has had a stroke! – but a concerned Adrian knew better; his father had a history of fainting at moments of great stress. A prostrate Hartwell was carried from the boardroom to his office, where he quickly began to revive. After summoning the company nurse, Hartwell's long-time secretary, Eileen Fuller, seemed determined not to let her attend to him. 'No ordinary medic is going to touch Lord Hartwell,' her voice rang down the corridor, insisting now that his personal doctor be summoned.

Colson suggested that this might be a good juncture for the meeting to adjourn. Suddenly, the gentlemanly Lord Camrose spoke, the rarest of occurrences during the endless meetings of the past weeks. 'What exactly is it you want my brother to do?' he asked. Colson took a deep breath, maintained his composure, and recited the terms of the agreement he had just finished explaining minutes earlier, and to which Camrose's brother had already acceded.

Back in his office, at about six p.m., Colson was preparing to relay the day's peculiar events to Black in Toronto when Montagu rang. Hartwell had called the audit committee chairman claiming he had not understood the deal. In spite of what he had said hours earlier, Hartwell had now told Montagu he would never agree to give Black voting control with less than fifty per cent of the equity.

Colson advised Black on the situation, and also spoke with Rogers and Evelyn de Rothschild. The consensus was that Hartwell was being influenced by Nicholas, who probably claimed there was another buyer. Twice more that evening Colson spoke with Black, who decided he would consider putting in £20 million immediately in return for 50.1 per cent, and doing away with the idea of buying only thirty-nine per cent now.

The next day, sensing the growing likelihood of the situation ending up in the courts, Colson spoke to Tony Hughes, the *Telegraph* secretary, to ensure that thorough minutes of the previous day's board meeting were taken, particularly Hartwell's opening remarks about accepting Black's proposal.

At four p.m. that Friday afternoon, Colson received a phone call from Rothschild to say that Hartwell wanted Black to buy eleven per cent of his *Telegraph* stock at 100p, now, instead of through options. A frustrated Colson noted that under take-over code, Black would probably then have to offer 100p to other shareholders, instead of the agreed 50p. 'Also, I pointed out that this was a totally new deal – again!' Colson later recalled.

When Colson explained the situation to him that night, Black agreed that Hartwell's counter-proposal was unacceptable. What he would consider, Black said, was buying eleven per cent from Hartwell now at 50p, and getting an option on ten per cent of Hartwell's remaining twenty-two per cent at 100p, with Hartwell having the right to put the shares to Black at that price in two years' time so long as the *Telegraph* wasn't insolvent.

Saturdays were quickly becoming somewhat of a routine for Colson – he would spend a good deal of the day in transatlantic conference with Black. Saturday 30 November was no exception. Colson complained, and Black concurred, that Hartwell wasn't getting the message.

On Sunday, Michael Richardson from Rothschild phoned Colson to say Hartwell was now willing to negotiate with Black and no one else. There would be no more talk of a white knight. The most recent approach had been from the Egyptian Al-Fayed brothers, owners of Harrods, whom Hartwell felt were not 'acceptable'.

On Monday 2 December Black's revised investment proposal was delivered by hand for Hartwell, his trustees and family to consider. Colson issued a warning through Michael Richardson: the time for negotiation and delay had passed. If there was no response by Wednesday afternoon, he would ask for a meeting with the banks – a subtle way of saying he would seek the banks' assistance to force out Hartwell.

Hartwell mulled over the proposal for a day and called a meeting in the *Telegraph*'s heavily panelled boardroom for Wednesday. Lord Camrose, Nicholas Berry, David Montagu and Hartwell's lawyer and financial advisers attended. Colson brought a telex from Black stating that Lord Hartwell should remain chairman and editor-in-chief for life, and once again Hartwell seemed agreeable.

Later, Colson met the banks, who insisted that regulatory approvals had to be obtained by the middle of the next week, that heads of agreement be signed by the following day, and that no repayment of the emergency funds that Hartwell had pumped into the company over the past few weeks to keep it afloat would be made without their consent.

From Toronto, Black ran through the points and added a few of his own. He was sensitive to a certain degree to the concerns of David Montagu and others about the effect his assumption of control would have on the family. As long as the family owned five per cent or more of the *Telegraph* shares, Black allowed, they could have four nominees on the board. He reaffirmed that Hartwell should retain the titles of chairman and editor-in-chief (but made it privately clear that they would be titles only, and Knight would exercise executive authority as publisher and CEO). Black also agreed with the banks that the company was not in a position to repay the loans to Hartwell's trust at this time.

The next day, Colson attended another key meeting in Rothsschild's boardroom in St Swithin's Lane, only to find Nicholas Berry and his personal adviser there too. Colson considered Berry uninvited; Berry said he was there at his father's request. Berry demanded that the trusts' loans to the *Telegraph* be repaid immediately. The meeting went downhill from there – 'a screaming match' in Colson's words – until Berry was ejected, but not before accusing Colson of being 'Conrad Black's colonial mouthpiece'. Berry soon after resigned from the board.

The night, around midnight, Colson received a call from David Montagu with Lord Hartwell's latest demands. Among them, he again wanted Black to buy shares now at 100p, not 50p, and he wanted the loan repayment made immediately. Colson talked to Black at around one a.m. London time, and Black agreed to repay the £3.3

million no later than 30 September 1989, but would definitely not buy shares at 100p then and there. It was to be Black's final concession.

On Wednesday 11 December, confirmation was received that there would be no referral to the Mergers and Monopolies Commission by the Secretary of State. It followed more crucial consent from the Panel on Take-Overs and Mergers that Black would not be obliged to make a take-over offer to all shareholders under City code, 'in view of the serious financial position of the *Telegraph*'.

Hartwell retreated to his office to prepare a 'personal' statement about the financing which appeared in the next morning's *Telegraph*. 'Details will be disclosed on Friday,' he wrote, 'and I very much regret that readers and staff have so far had to rely on incomplete reports in other newspapers.' Hartwell explained that as a 'main result' of complex arrangements, Black would own 50.1 per cent and his family's holding would be reduced from sixty per cent to a minority. 'I remain the chairman and editor-in-chief and I still remain responsible for the editorial policy of the newspapers.'

Black went to sleep on Thursday night sensing a victorious conclusion to his British foray. Early the next morning, an urgent phone call from an outraged Colson roused Black. A press conference announcing the deal and introducing Andrew Knight as the new chief executive had been scheduled for that afternoon, but Knight had not yet signed his service contract.

The difficulty of coming to agreement with Knight during the past weeks had been overshadowed by the more crucial wrangling with Hartwell and the banks. Black had already agreed to give Knight options over five per cent of the *Telegraph*'s equity, but they were arguing over the details. Now Black was listening to Colson's charge that Knight was trying to 'blackmail' him.

It had been widely leaked in the press that Knight would be the new CEO at the *Daily Telegraph*, but he was taking a hard line on his contract, often accompanied at negotiations by his brother Timothy, a lawyer. Colson had spoken to Black about Knight's demands several times the previous day, but no agreement had been reached.

From Knight's point of view, he realised that as editor of *The Economist* he had no particular executive experience in a situation of the magnitude or disarray of the *Telegraph*. But he was giving up prestige, security and possibilities elsewhere, and taking a fairly heavy personal risk in the process. Having brought the opportunity to Black, if he was now going to take the lead to turn the *Telegraph* around, he wanted to be properly remunerated.

The press conference was set for the afternoon of Friday 13 December 'and at eleven o'clock in the morning we were sitting in my office still dithering over his contract,' Colson recalled later. 'The one outstanding point was the stock option. Andrew had asked for a stock option over five per cent of the company, which I thought was outrageous. So finally, because I wouldn't agree to it, we called Conrad. It was six o'clock in the morning in Toronto, so you can imagine how thrilled Conrad was to hear from us.

'I told Conrad, in front of Andrew, that I thought it was outrageous that he should ask for that, and I thought it was particularly outrageous that he could be basically holding us up. I called it blackmail because Andrew was basically saying that if we didn't sign, he wasn't going to the press conference.'

But Black agreed to the terms put forth by Knight, and the conference went off at three thirty p.m. Under the deal announced, £20 million in new share capital would be issued, and the banks would provide an additional £10 million in financing. Hollinger would directly buy £14.4 million of new equity, and underwrite a £5.6 million rights issue (and in the end held fifty-seven per cent of the company after most of the institutions skittishly declined to pick up the new rights).

H. M. Stephen would retire in the new year, Tony Hughes would become financing director, succeeding a retiring R. J. Holland, and Andrew Knight would join in early February.

Hartwell coped as best he could with what was an obviously devastating situation – he maintained that nothing really had changed. In an interview with the Press Association, Lord Hartwell said of the paper's new owner, 'I do not know him very well, but I get on with him and he does not want to be a newspaper tycoon.'

Hartwell would point out repeatedly over the next years that he never actually sold the *Telegraph* to Conrad Black as many people believed; what happened is better described as a surrender. A perplexed Rupert Murdoch was among those who called up Hartwell, asking, 'Why are you doing this?' Recalls Hartwell: 'He couldn't understand it at all. He thought I was doing it on purpose.'

When questioned by one of his own reporters, David Graves, about the change of ownership, Hartwell explained it this way: 'The trouble is that we are a family with no other outside financial interests. Almost everyone else in Fleet Street has these interests on which to draw when the newspapers need money. Ours was a family situation and we were the last of them.'

The *Daily Telegraph* was the opportunity Conrad Black had been hoping for. And the shenanigans of the past few weeks had left him determined to impose some New World discipline on the venerable enterprise that had limped into his arms like a wounded hound. The company that would now be the centre of his business empire reported a loss of £16.3 million on turnover of £74.4 million in the six months ended 30 September 1985. Hardly an auspicious beginning, but a beginning nonetheless for a man determined to be both historian and history. Asked by reporter Diane Francis, then of the *Toronto Star*, about his initial impressions of doing business in England, Black did not tread lightly. 'The British as a matter of course have concentrated so heavily on questions of ritual and form, and comparatively little on performance and merit, that there's something slightly self-obsessive about their evaluation as to whether someone measures up or not,' he opined. 'This results in a fair amount of dead wood. They lack basic administrative standards and are still dealing with a delusional structure based on the envy of other nations.'

The implication, of course, was that Britain's newest press baron would have none of it. As another new year approached, Black flew to Palm Beach with his pregnant wife, young son and daughter to reflect on the remarkable changes the year had brought and to ponder what might lie ahead.

SIX

Waking the Giant,
Drowning the Kittens

'No one snubs the owner of the
Daily Telegraph'

Visitors to Conrad Black's Toronto mansion enter a two-storey entrance hall which leads directly to a sprawling living room, with French doors opening onto terraces and gardens. To the right is a large formal dining room, to the left, a sitting room. It is from the sitting room that a hallway leads to Black's inner sanctum, the place where he is most at ease: his library.

Containing fifteen thousand volumes, the design of the drum-shaped, domed structure was influenced by Renaissance Venetian architect Palladio and the Radcliffe Library at Oxford. And it was the *piece de resistance* of the new home Black erected in the early 1980s on the eight-acre estate, after tearing down the ageing mansion he grew up in.

To design the Georgian manor, Black enlisted Thierry Despont, a young French architect based in New York whose client list included designers Calvin Klein and Oscar de la Renta, and Wall Street high-flier John Gutfreund and his wife Susan. Despont was also retained to spruce up the Statue of Liberty. 'As Thierry was finishing up here,' said Black, 'he was just starting to work on the Statue of Liberty restoration, and I felt that in the brief overlap I got at least equal time with the world's most famous monument.'

Including the dome, the library measures a full twenty-six feet high, and twenty-two feet in diameter. Books are shelved on two levels, with the upper level, three feet wide and with metal railings, resembling a gallery. A secret staircase leading up to it is hidden behind the bookcases, complete with another passage leading off to the master bedroom suite. In the planning stages, Black was concerned the structure might look like an MX-missile launcher amid the grandeur of Toronto's ritzy Bridal Path neighbourhood. But he was not disappointed with the result. 'I'm not a great sportsman – my idea of relaxation is to go into my library and just start reading, and I find the room quite foolproof in that respect.'

It was in the Black library that Peregrine Worsthorne found himself on a blustery winter day early in February 1986. Worsthorne was in Toronto for one day and one reason, to meet the mysterious new proprietor of the *Daily Telegraph* regarding the position of editor of the *Sunday Telegraph*. Worsthorne had been with the *Daily Telegraph* since 1953 and had held the position of Sunday deputy editor for some years. But any aspirations he had for a full editorship dissipated after an incident in 1973 when he deliberately set out to say 'fuck' on BBC television – and succeeded. From then on, the ultra-proper Hartwell took a dim view of his prospects as an editor. So low were the self-deprecating Worsthorne's hopes that when CEO-in-waiting Knight invited him to lunch early in 1986, Worsthorne reckoned it was to pump him for ideas about who else might be right for the job.

The Black household Worsthorne arrived at was in an animated state, as Shirley Black had just given birth to their third child, James.* As Worsthorne recalled in his memoir *Tricks of Memory*. 'Perhaps because of all the excitement surrounding this happy event nobody had remembered to unpadlock any of the gates into the grounds, and after the airport taxi-driver had despaired of gaining access I had no choice but to climb over the fence and make my own way up to the mansion on foot.

'This was no easy stroll and I spent at least fifteen minutes stumbling through snow-drifts before eventually reaching the front door, my shoes ruined and soaked to the skin. Nor was there any time to improve my pathetic appearance because Conrad answered the door himself, distractedly showing me into a splendid library before rushing back upstairs to help with the new baby. By then I had developed a most fearsome headache, almost certainly through

* The births of the Black children seem to coincide with key events in his business life: His first son, Jonathan was born shortly before Black's dramatic 1978 take-over of Argus Corporation, and daughter Alana was born in 1982 amid the take-over battle Black was fighting with Cleveland-based Hanna Mining Corp.

nerves, and it was so bad that when Conrad returned in half an hour's time I felt compelled, almost reluctantly, to ask for a painkiller.

'More confusion ensued because the Conrad Black medicine cupboard did not run to such things and one of the estate's security guards had to be dispatched downtown, blue lights flashing, to buy a bottle. No, it was not a good beginning.'

A far less eventful meeting had taken place earlier at Black's office with Max Hastings, Knight's candidate for the key title of editor at the *Daily Telegraph*. Like Worsthorne, Hastings was an unorthodox choice. At forty, he was a respected and well-known reporter and military historian who had written several books and made a name for himself as a correspondent during the 1983 Falklands War.

Knight had met Hastings the previous summer, when, as Hastings recalls, Knight was 'thinking very seriously about some *coup* being possible towards the *Telegraph*'. Hastings, a tall, stern-looking man (dubbed 'Hitler Hastings' by *Private Eye*, in part because of his dictatorial *coiffure*) believed a 'complete clean-out' of the staff would reveal a fine franchise underneath.

As Black, too, is a military history buff of some note, it was likely that he and Hastings would get on. As soon as Hastings strode into Black's office he scanned the various military scenes adorning the walls. 'Ah, yes,' said Hastings, admiring one over Black's shoulder, 'HMS *Warspite* entering Narvik in April 1940.' Black had read a few of Hastings's books, and although in the ensuing months and years the two men would prove to have many ideological differences, Hastings would become a key ingredient of the *Telegraph*'s – and Black's – success.

Before Worsthorne had left London, Hastings had told him that his own meeting with Black had been fairly painless, 'except for the proprietor's almost obsessional preoccupation with abstruse points of nineteenth-century British political history'. Margaret Thatcher was campaigning for her third successive term as prime minister, and Black had asked Hastings: 'If Thatcher wins, when would there have been a prime minister before who won three successive terms in office?' Hastings had deflected Black's quiz, saying that Perry was the expert and he didn't want to steal his thunder.

At Worsthorne's meeting, the aspirins arrived and were washed down with a couple off stiff drinks. Sure enough, Black tried the trivia question on Worsthorne, stumping him. (The correct answer was Lord Liverpool.) Worsthorne felt the quiz was not intended either to catch him out or to show off. Rather, Worsthorne had written disparagingly in the *Spectator* of this mystery Canadian taking over the venerable *Telegraph*. Although Black did not mention the article, recalls Worsthorne, 'I think he was probably anxious to show that although he was a Canadian financier he was also a sort of educated chap.'

In any case, Black's right-wing views found a kindred spirit in Worsthorne, and it came out that Black was an acquaintance and fan of Worsthorne's friend William F. Buckley – indeed Worsthorne had once been described in *Time* magazine as the 'British Buckley'.

Both editors' appointments were subject to meeting Black in person, but Knight had insisted that the editors-in-waiting keep their appointments a secret; the rights issue which would formally install Black as proprietor of the *Telegraph* would take nearly three frantic months to complete after it was announced in December 1985. In the meantime, Lord Hartwell (wrongly) believed he would still call the editorial shots.*

Along with picking the editors, Black entrusted Andrew Knight with the task of assembling a new management team. Black knew from Knight and others that a showdown was looming between Britain's newspaper proprietors and the powerful Fleet Street unions, and sensed the paper had the potential to be profitable, although just how profitable was not clear. On Frank Rogers's advice, Knight enlisted consultant Joe Cooke, an industrial engineer whose gentle western Irish exterior conceals a hard-nosed pragmatist, to help devise plans to reduce the paper's 4,000-strong work-force. He also hired Stephen Grabiner, a member of Coopers & Lybrand's 'corporate care' unit which had been keeping the *Telegraph* limping along. Knowing that attracting younger readers was one of the keys to the paper's survival, Knight reckoned that the appointment of Grabiner as marketing director would 'break the mould' – and as

* Less reluctant to relinquish their roles were *Daily Telegraph* editor, William Deedes, seventy-two, and *Sunday Telegraph* editor, John Thompson, sixty-five, who both looked forward to semi-retirement, although Hartwell considered them young yet.

Grabiner was twenty-seven and had no marketing experience it certainly did.

More than 5,000 *Telegraph* subscribers were dying each month of old age, and this was a trend Knight did not think could be reversed by perpetuating the old Berry ways. But it was a delicate balance: Knight needed also to ensure continuity in order to retain the ageing upper-middle-class core readers.

Black took an avid interest in the personnel and planned editorial changes but saw no point in installing himself in Fleet Street. He considered what sort of a public image he wanted to convey in London, and opted for a low profile. Later, he volunteered, it would have been 'disastrous' for the paper's credibility and for his own reputation if he had appeared as 'another publicity-seeking, self-promoting Commonwealth person rushing across here with my coat tails trailing, seeking a peerage'. On the other hand, he felt he had to show that he was 'not just a materialistic caricature of a North American businessman with no respect for these institutions'. In other words, he was neither of the two famous Canadians with whom he was being increasingly compared, Lord Beaverbrook and Lord Thomson.

The antics of negotiating with Hartwell continued into 1986 and subsided little in the weeks leading up to the formal change of control. Knight wanted to make all sorts of urgent changes despite the fact that he could not officially take up his position until early February, but was frustrated at every turn by Hartwell's business-as-usual attitude. Black asked Knight to make do for the time being, as he did not want to jeopardise negotiations for options to purchase in the future further shares from Hartwell's family trusts.

Joe Cooke was asked to devise radical plans to reduce the work-force in the new plants, and Rogers and Knight enthusiastically championed them. No one, not even Alan Rawcliffe, the talented engineer who had designed the West Ferry Road facility, was confident the plans would work. Even before the unions could be confronted, the management-in-waiting met opposition from the old-style gentlemanly ways of Hartwell and his team. At one meeting on Sunday 22 December a majority of the board, which was still under Hartwell's control, rejected Cooke's plan for major cuts at the new

Manchester plant where the *Telegraph*'s northern edition was to be produced. Cooke later recalled the message conveyed to him from a livid Knight: 'They said when I had been in newspapers long enough, I would find out that all the money was made from advertising. You didn't make money from printing plants and I was very foolish to think you did.'

Knight and his group did manage to suspend negotiations with the Fleet Street unions, who were by this time operating without a contract. This would prove to be, in Knight's estimation, 'the most important single thing' they did in the early days.

Lord Hartwell was dignified and remote but in his way quite wily in his approach towards the strangers who had invaded his wood-panelled sanctuary on the fifth floor of 135 Fleet Street. After six decades of family ownership, he was not going to roll over. Certainly, he and his brother Lord Camrose had ceded control to Black in December by agreeing to the equity issue that would give Black's Hollinger and Ravelston companies at least 50.1 per cent of the shares. But until the deal was signed and sealed, Hartwell would cling to his beloved papers. It was a fine line to walk, though, since he too did not want to jeopardise his position in the talks to sell further shares to Black should the take-over go through.

In early January, Black's London lawyer and adviser Dan Colson got wind first that Hartwell was trying to sell his shares to a third party, and then that he had approached Coopers & Lybrand for information on the money-losing *Sunday Telegraph*, possibly with a view to selling it off to raise enough money to avoid the equity issue. From Toronto, Black spoke on the telephone to Colson on 10 January. By this point, only Colson's sense of humour and thick skin had allowed him to put up with what they viewed as Hartwell's increasingly erratic and unreliable behaviour.

Rupert Hambro, then serving as Black's representative on the *Telegraph* board, explains Black's relationship with Colson this way: 'He quite rightly sees that Dan's better at [negotiating] than he is, because Dan's got more patience than Conrad. Dan's . . . absolutely impossible to roll over and I think Conrad actually, to be honest, would get bored – and would probably honestly not do as good a deal as Dan would in the end.'

Nothing came of Hartwell's eleventh-hour gambits. But as if there were not enough strange goings-on, Colson received a call in the second week of January from Rothschild, informing him that executives representing the Australian financier Robert Holmes à Court and his advisers Lazard Frères were preparing a bid for the *Telegraph*. The head of the group, Sir Michael Clapham, asked to meet Colson and a meeting was set at Colson's office in Gresham Street at three thirty on Friday 17 January. Colson immediately called Black at home, in the early morning, Toronto time. But Shirley Black informed him that her husband was in the hospital with a ruptured disc in his back.

Rothschild reassured Colson that the equity deal could not be undone, so the lawyer was not in a receptive mood when Clapham arrived at his office at the agreed time. Clapham and his group confidently told Colson they reckoned Black had three options: 1) Talk to them about doing a deal, 2) Convince them that his position was such that they should go away, or 3) Do nothing, in which case Holmes à Court would independently decide whether to put another offer on the table.

Colson told them that, 'In our opinion, we have no doubt that we control the company, that we aren't impressed by thinly veiled threats and that we obviously couldn't preclude you from making us or anyone else an offer for their shares.'

He telephoned Black in his room at the Wellesley Hospital and explained the situation. The prostrate Black croaked that he was prepared to look at an offer, but would prefer it if they went away.

More and more information was filtering out about Rupert Murdoch's plans to take on the newspaper unions at his News International. Black wondered whether Holmes à Court was a front for Murdoch, who might want to merge the *Telegraph* with *The Times*. Black's hypothesis proved incorrect, but within a week developments at News International would forever change the firmament of British newspapering.

Black knew Holmes à Court would not gain any favour from the Berrys. Despite his desire to thwart Black, Lord Hartwell considered the Australians 'unsavoury'. Holmes à Court eventually withdrew.

Andrew Knight assumed his duties as chief executive on 3 February 1986, and quickly moved forward with major changes, having already covertly enlisted Hastings and Worsthorne. Finally, on 20 February, the rights issue was completed, albeit not without the directors having temporarily to retire Lord Camrose from the board, as, apparently, he was in such a state of inebriation that he was unable to sign the memorandum. (Illness was cited in the minutes and Camrose was reinstated soon afterwards.)*

With the rights issue in place, Hartwell was mildly supportive of Knight but oblivious of the showdown that was to come at a board meeting on the afternoon of 25 February. There, with Black's control absolute, Hartwell was given a letter from Black announcing the new editors. The normally reserved Hartwell was livid. 'I am still editor-in-chief!' he raged, arguing he should have been responsible for or at least consulted on such appointments. He had nothing against Max Hastings, who was then a columnist at the *Evening Standard* and feature writer for the *Sunday Times,* as editor, he just didn't know him and thought he should at least have had the chance to meet him. As for Worsthorne as editor of the *Sunday Telegraph,* Hartwell reiterated his long-standing view that he was a gifted writer but not up to the top job.

After retreating to his office for fifteen minutes, where he was joined by Lord Rawlinson and David Montagu, Hartwell returned and suggested the appointments be put to a board vote. H. M. Stephen, Hartwell's loyal managing director, quickly offered his support. Hartwell's son Adrian Berry, who had worked closely with Worsthorne and liked him, said he would not vote against his father and abstained. The half-hearted poll never made its way around the table, and even if it had it would have held no authority.

Hartwell's attachment to his newspapers was so powerful that he tried to swallow his intense feelings of loss and failure and resign himself to his fate as a powerless director. Although he would step down as chairman and Knight would take over as editor-in-chief in September 1987, he remains an at times cantankerous presence on the

---

* As a a result of the issue, at a price of 50p per share, the new ownership structure broke down as follows: Black's Ravelston held eight per cent of the shares, his Hollinger 49.8 per cent; the Telegraph Newspaper Trust held 21.9 per cent and Hartwell Cowley Charitable Trust 1.1 per cent; the newly created Daily Telegraph Group Pension Fund held 1.1 per cent; other, mainly institutional shareholders held 18.1 per cent.

  Black and Hartwell also agreed that until 30 September 1989, or a listing of *Telegraph* shares on the stock exchange, Hollinger would have an option to acquire up to half of the Telegraph Trust's shares at 100p each.

board to this day. 'I suppose if I'd had any guts, I ought to have resigned then,' he said in 1993 of the editors' appointments, long after the *Telegraph* had moved out of Fleet Street and Hartwell had installed himself in a St James's Park office which barely contained his ancient proprietor-sized desk.

He admits, as he did in an interview with the magazine *The Oldie*, that the financial benefits of the subsequent turnaround have dulled the pain. 'I think it has worked out for the best in the end,' he said. 'It has certainly benefited my family, because . . . we have made quite a lot of money out of the *Telegraph* and it's gone not to my brother and myself but to our nephews and nieces and their children. It has been more to their financial advantage than if I had soldiered on with no intention of selling anything.'

By early 1986, Fleet Street proprietors were emboldened by a renewed sense that they could break the iron grip the print unions held over British newspapers. The charge was being led by a wave of brash newcomers, among whom Conrad Black would come to be counted. The proprietors found an unlikely hero in Eddie Shah, an Anglo-Persian who had set up Britain's first non-union print shop, albeit a small weekly newspaper operation in Warrington, near Manchester.

Shah achieved this landmark victory on the back of hard-nosed trade union reforms introduced by the Thatcher government in 1980 and 1982, which specifically banned the usual and often menacing practice of sympathetic industrial action by non-striking workers. When the usual mobs materialised to picket at other operations linked to Shah or his advertisers, the National Graphical Association was fined more than £500,000 – the first time in anyone's recollection that a strike had cost the strikers more than the publisher.

In early 1985, Shah announced plans to follow his triumph at Warrington with the launch of a new national tabloid. His *Today* would be printed outside London, by non-union employees. Later that year, as Black edged closer to control of the *Telegraph*, the larger-than-life Maxwell capitalised on growing cracks in the unions' resolve and successfully negotiated the elimination of a quarter of his Mirror Group's 6,500 jobs.

Knight, who spoke frequently with Bruce Matthews, chief executive of News International, knew of Murdoch's covert plans to shift production of his newspapers to an east London site in Wapping. 'This is not the year of Eddie Shah,' Knight chirped to Black and his *Telegraph* colleagues, 'it is the year of Rupert Murdoch.' Black, in turn, asked his long-time friend, New York socialite Marietta Tree, to canvass Murdoch about his intentions towards the unions. The reply was a vague promise of something 'draconian'.

Rather than accede to Murdoch's demands for large-scale concessions, the London print unions, the NGA and SOGAT, had elected to strike on Friday 24 January. A few days without papers, they reasoned, would be enough to bring the rambunctious Australian's News International to bay. There was little cause for worry – after all, this approach had worked for as long as anyone could recall. But no longer. On the weekend of 25–26 January 1986, Murdoch moved production of all four of his titles, *The Times, Sunday Times, Sun* and *News of the World*, from ageing premises in Bouverie Street and Gray's Inn Road to the foreboding Wapping compound in London's docklands.

What the unions didn't realise was that News International had secretly enlisted the electricians' union, EECTU – which had its own axe to grind with the printers – to operate the machinery that would churn out papers from the Wapping factory.

Visually, Wapping evokes comparisons with the decrepit, abandoned chemical plant where the bad guys invariably hang out in shlocky Hollywood action movies. True to that image, Wapping would serve as the setting for British publishing's climactic showdown.

The News journalists, most of whom opted not to join the strikers, arrived at the newspaper factories in armoured buses, passing through massive gates joined to high fences topped with German razor wire, while security men, surveillance cameras and floodlights prowled the premises. As days passed, the picketers outside Wapping grew more numerous and more unruly, and at times violent, but nevertheless each night the trucks which Murdoch had engaged to bypass the traditional and vulnerable rail distribution route made their way down a massive ramp from the heart of the factory and out of the gates.

By the end of 1986, Murdoch had reduced his print work-force from over 2,000 to 570. The Wapping dispute would end a year after it had begun, with Murdoch employing the full force of Thatcher's new labour laws to pay the strikers less than he would have had to if he had merely laid them off.

The new bosses at the *Daily Telegraph* were inspired by the developments at Wapping, but as they laid their own plans to move production from Fleet Street to their new plant on the Isle of Dogs in February 1986, Murdoch's gambit was still in its early days, the outcome far from certain. And while draconian measures might have suited the rough and tumble Aussie, who could trumpet his triumph as a victory for all England in the racy tabloids his factory belched out, such behaviour was unbecoming to the conservative and genteel *Telegraph*. As Lord Hartwell's son, *Telegraph* science correspondent Adrian Berry puts it, 'It's a terrible bore to put barbed-wire fence around the office.'*

As far back as 1970, Joe Cooke had been plotting ways to deal with Fleet Street's unions. 'There wasn't the will,' says the pragmatic and taciturn Irish engineer. But he remained fascinated by the union puzzle, and became more so when Frank Rogers became chairman of East Midland and Allied Press and invited Cooke to join the board.

When he was asked by Rogers to 'clear the decks' in late 1985 to help out at the *Telegraph*, Cooke thought it would be a two-week assignment. Eighteen hectic months later he would join as deputy chief executive *en route* to becoming managing director.

Cooke developed a staffing model for the West Ferry Road plant that relied on what was a logical but, for pre-1985 Fleet Street, revolutionary notion: if the *Telegraph* were being printed by a sub-contractor, he wondered, how much might it reasonably pay? Then he worked out exactly how much the unions demanded per employee for the work, and compared it with how many people the manufacturers said were needed to operate the equipment. 'It sounds amazing,' says Knight, 'but that was an original concept at the time.'

Black was happy to remain in Canada throughout most of this period, which suited Knight as another element of his scheme was to

* Unlike his brother Nicholas, Adrian Berry harbours no resentment towards Black. In fact, he says that after the 1969 moon landing he was more interested in science writing than in following in his father's proprietorial footsteps.

portray Black as the 'distant ogre in Canada' who was inaccessible to the unions. Traditionally, the printers had insisted on face-to-face meetings with proprietors when negotiations reached a crucial stage, reducing the management to ineffectual puppets. 'Conrad played that role brilliantly, and he also played it *vis-à-vis* the outside community,' recalls Knight. 'There were all sorts of people in politics and the rest of Fleet Street, all dying to find out who this new mysterious owner was. And we deliberately cultivated around him an air of mystery.'

There were, however, some Britons to whom Black was not a complete stranger. One was Malcolm Muggeridge, with whom Black conferred after investing in the *Telegraph*. Black had met Muggeridge in the late 1970s, and they became friends. 'He's a man of considerable intelligence and very shrewd,' Muggeridge told the *Evening Standard*. 'I like him very much. He's charming and has none of that unpleasantness which you so often find in rich people.'

On Friday afternoons throughout February and early March, Knight, Cooke, Rogers, industrial relations manager Angus Clark, and senior department heads met to draft the plan to move production to the £70 million facility at West Ferry Road. The carefully selected date for the plan to be executed was Wednesday 26 March, Feast of the Annunciation, just before two bank holidays. At the last Friday meeting before 26 March, Knight was visibly anxious – his newfound career as a chief executive might be over soon after it had begun if the paper suffered strike action.

Unlike Murdoch's plan which was essentially to ignore and humiliate the unions, the *Telegraph* strategy hinged on presenting the job losses as a *fait accompli* and guaranteeing a reduced number of new jobs only if the unions pledged no industrial action.

Among the *Telegraph*'s lawyers the plan was code-named Operation Blackbird, which soon leaked to the unions whose representatives would enter negotiating sessions whistling 'Bye Bye Blackbird'. But this was merely cocky defiance: the unions had no sense of the master plan.

On 26 March, individual union chapels were called in at half-hourly intervals and informed that their production operations were being shifted to the new plant. All the printers were redundant, they were told, but if they wanted new jobs they could go down to the new plant and apply for them. The terms would be five days a week instead of four, and the payment per shift would be £80 pounds rather than the £125 they had earned in Fleet Street. Cooke knew it was virtually impossible to go to the Isle of Dogs without passing the unhappy throng at Wapping along the way. Moreover, the *Telegraph* printers were warned that if there was any work disruption as a result of the move, there would be no jobs for anyone. For all the nervous printers knew, the *Telegraph* had also quietly enlisted the EECTU or another union to man the new plant.

The bloated ranks of staff engineers would be offered no positions at the new plant, just the same redundancy payments of up to £45,000 given the printers. One of their leaders testily confronted Cooke, who cuts a deceivingly mild figure in his white short-sleeved shirts, demanding to know whether all of their ranks would be moving to the Isle of Dogs. 'Not quite all,' was Cooke's soft Irish reply. 'Actually, none.'

The transformation was remarkable. Before March 1986, the *Telegraph* staff had numbered 3,900, including part-time casuals and about 500 journalists. By 1993, the total staff would be slashed and whittled to roughly 1,000. The greatest number of redundancies – more than 1,500 jobs – came from the transfer of production to West Ferry Road. The move, in the summer of 1987, of the newspaper's headquarters out of Fleet Street and into gleaming new headquarters at South Quay near the plant, brought a further 900 redundancies with the introduction of a computerised pre-press production system that eliminated the need for 700 compositors who had done nothing but keystroke the articles after reporters had typed them or written them out in longhand.

Another key decision taken early on was to relieve the financial burden of the new printing plants by finding partners either to buy them outright and print the *Telegraph* on contract or to join the *Telegraph* as a partner.

The weekend after Andrew Knight's appointment as chief executive had been announced in December 1985, he, Rogers and Joe Cooke spent some eight hours negotiating the sale of the Manchester plant to Robert Maxwell. But, as so often happened, Maxwell appeared on the verge of agreeing to terms several times before declaring that he had just noticed a figure that showed the plant was worth less. Eventually, Knight secured a deal with Rupert Murdoch, which infuriated Maxwell.*

In the summer of 1987, Express Newspapers' new chairman Lord Stevens flew to Toronto from meetings in New York and met Black at his office where the two men hammered out a joint-venture deal that called for West Ferry Road to be increased from six computer-controlled web offset presses to sixteen and for both sides to own half of the resultant operation, the largest in the world outside Wapping and Japan. The joint venture is one of the most efficient newspaper plants in the world, with each press capable of 60,000 papers per hour, and a total capacity of 2.5 million copies per night of the *Express*, *Star*, *Telegraph* and *Daily Sport*. (One man's peculiar job while operating the sophisticated computer software that controls the presses' colour is to ensure that the shade and tone of the frequent naked breasts in the down-market *Sport* are just right.)

From the oil-splattered bowels of the old Fleet Street press room, only thirty-six pages in black and white could be produced with hundreds more workers. The new Goss Headliner presses could accommodate papers of twice that size, print at twice the speed, and include twenty pages of colour. In Fleet Street, the most fearsome union chapels were the paper handlers, who could simply elect not to bring fresh rolls of paper into the press room if their demands were not met. That role was now relegated to twenty-three robot reel-delivery vehicles which played no cards, took no tea breaks and raised not a murmur of complaint about their seven-day working week.

West Ferry Road became a testament not only to the opportunism of the *Telegraph*'s new owner but to the revolution that was taking place in Thatcher's England. From a pre-tax loss of £8.9 million in 1986, the *Telegraph* earned £620,000 in 1987, then £29.2 million in 1988, and £41.5 million in 1989. It was the death of Fleet Street, and the dawn of a newspaper cash machine capable of funding its owner's desire to pursue the acquisition of practically any newspaper in the world. In retrospect, rival publishers are astounded at the $67 million Black paid for control in 1986. Two years later the company generated almost that amount in profits and has done that or better every year since. Within four years, the *Telegraph* would be established

---

* In 1991 the *Guardian* assumed Murdoch's share of the Manchester joint venture.

as one of the most profitable as well as widely read titles on earth. Black likes to describe the *Telegraph* take-over as 'not the sort of deal you get two of in a lifetime'.

In 1987, Maxwell paid Black the backhanded compliment of having landed 'history's largest fish with history's smallest hook'. And in the early 1990s, Murdoch opined that if sold, what became The Telegraph plc would fetch £1 billion; by 1994 the company's market capitalisation on the London Stock Exchange approached that amount.

Having the *Telegraph* flagship would provide Black with not only wealth but stature to live the kind of life he had always envisioned for himself – not just an acquaintance of the international élite, but one of them. When he was younger, Black had confided to friends an ambition to 'internationalise' himself. Now, it was tantalisingly within reach. As he would later say, 'No one snubs the owner of the *Daily Telegraph.*'

Black arrived in London in April 1986 and applauded the *Telegraph* team on their early sucess with Operation Blackbird (final agreements would not be in place until September that year). It was only his third visit since investing in the paper, and his first since the previous October, having busied himself in Canada with the birth of his son, dealing with the remnants of the Argus empire, and back problems, all capped by a severe bout of bronchitis. One of his first appointments was to travel to Chequers with Knight for lunch with Margaret Thatcher and her senior foreign policy adviser, Charles Powell. It was, says Powell, 'Love at first sight – in a political sense'.

Thatcher was relieved to find not only a forceful personality behind what had been the flagship of Conservatism but somebody whose instinctive ideas were close to her own. Black spent large portions of the meal regaling the prime minister with his encyclopaedic knowledge of nineteenth-century Tory history. 'It became evident during the lunch that Conrad knew far more about the history of the Tory party than she did,' says Knight. 'Far more. And he didn't do it in an overbearing way but the conversation was fascinating because, you know, there she was, the leader of the party that he knew more about the history of than she did – certainly than I did too.'

Black was unrelentingly flattering. As he departed, he told

Thatcher that 'The revolution you have wrought in this country is more important by far than the episodes in British history that usually enjoy that description. After all, what are the decapitation of Charles I and the deposing of James II, particularly as described by that egregious utilitarian and Whig myth-maker, Lord Macaulay, compared to what you have done?' As Black later recalled, 'Mrs Thatcher is not particularly historically minded. When I described Thatcherism in such epochal terms, she blinked at me twice, demurely, patted me most considerately on the shoulder and said, "That is very good Mr Black. Do come back." '

Black's relations with his new editor, Max Hastings, got off to a shakier start. The previous December, before he was offered the editor's job, Hastings had set out his vision for the paper in a memorandum to Black and Knight. It was, says Hastings a 'sort of blueprint of what I did thereafter. And I said, "Although the *Daily Telegraph* always would be and should be a Conservative newspaper, in my view it should be an independent Conservative newspaper, and it should clearly be perceived not to be a house magazine for the government, and we should simply judge issues on their merits." '
This was a significant shift for what was known as the 'Torygraph', and Hastings knew it was essential if younger staff who would inject new vigour into the paper were to be attracted.

His first few weeks were difficult. In the days before the American bombing of Libya in the spring of 1986, some of the staff suggested the *Telegraph* send a reporter to Tripoli to monitor the U.S. airbase there. Hastings was anxious to save money and didn't – and later admitted he had make 'a bad call'. The episode got worse when the *Telegraph* published a leader condemning the U.S. action, and a similarly negative opinion piece by Ferdinand Mount. An irate Black called up Hastings and told him both were 'seriously fallacious analyses of what really happened'. The episode made Hastings visibly uneasy, but time would show that the outburst was a rare exception from the new proprietor, rather than the rule. Indeed, Black grew to appreciate Hastings because he was, as Black put it, 'good at drowning the kittens'.

It was said that if one opened cupboards in 135 Fleet Street, old journalists fell out. The 1930 building was a rabbit's warren of cubby-holes, and since Hartwell had held no editorial meetings the only place most of the staff would see one another was the pub. One of Hastings's first tasks was to go through the staff list, which he would read on the train home at night, ticking off names of people he thought he should get rid of. In the arts section, for instance, he noted there was no one under the age of seventy. As a man who had never been an editor, working for an editor who had never been a chief executive, who was working for a financier who had never been a major press owner, Hastings felt a growing sense of terror as he realised he had marked off about half the names on the list.

'One morning after I became editor,' Hastings recalls, 'I came up to my office and I found a tramp sleeping outside the door, wrapped up in insulating material from the switch-board box that he had yanked out. And he complained like hell about being kicked out, because he said he'd been sleeping there on and off for years. This sort of thing went on. I mean, the whole place was a lunatic asylum in that sense.'

Nonetheless, a determined Hastings adopted his best war correspondent's demeanour and coolly set about eliminating large chunks of the staff, some of whom were happy to retire anyway and had not had a proper pension under the old *Telegraph* but did now. The first new people he hired for the paper were newspaper designers, because it sorely needed a contemporary look, and this was an area in which Hastings had no knowledge. One of the key lay-out people he hired was Don Berry, an assistant features editor who had resigned from the *Sunday Times* after refusing to move to Wapping.

Next, Hastings needed to introduce the alien concept of editorial budgets. One of the first people he recruited for the task was Jeremy Deedes (son of former editor and now columnist William Deedes) with whom Hastings had worked for some twenty years. A relentlessly suave man with a taste for Silk Cut cigarettes, Jeremy Deedes recalls meeting Hastings for lunch in early 1986: 'I got in the car with him, and he said, "You'd better have a look at the staff salary list." And he reached into his briefcase and he gave me these sheets – I thought he was joking. They were written in fountain pen. And these were kept up-to-date each month. The guys' names were actually written in copperplate, with the salary written on lined ledger sheets. And that was the staff salary sheet, in 1986. In 1921, you might have thought,

"Well that's how they keep the books." And, I say, I thought this was his little joke. It wasn't.'

Deedes came from a senior role at Eddie Shah's *Today* and was inspired by the freedom he had enjoyed at Britain's first union-free shop. Appointed executive editor, he was essentially the taskmaster who presided over managing editors who were not long for the *Telegraph*. 'The primary brief was to introduce budgeting and some sort of financial order, but at the same time obviously Max was wanting to get rid of a lot of people, put some new blood into the place. So I was helping to, in Conrad's words, "drown the kittens".'

Hastings reckons most of the names he had ticked off on the train ride home were gone within six months. One member of the feature staff whom Hastings felt did not fit with his vision of the *Telegraph* was Carol Thatcher, the prime minister's daughter. Hastings approached her and suggested she might like to look quietly for a job elsewhere. This particular kitten roared. 'Well, you've sacked lots of other people, if you really want to sack me, sack me,' she told Hastings. 'But I'm not going to make it easy for you.'

Hastings did indeed fire her, and the prime minister was livid. Margaret Thatcher believed it was a mean-spirited act by a new editor seeking to distance himself from the 'Torygraph' label. She was sceptical of Hastings anyway, whom she viewed as a proponent of the tweed-suited, hunting and fishing, old-style country gentleman Toryism, not the hard-edged Conservatism she championed.

Indeed, Thatcher would not speak to the editor of the Conservative Party's flagship newspaper for as long as she was Prime Minister of England. Says Hastings, 'Given Conrad's devotion to her, I greatly respected the fact that Conrad never, as far as I know, gave any encouragement at all to those around Thatcher who would like to have seen me go.' Black says he 'took a fair bit' of heat, but Thatcher accepted his position. 'You have to defend your editor. She defended her daughter and I defended my editor. We agreed that we had different roles to play in that case.'

Other key people Hastings added to the staff were Veronica Wadley, John Keegan and Robert Fox, Neil Collins, Trevor Grove, and Hugh Montgomery-Massingberd, whose idiosyncratic style transformed the *Telegraph*'s moribund obituaries page into a must-read. The changes spearheaded by Hastings began to produce results.

Circulation at the daily increased in 1987, despite the launch in October 1986 by three former *Telegraph* journalists of a new broadsheet, the *Independent*. As it happens, the circulations of *The Times* and *Guardian* suffered worst from the *Independent*'s competition. In the same year, Worsthorne's *Sunday Telegraph* enjoyed a gain of almost 50,000 subscribers.

Although the loss of readers was staunched, the readership profile in fact grew increasingly old, with readers aged fifty-five and older accounting for 44.1 per cent in 1989 as opposed to 38.4 per cent in 1986. On a random day in September 1993, the *Daily Telegraph* published five birth and forty death notices, compared to four births and fourteen deaths in *The Times* and one death in the *Guardian*. Indeed, the paper even played to this strength by offering a mail-order '*Telegraph* Willmaker' service in the classified ads near the death notices. 'The *Telegraph* offers its readers a reliable and efficient will writing service by post, supported by a telephone helpline.'

In Black's view, the growing success was a result of cutting non-editorial costs and reinforcing the formula perfected by the first Viscount Camrose, which he described in a 1991 speech in Toronto: 'This consisted of a good, informative newspaper, concise, fair, and covering all the news, but enhanced in its appeal to the British middle-class by heavy emphasis on bourgeois sports and pastimes, and a relentless truckling to the Royal Family. I scarcely recall an edition of the newspaper in the nearly six years of my association with it, when there wasn't a flattering photograph of some member or other of the Royal Family. Not for the *Daily Telegraph* the lurid propagation of vapid gossip about every aspect of their sex and marital lives.'

Along with 'recitations of life's quirky episodes', it seemed to Black one of the paper's great traditional strengths was its 'practice of presenting Britain's gamiest, kinkiest, most salacious and most scatological news with apparent sobriety, but with the most explicit, almost sadistic, detail, including carefully selected extracts from court transcripts. Middle-class commercial travellers from Manchester and Birmingham may still be seen on the verandas of the Victorian railway hotels, in Russell Square, as they were fifty and a hundred years ago, reading in our newspaper unashamedly of the indiscretions of deviant clergy, the activities of paid flagellators, and the rest of the vast English supermarket of unconventional sexual titillation.'

*

Throughout his early career, Conrad Black likened his business strategy – or the apparent lack of one – to military historian Sir Basil Liddell Hart's 'expanding funnel' theory which was based on 'the unpredictable downhill course of water in ways that were unforeseeable'. It might be added that Black has thrown a lot of water down a lot of hills, to ensure that no opportunity escapes at least a trickle of his attention.

In late 1984, a full half-year before the notion of investing in the *Telegraph* came to light, Black's partner David Radler had been running a small advertisement in the back of *Editor and Publisher*, the American trade magazine, under the heading 'newspapers wanted':

'Well respected, growing Canadian daily newspaper with cash seeks to purchase smaller newspapers (5000–10,000 circulation). Write or phone Arthur Weeks, Sterling Newspapers Ltd, PO Box 10079, Pacific Center, Vancouver B.C. V7Y1B6 (604) 682–7755.'

Soon after Black took over the *Telegraph*, the ad snared Radler (who has an almost demonic aversion to spending money and would not run the ad every issue) a big deal: Thirty-four small-town papers in the United States for $106 million. Small newspapers were, after all, Conrad Black's and David Radler's original business. They named their new subsidiary American Publishing Co. Combined with their continuing ownership of nine small Canadian papers in the Sterling chain, they now had a foothold in three countries. The *Telegraph* would be the centrepiece. Hollinger declared itself an 'international newspaper company' in search of acquisitions at home and abroad.

SEVEN

Citizen Black

'I want to build a first-class international
newspaper company, and I think the
omens are favourable'

'Jesus, this could be *embarrassing*,' Conrad Black muttered to an
acquaintance. It was Friday evening, 24 October 1986, and Black was
reviewing his lines. As the crowd gathered in the Centennial Ballroom
at Toronto's Inn on the Park Hotel, Black was starting to regret
having volunteered to be one of sixteen Toronto society stars acting
out a dinner theatre farce entitled 'Much Ado About Something'.

At a tax-deductible cost of $200 per person, the evening's goal was
to raise money for the Stratford Festival, an annual theatre festival in
the hamlet of Stratford, ninety minutes west of Toronto by car.
Shirley Black was one of the event's co-chairs, and had hosted the final
rehearsal at their home. But her husband had missed it because of
meetings in London, at the *Daily Telegraph*.

Even though he had re-written part of his lines while aboard the
Concorde flight back, his misgivings about the show were under-
standable: his performance required him to wear a crown of laurel
leaves while his wife played the role of the pop-cultural stereotype
momentarily in vogue, the Valley Girl.

The spoof was, if nothing else, an exaggerated illustration of the
Blacks' contrasting public personas. Shirley's lines called for such
outbursts as, 'Barf me out, airhead! You're, like grody to the max.' Of
her husband she exclaimed, 'Fur sure, I mean this dude is totally
awesome.'

Conrad's script, initially penned by Canadian actor/comedian
Don Harron, called for him to declare: 'Greatness knows itself, and all
the course of my life shows that I am not in the roll of common

men. . . and at my birth the frame and huge foundation of the earth shak'd like a coward.'

The Blacks were joined on stage by Trevor Eyton, one of the top executives in the many-tentacled Brascan empire controlled by Toronto tycoons Peter and Edward Bronfman. Eyton took the stage and stiffly declared of forty-two-year-old Black, 'I never knew so young a body with so old a head.' Further barbs were aimed at Black's recent investment in the British newspaper and apparent withdrawal from Canadian industry.

In a $300-million deal, Black had recently sold to the Bronfmans Hollinger's forty-one per cent interest in its resource group, Norcen,* completing the transformation of Hollinger into a newspaper company. The Bronfmans' reputation for complex dealings rivalled Black's, and under the convoluted deal Hollinger received among other things $137 million in cash and shares in the Bronfmans' Hees International Bancorp. Black soon sold his Hees shares at a profit, but not before giving some the short-lived impression – insulting to him – that he was becoming another cog in the Bronfman wheel.

The climax of Black's stage performance featured Eyton and Black's friend Hal Jackman pulling daggers on Black. ('Like I am totally bummed,' Shirley aped.) Black responded by making a grand gesture with his hand, causing his attackers to impale themselves on their own daggers.

Few in the audience would have been aware that Black felt he had spent a good portion of 1986 evading real daggers. Earlier that year, just as Hollinger invested $47 million in London for the *Telegraph* rights issue which crystallised its control over the paper, the Canadian Imperial Bank of Commerce called in a $40 million Dominion Stores' loan while the Supreme Court of Ontario ordered Hollinger to return some $40 million to Dominion's superannuation funds. This created a cash crisis at Ravelston that was the closest Black had come to outright financial disaster. This was particularly shocking, since Black carried some weight around the Bank of Commerce as one of its directors. He laid the blame on 'lesser echelon' loan managers who

---

* Despite Black's earlier efforts to build a resource group and his hard-fought investment in Hanna, he says he decided to sell Norcen when Henry Kissinger warned him that oil prices were going to decline. 'If I hadn't had the relationship I had with Kissinger, I wouldn't have got out of Norcen in time,' said Black.

had doubts about his companies' balance sheets. 'I'm afraid some of the senior managers were trouble as well,' says Hollinger deputy chairman Dixon Chant. 'We needed just a bit of time.'

Black quickly visited Commerce president, Donald Fullerton, asking him to 'get these guys off my back and I'll clean it up'. Fullerton agreed and the bank executives backed off. But Black had to make quick, drastic cuts, which included selling the Argus jet and the security guard company Ravelston had bought. Black later acknowledged the episode as a cautionary tale for any borrower who does not happen to sit, as he did, on the board of the bank. 'You can't trust these banks once they decide there is a problem.' Black reflected. 'I'll tell you what it's like: it's like that mentality I encountered with the police a few years before.'

At one point during the nerve-racking period, Black approached Douglas Creighton, chairman and chief executive of Toronto Sun Publishing Corp. about the Sun taking an interest in the *Telegraph*. Creighton was interested in an investment not unlike Black's own *Telegraph* deal, where the Sun might acquire rights to gain eventual control of the British paper. But the Sun's controlling shareholder Maclean Hunter Ltd was lukewarm about the idea, and it never went beyond informal discussions. Had Black not worked his way out of this predicament, his dream of a media empire would have been over before it began. However, the sale of assets and Hollinger's austerity programme soon restored the balance sheet to levels acceptable to the bank.

Over the next three years the improving financial health of Hollinger was fuelled by the remarkable turnaround of the *Daily Telegraph*. Now, Black and his associates could pursue print media acquisitions at a blistering pace.

Changes in U.S. federal tax laws on the treatment of capital gains, which were introduced by the Reagan Administration, inspired long-time owners to sell. David Radler, the executive responsible for the assembly of the U.S. chain, fielded a constant stream of phone calls from newspaper brokers. Between 1986 and 1992 the group would spend US$302.1 million acquiring 288 titles. Like Roy Thomson in his early newspaper days, American Publishing focused on papers with a circulation of 4,000 to 25,000. With every deal, Radler would send his lieutenant, Sterling general manager Arthur Weeks, ahead to scout a newspaper property. But Radler would never complete a deal without physically checking out the premises himself. In fact, at some point he would invariably turn to his colleague and say, 'Arthur, count the chairs.' Radler's Sterling experience told him chairs – not official head counts that might not include part-time and contract staff – told the true story of a paper's labour costs. It also told him that, often, fully half those chairs could be thrown out without what he considered a noticeable decline in quality or productivity. Following American Publishing's first purchase, the *Wapakoneta Daily News* in Ohio, Hollinger quietly but steadily became the owner of such papers as the *Morocco Courier* in Morocco, Indiana (circulation: 1,400), the *Hawaii Pennysaver* in Honolulu (circulation: 22,500), the *Punxsutawney Spirit* in Punxsutawney, Pennsylvania (circulation: 6,000), and *Stamps Magazine* in Hornell, New York (circulation: 14,000). In 1988, the group bought a forty per cent interest in the *Caymanian Compass*, the daily journal of the Cayman Islands, which Black likes to joke features 'a swim suit issue every week'.

Radler, whose style makes him fit in as easily at the Kiwanis Club as at the Vancouver Club, is well tanned from his sojourns in Palm Springs. He is flip and sarcastic, but engaging; like Black, he enjoys a good verbal joust, and he calls negotiations a 'grind'. He worries a lot. He hates to fly, but he hates even more not making the rounds to meet publishers and advertisers in specks across the American map. To add emphasis to his statements, he often transforms them into questions, usually ending with 'okay?' or 'all right?'

There is a glint in his narrowed eyes, a sense of whimsy in his manner and in the decor of his comparatively shabby office, which, situated off Vancouver's beaten path, contains an old Dominion Stores toy truck, baseball caps and fighter aircraft models and a Terence Gilbert print of Queen Elizabeth and Ronald Reagan on horseback at Windsor. Behind a massive desk, he can sometimes be found sucking loudly on a candy or digging into a box of gumballs. At five thirty p.m. on one Friday afternoon, Radler is on the phone and his secretary Barbara pops her head around his door to signal that she and the other secretaries are leaving. 'Where are you guys going?' Radler asks in mock astonishment. 'We've been so successful, *is that it*? It's been a good day, *is that it*?' Radler pauses a moment for effect, then shrugs. 'We fired three and didn't hire anyone, so I guess it is a good day.'

Radler sees no great mystery in what he does, or, for that matter, what any other businessman does: 'What do you think motivates any one of us? You go out and you try to make a living for your family; pre-marriage you try to make a living just to have a family. And these are basic desires, *okay?* The desire to eat, the desire to have things, the desire to accumulate, those kinds of things. It's not terribly complicated.'

Like his long-time friend and partner Black, Radler once suffered from anxiety attacks. Radler does not search for historical analogies to explain this. It was back in the early 1980s, when the Sterling offices were in the Pacific Center. As Radler walked into the office complex, he would feel light-headed. 'I remember one day I was walking up Granville Street and suddenly I felt faint,' he recalls. 'I had to sit on a bench. And I never felt the same. I got back up, it was like you were afraid you were going to fall. Then of course I couldn't sleep. I kept on going to the doctors and they kept saying there's nothing wrong. So then I thought, "I've got cancer." One day I had a nightmare that my wife knew and I didn't, that kind of stuff. Finally, I couldn't take it any more and I went to one doctor and said "I can't function." ' This time, the doctor prescribed a 'nerve pill', and Radler spent a month in Florida. Three weeks later, taking declining doses of medication, he was fine. And has been fine since. 'By the way, this is not unusual,' he says, pointing to the stresses of running big companies as the root of his, and possibly his partner Black's, one-time anxiety-related difficulties. 'I think you pay a toll, remembering everything. Our styles are similar: remember everything in your head, never write anything down. I think it does come from something, and I suppose if you go under deep psychoanalysis you might know.' But Radler shrugs that he had no interest in knowing such things. 'One of the things I learned is that every once in a while you've got to take a pill.'

In Ravelston, the private company which controls Hollinger, Radler is the second-largest shareholder with something around fifteen per cent, compared to Black's 67.5 per cent.* Despite the fact that the two men are separated by thousands of miles, says Radler, 'I

* The other shareholders in Ravelston are Peter White and Dixon Chant.

know what he thinks and he knows exactly what I think. We run on a certain wavelength.' That is not always apparent to those who know both men. 'Black and Radler are like day and night,' contends one Hollinger director. 'They have absolutely nothing in common. David is a small-town newspaper guy. Black never gets involved in the nitty-gritty. He's a big-picture guy.'

Although holding the title of president and chief operating officer at Hollinger and chairman at American Publishing, Radler describes the Hollinger style as 'probably closer to an American-style brokerage company where guys have their own kinds of deals' than a hierarchical corporation. The rule of thumb is that whoever 'does the deal' within Hollinger looks after that particular business. The *Telegraph* was Black's deal, while Sterling was predominantly Radler's, and American Publishing was Radler's alone. Although he is the guy who closed the one hundred separate deals – a pace of almost one per month – that built American between 1986 and 1995, Radler is quick to share credit with the publishers who manage the far-flung papers. Thirteen of the eighteen district managers are former owners of papers absorbed by American. Larry Perrotto, the company's president, is one of five original owners of the sixteen-paper chain with which Hollinger launched its foray into the U.S. To suit Perrotto's frugal Radleresque style, American's headquarters is maintained in a small drab office off the main street in West Frankfort, Illinois.

Editorially, American's approach to newspapering is equally uncomplicated: plenty of local coverage, with as many names and photos as possible. If readers want to know what's going on in the greater world, they can get that from television or magazines. Only the local paper can deliver what's happening on Main Street. 'Success,' says Radler, 'is defined by the public putting down their fifty cents.'

Overall, Black explains the American Publishing strategy this way: 'Sensibly selected,' a package of local newspaper semi-monopolies should have an ultimate value only 'modestly' below that which a large metropolitan daily with the same overall circulation would command. Generally, titles acquired would generate operating cash flow in the second year of ownership of between fifteen to twenty per cent of the original purchase price.

To accomplish this, the cost-cutting techniques perfected by

Radler at Sterling were exported to the U.S. small-town newspaper market. The first tenet of American's profit improvement strategy is that labour costs as a percentage of annual revenues should not exceed thirty per cent, whereas U.S. industry norms for papers with circulations up to 20,000 range from thirty-nine per cent to fifty-one per cent.

In a typical American Publishing acquisition, step one – after the chair count, of course – is to cut jobs. After all, this is the surest way to boost operating profit margins. Tying a new paper into regional advertising sales groups and bulk newsprint purchases also saves money. In addition, presses are often upgraded, and, in some cases, weeklies are turned into dailies.

As a result of these measures, the forty-four newspapers acquired by American in 1988, which were already generating a fairly impressively gross operating margin* of sixteen per cent as a group, produced an average twenty-three per cent margin in 1993; papers acquired in 1989 improved their margins from thirteen per cent that year to twenty-four per cent in 1993; and papers purchased in 1990 improved their gross operating margin from twenty per cent to thirty per cent in 1993.†

There is no mystery to American Publishing's formula, except for the fact that Radler would often buy papers so small that no established player, such as Thomson, would bother with them.

Of course, Black likes to place the American venture in a greater historical context. 'My associates always essentially believed in

---

* Gross operating profit is roughly defined as revenues less operating costs and general and administrative costs.

† American distributes to its publishers a simple piece of paper with the heading 'Guidelines for expense allocation'. The breakdown is as follows:

Expense	Percentage of total revenue
1: Composition	4
2: Advertising sales	10–12
3: News (editorial)	10–12
4: Circulation	14
5: Pressroom: press operation	5
newsprint	11–13
6: Adminstration	15
TOTAL EXPENSES	69–75
PROFIT	31–25

Reaganomics. We always believed in the economic recovery of the so-called Rustbelt, and we knew that daily newspapers could be profitable down to 4,000 circulation or even less.' For American's official motto, Black asked a classics scholar to translate into Latin the phrase 'in rust we trust'. Black compared the development of the network of monopoly papers that American was amassing to 'the methods of cable television industry, where the multiple system owners have added subscribers wherever they found them to build their companies'.

The acquisition of Quebec's UniMedia Inc., in the summer of 1987, was Peter White's deal. He had known the company's majority shareholder and chief executive Jacques Francoeur for more than two decades – indeed, a Francoeur paper, the *Granby Leader Mail*, at one time printed White's and Black's first venture, the *Eastern Townships Advertiser*. UniMedia owned three daily newspapers, twenty weeklies and four printing plants. Since it operated three French-language dailies, most notably *Le Soleil* in the provincial capital of Quebec City, the notion of selling to any anglophone, let alone Black, was controversial. Hollinger bested established Quebec media players including Paul Desmarais' Power Corp., which owned Montreal daily *La Presse*, by representing diversity of ownership. But in order to complete the $50 million buy-out, Hollinger had to give the Quebec government an assignable right of first refusal, should they propose to sell either *Le Soleil* or the group's third-largest paper, *Le Quotidien* of Chicoutimi, to a non-resident of Quebec, or should a non-resident propose to acquire control of the whole company. Protecting the paper from the clutches of non-Quebecers was a somewhat ironic gesture given that Black and Radler were both born in Montreal.

Le Soleil is the largest paper within UniMedia, with a weekday circulation of about 110,000, exceeding 140,000 on Saturdays. Black and White vowed to turn it into the *Washington Post* of Quebec, but a number of journalists complained that the paper's coverage softened after UniMedia appointed a former Quebec deputy minister, Robert Normand, as publisher. Peter White became UniMedia's chairman, and as chief executive he and Black recruited Pierre Des Marais, a former executive of Carling Breweries of Canada, which as it happened was the successor to the brewery that Black's own father had run in the 1950s.

Less than a year after the deal, the Hollinger operating style was evident: a ten-week strike closed Ottawa's *Le Droit*, second largest of UniMedia's dailies, after the new owners revealed plans to convert the paper from a broadsheet to a tabloid. By 1989, more drastic measures loomed. Despite the new format, the paper was losing $1 million annually and Hollinger gave serious thought to closing its doors. With collective agreements expiring at the end of 1989, *Le Droit*'s printing plant and office were sold, editorial moved into leased premises and printing was assumed by another UniMedia plant across the river in Hull, Quebec, where *Le Droit* found the market for the bulk of its copies. From more than 300 employees at the time Hollinger took over, the staff was slashed by more than a third by 1991. By that time, *Le Droit* was heralded as a pioneer in the field of desktop publishing for newspapers. Gone was the necessity for a large production staff; reporters wrote on Macintosh computers and sent their stories online to an editor who integrated pictures onto a computer-generated "dummy" page. It was, in effect, the same revolution, though on a much smaller scale, as had transpired overseas at the *Daily Telegraph.*

Black later claimed that the disposal of 'secondary assets' at UniMedia, such as printing plants and real estate, yielded more than the entire $50 million purchase price. 'Even allowing for a discount for the problems inherent in doing business in Quebec,' Black said, 'this has proved quite a bargain.'

One of the lesser-known assets acquired in the UniMedia deal was Novalis, a publisher of Catholic periodicals in French and English. Under a licence agreement with St Paul University in Ottawa, Novalis delivers more than two million copies of its religious periodicals in Canada and the United States via parishes, congregations, and subscriptions. The largest English-language periodical of the group is the monthly *Living with Christ*, with a circulation of about 107,000. The French weekly *Prions en Eglise*, is distributed in Canada to 414,000 readers.

As it happened, Black had converted to the Catholic faith in the summer of 1986, a year before the UniMedia acquisition. Raised an Anglican, he had never been particularly religious, but his interest in Catholic figures such as Cardinal Leger in Quebec, Cardinal Newman in England and his close association with Toronto's Cardinal G. Emmett Carter, were well known.

In describing former Quebec premier Maurice Duplessis' Catholicism, Black had written a decade earlier that Duplessis 'had nothing against Protestantism; it just didn't mean anything to him. It was indistinct, full of compromises, and not sufficiently uplifting. . . . Catholicism to him, apart from all its institutional importance in Quebec, was the link between the mundane and the celestial and was to be embraced with fervour.' But Black's own views towards the subject were not quite so spiritual. 'I look upon it,' he explains, 'as more of an academic subject and one that has absolutely *nothing* to do – *nothing* – with my own cultural heritage or my ancestry at all.'

In his own case, Black explained that either one believes in the basic concept of Catholicism 'or you don't. And there's nothing wrong with it if you don't and I eventually came to the conclusion that I did – but by a fairly narrow margin. And I'm not a zealous or pious person and I don't make all sorts of displacements involving religious matters.'

Another take on Black's religious attitudes may be found in an extract from an article he penned in the *Spectator* magazine several years later: 'Those who find trendy and undignified the Anglican tendency to agonise in public deliberations over every contemporary moral issue, and who detect a tendency to strip the faith down to feel-good, love-thy-neighbour handclapping as our pal God jogs along beside us, may find Rome more appealing'.

Not long after his conversion in June 1986, Black described the occasion to an acquaintance, author Ron Graham. It took place in Cardinal Carter's private chapel. Apparently Black told the Cardinal he was ready to join, and Carter said he would be welcome.

'Ah,' Black replied, 'but would I be invited?'

'All right,' the Cardinal responded, 'I invite you.'

A debate ensued over the The Truth. Eventually, an agreement was struck. 'Then Emmett called for champagne, to celebrate,' Black recalled. 'So I didn't exactly go to them on my knees.'

The acquisitions of small newspapers in the United States and UniMedia were giving Black a growing presence in the media aristocracy of his native country. But no newspaper in the UniMedia or Sterling chains could command the respect of the élite among whom Black felt most comfortable. *Saturday Night*, magazine, however, could. Black had long been interested in the venerable but perennially money-losing monthly magazine which focused on literary and political matters. Black had looked at buying it in 1973, when he even wrote to William F. Buckley seeking advice on transforming it into a Canadian emulation of Buckley's right-wing journal, the *National Review*.

Norman Webster, scion of a wealthy Montreal family and editor of the *Globe and Mail*, and two of his siblings had purchased the magazine in the late 1970s through a company called Dascon Investments Inc. Throughout eight years of ownership, the magazine never made money, although it reaped more critical acclaim and literary awards than any other Canadian magazine. With a paid circulation of 135,000 in 1987, however, the magazine remained unviable. Webster liked to point out that on a per capita basis, that level of circulation 'would have made us a champion in the United States', a country with ten times the population. But such were the realities of publishing in Canada that, as *Saturday Night* marked its centenary, the Websters had lost millions on the venture and were losing money at an accelerating pace. They wanted out, and Black was a willing buyer on the right terms.

On learning on 18 June 1987 that the magazine was to be sold to Conrad Black, some staff were disarmed by the date's proximity to the anniversary of the Battle of Waterloo. Publisher John Macfarlane, who had been with the magazine since 1980, had only recently told Webster that the magazine would not be profitable in its existing state. It needed a large investment to boost its circulation to the 200,000 level, at which it could command national advertising rates and attention that would make it profitable. Macfarlane had bluntly told Webster: 'Invest or divest.'

Webster chose the latter, but a dispute with Black threatened to scuttle the deal. Under terms Webster negotiated with Peter White, Hollinger agreed to buy the assets of the magazine, but did not want its associated publishing services business, nor was it willing to assume the magazine's debts. Webster assumed Hollinger would be picking up the debts as well. 'There was a hitch,' recalled Webster, 'because the initial agreement had been drafted loosely, and the lawyers on the two sides looked at it and said, "Well, what was our intention?" The intention on both sides was to close clear [of debts]. So we went ahead on that basis. They bought it for $1.4 million, but they bought the assets of the magazine, i.e., they did not buy all the debts the magazine had. We had to eat those.' He will not say how much the debts were but both seller and buyer deny the story that went around at the time contending that Webster ended up paying Black to take the magazine off his hands.

Toronto was abuzz with talk that *Saturday Night*'s new owner would turn the magazine into a tout-sheet for his well known conservative proclivities. Black invited Robert Fulford, the magazine's eminent editor of nineteen years, to lunch at 10 Toronto Street. Members of the journalistic establishment were sceptical of what would come of it. Employees were already rattled by the way respected publisher Macfarlane had been treated – he was not asked to stay on at the magazine, but was offered a lesser job by Webster of running the publishing business that was not part of the Hollinger deal.

When asked by the *Globe and Mail* what elements of the magazine Black ought to preserve, radio broadcaster Peter Gzowski simply said, 'Fulford.' He added, 'If he stays, it should be fine. If he doesn't, I'd be worried. When something happens to an important and fundamental part of the country, you worry.'

Fulford possessed no personal animus towards Black and, unlike many journalists he knew, actually believed in the principles of capitalism and was a follower of neoconservatism. Besides, Black was not the first flamboyant tycoon to take a stab at owning the magazine. But the editor reckoned even before meeting Black that his departure from the magazine was likely, if not inevitable. The day after Black's purchase was announced, author Peter C. Newman dropped in on Fulford's office to give him a copy of his 1982 biography of Black. 'Bob, do not go tiger hunting with this man,' Newman signed it.

'When I arrived at Toronto Street I was inspected by a secretary and a security guard and then taken upstairs to a sitting room,' Fulford recounted in his book, *Best Seat in the House*. 'A woman in a maid's costume came in, said we were having steak for lunch, and asked how mine should be cooked. I said "medium", a serious mistake – it was close to inedible when it arrived. Indeed, the cuisine at Hollinger was in all ways a disappointment. Truman Capote once said, "The real difference between rich people and regular people is that the rich people serve such marvellous vegetables. Delicious little tiny vegatables . . ." By Capote's standards, Black is not a rich person.'

Fulford waited for twenty minutes before Peter White came in, and at one point White suggested the magazine do a piece on the deteriorating public service in Ottawa. Fulford said it already had one in the works, to which White said, 'I'd like to see that before. . . .'

'Perhaps he saw a look on my face,' recalled Fulford. 'He didn't finish his sentence. But I understood immediately that things would quickly change at *Saturday Night.* In eight years, so far as I know, Norman Webster never asked to see an advance proof of an article, even when people he knew well were the subjects.

'Finally Black joined us. In the conversation that followed he seemed particularly interested in telling me about his friend Andrew Knight, the former editor of *The Economist*, who was now running Black's *Daily Telegraph* and *Sunday Telegraph* in London. I mentioned that I'd never met him.

' "The amazing thing about Andrew," Black said, "is that he knows everyone."

' "It's true," White said. "I do believe Andrew Knight knows every important person in the whole world." Suddenly it occurred to him – his face is like that electric sign on Broadway that gives the news in giant capital letters – that he might have insulted me, a wretched fellow who had reached the age of fifty-five without once shaking the hand of Andrew Knight. "Sorry, Bob, I didn't mean that. . . ."

'Black went on, "Everyone asks about him. When I saw Katharine Graham the first thing she said was, 'How's Andrew?' And when I was speaking to George Shultz he asked me, right away, 'How is Andrew?' And so did the Aga Khan. And Henry Kissinger, when I saw him, he said [here Black went into a German accent], 'Howss Undrew?' " '

'He sat back, well satisfied. He had dropped the names of Katharine Graham, George Shultz, the Aga Khan, and Henry Kissinger, all in one paragraph. It occurred to me that I might never see this feat equalled in my lifetime.'

In general, the lunchtime discussion was amiable, but Fulford's discomfort was undeniable. He was particularly put off when White and Black each pulled out copies of the magazine's payroll list and asked the editor to go through it and grade employees as Excellent, Good, or Fair. Despite their expressed hope that he would stay on, Fulford resigned the next day, but agreed to continue until a successor was named and to contribute to the magazine thereafter. Fulford's lingering impression of his encounter with Black was that the magazine's new owner was 'an extremely uncommon millionaire, not so much in the content of his conversation as in his manner. He was more theatrical than any other businessman of my acquaintance. His personality had a staged, directed feel to it. It was also oddly familiar. Where had I seen it before, a large, handsome man with a supercilious and condescending manner and a baroque vocabulary? Of course: Orson Welles in *Citizen Kane*. I was talking to Citizen Black.'

Black's choice to succeed Fulford as editor was John Fraser, his former classmate from Upper Canada College days and, since the summer of 1984, London correspondent for the *Globe and Mail*. Somewhat the dandy in manner, Fraser possesses a quick wit balanced by an openly mischievous nature and a marked fondness for gossip. His working experience included stints as a China correspondent and dance critic for the *Globe*, a task he enhanced with usual elan by helping Mikhail Baryshnikov defect. Fraser was widely regarded as a gifted writer, but at no point in his career had he edited a magazine. He accepted Black's job offer on the proviso that Black sign a codicil to his employment contract ensuring him full editorial independence. Fraser held no real concerns that Black would impinge on his autonomy, but wanted to wave around the formal documents to quell such talk.

In drafting the clause, Fraser borrowed some heavy phrasing from a volume on the correspondence of William Pitt during his term as prime minister of England. 'He was talking about the role of the monarch and the executive, essentially a system in which the cabinet was only emerging, and I used a bit of his language,' recalled Fraser. 'Conrad caught it. He said: "I know where you got that from – and George III was mad at that time." ' Fraser was not surprised that his new employer identified the reference. 'It was put in there partly for amusement and partly as a test. But I had to look it up – he knows this shit off the top of his head!'

The two men enjoyed a good working relationship, and Black was the proud owner of a respected magazine in his own country. Fears of a right-wing agenda did prove to be overstated, if not unfounded. And, unlike Webster, Black was willing to invest in the magazine.

Black was not always happy with Fraser's story selection, for example when the magazine ran a controversial cover story purportedly exposing American 'death camps' under Eisenhower. One of

Fraser's favourite Proprietor Stories is of the time he told Black about the cover story in the May 1989 issue, a profile of Member of Federal Parliament Svend Robinson, who was then rumoured to be a federal leadership hopeful for the socialist New Democratic Party. The story was entitled 'Canada's Gay MP'. Fraser informed Black of the story a couple of weeks before publication. 'What, that faggot?' Fraser recalled Black saying. 'Yeah, you know, the NDP guy.' Black was then floored to learn that Fraser was putting the story on the cover, mustering only a 'Wow'. As he often did, Fraser handled the situation with cheek. 'Conrad, you know you're going to sleep easier knowing you did your bit to help Svend Robinson get the leadership of the NDP.' Black replied, 'I can use that line.'

Several years later, on Brian Mulroney's retirement from politics in 1994, Mordecai Richler authored a satirical cover story in *Saturday Night* marking his departure. In a subsequent column in the magazine, Richler wrote that Mulroney had called Peter White – who took a sabbatical from Hollinger to serve as the prime minister's principal secretary – to complain about the piece before its publication. Richler's depiction of his conversation with White seemed to indicate that Mulroney knew about and had perhaps even read the article before publication. Was this a case of the common newsroom fear that powerful proprietors with friends in high places interfere in editorial matters when those relationships are jeopardised? The matter was debated at a Canadian Association of Journalists conference where Black spoke in 1994, shedding light on the code he developed as a publisher. According to Black, the much-pilloried prime minister had in fact phoned him, not White, and said: 'If it was a very hostile article could we try to make it less hostile?'

Black said he 'never dreamed of showing it' to Mulroney and Mulroney never asked him to see the article in any case. 'So I had a look at it, I read it,' Black went on. 'I called him back and I said, "Look, you're not particularly going to like this but it's not that bad. It's very entertaining and it's not that bad. And in any case there's nothing I can do about it. If it's defamatory I can do something, but it isn't. And we can't seriously expect to interfere with a writer, especially one as eminent as Mordecai." He said, "No, that's fine." He never mentioned it again.'

Black said it was his or Peter White's job 'basically to say "nothing can be done" as politely as we could. That's what we did do. On the broader question of this sort of thing, I think the response should be exactly the one we made. We were right to take Mulroney's call, we were right not to make a massive issue out of it. I was right to read the article so that I could say to him authoritatively what I thought of it. And I was right to decline to request any changes in it. I mean it sounds sanctimonious but I think the right thing was done.'

If Black had thought Richler's piece too negative, would he have reacted differently to the call? Only, he replied, if it was in 'unimaginably bad taste'. 'Frankly, I looked into it to humour the prime minister because he was the prime minister. I thought the chances of my asking Mordecai Richler to make a change in his copy were awfully close to zero.' Ultimately, Black said he was 'humouring' the prime minister because of their thirty-year acquaintance. 'As a practical matter,' Black noted, 'you rarely take a phone call from the prime minister, no matter who he is, and say "To hell with you" and hang up.'

Though it represented only a small fraction of Black's expanding publishing interests, with *Saturday Night* he was finally playing a part in quality English-language Canadian journalism. Despite the magazine's continuing losses, Black would come to regard it as a good investment: prestige and journalistic legitimacy acquired in his native country at a bargain price. He would describe the magazine's losses at one Hollinger annual meeting as a 'pin prick' in the overall corporate scheme. Yet he would not tolerate them indefinitely.

Black continued his 1987 buying spree by acquiring a fifteen per cent interest in the *Financial Post*. The $6.9 million investment was made after Black suggested to Toronto Sun Publishing Corp. chief Doug Creighton that the Sun buy the eighty-year-old weekly from the Sun's parent, Maclean Hunter, and turn it into a daily. Black believed the paper could be a strong competitor with the *Globe and Mail* and its *Report on Business* section, then the only widely read business report; he also met Frank Barlow at the *Financial Times* of London, which took a twenty-five per cent interest in the venture.*

Several months later, Black added the 160-year-old *Spectator*, a weekly British magazine with a reputation comparable to *Saturday*

---

* Hollinger and the *FT* later adjusted their stakes to own 19.9 per cent each.

Night both in terms of prestige and woeful financial performance, to the *Telegraph*. Several *Telegraph* scribes also freelanced for the *Spectator*, and Black rationalised that the magazine would ensure the paper had access to a talented writing pool. The *Spectator* acquisition was all the more intriguing because Black had been pilloried in print in the magazine on more than one occasion, including in a piece by its then editor, Charles Moore. But unlike *Saturday Night*, there would be no editorial upheaval as a result of the change of ownership, and the magazine would soon become profitable.

'He brought a sinister reputation in front of him,' recalled Moore. 'We'd heard stories about business dealings in Canada that made him sound very ruthless. Also, we heard that he had very strong political views. Of course, if a journalist hears that about a proprietor, he gets nervous. And when you first meet Conrad, that impression can be confirmed – because he's so full of views, and he expresses them so forthrightly, you think, "Christ, he's going to trample all over us."

'But in fact you quickly discover two things. One is that he's professional in the way he runs his organisation. He knows that he's not a hands-on chap anyway, and he knows it's ludicrous to come into the office every day and tell everyone what to do in detail. It just doesn't work. It's not good journalism, so he never tries to do that. The other thing is, though he likes holding forth, he doesn't make you feel a worm. I think one of the things Rupert Murdoch does – though he's a very charming man often – is that he uses conversations with journalists in a manipulative way. He tries to make one journalist feel small in order to make another one feel big and it's all a great big complicated game. And you don't feel that with Conrad. Though he can be an intimidating presence when you meet him, you actually find that if you have a conversation it's pretty relaxed. You feel that he wants to have the conversation just because it's a conversation, rather than in order to lay down the law.'

Black's ownership of the *Spectator* did not end his unusual habit of writing letters to the editor for publication. In October 1991, he fired off a missive against an 'unbalanced attack' by *Telegraph* Washington correspondent Stephen Robinson against U.S. president George Bush which reminded Black of Christopher Hitchens's 'demented ravings against Ronald Reagan' in the magazine that had prompted a letter from him six years earlier. 'In recent years,' Black wrote, 'the

Spectator has published an error-riddled cover piece on the Reich-manns and Canary Wharf and a gratuitous sketch of Lord Carrington [who had become directors of Hollinger and the *Telegraph* respec-tively].

'Lord Carrington and Paul Reichmann would have the right to expect to be treated fairly by the *Spectator* even if they were not directors of the companies that ultimately owned it and friends of its proprietor. It is not normally the duty of the proprietor to distinguish between intelligent controversy and bile.' A year after that, Black added a twist to his letter-to-the-editor repertoire by partially recanting his previous letter, given that Bush had lost to Bill Clinton and Canary Wharf's financial troubles led to the bankruptcy of the Reichmanns' main company, Olympia and York. The letter ran under the headline, 'It takes a big man': 'While I continue to believe that President Bush's conduct of foreign policy was quite successful and that the articles about the Reichmanns and Lord Carrington were unnecessarily snide, subsequent events demonstrate that Stephen Robinson was not mistaken in taking the Democratic quest for presidency seriously and Edward Whitley, the author of the Canary Wharf piece, was essentially correct in his financial prognosis for Canary Wharf. I would like to retract those aspects of my letter of 12 October and apologise to Mr Robinson and Mr Whitley for them.'

The letter prompted a surfacing of the long-simmering feud between Black and Christopher Hitchens, who took to the *Guardian* to publish an open letter to Black. 'From my observation of you,' Hitchens sniped, 'I would say that you knew at least as much about the American presidency as you do about the delicious world of Canadian real estate. So what's the use of an apology when all can plainly see that Bush and the Reichmanns have lost out? Do you mean us to understand that until last week you thought Bush was fine, the Democrats washed up and the Reichmanns on the level? If your reporters followed your example, there would be room for nothing but grovels, Canossas and *mea culpas*. And by the way, since you don't mention the Carrington editorial again, are we to suppose that you think he retired with honour from the former Yugoslavia? Can we expect a tortured rethink about your recommendation of John Major? Of Brian Mulroney? I would say – stop now before you kill again. Think of the apologies *before* you write the letters, or the editorials.'

After buying the *Spectator*, Black also effectively aquired *Encounter*, a right-wing journal once funded by the CIA. Commercially, the magazine was intriguing because, although based in Britain, more than eighty per cent of its sales were in the U.S. However, Black and his lawyer Dan Colson, who served as a director of the magazine, quickly found its editorial product wanting and the editors unyielding to change. 'The thing basically lost its way,' recalled Colson. 'After communism started to come apart in Eastern Europe, these guys were still looking for reds under the bed everywhere.' About two years later, Black gave his shares in *Encounter* back to the money-losing magazine which failed to find another buyer and folded. All through this period, David Radler criss-crossed America in search of more newspapers.

'We have effectively approached several situations,' Black later said, 'with a view to moving slightly ahead of the conventional wisdom, which held, among other things, that money could not be made in the British national newspaper industry, that English-Canadians could not own and operate French-Canadian daily newspapers, and that daily newspapers of under 10,000 circulation could not be made adequately profitable to justify the administrative complications required to administer them.' Indeed, by 1987, much to Black's satisfaction, he appeared to be defying those who only two years earlier had criticised his business career as being that of a man who was a mere shuffler of paper rather than a builder of companies.

Black's first public speech in London was before the Canadian Club on 1 July 1987. It was Canada Day, the holiday in his native country marking the forming of the Canadian dominion. The Canadian high commissioner in London at that time was Roy McMurtry, whom Black had labelled a 'cockroach' during the 1983 police investigation into his affairs while McMurtry was Ontario's attorney general. McMurtry declined to attend, citing the club's male-only membership policy, which Black allowed was a plausible excuse. 'The last time Roy was invited to a dinner at which I was speaking,' Black quipped, 'he declined my invitation because, he said, he would be studying penal reform and the humane interrogation of detainees, in Pakistan.'

The comment was a classic Black barb – an inside joke delivered in sufficiently colourful language that much of his audience would chuckle despite being unsure what exactly they were laughing at. Among those listening to the speech was a rather bored-looking Robert Maxwell, proprietor of the Mirror Group and the grandiose Maxwell Communications Corp.

In his speech, Black launched into a defence of Ronald Reagan and an attack on much of the British press's coverage of the Iran-Contra affair. Black had already banished the use of the word 'Irangate' from the *Telegraph*'s pages in a rare proprietorial edict. He also took time to express 'a few words of gratitude' over the recent re-election of prime minister Margaret Thatcher, 'a social and political champion of unheard-of determination'.

'There is, in Mrs Thatcher's policies and in her demeanour,' Black gushed, 'not only the triumph of Victorian middle-class values but also a hint of the grandeur of Elgar, and even of Kipling.' Black praised Thatcher for promoting the concept that the honest accumulation of wealth is admirable. 'It is not,' he noted, 'an indecent ambition to seek material wealth, and the ranks of those who achieve that status in this country should not be confined to the most fortunate inheritors and the most ingenious outsiders, such as my ineffable friend, Bob Maxwell.'

Spending the summer of 1987 in London in a rented house with his family, Black was gradually shedding the mystique of the shadowy man in the back of the 1954 Rolls, as Andrew Knight had portrayed him. Slowly, the Blacks began to make the rounds of British society. When Queen Elizabeth visited the *Telegraph*'s new offices on the Isle of Dogs after the opening of the Docklands Light Railway, Conrad and Shirley were there, although in the photo that ran in the next day's *Telegraph*, Andrew Knight was most prominent; Black's head was obscured by the top of the monarch's hat. Meeting Sarah Ferguson, the Duchess of York, on another occasion, Black was so enamoured that he sent her a copy of *Duplessis*.

In September 1987, Black formally donned the mantle of British newspaper proprietor when he became chairman of the *Telegraph*. Granting an interview to the *Financial Times*'s Raymond Snoddy, Black revealed that 'my greatest pleasure beyond the satisfaction of basic appetites is to sit at home with my family and my cats and read my books.' But it was clear that Black was doing more than retiring to his library and poring over volumes while stroking a feline. 'I want to build a first-class international newspaper company,' he allowed, 'and I think the omens are favourable.' Indeed, cash provided by Hollinger's operations increased from a deficit of $7 million in 1986 to a positive figure of $45 million in 1987, $99 million in 1988 and $106 million in 1989.* Along with it rose Black's international profile, his influence and his desire for more.

Hollinger's board of directors began to reflect both the company's growing structure and Black's affinity for celebrities; in addition to Carrington and Reichmann, Henry Kissinger and Canadian moguls Peter Bronfman and Robert Campeau were enlisted.

It was also time for Black to raise the profile of his annual fête for the good and the great, the Hollinger Dinner. The dinner had in fact been around since 1929, when the original Hollinger – a man known as Benny, whose first mine was in Timmins, Ontario – founded it as a gathering for his rough-and-tumble mining crowd. Through the Argus era of E. P. Taylor and Bud McDougald, the event became more of a Toronto society outing, and after Black took over Argus he decided to update the evening by bringing in speakers and inviting more politicians and international guests. One year in the early 1980s featured a political debate between Conservative parliamentarian John Crosbie and future Liberal prime minister Jean Chrétien. The first big international speaker was Kissinger in 1983, who along with Black and David Rockefeller was *en route* to a Bilderberg meeting in Montebello, Quebec. Black enlisted Kissinger to come to the dinner and give a talk and Kissinger later became a fully fledged Hollinger director.

Black set a high standard for speakers that he worked hard to maintain. On 21 June 1988, during a meeting of the leaders of the Group of Seven industrialised countries held in Toronto, Margaret Thatcher was Black's guest of honour at the Toronto Club for the

---

* Along with operating profit margins, cash is the benchmark typically used to judge the performance of media companies. Cash flow relates to the actual amount of cash coming in and going out of the company, while net profit figures include depreciation, amortisation and other non-cash charges that can have more to do with accounting than the state of the business.

dinner. In attendance were Canadian Prime Minister Brian Mulroney, Governor-General Jean Sauve, and Kissinger, whom Black
introduced to the black-tie crowd as 'the only director in our history
not to appear at our annual meeting because of a long-standing prior
engagement with the King of Morocco'. Black's panegyric on the
British prime minister ran for eight minutes but seemed, to some
guests, considerably lengthier. Black praised her for reducing
corporate tax rates, championing privatisation, increasing general
productivity, and for bringing about 'the abstract renewal of British
greatness . . . the revival of Britain's capacity for moral leadership. . . .'

Thatcher began her own lengthy remarks by jesting, 'I really don't
think you've left very much for me to say . . .'

'Of course, we're used to Canadians in Fleet Street – Lord
Beaverbrook and Lord Thomson – and Conrad Black is continuing a
great tradition.' It was a crowning moment for Black – a ruling British
prime minister praising him at his own dinner before a glittering
crowd in his home town of Toronto. At the end of Thatcher's speech,
described by one jaded guest as 'her Cheltenham Women's Garden
Club Address No. 3', the guest of honour was thanked by Henry
Kissinger.

'I must say I listened to Conrad Black's beginning with mounting
panic,' Kissinger deadpanned in his gravelly monotone. 'Because I
thought, "If this is what is being said before the prime minister has
spoken, what can I possibly say after the conclusion of her remarks?" '
Of course it was usual that the owner of the *Daily Telegraph* – traditional
pipeline between the Tory party and the lawn-mowing classes –
should enjoy some sort of relationship with the prime minister. But it
was clear Black had a special personal affinity for Thatcher, and she in
turn remarked that Black made her feel like a 'wet'. In a very
meaningful sense, her revolution was also his.*

'The *Telegraph* was not always a strong ally to the sort of
Conservative government that Mrs Thatcher was running,' observed

---

* Before another dinner, in London, Black arranged for Hollinger's entire board
of directors to meet the prime minister at 10 Downing Street. 'We all sat in the
cabinet room and she gave us a nice chat, answered questions,' Black recalled
fondly. 'She was sitting there under the painting of Walpole and she was very
generous with her time.'

Sir Charles Powell, who served as her senior foreign policy adviser. 'But on the crucial moments – I mean, a) election times, b) some sort of international crisis – it generally was. And Conrad saw to that.'

Not all of Black's investments work out the way he plans. His partner Radler likes to say that 'you can't buy what's not on offer, that's a fact'. This principle does not prevent Black from pursuing what he desires. During the summer of 1985, in the early days of his global newspaper hunt, he attempted to take a friendly position in Southam Inc., Canada's largest publisher of daily newspapers. Amid the terminal illness of its chief executive, Gordon Fisher, the venerable company was rumoured to be the object of hostile but unspecified acquisitors. At stake were some of Canada's bedrock metropolitan newspapers – the *Ottawa Citizen, Montreal Gazette, Edmonton Journal, Calgary Herald* and *Vancouver Sun* among them – plus various other interests in publishing, printing, cable-television and broadcasting. Black approached Southam chairman St Clair Balfour with an offer to play a role as white knight. Having noted the negative press some of Black's Argus deals had received, Balfour felt uncomfortable about him as a partner, and gently rejected Black's approach. Instead, Balfour sought a controversial investment arrangement with Torstar Corp., publisher of the *Toronto Star*. Black's interest in Southam did not disappear altogether; he shrewdly sold his five per cent stake in the company in late 1989 when the shares were near an all-time high, but retained ambitions towards the company which would smoulder until the time was right several years later.

In January 1989, Black made a friendly overture similar to his Southam gambit to Lord Stevens of Ludgate, executive chairman of United Newspapers, which included Lord Beaverbrook's vaunted mid-market titles the *Daily Express* and *Sunday Express*. The former David Stevens had emerged at the helm of United Newspapers at roughly the same time as Black had acquired the *Telegraph*.* The *Daily Express* had sold four million copies daily in Beaverbrook's era, but circulation had declined steadily to less than a third of that tally by the time Stevens assumed the helm.

* Until autumn 1985 United had been a chain of provincial newspapers, which acquired the former Beaverbrook newspaper empire, then known as Fleet Holdings.

The *Telegraph* already had a relationship with United through their successful West Ferry Road printing joint-venture, but Stevens was sceptical of Black's suggestions of a closer relationship. Hollinger had already acquired about one per cent of United and was en route to becoming its largest single shareholder with nine per cent of the stock. As with Southam, Black described his role as a 'white knight', although this time it looked as though the largest threat to United's independence was Black himself. Black explained to Stevens that, in any case, he considered United a bargain amid all the newspaper companies he constantly scanned in Canada, the U.S., and the U.K; it was selling at a low multiple of about seven times cash flow, had strong assets, and no controlling shareholder.

In the following months, Stevens amiably discussed various proposals put forward by Black: a reverse take-over of the *Telegraph* that would have left Black in control of both firms, and a management buy-out that would have seen Stevens and Hollinger divvying up United's assets. Andrew Knight, for one, thought United's stable of provincial newspapers and maybe its magazines would well complement the *Telegraph*; this interested Black, but so did the more dicey prospect of the *Telegraph* getting the *Express* titles and United's downmarket tabloid, the *Star*, a move which would have been eyed sceptically by Mergers and Monopolies officials.

After a while Black began to feel that Stevens was doing little more than putting on a show of interest to keep him at bay. So Black held serious discussions about launching a tender offer for all of United with several parties including the Dutch group Elsevier, the British publisher Reed, and the East Midland Allied Press. No luck: Elsevier and Reed decided to merge and the talks with EMAP petered out. So too, after a while, did United's share price. Stevens's stall worked, for in April 1992 Black sold the stake at a $38 million loss.* This did not turn out to be one of Black's shrewder moves: the shares he bought at an average price of 458p and sold at around 350p were trading at 427p two months later.

In conceding a strategic retreat, Black tipped his hat to Stevens.

---

* In 1990, Black took a similar ten per cent interest in Trinity International, the British publisher of the Liverpool *Daily Post* and *Echo* newspapers. (Trinity also owned several small papers in Canada, including the *Richmond Review*, sold to it by Sterling.) This, too was eventually sold, but at a gain of $13 million.

'What he managed to do, I think, is turn a weakness to a strength,' Black later reflected. 'He managed to use the perceived weakness of the *Express* titles as a disincentive to others to make a bid for his company even though his company appeared be undervalued. . . . It's hard to do it, but it's very cunning the way he did it, I think.'

Black had never liked to think of himself as a mere businessman, and the late 1980s were arguably his most prolific as a published commentator. For almost two years, Black was a regular columnist in the *Report on Business* magazine, and, for a time thereafter, in the *Financial Post*.

Black's regular missives in Canadian publications were an interesting outlet for his forthright opinions and his prose style which could achieve deep shades of purple. It was clear to followers of his writing that certain words enjoy a preferred status in the Black lexicon: Workforces tended to be 'slovenly', steps taken to reduce them were 'draconian', governments were likely to be in a state of 'torpor'. 'The man is a walking *Roget's*,' noted John Allemang, writing a column on language in the *Globe and Mail*. 'Black's use of words such as "prodromal", "velleities", "ziggurat", "rodomontade", all testify that it pays to increase your word power. His storehouse of allusions . . . remind us that while we sniffed flowers in the sixties young Conrad was nosing the grindstone.'

Politics, religion, business (including his own), even sports were subjects on which Black also displayed a unique stylistic approach. For instance, in the *Financial Post* he wrote that the Toronto Blue Jays baseball club's 1988 season was 'like Pierre Laval at the Vichy Casino, one of the most ludicrous débâcles since the fall of France in 1940'.

Another time, Black grudgingly paid a compliment to the Jays, noting that 'a number of players exude circumstantial evidence of enhanced motivation'. But Black's prose seemed most honed when on the offensive. 'Instead of being an enjoyable pastime to share with my son,' he wrote in 1990, 'the Toronto team is an object lesson I regularly cite to him on the evils of defeatism, selfishness and cowardice.'

Black's most intriguing venue was the *Globe and Mail*'s monthly *Report On Business* magazine. Here was a paper he did not own and thus was hired solely on his merits. Moreover, he had the rare distinction of

suing the newspaper for libel during his period as a contributor. The
suit did not affect his relations with his editors, but it was clear in more
ways than one that Black was no ordinary hack; one *Globe* editor
recalls having to negotiate changes to one of Black's columns through
Black's lawyer. Nor was he afraid to bite the hand that 'fed' him; he
took a swipe at the *Globe* in one missive, writing, 'It expresses so
faithfully the English-Canadian characteristic I have often decried in
this and other places, of smugness and sanctimony, tinged with envy
and suspicion of success. Unless a person is a septuagenarian, a
professional hockey player, or one variety or another of social worker,
success is unbecoming, suspect, and even un-Canadian.'

A high point was a column Black wrote in 1987 on the social
teachings of Canada's Roman Catholic bishops – 'all sorts of
unfounded and hysterical predictions' – which was nominated for a
national magazine award. 'With passing years, the bishops have
become more trendy, biased, misleading and desperate for attention,'
Black wrote. 'Of course, the church has the right, and often the
obligation, to speak out on secular issues that have moral implications.
I am not so convinced that the local successors of the Apostles have an
unarguable right to do violence to the credibility of their venerable
institution by identifying it with a sophomoric mish-mash of false
prophecies, factual errors, reflexive prejudices and naïve velleities.
Their reckless guilt-mongering has given new meaning to Malcolm
Muggeridge's description of the "great liberal death-wish".'

The article did not win the national magazine award, losing to a
profile in *Toronto Life* by journalist Elaine Dewar about the secretive
Reichmann family, which had assembled one of the world's largest
real estate empires. Black thought Dewar's article 'nasty', 'obnoxious'
and 'uncalled for' but wanted it made clear that 'I hold no ill-will or
grievance against the fact that she won the magazine award ahead of
me.'

Before the awards ceremony, the Reichmanns had launched a $90
million lawsuit against *Toronto Life* and Dewar. Black – no stranger to
libel litigation – played a cameo role in the suit's settlement. *Toronto
Life*'s largest shareholder, Michael De Pencier, who had played bridge
with Black's parents and known him for most of his life, sought Black's
advice on ending the lengthy litigation. Black suggested, and
arranged, a meeting between De Pencier and Paul Reichmann, a

Hollinger director, and eventually the magazine settled, publishing a large apology.

In another of his relentless deals, Black later agreed with De Pencier to invest in Key Publishers, *Toronto Life*'s majority owner, taking a ten per cent interest. In return, he also gained the right to force Key to take *Saturday Night* off his hands should his ownership of the magazine not work out. In this way, Black ensured that he would not be remembered as the man who killed off a Canadian cultural institution.

Read in totality, Black's columns composed a guidebook to his intellect, each month's instalment, like the nineteenth-century serials of Dickens or Poe, revealing another facet of his mindset. The tone was usually lecturing, sometimes brow-beating, the language heavy as an anvil, delivered with the punch of a campaign speech directed against a ruthless opponent. Black railed against the increasing power of unions in Canada. He saw capitalism as 'the only effective engine for reform in South Africa' noting that 'much of the Commonwealth is now a rag-bag of petty tyrannies and receiverships'. He was not in favour of capital punishment because its proponents 'usually resolve themselves into a rational assumption that irrational psychopaths will respond to what would impress rational people, were they to contemplate capital crimes'.* On abortion, Black opined, 'Obviously abortions take place, and any attempt to stamp them out altogether will be no more effective than have been comparable efforts in the past to abolish well-established behavioural practices such as prohibition . . . More offensive to me than the practices themselves is the studious tendency to repress and disguise the nature of acts of life-taking.'

One of Black's favourite lecture and writing topics was the long-standing divisions between French and English Canada. Black was a keen follower of what is known in Canada as the French Question. In late 1988, he picked up his pen to oppose a new Quebec law which was brought in by Premier Robert Bourassa and stipulated that outdoor signs on businesses must contain only French, no English.

---

* 'Conrad thinks hanging is too good for them,' is how Dan Colson summarises his friend's views on capital punishment.

This Black saw as a 'reduction of liberty of expression, a discouragement of any spirit of *bonne entente*, severe treatment of a minority and a symbolic and ineffectual response to a demographic problem'. Black's views were not always well received by French-Canadian commentators, who considered him an English meddler in spite of his credentials. In a puzzling development, Black's pronouncements also incurred the bluster of fellow proprietor Robert Maxwell, who had several investments in Quebec and happened to be there in early 1989 for the launch of an ill-fated English-language Montreal tabloid which he had invested in with Quebec tycoon Pierre Peladeau. Maxwell publicly took issue with Black's comments, arguing that by predicting that the Quebec English would flee the province because of persecution, Black was comparing them with the Jewish diaspora.

The debate led to a fiery exchange of letters published in the *Financial Post* in early 1989. 'As you are aware,' Black wrote, 'it has been my policy as a British national newspaper proprietor never to encourage or even tolerate ungenerous reflections on my fellow newspaper chairmen. I do not intend to vary that policy, but I would be remiss if I allowed to pass without comment your buffoonish and demagogic insertion of yourself, at my expense, into what is a serious question of public policy of legitimate interest to all Canadians.'

'We missed you at Davos,' he concluded. 'Best wishes to your family.'

Maxwell wrote back, 'I am sorry that you are in such dudgeon; but I really see no reason why people like you and me who are prominent in public life should not trenchantly and publicly debate their opinions on public policy, while remaining perfectly good friends and colleagues in business. I am sure that you are perfectly capable of looking after yourself and will, no doubt, give as good as you get.' Maxwell clarified that he did not quote Black using the word diaspora, but insisted it was a 'perfectly accurate encapsulation of what you did say'.

'The facts remain,' Maxwell wrote, 'that you have placed yourself in vigorous and public opposition to the Bourassa policy and that you have threatened – some might say proposed – that the English-speaking population will leave Quebec step by step as reported in the press. . . .

'As a substantial investor in Quebec and friend of Premier Bourassa

I can see no reason why I should have abstained from expressing these views in public in Quebec. I shall vigorously stand up for your right of free speech in Britain. I shall continue to prefer open disagreement to private backstabbing.'

What the exchanges did not reveal – a fact which underscores the mischief behind Maxwell's drawing the diaspora analogy and an unspoken reason for Black's exception to it – was that on the other side of the world Black and Maxwell were bidding against each other for ownership of the *Jerusalem Post*.

EIGHT

Uprising

'This is not a left-right bullshit thing,
okay?'
DAVID RADLER

When approaching the *Jerusalem Post* by car from the rear, turn into
the parking lot at the first sight of the primer-painted car chassis
ranged on the roof of an adjacent autostop. The three-storey
newspaper building, approached from this angle, is just as uninspiring
as its environs – it's a former dairy, and a shambles. Inside, the *Post*
newsroom exudes the ambience of a bunker. This is somehow
appropriate, considering the strife the paper has endured over the
years, including the February 1948 bombing which left its original
office at the top of Hasolel Street in smoking ruins – but did not
prevent the next day's edition from being published. Inside, among
the reporters and editors in short-sleeved open-necked white shirts,
the wallpaper is peeling, the computer terminals need a wash, and the
editor's office is distinguished by a clock radio and an aluminium pie
plate holding the dregs of pretzels and biscuits served at the two p.m.
story conference.

Founded by editor Gershon Agron during the British Mandate on 1
December 1932 as the *Palestine Post*, the journal's first edition ran to
four pages and sold 1,200 copies.

Agron's *Post* was first and foremost a Labour Zionist paper, with the
commercial imperative taking a back seat. 'The aim of this paper,' he
once said, 'is not to lose money, but not to make a penny at the
expense of the staff. The staff come first, not profits. If we can make
our way, preserve our reputation and serve the country, I and the
board of directors will feel ourselves well rewarded.' Chances are,
Agron would not have fared well as a Hollinger publisher.

In 1950, two years after the creation of the State of Israel, the paper was renamed the *Jerusalem Post.* In 1959, it introduced a weekly overseas edition, precursor to its influential international edition, which sells largely in the United States and is credited with shaping overseas perceptions of Israeli affairs. In the mid-1970s, the paper came under the stewardship of co-editors Ari Rath and Erwin Frenkel, who established and maintained the paper as the thoughtful voice of liberal Israel. As the country's only English daily, its audience was limited, and, in relation to its size, its influence phenomenal.

The *Jerusalem Post* was David Radler's deal. Radler is Jewish, but he is neither a religious man nor was he well known in Israeli circles. But, as he says, 'You're going to send the Italian guy to Rome, aren't you?' He had travelled to Israel a number of times on holiday, and on one trip during the Argus years he bought a subscription to the *Post*'s international edition. Later, he gave a *Post* subscription to Black as a gift.

In 1988 when in Jerusalem with his wife Rona and two daughters, Radler proposed, as a major Canadian publisher, to pay a visit to prime minister Yitzhak Shamir. He was not available, so Radler instead met with Shamir's political secretary, Arye Mekel, at his office. Through the course of their conversation, recalls Mekel, 'He told me about the fact he owns a few hundred newspapers in Canada. He said that he was a conservative himself, and that he supports the policies of Mr Shamir, and, as I recall, he may have mentioned the fact that maybe he would want to buy a newspaper in Israel.' One story going around Jerusalem was that Radler had asked what he could do for the right-wing Likud Party, to which Mekel replied something to the effect of: 'Buy the *Jesusalem Post* if it's ever for sale, because every morning when Shamir reads it his blood pressure goes up.' It's a good story for those who believed Hollinger's interest in the *Post* was politically motivated, but neither Mekel nor Radler recalls this. Nevertheless, such stories are part of the folklore that surrounds Hollinger's acquisition of the *Post*, in which Conrad Black was accused of imposing his right-wing ideology on one of the world's great newspapers.

At the time of the Radlers' 1988 visit, about sixty per cent of the *Post* was controlled by Israel Investors Corporation, a U.S.-based subsidiary of Koor Industries, an ailing Israeli conglomerate ultimately owned by Histadrut, the Israeli Labour movement. By 1988 Koor was in peril, weighed down by debts of US$1.2 billion, and had lost nearly a half-billion dollars in two years. Under pressure from its lender, Bankers Trust, its board was in a scramble to sell off assets, including a stake of almost sixty per cent in the *Post*. The other forty per cent of the paper was owned by Bank Hapoalim, Koor's biggest creditor.

Yehuda Levy read about the *Post* being for sale in a Hebrew newspaper and called his friend Radler in Vancouver. After twenty-six years in military service, Levy, having attained the rank of colonel, retired from the Israeli Defence Force and entered civilian life in 1978 to work for the Jewish National Fund as its Western Canadian representative. Based in Vancouver for three years, he met and became close friends with Radler, who appreciated Levy's brisk, authoritarian mien. In 1981 Levy returned to Israel to set up a tour company, but the two men would still get together when Levy travelled to Canada. The closest thing Levy had to media experience was a stint as a media spokesman for the Israeli Defence Force in Beirut in 1982, and periodic freelance articles on international terrorism for Jewish periodicals in Canada and the United States.

When Radler received Levy's call in early 1989, he asked him to send the material on the *Post*, then retained him to look into the deal. At one stage he flew over to see the operation and discovered what little interest its owners had in the *Post* as a commercial enterprise: The Koor executive charged with escorting Levy and Radler had to stop for directions to locate the newspaper's offices.

Nonetheless, by 1989 the *Post* had achieved a daily circulation of 25,000 rising to around 45,000 on Fridays, and the weekly international edition sold a further 60,000 copies. Radler thought it had potential. Black's London lawyer Dan Colson, who had handled the *Telegraph* deal, was brought in to draft the formal bid. Colson recalled first hearing about it on a Sunday afternoon, speaking to Radler in Vancouver by telephone. Colson and Black had been to Mass at the Brompton Oratory, near Colson's Kensington home. There was, he recalled, 'a certain irony after being at High Mass, we walked over to our house around the corner and then we proceeded to have a chat about buying the *Jerusalem Post*'.

The paper attracted six or seven serious bidders, but Radler and Colson were mainly concerned about whether the business could be viable; it was clearly overstaffed, with some 450 employees, but it was less certain that Radler could lop jobs out of the operation as he had in the U.S. It was on its way to losing $2 million in 1989. And this was not a typical North American-style paper – a much higher percentage of its revenue was generated from circulation than from advertising. The *Post* was probably unique in that, through its international edition, its readership was greatest outside its home country. Moreover, as the bombings of the past and the rain of scud missiles during the coming Persian Gulf War would demonstrate, the region's politics could have a sudden and dramatic impact on the bottom line.

On the other hand, the franchise was internationally renowned and undermarketed. It also derived a larger proportion of its profits than other Hollinger papers from commercial printing, and held a potentially lucrative twelve-year contract to print the Golden Pages (Jerusalem's equivalent of the Yellow Pages). Alan Rawcliffe, the *Daily Telegraph*'s printing press guru, flew to Jerusalem to assess the operation, and eventually Hollinger would invest $10 million in new presses, giving it the only commercial printing plant in Jerusalem.

Rival bidder Robert Maxwell had cobbled together an offer with Canadian alcohol magnate Charles Bronfman. It seemed that wherever Hollinger turned, Maxwell was there. The previous year, Hollinger had tried to buy Melbourne's *The Age* from the Australian John Fairfax Group, only to have Maxwell top its bid by a considerable margin. A public outcry against potential ownership by the controversial Czech-born publisher prompted the Australian government to make it virtually impossible for a foreigner to own the paper. The *Post*'s editors published a front-page article making it clear that Maxwell was just as unwelcome in Israel.

Hollinger outbid the field by paying US$17.5 million for seventy-eight per cent of the *Post*.* A year later, it spent another US$4 million to buy most of the rest of the shares.

According to *Post* editor Ari Rath (who himself had failed to put together a 'Jewish liberal consortium' to bid for the paper), when the Hollinger bid envelope was opened by Koor in April, the amount enclosed was so much greater than the nearest bid, 'they thought it

---

* Hollinger was later refunded US$1.15 million because of a 'clawback' arrangement based on auditing the financial results on which the bid was based.

was a typo'. Maxwell put out word that he and Bronfman had bid only US$3.5 million which fuelled suspicions that Hollinger had an ulterior motive. Few in Israel had heard of Hollinger; one theory had Black and Radler as a front for Hollinger director Paul Reichmann. Another hypothesis blended Black's ownership of *Encounter* and friendship with Henry Kissinger into a frothy fantasy that the CIA was somehow behind it.

Black dismissed these theories in his usual thumping manner when he paid his first visit to the paper almost a year after its acquisition: 'It wasn't that our bid was higher than it should have been; the other bids were lower than they should have been.' Black contended that the other bidders were trying to have a controlled auction and keep the price down. In fact, he claimed, the price Hollinger paid wasn't excessively greater than Maxwell's offer, nor did the economic rationale behind the bid differ much from other Hollinger papers.

'This part of the world is most historically prone to discussions of conspiracies, hidden agendas and esoteric motivations,' Black offered. 'In this case, these tendencies were undoubtedly inflamed by the sour grapes of the defeated bidders. Crestfallen after the breaking up of their closed auction, they confected the theory that we had been taken completely over the barrel by the vendors. But, on our record, we seem too astute for that. So they spread the rumour that perhaps it was just some heinous plot to produce a Likud propaganda sheet and bring Israel to extreme Orthodoxy – the whole male population would have to go around in peyot and phylacteries.'

Black went on: 'I consider Bob to be the main author of those wild rumours. Bob Maxwell is a sort of friend, and he put out the story that we overpaid, because he was particularly horrified at having his bid topped. Also, there was some lack of enthusiasm around here about working for Bob, because for all his merit – and he has a lot of merit – he is known as an overbearing proprietor. Not everyone at the paper was enchanted at the thought of coming to work here like happy little elves singing, "Heigh-ho, I'm working for Bob Maxwell".'

Indeed, at no time was Black more aware of Maxwell's penchant for mischief-making than when, on the day Hollinger closed the deal at the end of June 1989, Maxwell held a press conference at the Jerusalem Hilton, where Colson was staying. 'I was standing in the lobby and I saw all these journalists arriving, including a couple who

I'd met from the *Jerusalem Post*,' Colson recalled. 'And I said, "What's going on here?" And they said, "The big press conference – Mr Maxwell." So I went in and sure enough the late great captain proceeded to stand up, and claimed that our deal had come unstuck in New York. "Negotiations in New York have come off the rails," he said. There were no negotiations in New York! The negotiations had been taking place for two solid weeks in Tel Aviv, and the deal had already been done, and he was there claiming he'd been invited back by the vendors to rescue the deal. The nerve, the *gall*, was unbelievable. I just laughed, I mean, what could I do? I don't think anybody took him particularly seriously. I was outraged by the whole thing, but what the hell could you do?' As Black told it, Maxwell capped the escapade by quietly offering to take the paper off Hollinger's hands for more than it had paid, while at the same time publicly proclaiming Black had 'overpaid'. Then Black asked Maxwell, and he agreed, to join the paper's board of directors. 'I think it was to shut him up,' said Colson.*

After the deal closed in June, Radler met Frenkel and Rath and said there would be no dramatic change in the paper's direction. There would, however, be greater emphasis on running it like a business: Staff would have to be let go. Rath, who had been with the newspaper for thirty-one years, said Radler told him he could stay on despite the fact he would be turning sixty-five in January 1990. Certainly, Radler had initially given interviews saying that the editors would retain their jobs and would continue to dictate editorial policy. But at the same time, he made no secret of his vision of the role the publisher plays: 'They have a responsibility to be aware of what they're publishing and to influence it. They can't hide behind the concept of "journalistic independence" and pretend that they are not aware of what is going on in their paper.' Radler, Rath and Levy, in their open-necked shirts, looked casual and content for a *Post* photo shoot. But, as happens so often in the Middle East, peace would be short-lived.

The first question the editorial staff asked Radler was why had he

* On returning from one trip to Israel, Colson was subjected to a long interrogation by an airport security officer before being cleared to board his flight to London. The officer summoned his supervisor, who asked Colson – now for the umpteenth time – why he was in Israel. 'To buy the *Jerusalem Post*,' Colson replied. 'What?' the supervisor snapped. 'You can't buy that in London?'

spent so much money on the *Post*. 'We don't buy newspapers for the physical plant,' one *Post* editor recalled Radler saying. 'What I'm really interested in is the people.' Radler said the *Post* was one of the great titles of the world, not something you normally had a chance to buy. In his flip way, he talked about the financial criteria Hollinger applies to acquisitions – it never paid more than five times cash flow in the third full year of operations – and recounted anecdotes going back to his *Sherbrooke Record* days with Black. One editor, Hanan Sher, recalled the impression left after the meeting: 'Somebody said to me, "He's just the kind of guy who will leave us alone. Certainly we'll have to worry more about money than we have in the past. But we're doing more for him than he's doing for us. We're putting him in the big leagues." '

Added Sher: 'We couldn't have been more incorrect.'

At a reception at the Hilton introducing the well-tanned Radler to the community, Rath thought him non-committal, almost cool when discussing plans for the paper. Then Radler introduced Yehuda Levy as the *Post*'s new president and publisher. Levy not only had negligible media experience but had rarely if ever read the *Jerusalem Post* in the eight years since he had returned to Israel. But Radler liked the way Levy bridged the Israeli and North American business cultures, and 'He proved his courageousness in the battles.'

The *Post*'s long-time editors did not deny that the paper was in administrative disarray and overstaffed. But they were not ready for Levy. With a voice like a sonic anvil, Levy has a stern but uncomfortable demeanour that is perhaps emphasized by the recurring back pains he suffers from an old parachuting mishap. Reflecting on the situation much later, while puffing cigarettes and sipping soda water in his office, Levy sat behind his desk clad in black jeans rolled up 1950s-style over black leather shoes and a short-sleeved shirt open so as to leave very little chest hair to the imagination.

'The whole spirit of the operation, attitude, and relationship between employees and so-called employer, were more than just regular socialistic,' Levy said. 'It was like a big kibbutz.'

What followed soon after he took over command at the *Post* has been portrayed by former *Post* journalists as nothing short of the imposition by Black's and Radler's hired hand of a new right-wing order on the bastion of Israeli liberal journalism. *The Times* of London billed it a fight 'over the soul of Israel'. No one disputes that there was a sudden and dramatic shift in the paper's editorial direction. Radler argued it was merely a case of repositioning the paper to reflect its readership more accurately. 'Let's not play games,' Black huffed. 'It was universally perceived to be a very left-wing paper before. Well, the far-left isn't the only game in town.' For Levy it was a tale of office politics, a 'struggle for power'.

One of Levy's first actions was to install a time-clock for employees. Journalists claim the publisher paraded around the newspaper calling it a 'factory'; Levy said the term he used was 'company', which was more than the journalists could stomach in any case.

Ari Rath's and Erwin Frenkel's suspicions were piqued when they discovered that Levy was taking Radler to meet various right-wing figures such as Yitzhak Shamir and Ariel Sharon on the latter's farm. As Frenkel later told the *Independent*, 'I knew it was over a few weeks after Levy joined. I had a sick feeling in my stomach.' Added Rath, 'I said, "I smell a rat here." '

As Radler recalls it, he thought Rath should stay but never expected him to retain the editor's post – it was absurd that a paper the size of the Meridian Mississippi *Star*, which American Publishing acquired shortly after the *Post*, should need two editors. In the weeks after Levy took over, he and Rath clashed over various minor issues, and Levy noticed Rath had taken on a silent sulk at meetings. The last straw came at the beginning of August, when Rath saw Levy meeting Hirsh Goodman, a former *Post* defence correspondent. Rath thought Levy was making editorial personnel decisions behind his back, and he'd had differences with Goodman in the past. According to Levy, Rath summoned the publisher to his office and shouted at him, 'You're stabbing me in the back.'

'Enough is enough,' Levy replied. 'I now can see that we will not be able to work here together. I'm not going to ask your permission with whom to meet and with whom to speak, and that's beyond my understanding, and so I think it will be a good idea if you just left. If you just leave the place, its about time. You're sixty-five. Retire, and that's it.' A calmer conversation the following day wound to the same conclusion.

Rath sent an urgent fax to Radler asking if he knew about this development, to which Radler responded by phone and told him to do nothing until his next planned visit in four weeks to take over as chairman of the paper.

Before Radler's arrival, Rath called a friend, the London *Times* columnist Barbara Amiel, who knew Conrad Black and was then linked socially to Rath's and Black's mutual friend Lord Weidenfeld. 'Ari, if anything is happening, I can talk to Black,' Rath recalled Amiel telling him. 'Better still, George Weidenfeld can talk to Black. This is ridiculous.' If there was an intervention, nothing came of it. Radler arrived at the Jerusalem Hilton via a Hollinger board meeting in London, and found a letter from some of the *Post*'s senior staff awaiting him:

> Dear Mr Radler,
> We, members of the *Jerusalem Post* editorial staff, wish to draw your attention to the considerable damage done to the paper by Mr Yehuda Levy's brusque and ill-considered treatment of Mr Ari Rath, its long-time co-editor.
> Aside from the human dimension, it is the devastating effect on the prestige and reputation of the *Jerusalem Post*, in Israel and beyond, that dismays us.
> The political and journalistic community of this country is learning, to the *Post*'s embarrassment, that the man who has virtually personified the paper for many years was summarily fired by the new publisher.
> This action surely does not accord with your public protestations regarding editorial integrity.

It was a clear sign of how little the *Post* journalists knew Radler that they could have conceived that he would not stand behind his friend and hand-picked manager. Indeed, Radler took time to chastise one of the letter's chief authors, *Post* magazine editor Joanna Yehiel. In Tel Aviv that week, at the *Post* board meeting where Radler was appointed chairman, Frenkel and Rath were in attendance. At one point, Radler turned the floor over to Levy to discuss retirements of senior staff. In Hebrew, as was usual at such meetings, Levy ran through the retirements of the treasurer, advertising manager and business manager. Then, to Rath's surprise, he added, 'And a similar such thing is taking place with regard to Ari Rath.'

'Would you proceed in English because of Radler?' Rath piped in. 'Would you care to elaborate – what do you mean by "similar such case"?' Radler became very impatient: 'We have discussed this before. This is no place for bickering.' The meeting moved on to the next agenda item, and Rath never spoke again to Radler, during the meeting or after. Levy later asked Rath if he could vacate his office by 1 December.

Radler may have returned to Vancouver thinking things would now settle down at the *Post*, but three weeks later Erwin Frenkel resigned. In Radler's view, Frenkel had little appetite for the job-cutting task which lay ahead. But to the outside world and many within the *Post*, it was again the meddling and right-wing agenda of Yehuda Levy that was at the root of Frenkel's departure. Levy liked to recount that when he took the *Post* job, he was summoned to a meeting by Yitzhak Rabin, then Israel's defence minister. Rabin told him, 'Yasser Arafat could never dream of a better propaganda tool than the *Jerusalem Post*.'

Practically every week there were new stories of Levy's incursions into the newsroom. Though such behaviour – and the departure of editors following a change in ownership – would come as no surprise to Western journalists who have worked for publishers who keep a hand in editorial, for *Post* veterans such actions were unprecedented. Yehiel, for example, recoiled when Levy began suggesting friends of his as profile subjects for the weekly magazine she edited.* Michal Sela, a reporter covering the Gaza strip, learned from her editors that Levy had complained that her feature-writing was not even-handed, and had requested her dismissal. Sela had never met Levy and confronted him in the corridor. According to Sela, Levy defined himself as belonging to the extreme right (which was in favour of Israel keeping the occupied territories) and asked her not to use the term 'gunman' but instead to employ the term 'terrorist' when referring to

---

* Levy recalled telling Yehiel, 'Joanna, it's about time we make it look more like a magazine. Let's put more colour. Let's stop with the holocaust stories every week, and so on. Let's make it more lively, more life stories on Israel.' Levy said he suggested some of the new generation of recently elected mayors and some other military officials. Levy said he could open some doors. He said later, 'Some of them are my friends, it so happened that they were my friends from the Army. So what? It's a big crime.'

Arabs in Gaza who carried out assaults against Jews. Levy recalled saying, 'I believe that you cannot call a terrorist who kills children and women a gunman or a guerrilla fighter, etc., and we'd better use more accurate terms.'

Another journalist, Hami Shalev, recalled Levy taking issue with an article on deputy foreign minister Benjamin Netanyahu, which Netanyahu later claimed misquoted him. Shalev told Levy he had recorded the comments but Levy declined to listen to them. Instead, Shalev said Levy told him that the words and feelings of public figures should be respected and he might have to apologise to Netanyahu's spokesman.

The bulk of journalists at the *Post* did not have such encounters with Levy, but Frenkel's departure shredded whatever morale remained in the newsroom. In November 1989, the *Post*'s coverage of a visit to the U.S. by Likud prime minister Yitzhak Shamir portrayed the trip as a failure, with cool receptions by President Bush and American-Jewish leaders. On his return to Israel, in a speech at a meeting of the Likud Knesset faction, Shamir attacked the *Post*, claiming it was defaming the country abroad. Frenkel responded by writing an editorial defending the press's right to dissent from the government, and, reiterating the long-time stance that the paper had consistently held, advocating political and territorial compromise over Gaza and other areas captured during the 1967 Six-Day War as being of 'vital interest for the ultimate security and welfare of the Jewish State'.

'In sustaining its independent editorial views and because of its reach abroad as well as at home, the *Jerusalem Post*, like the rest of the Israeli press and the free press everywhere, ministers not to the government or party in power, but to the nation which the government serves. And just as the press is weighed by the responsibility of that task, so a democratic government and a democratic political party, and its leader, even in an embattled society like Israel, are enjoined to uphold, not discredit, the legitimacy of that task.'

Levy took issue with the editorial on the grounds that he thought it should have been a signed opinion piece, rather than an unsigned representation of the paper's views. At Levy's request, the editorial was pulled from the paper's international edition. The final straw for Frenkel came a month later when Levy wrote to the secretary-general of the Editors' Committee, a select group of editors from the nation's newspapers which is given off-the-record briefings by senior political and security officials. Taking a greater interest in editorial operations after Rath's departure, Levy learned that other Israeli proprietors were members of the committee, and sent an application to join. Hanna Zemer, the committee's secretary-general, told him that he needed the approval of his editor to join. 'What, are you kidding me?' Levy replied. 'You don't understand that things have changed in this building? There is a new ownership here. The editor is not the top person in the pyramid, it's me. You're saying ridiculous things that I need to ask the permission of my editor.' Levy was told that the editor should approve additions to the committee, but was invited to explain his situation in writing. On 12 December Levy sent a letter to Zemer explaining that as president and publisher of the *Post*, 'I want to be very much involved with editorial work, with everything this term may imply. At the same time, I have decided to refrain at the present stage from appointing myself responsible editor, so as not to undermine the status of the editor, Erwin Frenkel.'

Frenkel received a copy of the letter from someone at the committee, and immediately composed his resignation, which he sent to both Levy and Radler on Christmas Day 1989. Levy's letter to the committee, Frenkel wrote to him, 'placed me in an invidious circumstance in relation to you and to my fellow editors: I had the choice of either humiliating you by denying your attempt to be named to the committee, or denying my standing as the editor of the paper.' The fact that Levy said he was not naming himself responsible editor 'at this stage', Frenkel continued, 'wholly undermines my position within and without the offices of this newspaper, making it impossible for me to continue'. Levy asked Frenkel to reconsider. He would not, but agreed to stay on for a time to ease the transition to a new editor.

On the morning of Sunday 31 December 1989, about ten senior *Post* editors and writers, led by managing editor David Landau, met at a coffee shop on Mea Shearim Street. They formulated a plan which hinged on an ultimatum: Thirty journalists would resign unless Frenkel were reinstated (even though it was not clear that Frenkel, aged fifty-six, wanted this), Landau was installed as editor, or Levy removed as publisher. Weekly supplement editor Joanna Yehiel, who seemed to get on with Radler, would call him in Vancouver to explain the situation. She and others again thought Radler would be sympathetic, based on his comments several months earlier about people being the *Post*'s true assets.

On the morning of 2 January 1990, Yehuda Levy arrived in his office to find the first resignation letters from the journalists, including Landau and Yehiel, on his desk. Each letter was identical, citing 'a substantial deterioration in the terms of my employment', leaving the writer 'no alternative but to ask to be relieved of my duties at the newspaper' but giving thirty days for the publisher to respond. After some consultation with Radler – which included the Hollinger president telling Yehiel she was making a mistake and trying to talk her out of resigning – the resignations were accepted, just two days later. Levy ordered that power to the newsroom's computer terminals be shut off and all those resigning vacate the building within two hours.

The official version of events, given in the 1989 Hollinger annual report, summed up the tumultuous events at the *Post* thus:

'The changes that have been instituted have not been introduced as quietly as we would have hoped. The editor resigned after his sole ability to commit the newspaper irrevocably on matters of the utmost national importance to Israel was slightly curtailed. The managing editor, after his participation, while physically at the *Jerusalem Post*, in a competing overseas news service was challenged, declared a "labour dispute" under Israeli law and demanded that Hollinger name him the new editor and fire the publisher. When we declined to submit to this initiative, the managing editor resigned, taking about twenty-five other editorial people with him. As editorial ranks had swollen from roughly fifty to one hundred since 1986 without any corresponding increase in editorial product, this was not an altogether unwelcome development. The departing personnel used their contacts in the international press to stir up an unwarranted volume of overseas comment, some of it, especially in Canada, rather uninformed and tendentious.'

Levy was an easy target for editorial caricature. Invariably articles about the *Post* dispute scrutinised his military career, particularly a stint in Uganda training paratroopers under the regime of dictator Idi Amin. 'I was there three years as a major in Israeli uniform,' says Levy. 'Idi Amin was chief of staff at that time, yes. But that makes me a mercenary of Idi Amin, together with fifty-five other Israeli officers? Anyway, [the *Post* journalists] did use all their contacts, and all their journalistic talents to make me look like a monster. And they succeeded in a way, I must admit.' Indeed, Levy attributes a 'lack of experience' to the way he tried to ignore the worldwide press attention. 'Journalists would call me at two o'clock in the morning, I would slam the telephone down in their face.'

The real issue behind the mass resignations, as Radler and Levy saw it and the Hollinger annual report told it, was the ambition of managing editor David Landau to become editor of the newspaper while ensuring that he and other top *Post* journalists could freelance for other media outlets.

Since 1972 Landau had been operating the Jewish Telegraphic Agency wire service part-time from a room on the upper floor of the *Post*. Like many Israeli journalists, Landau served as a stringer, or freelance contributor, for several other papers around the world, including the *Toronto Star* and, ironically, the *Sunday Telegraph*. This was unacceptable to Radler who was concerned that articles which appeared in the *Post*'s International Edition could be read in other major papers, particularly Jewish journals served by the JTA. 'I'm not against freelancing, I'm against freelancing where there's competition. They can freelance on their own time, and not my articles.'

Landau was astounded that the Hollinger executives zeroed in on the wire service as the key issue behind the resignations, and later claimed that in fact Levy had asked the JTA to vacate the office it rented, but had never asked Landau to stop writing for it.

Though the *Post* was Radler's brief, Black would no longer stay quiet. The resignation débâcle was attacking his credibility at a time when his profile was on the rise in London. Writing in the London *Jewish Chronicle* on 12 January 1990, columnist Chaim Bermant repeated the Maxwell-inspired line that the price Hollinger had paid for the *Post* 'bore no relation to its commercial prospects and they obviously bought it for ulterior motives'. Of the departure of the editors, he concluded: 'Mr Shamir is, in effect, demanding that the paper should either ignore the truth or be prepared to doctor it, and it looks as if Yehuda Levy is willing to fall in with his wishes.'

Black responded in the *Chronicle*'s letters column: 'The *Jerusalem Post* will not be a mouthpiece of any party or faction and Mr Bermant will find that his dire predictions to the contrary are not justified. Mr Rath retired at the normal retirement age, and Mr Frenkel retired from fatigue, as well as concerns, that he now acknowledges were exaggerated, about the political tendencies of the publisher.' Black noted that the resignations, 'as far as we can discern', were because of Landau's operation of the 'competing overseas news service' and 'insolent demand' that Levy be dismissed and himself named editor.

A response to Black's letter from Erwin Frenkel in Israel, was sent to the *Chronicle*: 'Citing "fatigue" as the reason for my resignation as editor of the *Jerusalem Post* . . . has evidently become the official line of Hollinger, the new owners. It is certainly more convenient than the truth. Nor have I acknowledged, as Mr Black claims, that my concerns about the political tendencies of the publisher were "exaggerated".'

Frenkel said he regretted that Black had 'distorted' his action and meaning. He also refuted Black's explanation of the motivation behind the mass resignation. 'To sustain the *Jerusalem Post*, to which they had given so much, they made a stab at staying put, under the editorial leadership of the managing editor. When negotiation with the publisher failed, they resigned. . . . That management, the staff members who resigned, and those who choose to remain, made the *Jerusalem Post* the newspaper that attracted Hollinger's considerable investment. It is the *Post*'s future performance under Mr Black and his associates, not rewriting of the past, that will determine whether that investment was justified.'

Joanna Yehiel, who had worked at the paper for twenty years, sued the *Post* for severance pay in an Israeli labour court, and ultimately won. The forty-six-page ruling by Judge Elisheva Barak, delivered on 25 April 1993, concluded that Levy's interference in the workplace made it impossible for Yehiel to carry out her duties. Barak ruled that the mass resignation was not a resignation at all, but that the resigning employees had hoped the management would make changes and ask them not to leave. From a journalistic perspective, it was a remarkable judgement, basically saying that the editors' and writers' freedom of expression superseded that of the owners and publisher. At the same time, it seemed to suggest that if Levy had simply made himself editor in title, any interference he subsequently made in editorial matters would have been perfectly acceptable. The defendants had not been optimistic of the *Post*'s chances in an Israeli labour court but appealed against the decision. Radler reckoned the appeal would eventually be lost too; the case was 'mishandled' and different lawyers would be representing the *Post* in the future. Said Radler, 'I was sympathetic to Joanna's complaints, but they weren't true – still aren't. I don't care what the court says. This is a real *shlomazl*, because I was never called as a witness, and I'm the guy who dealt with Joanna!'

After the departure of Frenkel, Levy brought in David Gross, a sixty-six-year-old retired *Post* veteran with a decidedly right-wing attitude, as acting editor. The man who would officially succeed Frenkel as editor, David Bar-Illan, was first hired as an editorial writer in early 1990. A native Israeli and concert pianist by training, Bar-Illan lived in the U.S. for many years and was also a veteran commentator on Israeli affairs in American newspapers and maga-zines such as *Commentary*, *Foreign Affairs* and the *National Review*. A self-described 'hawk', his career included writing speeches for Yitzhak Shamir. In 1988, Bar-Illan tried his hand at newspapering by launching a Hebrew weekly, *La'Inyan* (The Truth), in Tel Aviv with the backing of Rupert Murdoch. Running into his own financial difficulties, Murdoch withdrew his support before the first edition, so Bar-Illan phoned Black and met him in London in late 1989 to see if the new owner of the *Jerusalem Post* would consider backing the venture. 'My meeting with Black impressed me,' Bar-Illan recalled. 'I'd been used to meeting people in this business, but it was on a completely different intellectual level from most of the people that I knew. He impressed me also with his very penetrating knowledge of what was happening in Israel, which I didn't expect.' Black explained that the *Jerusalem Post* was Radler's domain, and Bar-Illan later met Radler and Levy in Jerusalem. Bar-Illan's paper folded at roughly the same time when Levy desperately needed to replace the bodies who had resigned *en masse*. 'Generally speaking,' said Levy of the hiring, 'I knew we were standing more or less with the same views on the most important issues, and I knew he was a very good writer.' But Levy insists it was not a conscious turn to the right and that neither Radler nor Black tried to dictate any change in the paper's political line. The only push was to make more money. Said Levy: 'They wanted results, period.'

Says Radler, 'This is not a left-right bullshit thing, okay? The reason David Bar-Illan is there is not because he's right-wing, it's because he's probably the greatest editorial writer I've ever seen – it does tend to be right-wing, but it's good.' And in the modern newspaper business, it is the proprietor who ultimately decides what is good.

Consciously or not, with Bar-Illan writing editorials and Gross as editor, the paper did indeed take a 180-degree turn from dovish to hawkish. Among the changes under the new regime was that the paper now referred to the area known as the West Bank by their historical designations Judea and Samaria, which Bar-Illan concedes is a 'code' which identifies a viewpoint to the right. In Israeli affairs there is no subtlety. 'The point is, if you call it the West Bank, you offer compromise,' explained Bar-Illan, who became editor in 1992. 'If you call it Judea and Samaria, you are a fanatic right-winger. All I do is try to do it correctly. This is the area of Judea and Samaria geographically.' The same goes for the terrorist versus guerrilla debate. 'You don't use terrorist indiscriminately, because you lose the impact of the meaning of the word when you should use it – when the attack is on a bus in Jerusalem and on the passengers of a civilian bus. My main complaint is that the British have absolutely no compunction calling the IRA terrorists, even if they attack army barracks. Terrorism is a very definite thing. It's not just a pejorative word. It's a describable, definable thing – it's attacking civilians in order to spread terror, in order to spread fear, in order to achieve political means.'

The argument that Black was pulling the editorial strings from afar didn't accord with the reality that Bar-Illan's views were somewhat more hawkish than Black's. 'My own inclination, for what it is worth and you're not likely to read it in the *Jerusalem Post*,' Black said in a 1990 speech to the Canadian Friends of Hebrew University, 'is that Gaza should be abandoned sooner rather than later.'

David Horovitz, a London stringer for the paper who moved to Israel in 1989 and was among those who quit, said the story of the *Post* is as complex as the country in which it operates. In his case, he couldn't stomach the *Post*'s new line advocating the continuing Palestinian occupation. 'It's not just a job and it wasn't just a power struggle – although that was part of it,' says Horovitz, now managing editor of *Jerusalem Report*, a weekly backed by Charles Bronfman which launched around the time Hollinger bought the *Post*. 'The fact was that these are existential issues for people who had come to live in this country with certain beliefs. The paper was no longer representing why they were here.'

The *Post* under Hollinger may not be a representative paper for Israel, but then again, concedes Horovitz, perhaps it was not before either. 'One of the arguments advanced when we left was that the paper had lost touch with its readership, that this was a left-wing paper for an English-language readership in Israel that was overwhelmingly right-wing,' said Horovitz. 'Most immigration from the West tends to be religious, right of centre Jews. I think probably the *Jerusalem Post* readers now have the paper that they want. I think it's a shame. I don't think it's the paper that Israel deserves for its sole English-language daily. But it's probably more fitting for its readership than the paper we ran. I'm disturbed.'

Jerusalem Report editor Hirsh Goodman is a harsh critic: 'Conrad Black is a professional. He produces professional papers all over the world. The current *Jerusalem Post* is a disgrace. It's got no competition, it's the only view of Israel that every foreign correspondent, every diplomat sees, every visitor sees, and it's bad. Its editing is bad, because the guys aren't professionals.'

As far as David Radler is concerned, the *Post* is an unqualified success. While it would not produce profits on the scale of comparable American Publishing titles, the operation did begin to generate profits after the 1991 Persian Gulf War. Staffing levels were pared virtually in half, from 130 journalists on the payroll in 1989 to sixty-two in 1993; overall headcount was slashed to 210 from 450. Some $10 million was invested in upgrading the plant, which made for a better-quality paper and more commercial printing work. When the building is approached from the front it now looks more like a gleaming red-brick mid-American newspaper than a bedraggled former dairy operation. In comparison with the newsroom, the *Post*'s advertising and other offices are modern and luxurious. And in autumn 1993 Levy was making plans to renovate the editorial department. A French-language edition of the *Post* was introduced in 1991, and the paper logged a gross operating profit of US$3 million on revenue of US$18.6 million in 1993, a respectable margin of sixteen per cent. The *Post*'s editorial content is debatable; its bottom line is not.

'Has the *Post* been a headache?' David Radler reflected five years after buying it. 'Yes. Would I have done the deal? Yes. We're talking about an operation that makes a lot of money. I never expected it to make what it did.' Despite all the turmoil, in 1991 a British Broadcasting Corporation radio series proclaimed the *Post* one of the world's six great newspapers. Does it remain one? 'My opinion is it's a better paper today than it ever was,' says Radler. 'If it's not a great paper of the world by someone's definition, then it never was.'

NINE

The Proprietor

'We have created a kingdom. Now it's
time the king took over'
ANDREW KNIGHT

The guest speaker at the Hollinger Dinner on 29 June 1989 was Ronald Reagan, a favourite whom Black once described as 'one of the most important and successful presidents and one of the most formidable political leaders in US history'. In the early days of Black's ownership of the *Telegraph*, cartoonist Nicholas Garland recalled a colleague saying, 'Black once said that he was prepared to let his editors have a completely free hand except on one subject. He forbade attacks on American presidents in general and Ronald Reagan in particular.' For the event, Black introduced a musical element and hired a local tenor, John McDermott, to sing a stirring *a cappella* rendition of 'Danny Boy'. The triumphant evening was a fitting sequel to Thatcher's appearance a year earlier and a further display of Black's burgeoning international VIP status.

Milling around during the after-dinner drinks, Black chatted in a clique that included Toronto Sun chairman Doug Creighton and *Financial Post* editor John Godfrey. Witnesses observed a curious scene. Earlier in the day, Black had filed a column to run in the *Sun* and the Sun-controlled *Financial Post*. In the article, in one of his more memorable outbursts, he described investigative journalists as 'sniggering masses of jackals' and in particular blasted *Globe and Mail* reporter Linda McQuaig as a 'weedy and not very bright leftist reporter'. Black had asked Creighton to ensure that the column ran unedited, and Creighton had left those instructions with the various editors. The column ran intact in the *Sun*. But Godfrey had problems with some of the language and, after consulting the *Post*'s libel lawyer, thought the 'tweedy and not very bright' reference ought to be taken out, as well as the word 'mendacious'. Black, however, is not a typical columnist – he has his own libel lawyers.

'So did you receive my column?' asked Black.

'Indeed,' said Godfrey.

'Is it running tomorrow?'

'Indeed.'

'Is it running without changes?'

'No,' Godfrey replied, explaining that the references were removed on the advice of the *Post*'s libel lawyers, and that as editor he didn't think it appropriate to attack a journalist personally the way Conrad had set out to. Creighton fumed. Black's expression darkened. He had already run it by his own libel lawyers, he thundered, which was why the instructions were to run it unedited. As a result, Black, for a time, stopped writing for the *Financial Post*, a paper he partially owned.

For her part, McQuaig was amazed at Black's animosity towards her, which dates back to her coverage of the regulatory and police investigations into him. 'I thought Ms McQuaig should have been horsewhipped,' Black once commented to radio interviewer Peter Gzowski, 'but I don't do those things myself and the statutes don't provide for it.' McQuaig says she was initially hurt by Black's denouncements, but that quickly passed. 'The kinds of attacks are so extreme and kind of bizarre,' says McQuaig. 'When you get over the initial hurt, you end up thinking "Wow, that's kind of interesting. He's made me into a character".'

The evening with Reagan and the jibe at McQuaig were Black's final goodbyes to Toronto, and to being a Canadian resident. The next day, he jetted off to England, this time for good. After renting a house and spending the previous three summers in London, Conrad and Shirley had decided to make London their primary residence. They took with them their children, Alana, seven, and James, three, while the eldest, Jonathan, eleven, elected to stay at school in Canada. From then on, Black would spend at least seven months a year in London.

Black reasoned that the *Telegraph* was by a large measure Hollinger's major asset, and he ought to take a more active role in its affairs. Besides, he had always wanted to 'internationalise' himself, and London would prove a more interesting venue than Toronto. The incessant controversies of the past would be left behind; instead,

Black would physically preside over arguably the most important journal in Britain. 'As a Canadian, I wish I could sit here, hand over heart and tell you otherwise,' he told one interviewer. 'But the fact is, London is more interesting than Toronto. It's an endless sequence of sumptuous lunches and dinners with terribly interesting people from all over the world.'

And Black would not disguise his appreciation of the special status bestowed on British press proprietors: 'Do you realise that anyone who owns the *Telegraph* has access to anyone in the world? Even Gorbachev passes through here. It's remarkable.' Still, according to Peter White, Black was concerned about how people would view his 'abandoning Canada'. White told Black that a person of his stature didn't have to live in one place. Said White, 'Where does Richard Nixon live? Or where was he from? He was from California, he was in Washington, he was in New York – who knows where he was from? Bush in a sense was like that too . . . Conrad, you can have a residence in London, you can have a residence in Palm Beach, you can have a residence in Toronto . . . You haven't changed your citizenship, you just travel around.'

Black's trepidation passed quickly. 'He loves the atmosphere over there,' says White. 'He absolutely adores being a newspaper tycoon, and that's the place to do it. He's lionised over there and that's very much to his liking.' London's social rounds suited Black well. On a typical day he would sleep until mid-morning, lunch, work at his Docklands office until the evening, then go off to a 'function'; in London he discovered a fondness for opera and ballet.

Prominent Londoners were initially interested in Black because of his position as *Telegraph* owner, but Black slipped quickly and easily into the ranks of British tycoons. 'He charmed an enormous number of people in this country,' says his friend Rupert Hambro, 'by sitting next to them at dinner or by talking.'

'I think he's gained enormous respect,' agreed *Telegraph* editor Max Hastings. 'In the early stages, not many people knew a lot about him, and I think, yes, quite a lot of people were inclined to laugh at him. First of all, he himself has changed. He was quite nervous and unsure of himself . . . when he first came here. Now he's much more relaxed, he's much more sure of himself and his own position. As a result he comes across very well.'

Conrad and Shirley's new home in Highgate, north London, sat in two acres of land and was somewhat smaller than their Toronto home. As is often the case with Black acquisitions, it was soon expanded. He added a conservatory, which could serve as an extra dining area for entertaining – at first the house could only accommodate sixteen for dinner or twenty for a buffet – then bought the house next door and tore it down in order to add a library. 'Conrad needs, I think, to have "big" around him,' observed a friend.

Black arrived in London at a time of upheaval and unease at the *Telegraph*. The paper was undergoing a restructuring to introduce seven-day publishing and a five-day working week. In *Quaynotes*, the internal *Telegraph* newsletter, Black made it clear that he had not arrived to bask in the reflected glory of the *Telegraph*'s successes. 'The fact is, if you don't stay reasonably dynamic, things stagnate. If I adopted the view that "we've done, we've made it, we're home and dry, so we can rest on our oars", we would be overwhelmed by the competition. We've got to move on to other challenges as a company and as a newspaper. But they should be rationally conceived and not compulsive and they should not be motivated by obscene ambitions or Napoleonic ideas. I mean, I'm not marching on Moscow – I'm just trying to build our company in an orthodox and dignified way.'

That said, between sips of iced tea, the newly arrived proprietor managed to confirm the well circulated view – this time in his own newspaper's employee newsletter – that he was no champion of the working press. 'I have made all sorts of unflattering remarks about the media in general, and I hold to them. I used to see a lot of journalists in Canada (in the contentious period of the 1960s) and it was in that context that I was commenting. I'm not a particularly great admirer of journalists. A great many of them are irresponsible. They have huge power, and many of them are extremely reckless.' However, on this and other subjects, Black tempers point with counterpoint. 'But like people in all other occupations, many of them are outstanding professionals, competent and conscientious people. So I would avoid generalisations about them – and let me add that there are very high standards at this newspaper and, indeed, at other quality broadsheet newspapers.'

For most *Telegraph* employees, journalists and others, the interview was the closest they would come to a personal encounter with the proprietor. He made no pretences to a chief executive's role at the *Telegraph.* There were no annual addresses to the troops, no general memos to staff, no strolls through the newsroom to see what the team was up to. 'He's very remote,' observed Charles Moore, who joined the *Daily Telegraph* as deputy editor shortly after Black's move to London. 'There can't be very many people among the journalists who know him at all well. I think if you were a normal journalist, you wouldn't expect to go see Conrad about something.' The normal protocol would be for an editorial employee to talk to the editor or maybe to managing director Joe Cooke. If a matter demanded Black's attention, he might hear about it at the regular Tuesday senior management meetings held in his office. 'There are no formal occasions on which people can be certain of meeting him,' explained Moore. 'He does give parties for all sorts of people at which some of his senior journalists might attend, that type of thing.'

This is not to say that Black did not take an active role in the newspaper's affairs.

By the spring of 1989, after a string of strategic and financial successes in the three years that Andrew Knight had been guiding the *Telegraph* as chief executive, things suddenly were out of kilter. There was infighting among the management team, and Rupert Murdoch was rumoured to be courting Knight to work for him at News International, effectively the *Telegraph*'s main competitor. Knight told *Telegraph* deputy chairman Frank Rogers that he had been approached by Murdoch to be News International's managing director, but had declined.

The unease began building in March 1989, when Knight demoted Peregrine Worsthorne from his editorship of the *Sunday Telegraph* to editing only the Sunday paper's comment pages.

After rising steadily under Worsthorne's stewardship since 1986, the *Sunday Telegraph*'s sales had dropped from a peak of about 750,000 in the autumn of 1987 to 664,000 by February 1989. During the same period, the *Daily Telegraph*'s circulation had fallen about one per cent to about 1.1 million copies daily, but that was against a cover price increase of thirty per cent and the launch of the *Independent.* While the *Daily Telegraph* continued to have a circulation only marginally lower than those of the *Guardian, Independent,* and *Times* combined, the *Sunday Telegraph* was third in a field of five (which included the ill-fated *Sunday Correspondent*).

Unlike their North American counterparts, British newspapers maintained wholly separate editorial operations for their weekday and Sunday editions. Invariably, the Sunday paper had a different character and personality to the weekday product.

Since the *Sunday Telegraph* had never been anything more than marginally profitable since its inception in 1961 – and the *Sunday Times* seemed an immovable juggernaut with sales of almost 1.3 million copies – Knight and his executives began forming a new game plan in autumn 1988. 'Our first job is to bolster strength,' said Knight. 'Our second is to remedy weakness. As far as we can see the Sunday market is stagnant, and as number three in it we're hurting badly.'

Monday was also a 'black hole' in *Telegraph* sales, and the strategy was formed to beef up the Saturday and Monday products to envelop the mighty *Sunday Times*. Several months earlier, the *Sunday Telegraph*'s colour magazine has been transferred to the Saturday paper. Concern had been expressed by Black that this would cannibalise the Sunday, and certainly Worsthorne felt the loss of the magazine was responsible in good measure for the continuing slippage in his sales.

'Black,' recalled Knight, 'quite rightly worried about what the consequence was for the Sunday. So we felt we had to do something dramatic about Sunday.' The answer: appoint Max Hastings to edit all seven days of the paper. Hastings himself was not keen on the idea – he could work only so many days a week – and the Sunday paper's distinct character would be jeopardised by such a move. On the plus side, the sharing of resources between the daily and Sunday product improved the *Sunday Telegraph*'s foreign and sports coverage. And it set the stage for a reduction in the Sunday staff, which Black felt was unjustifiably large. Managing director Joe Cooke and a consultant, Dick Herbert, put forward different models for cutting editorial jobs, which Max Hastings adamantly contested. Debate and argument on the issue dragged on for weeks. Absolute decision-making would have fallen to Knight in the past, but Black's impending arrival and swirling suspicions about Knight's future made for a sullen mood of resistance on the *Telegraph*'s executive floor. Though Knight had been largely responsible for putting in place the executive team and leading the paper's turnaround, other executives and directors increasingly found him difficult, characterising him as 'prickly', and 'complicated'.

'You never knew quite where you were with Andrew,' says Rupert Hambro, who sits on the *Telegraph* board. 'And then Conrad started to get at him about improving the product on Sunday. It needed a facelift; he didn't do very much about it, so Conrad then kept going back to this subject. And Andrew, without seemingly thinking it through, had this sort of knee-jerk reaction of the seven-day newspaper. . . . He just got it completely wrong, and lost the confidence of all the people.'

As far as Knight was concerned, the only issue was Black's growing presence in London – which he had encouraged – and its effect on the chain of command. He recalled Black telling him that it seemed that a 'Bermuda Triangle' was forming on the executive floor where decision-making mysteriously disappeared. Knight, watching his senior executives pass by his office on the way to see the newly arrived proprietor, agreed. The seven-day concept, concedes Knight, 'didn't really work out'. Hastings calls it 'probably the most significant wrong-turn we took in the last seven or eight years'.

In late July 1989, Knight arranged to sell 2.1 million of his *Telegraph* shares to Caledonia Investments, the investment arm of the Cayzer family. He did not reveal any intent to stand down during a ninety-minute meeting with Caledonia. Knight reasoned it 'wholly improper' to do so, but spoke at some length about his enthusiasm for *Telegraph* management if he were to be 'run over by a bus'.

The following month, Knight visited Black at his home in Highgate and told him, 'I actually think I ought to step aside.' 'You'll stay on the board, won't you?' Black asked. 'Would you like to be deputy chairman?' At first, Knight reluctantly agreed that he would, but was uneasy about it and a few weeks later he changed his mind even about being a director, citing the fact that he had been in charge and had difficulty merely coming in for board meetings.

In September, Black announced that he would be taking the role of executive chairman and that Knight would be standing down as CEO. 'We have created a kingdom,' proclaimed Knight. 'Now it's time the king took over.'

One of the king's first managerial tasks was to resolve the festering debate over the seven-day operation. Under the compromise Black worked out among his executives, the *Telegraph* announced thirty-three redundancies and a new five-day working week. This prompted a thirty-six-hour lightning strike. 'That may be good for him,' complained Lynne Edmunds, a features writer, 'but what about the quality of the two newspapers?'

Black saw the scattered pickets in front of the *Telegraph*'s South Quay offices as 'a rather picturesque illustration' of 'the penchant of many journalists to masquerade as a learned profession while behaving like an industrial union'.

He later recalled sardonically, 'I brought my hobnailed jackboot down on the necks of our journalists by proposing the Dickensian bleak house of a five-day work week. The *UK Press Gazette* instantly reverted to being an N.U.J. [National Union of Journalists] tout-sheet. Serious financial journalists, with whom it is usually possible to have a sensible conversation, became hysterical muck-rakers, febrile with righteousness, as if they were exposing the most repulsive abuses of the Victorian sweatshop. On that occasion the widely retailed theory of my implacable hostility to journalists was noisily revived.'

According to Knight, on 13 December 1989 Murdoch invited him to his office at Sky Television and offered him the executive chairmanship of News International. Knight would effectively replace Murdoch at the head of Wapping's five newspapers because the mogul was spending an increasing amount of time in the United States.

In late December, Black received a note from Knight saying Murdoch had made him an offer he could not refuse. An annoyed Black claimed Knight had only three days earlier denied the latest rumours to him. Black didn't begrudge Knight the £14.5 million in shares he had earned through his option over five per cent of the company arranged back in 1986. But the flip side of Black's immense loyalty is that when he perceives betrayal, he does not take it lightly.

The combative Dan Colson sensed another motive behind Knight's departure. 'I think he could smell the money,' says Colson. 'I certainly had no idea he was going to go work for Murdoch. I was appalled by that when I heard it. But I wasn't surprised when he decided to pack it in.'

Lord Cayzer expressed 'great surprise' that Knight had sold his family two million of his *Telegraph* shares without letting on that he was planning to step down. 'If you lose one of your best managers it is bound to make a difference,' he told the *Sunday Correspondent.*

Throughout the months of planning his departure from the *Telegraph* Knight had been concerned that it should not appear as though Black had fired him. Black also had to worry about appearances; the defection of the *Telegraph*'s chief executive to its main competitor so soon after his move to London could reflect badly on Black. He had much experience of defending his reputation in public and would not allow this. Consulting with deputy chairman Frank Rogers, Black elected to dispense with his low British profile and to fight this battle on familiar turf – through the papers.

Rogers sent the correspondence over Knight's defection to the *Observer* and *Sunday Telegraph*, and Knight later provided his letters to the *Sunday Times* on the proviso all the letters be published in their entirety. The first was a note from Knight to Black dated 20 December:

Dear Conrad,
   I quite agree about the 'decent interval' – I have said to you from the outset that I regard the earliest date for starting *any* new job (competitive or not) as being spring. One condition put to Murdoch and others has accordingly been that I will not entertain any starting dates before mid-March 1990.
   If you feel inclined to call, I would *welcome* your counsel.
Yours,
Andrew

Conrad's reply was a handwritten fax from Palm Beach dated 2 January 1990:

Dear Andrew,
   Now that Rupert Murdoch's long-awaited announcement about you has come out, I would be remiss if I did not offer some parting thoughts, especially in reply to your last facsimile letter to me of December 19, in which you volunteered that 'It would require an act of Parliament to prevent us from being friends.' In the same letter you also gave your idea of a 'decent interval' that should elapse between leaving us and joining Murdoch.
   You will recall that you retired as chief executive on September

19, a week after selling two million *Telegraph* shares to the Cayzer
family after extensive discussions in which you apparently gave
them to understand that you would be continuing indefinitely
with us. In view also of the fact that you remained as a director of
the *Daily Telegraph*, receiving board papers and giving
management advice until December 21, and on full pay until
December 31, and that you proposed to backdate your
resignation from the board (an initiative that would have been
illegal as well as in questionable taste), it would seem that you,
too, are aware that March 12 may be premature to the point of
unseemliness as a starting date for your new employment. As
Frank Rogers has told you, six months from December 21 would
have been quite acceptable to us.

I must emphasise, as I have before, that my only interest in
these matters is in the avoidance of unnecessary damage to your
reputation. We have been friends for many years and you did me
the honour of asking me to be a godparent of your daughter, and
it is in that spirit that I must tell you that I fear that this transition
has not been handled with your customary thoroughness and
probity.

Rupert Murdoch's entourage intermittently announced your
imminent arrival at News International through most of 1989.
You repeatedly assured me and other colleagues that there was
no truth to these reports. I know of no one who believes that this
new venture really originated at the Reuters meeting in autumn.

It seems to be a universal view, among people whose friendship
we both value in Britain, Canada, and the United States, that
your prolonged (if sporadic) courtship with our principal
competitor while continuing as the ostensible chief executive of
the *Daily Telegraph*, leading to a consummation just eighty days
after retiring (awkwardly) as a director of ours, and with your
pockets loaded with a net fourteen million of free *Telegraph*
stock,* raises substantial ethical questions.

Our success at the *Telegraph* has been so comprehensive that the
manner of your leaving seems doubly unfortunate. I did not
dissent at all from your suggestion in August that you retire and
wholeheartedly supported your efforts to quell malicious gossip to

---

* The stock was not, technically, free. Knight's option was to acquire up to five per
cent of the stock at a price of 100p.

the effect that there had been a dispute between us. I always said that I had no objection at all to your joining a competitor if the transition was executed with appropriate timing and the necessary elegance.

That it has not been astonishes and disappoints all of us at the *Telegraph*, particularly given your well-known care for your own public relations. It brings back, not without some irony, your assurance to me in 1985 that a non-compete agreement would be 'unnecessary and inappropriate' as you told me then that it would be 'unthinkable' that you would move overhastily to a competitor.

I do not, and will not, forget that you brought me the *Telegraph* as an investment possibility in 1985, even if I did not follow your advice on how to pursue that investment. If I had, neither Michael Hartwell nor I would have been in control of the company; (I had to propose that and similar corrections to Duff Hart-Davis recently when I read some of your reflections in galleys of his book about the *Telegraph*).

Nor do I, or will I, forget your contribution to the *Telegraph*'s revival, especially in recruiting talented personnel, encouraging and supporting radically innovative thinking about demanning, and helping to stabilise the company in its most difficult days. I agree with your very optimistic prognosis for the company; your services in achieving that transformation were valuable and you were well-appreciated and amply rewarded for them.

If I could not quite subscribe to your September 17 draft of a press announcement referring to yourself as the ' greatest thing since sliced bread', it is equally true that I thought you were being uncharacteristically self-deprecatory when you described yourself in July at Brooks's Club, in industrial relations matters, as a 'busted flush'.

For every personal and corporate reason, I will always endeavour to give you the benefit of the doubts that have arisen. Unfortunately, many will not.

Finally, it would be churlish of me not to wish you well in your new endeavours, which I surmise consist largely of trying to alleviate News International's widespread, and in my view, not wholly deserved reputation as a cynical and somewhat down-market operation. Good luck! Max Hastings has asked me to commend to you the merits of combining *The Times* and the

Sunday Times.

To be entirely serious, I do wish you and Sabina well, and will always remember the pleasant times we had together.
Yours sincerely,
Conrad

5 January 1990

Dear Conrad,
You have widely circulated your views without checking the most crucial facts – which are incorrect. Your charges are very grave, and I hope you might ask those friends to whom you have shown them to suspend judgement until I have been able to respond in a few days.

Meanwhile, I remember only our friendship and achievement.
Yours,
Andrew

7 January 1990

Dear Conrad,
On January 2 1990 you sent me an emotional and inaccurate letter. You wrote that your 'only interest in these matters is in avoidance of unnecessary damage' to my reputation. Three days later I learned you had sanctioned your letter being used by one of your own newspapers, from where it found its way to other national newspapers.

I will reply only to the wildest inaccuracies in your letter: First, you refer to my 'courtship' with Rupert Murdoch while I was chief executive of the *Daily Telegraph*. The truth is that during the autumn I told you, the deputy chairman, many *Telegraph* staff and outsiders that I had been under offer to be managing director at Wapping from Rupert Murdoch at various times. And that I was not going.

Rupert Murdoch appointed Gus Fischer as managing director. After this appointment, and long after I had ceased all executive functions at the *Telegraph*, he made me a new offer involving a different job, executive chairman, as his own replacement in Britain. This I accepted.

Second, you criticise me for taking up the appointment by a competitor too hastily. I ceased to be chief executive in October 1989, remaining thereafter as a non-executive director. I wrote to you on December 20 informing you that I would not entertain any starting date for the NI [News International] or any new job before mid-March 1990. I specifically mentioned that I would welcome your advice on the matter. For two weeks I did not hear from you and the announcement of my appointment was made on January 2.

There has been no indecent haste and you declined even to discuss the matter of a starting date when I suggested you do so.

Third, you say that when I sold a portion of my shareholding in the *Daily Telegraph*, I gave the purchaser to understand that I would continue indefinitely with the *Telegraph*. You assert that I did this only a week before announcing my retirement as chief executive on September 19.

This again is completely untrue. I sold the shares almost two months before the announcement of my retirement as chief executive. The sale was long prior to and completely unconnected with my retirement. You and I did not begin to discuss the consequences for me of your residence in London until August.

You were initially unwilling to talk yourself to the proposed purchaser of the shares when I said they wanted to meet you. When I spoke to them I emphasised my own enthusiasm for the *Telegraph*. But I also described at length your strength as the newly resident chairman, the role of the new managing director and the tremendous management and editorial strength I had installed.

You have provided a very jolly story for the newspapers but your letter says more about you than me.
Yours sincerely,
Andrew

In a further exchange of letters, Black responded: 'I advised you again and again to execute your departure without harm to your reputation. You followed your own counsel, and, demonstrably, your reputation has suffered. I didn't provide a "very jolly story for the newspapers". You did. In addition to being jolly, it is rather tawdry and disappointing.' Knight replied that he had been 'deluged with so many calls and notes of outrage at your conduct'. The same day as the first letters were published in the *Observer*, an un-bylined profile in the *Sunday Telegraph* (written by Worsthorne and another journalist, Frank Johnson) incorporated Black's lengthy first letter as part of an article headlined, 'The constant smiler with the knife'. It was accompanied with an illustration depicting Knight, in suit of armour, with weapons laid down, embracing a dragon with the head of Rupert Murdoch. It noted of his defection to News within an 'astonishingly short' period of leaving the *Telegraph* that, 'Among quality newspapers, only relatively junior employees would normally make so swift a change.' Ostensibly a profile, the piece ran brutally through Knight's career, remarking that in his previous incarnation as editor of *The Economist*, 'Knight's enemies would say that his bland *Economist* was a reflection of his personality.' Without any hint of irony, the article portrayed Knight as possessing 'a gift no so much (or merely) for buttering up the great and the good, the rich and the powerful, but for making them feel secure. He has long been an assiduous attender of those staging posts of the conventionally ambitious – international conferences. His contemporaries on the same circuit still talk of his technique, perhaps enviously: to wait for the most powerful people present to speak, then to agree with them, then to reinforce that agreement over cocktails afterwards. His is a world whose inhabitants describe themselves as "friends" of one another but really just know each from conferences.'

Conrad Black, the article noted, was 'Knight's luckiest contact'.

In the same day's *Sunday Times*, business editor Ivan Fallon described the piece as 'one of the most poisonous, score-settling pen profiles seen in journalism in recent years' while Knight deflected Black's attacks as 'the rather sad inaccuracies of a wounded lover'. William Rees-Mogg wrote in the *Independent*, 'Surely it cannot have been read by the *Sunday Telegraph*'s lawyer, who must know as well as anyone that malice invalidates a fair-comment defence to libel. This profile breathed malice in almost every paragraph.'

To Black's satisfaction, much of the London Establishment with whom he was becoming a regular supper guest or black-tie companion rallied around him. Within the *Telegraph* some executives expressed, as Max Hastings did, dismay that Knight had 'become chief apologist for somebody whose newspapers are daily doing things that I for one couldn't be party to'. Knight, meanwhile, put the episode behind him and set up his affairs in a commodious office at

Wapping, which included a comfortable living area complete with rocking chair, a space-age desk with a rack of News titles beside a wall of Sky Television screens, and a huge reproduction of one of the *Sun*'s classic front-page headlines: 'Freddie Star Ate My Hamster.'

At Hastings's urging, Black quickly unravelled the seven-day newspaper arrangement by first installing a separate editor of the *Sunday Telegraph* (although he did leave Hastings as editor-in-chief responsible for both titles). Despite the stumble of the seven-day notion, the strategy of moving the magazine to Saturday was paying off. By 1990 the *Saturday Telegraph* was outselling the *Sunday Times*, while the *Sunday Telegraph*, despite a declining sale, surpassed the circulation of the *Observer* to move from third into a distant second to the *Sunday Times*.

Now physically at the helm of the *Telegraph*, Black showed he could tolerate some journalists who had crossed him in the past. One was Charles Moore, who joined the *Telegraph* as deputy editor from the *Spectator* and became *Sunday Telegraph* editor in 1992. Moore's move to the *Telegraph* was intriguing because (even though his plans to join the *Telegraph* were already in the works) he had written critically of Black shortly before Black's move to England. And, as *Spectator* editor, he had commissioned the scathing 1985 John Ralston Saul profile of Black. When Moore criticised him, Black phoned and complained loudly about the piece, then wrote a letter for publication. 'Shortly after that,' recalls Moore, 'my twins were born prematurely and they nearly died. So Conrad sent me some flowers and good wishes about that, after all this stuff was published. And I wrote back and said, "It was very nice of you to send the flowers, etc. etc., I'm most grateful and I'm also very grateful for the sabbatical and the job that's coming up, and I think I've been treated generously when I didn't really have to be, in view of the fact that I've been pretty cheeky." And he wrote back, "Yes, that's right, you have been pretty cheeky." And you know, it's all over. Since then, fine. So he's sort of quietly buried the hatchet.'

Black had also been unimpressed with Moore and cartoonist Nicholas Garland over an entry Garland made in his subsequently published diary in 1986. It recounted a story Moore told after attending a dinner at 10 Downing Street for the retirement of former *Telegraph* editor Lord Deedes. 'Charles was very funny about Bill's dinner at Downing Street,' Garland wrote. 'At one stage of the evening the lights were dimmed in the drawing room so that the company could watch the Guards beating the retreat or flashing their colours or whatever they do. Everyone stood spellbound. But Conrad Black's act is apparently to be the one who knows everything, and he completely ruined the spectacle with an interminable monologue about the history of the uniforms and the origins of the ritual before them. Charles gave his spluttering laugh. "And it was so boring and pointless." ' Yet even after Garland defected to the *Independent* and his diaries were published as a book, Black approved his re-hiring by Hastings. To this day, Black has never spoken to Garland, but his satisfaction at raiding the *Independent* outweighs his feelings towards the book. 'I approved hiring him back from the *Independent* at an astronomical price but I refused to welcome him with open arms,' Black explained. 'If I met him I'd be perfectly civil. He's a good cartoonist. I wouldn't begrudge him anything – but that was an appalling book.'

After the Knight affair, Black reverted to his low British profile. Nonetheless, he was an object of growing curiosity in a country obsessed with press proprietors. 'Unlike, let's say, Rupert or unlike a lot of tycoons, Conrad loves to play,' contends Max Hastings. 'He adores to talk all night. One of the problems can be that his staying power is a good deal greater than mine as regards all this all-night gossiping.'

'I think the best way to describe it is he's not Rupert Murdoch, he's not Vere Rothermere,'* says Evelyn de Rothschild. 'I wouldn't say Conrad is a hands-on proprietor. I think he is interested intellectually in the content of his newspaper. I think he's quick to praise certain areas of good and bad. I think he's very interested in the standard of production, the quality of the paper. I think he's very interested in the type of people who work for him. But, at the same time he's also a businessman. He's interested, obviously, in the capitalist system of using funds to the best advantage.'

In London, many of the old Canadian myths about Black persisted, such as the notion that Black has a fanatical interest in Napoleon. This misconception may have been aided by the way Black often employs

* Rothermere's Associated Newspapers own the *Daily Mail* and *Sunday Mail*.

Napoleonic analogies to describe his business dealings, or by the fact
that he hung a portrait of the Emperor in his office, alongside various
naval battle scenes. 'His [Napoleon's] talents as a military
commander are, to say the least, rather impressive,' explained Black.
'His career was just so prodigious. His origins were so obscure and his
impact on Europe was so great that he's automatically an interesting
phenomenon. And add to all that, he obviously had enormous skill as
an administrator to maintain some sort of authority over so great an
area. And, finally, his talents as a myth-maker, as a self-romanticist,
are astonishing. How he managed to persuade the French public to
become nostalgic about him after all the carnage for which he was
largely responsible, is an amazing thing. Selling glory is a little hard
when the sole beneficiary of the glory is yourself – I mean, selling it to
the people who give up their lives and limbs for you. But all that said,
I've never found him an attractive personality, just a great talent. I
wouldn't go so far as Clarendon's statement of Cromwell, "He was a
great bad man." I don't think Napoleon was bad, but he had
psychopathic tendencies. He was indifferent, I think, to the misery
that arose at least partly in consequence of his policies. In certain areas
he was surprisingly unimaginative. As a statesman, he had no policy
really except making war.'

Indeed, Black says his greatest hero is Abraham Lincoln. 'Now
there was a man associated with a terrible war, but whose solicitude
for the victims was very real. And yet he made the conscious and no
doubt the difficult decision of pursuing the war to absolute victory in
the name of a just cause.'

One day, a London auction house announced that it was selling a
cache of exotic Napoleonic memorabilia including, apparently,
Bonaparte's preserved penis. A rumour swept through media circles
that Black had purchased the body part in question. Francis Wheen,
writing for the *Independent on Sunday*, phoned Black's office to ascertain
whether there was any truth in the rumour. Rosemary Millar, Black's
stoic assistant, said she would speak with the chairman about this
matter. She soon rang back with a prepared response: 'The proprietor
of the *Daily Telegraph* would like to go on the record to say that he does
certainly *not* own Napoleon's penis.'

Just as the Hollinger board had become a more high-profile
assembly with the likes of Campeau and Reichmann, so the board of

the *Telegraph* began to reflect Black's growing stature in British life. In August 1990 he added Lord Carrington, financier Sir James Goldsmith, the chairman of Jardine, Matheson Holdings Ltd, Henry Keswick, Evelyn de Rothschild, and British Airways chairman Lord King of Wartnaby. The addition of Goldsmith was particularly infuriating to Lord Hartwell, who remained on the board and had long despised Goldsmith for a hatchet-job written about Hartwell's wife Lady Pamela in a magazine once backed by Goldsmith. 'I couldn't and can't stand that man,' grumbled Hartwell. Black says that, as a courtesy, he spoke to Goldsmith about Hartwell. 'Jimmy assured me [that article] had nothing to do with him,' recalls Black. 'It was the editor who ran it and he didn't know he had run it. And I told Lord Hartwell that, and I don't know whether he believed me.' Nonetheless, Hartwell saw no need for the new faces around the board. 'I don't think non-executive directors are all the shout,' he said. 'If the company is controlled by one shareholder, there's no point in having non-executive directors. They might come up with some interesting idea, but as far as I can see they don't.'

The objection to Goldsmith was just one of the frequent protestations that the embittered Hartwell would make at board meetings. 'Hartwell goes out of his way to be irritating to Conrad,' says one *Telegraph* director. 'He likes being a naughty boy.' Another director said Hartwell was not the only director surprised when Black began to expand the *Telegraph* board a year after his move to London. 'Conrad, as is his way, suddenly announced he had a new slate of directors he wanted to add,' recalled the director. 'I think we have the biggest board in the country!' The same claim may have been true in Canada, where in 1990 the main board was twenty strong and Black created an additional thirteen-member International Advisory Board, a star-studded assembly of tycoons and pundits with whom Black could hold his own Bilderberg-style think-tanks. One observer described the board as 'a sort of *Almanach de Gotha* of the international right'.

The International Advisory Board brought together Dwayne Andreas, chairman of U.S. agricultural giant Archer Daniels Midland Co., Lord Hanson, Goldsmith, Lord Rothschild, former U.S. Assistant Secretary for International Security Policy Richard Perle (architect of Reagan's Star Wars initiative), former Canadian ambassador to the U.S. Allan Gottlieb, former Chairman of the U.S.

Federal Reserve System Paul Volcker, former assistant to the President of the U.S. for National Security Affairs Zbigniew Brzezinski, and well known American pundits David Brinkley, William F. Buckley Jr, and George Will. Henry Kissinger and Lord Carrington moved over from the main Hollinger board as Senior International Advisers. Additions in subsequent years included Fiat Chairman Dr Giovanni Agnelli, former president of Israel Chaim Herzog, and Dr Josef Joffe, editorial page editor for *Suddeutsche Zeitung*. Black's crowning catch was Margaret Thatcher, who, three years after her departure from politics, was placed at the top of the list as Honorary Senior International Adviser. The only living person whom Black would like to have on board but who politely declined his invitation is billionaire Berkshire Hathaway Inc. chairman Warren Buffett.* 'Conrad's role to some extent is to ingratiate himself in certain circles, and this does help,' says David Radler. 'Every one of these guys are pros at putting in off-the-record stuff. They do it for a living.'

The International Advisory Board meets once a year, holding topical round-table discussions on world political and economic affairs during the day and a dinner at night. Its members are paid like ordinary directors, which could be seen as a bargain when compared with the sums they command for public speaking engagements on the rubber chicken circuit: according to *Forbes Magazine*, Thatcher commands a bit less than US$60,000 for an appearance, Kissinger US$40,000, Brinkley US$30,000. And as advisory rather than regular board members, they do not share corporate directors' liabilities for such matters as signing off prospectuses and other company documents.

At the International Advisory Board meetings, the discussions, led by Black, are quite intense, says William F. Buckley. 'They're almost too rich, when you put those ten or twelve people in a room, convene at ten, have a lunch and get through it by three thirty or four,' says Buckley. 'A little bit *dizzy*, the amount of talent that can only be given ten or fifteen minutes each because of the hectic schedule. I guess the reasoning behind it is that you can't get people who include Kissinger and Thatcher and Brzezinski and George Will and so on and hang on

* Before Nixon's death in 1994, Black ventured he also would have liked to include him, 'if he were younger and more gregarious'.

to them for more than a day, day and a half. As I say, it's a little bit too rich for satisfactory exploitation – that is a little bit frustrating. Otherwise, it's a little bit bracing to run into each other and say hello.'

The meetings are held in different venues each year. In 1994, for instance, the meeting was held in Washington, D.C. with Republican presidential candidate Robert Dole as dinner speaker and Democrat Lloyd Bentsen at lunch. 'It was an experience, for me, second to none,' said Hollinger director Peter Munk. 'To have the president of Israel and Kissinger debating with Volcker and the head of Archer Daniels Midland – I mean, it's spectacular, it's informative, it's just fascinating.'*

The advisory board, says Black, is not a vanity collection of celebrities but a key ingredient in Hollinger's corporate success. 'Frankly,' explains Black, 'a lot of the use of these boards is to load them up with important people who can be helpful to you. I realise the allegation is about that I am somewhat of a seeker of celebrities, and in one sense I suppose that's true. But my purpose is that celebrities who are justly celebrated can be very useful to you. I'm interested in relationships that can be useful. I'm not interested just in trotting these people around.'

'The newspaper industry in London has long attracted proprietors of immense ego.' So began Black's review of a biography of Lord Beaverbrook in *Saturday Night*, which also noted that 'megalomania is an occupational hazard'. There was always a temptation to compare Black with the famous Canadians who had preceded him on Fleet Street and entered the House of Lords, Roy Thomson and Max Aitken. Like Black, Lord Thomson was devoutly committed to the bottom line. Unlike Black, Thomson had little interest in public life. Max Aitken, who became Beaverbrook, held more surface similarities to Black: he was a financier who moved to London in 1910 after unsuccessfully trying to buy a newspaper in Montreal. In 1917, he bought control of the *Daily Express*, and, at age thirty-seven, was elevated to the House of Lords. Like Black, Beaverbrook regarded himself as a historian. Unlike Black, Beaverbrook was known for a

---

* Soon after, Munk's Barrick Gold Corp. started its own international advisory board.

frenzied romantic life, maintaining a 'black list' of people banned from the pages of his papers, and for his statement that he ran the *Express* 'purely for the purpose of making propaganda'. Black said Beaverbrook 'will always remain a model of the panache and influence an aspiring media proprietor may seek to achieve, and some of the excesses and frailties of character and judgement one would wish to avoid'.

Charles Wintour, a former *Evening Standard* editor who worked for Beaverbrook, found after interviewing him that Black's style is quite different. 'He's very interesting in private conversation, but he's an extremely orotund and boring public speaker,' said Wintour. 'Whereas Beaverbrook was one of the great platform speakers of his day.'

Black did put on a performance reminiscent of 'the Beaver' in his staunch speech at the Centre for Policy Studies meeting at the Tory Party's Bournemouth conference in October 1990. Black warned against subsuming Britain's identity and currency through its participation in Europe, and that monetary union in particular would mean 'the British government would have lost all power over the currency, and all the ramifications of that power.' Indeed, Black thundered, if the House of Commons were to agree to such a thing, 'that ratification would be the last properly soverign act of our parliament'.

It was clear that Black had quickly adapted to his new role as a defender of Conservatism in England: during the course of his Bournemouth speech he used the words 'we', 'our', and 'us', no fewer than eighty-six times. This only added to growing speculation that Black would soon be following the other Canadians into the House of Lords. The gossip was fomented, in part, by Shirley Black's decision to change her first name. In fact, this was Shirley's decision and unrelated to her husband's ambitions. She simply never liked her name.

The subject arose during the summer of 1990, over dinner at the home of Sir Evelyn and Lady Victoria de Rothschild. At one point, Lady Rothschild said, 'I wish people would stop calling me Vicky. I would like to be called Victoria.' To which Shirley Black replied, 'What would you do if your name was Shirley?' Lady Victoria thought momentarily. 'Change it,' she said. As Conrad and Shirley rode home in the limousine, they ran through names. Her first thought was Catherine. 'Oh no. That's too common,' Conrad replied. Then she thought of the name she had wanted to call their daughter – Joanna – but didn't because it would have been too cute in tandem with brother Jonathan. She finally settled on Joanna Catherine Louise. When the Canadian press caught wind of her name change there was much fuss made about how 'Lady Shirley' did not roll off the tongue.

Black has always publicly played down the notion of a peerage, and he certainly would not pay for one as others had. That said, he privately ran through various titles he might like to be called if one were ever bestowed. He had not particularly liked his name to begin with, he joked, and did not wish to be called Lord Black. Perhaps 'Lord Ravelston', after his private holding company; 'Lord Haven-wold', after the name he christened his Toronto estate when he had a Black coat of arms created.* 'If Thatcher would have offered it,' says a close friend of Black's, 'he would have accepted it with enthusiasm.' All such musings, however, both public and private, faded when Thatcher was ousted as Tory Party leader and replaced by John Major. Black's, and the *Telegraph*'s, tepid feelings towards Major forestalled, for the moment, any suggestion of Black's being rewarded with a seat in the House of Lords. 'I used to see more of Thatcher. I used to call on her fairly often,' says Black. I always found her extremely stimulating until very late on in her term when she was a bit beleaguered and it was not such a pleasant experience. I mean she was perfectly nice but I felt like I was imposing on her a bit because she was so harried by events. But I see her a fair bit now.

'John Major, I don't call upon him in the same way. He invites me over sometimes and I do see him. I always enjoy talking to him, he's a perfectly nice man. He purports to agree with me on a lot of things. I don't have any great ideological problem with him. . . . While our relations are perfectly cordial there's not the same or even slightly comparable rapport that there was with her. I had considerable admiration for her and she knew that. And she was much more

---

* The coat of arms incorporates a book, an eagle, a plumline representing the fact that his family had come from abroad, sheaves of wheat for western Canada and fleur-de-lis for Quebec. The crest was hung above the front door at Havenwold and was incorporated in a large gold signet pinkie ring, a gift from Joanna.

comfortable with people in my – if I may put it this way – socio-economic echelon, and with John Major there have been times when I've exchanged real pleasantries with him, and I always do enjoy talking to him – there's no coolness or anything, everything's fine – but there isn't as automatically or spontaneously positive a basis to our relations as there was with his predecessor.'

Peerage or not, the beginning of the 1990s was a prosperous time for Black. Despite warnings of an oncoming recession, the *Telegraph* was performing well, with cash flow approaching $100 million. It had increased its cash in hand by selling its Reuters shares for £35 million and by selling its London office building in South Quay at a £14 million profit as part of an arrangement with Paul Reichmann to move the *Telegraph* into four floors of his struggling Canary Wharf development. *Telegraph* staff who bemoaned Docklands' remoteness from the City and the former Fleet Street joked that nearby Canary Wharf was at least 'a hundred yards closer to civilisation'.*

From his new perch in Europe's largest building, Conrad Black's horizon for newspaper acquisitions could extend virtually to the ends of the earth. 'Our cash flow,' Black mused, 'is almost entirely available for acquisitions and my associates and I may even some day be entitled to say, as Roy Thomson famously did when asked why he wanted to buy more newspapers: "To make more money"; and when asked why he wanted more money: "To buy more newspapers".

---

* A separate office for the City (business) section was opened closer to the action after much protesting about the lengthy cab and train rides required to get to interviews and lunches.

TEN

Australia's Newest Press Baron

'Who is better than Conrad Black at
running the Fairfax group?'
KERRY PACKER

On 9 November 1991, Warwick Fairfax flew from La Guardia to
Toronto's Lester B. Pearson Airport, where a car waited. Desperate
to salvage his control of a family empire incorporating Australia's
most esteemed newspapers, the dishevelled, bespectacled Fairfax was
en route to the neo-Grecian pillared façade of 10 Toronto Street. With
him, Bill Beerworth, his Sydney-based adviser, and Luis Rinaldini of
Lazard Frères, the New York investment bank.

The drive from the airport to Conrad Black's Toronto office takes
about half an hour. The small, three-storey building is tucked away on
a central side street, and behind it, a rarity in the city's business
community, it retains its own ground-level parking lot. Since moving
to London in 1989, Black had been an infrequent sight at 10 Toronto
Street. But on this gloomy, overcast day, his polished navy Cadillac
was stationed in the car park.

The grey-haired, grey-jacketed sentinels who watch over Black
Central ushered Fairfax through the double set of bullet-proof doors,
into the small reception area and upstairs to an ante-room near
Black's office. On offer was a stake in Fairfax's vaunted titles,
including the *Sydney Morning Herald*, Melbourne's *The Age*, and the
Australian Financial Review. Fairfax papers boasted a combination of
prestige and some of the richest operating profit margins in the
Western world. The problem was that three years earlier, Warwick,
then aged twenty-six, had borrowed A$2.1 billion to take the family
company private in the largest take-over in Australian history. It had
seemed like a good idea at the time.

In search of an investor, the Fairfax entourage had already trod similarly opulent corridors at some of the top North American newspaper groups – Washington Post Co., Tribune Co., New York Times, and Thomson. So far no takers. The lack of appetite was a testament both to the peculiar state of affairs at Fairfax and the fact that Black's Hollinger was one of the few newspaper groups with aspirations to global empire building. 'It didn't seem to appeal to us as an attractive financial opportunity, so we didn't pursue it,' said Ken Thomson. 'Now Mr Black is another story.'

'I would be a little bit leerier than Mr Black is about acquiring papers overseas,' observed New York Times chairman Arthur Sulzberger Sr. 'Papers are rather a personal thing to the community. I'm not sure that we can run a paper in Prague or the *Irish Echo* or whatever else it is going to be. We'll sell them our news service, but I think they have to be pretty home-grown.'

For others, the lack of interest in Fairfax was attributable to the Australian government's policy on foreign investment in the media – which was as woolly as a koala. But perhaps the largest deterrent for prospective investors in Fairfax was the dismal state of the Australian media industry. Virtually every well-known member of that country's legendary slate of media moguls was out of the running for Fairfax; they had either left the country, buckled under avalanches of debt (like Alan Bond), or, in one case (Robert Holmes à Court), died. Even Australia's most famous media baron, Rupert Murdoch, was in the throes of a debt crisis. If Warwick Fairfax didn't find capital soon, his would be the most spectacular disaster yet.

A quarter of an hour late, Black made his entrance. He spoke with familiarity about Fairfax's predicament, peppering his dialogue with a couple of military analogies. His visitors gained the distinct impression that Black was a tough businessman and negotiator, nobody's fool, and impossible to predict. Fairfax and his advisers pressed their case; Black's expression remained stony. If he was interested, he wasn't about to let on.

But Black had been eyeing Fairfax for some time. *Telegraph* chief executive Andrew Knight was quite taken with the Fairfax papers as early as 1986, when he flew to Sydney to negotiate the sale of part of the *Telegraph*'s Manchester plant to Rupert Murdoch. In those early days of Black's control of the *Daily Telegraph*, Black suffered from numbing bouts of trans-Atlantic jet lag. Half in jest, Knight raved to

Black from Australia about how the *Sydney Morning Herald* was bursting with advertisements on the day he was there. 'This Fairfax company is unbelievable,' Knight had gushed to Black over the phone. 'It's got the most fantastic classified advertising business I've ever seen in my life.'

'Andrew,' Black interjected, 'I find it hard enough to get on the airplane to come to London. Certainly you *can't* imagine me going back and forth to Australia.'

Two years later, Black was willing to make the sacrifice of trans-Pacific travel. In early 1988, Warwick and his then chief executive Peter King had visited Black at his Palm Beach home to solicit a bid for Melbourne's *The Age* newspaper. In April of that year, Black bought the *Spectator* from Fairfax, for about £2 million, and bid about A$500 million for David Syme & Co. Ltd, *The Age*'s publisher. The deal dissolved when Robert Maxwell bested Black's offer. This prompted a flurry of anti-Maxwell sentiment among *Age* journalists and prominent Melbournians, and the Australian government tightened foreign-ownership rules. The paper was taken off the auction block, but not before the *Telegraph* had completed the *Spectator* deal, which Fairfax had offered as a 'sweetener', recalled Dan Colson, Black's lawyer and chief deal adviser in London. 'In the end we took the bait but not the hook.'

Now Fairfax was available again, and Black assumed there would be other groups keeping watch as Fairfax circled the drain. Who else might be interested, he asked Warwick's crew? One of the advisers volunteered that Kerry Packer, Australia's richest man and a long-time Fairfax rival, would no doubt have his eye on the *Sydney Morning Herald* and perhaps other properties, despite having potential cross-media ownership problems. 'Oh, Kerry Packer,' Black nodded, 'Didn't he *take* a coronary?' The unusual construction stuck in one of his visitors' minds. 'From this, it seemed that Black didn't know Packer, but I suspect he knew him very well,' he says. In fact, Black had been introduced to the garrulous Australian five months earlier over dinner at the London home of financier Sir James Goldsmith, a mutual friend and *Telegraph* director. Packer's famous coronary had occurred in 1990 while he was enjoying one of his favourite pastimes, polo. He was carried from the Sydney polo field, was technically deceased for several minutes, but recovered and discharged himself from St Vincent's Hospital six days later. The episode had granted Packer a particular place in Australian lore – plenty of moguls are larger than life, but Kerry Francis Bullmore Packer was larger than death.

At Goldsmith's, Black and Packer had actually discussed the deteriorating Fairfax situation and agreed to stay in touch.

Black's meeting with Warwick was inconclusive. His advisers thanked Black for his time, and he thanked them for coming. Fairfax and his group took the limousine directly to the airport, where he and Beerworth grabbed the next available flight to Los Angeles, then Sydney.

Warwick Fairfax was named after a dynasty and the town that spawned it. John Fairfax, after whom the company was named, was a god-fearing man from the town of Warwick, in the heart of Warwickshire, England. Early printing and newspaper ventures left him a penniless man with a family to support. In 1838, with few immediate prospects, the thirty-two-year-old Fairfax secured passage for himself, his pregnant wife and three children, to Australia.

With ten pounds in his pocket, Fairfax found work, and soon rekindled his interest in the press. Three years later he and a court reporter from the *Sydney Morning Herald*, Charles Kemp, purchased the decade-old *Herald* for £10,000, most of which they borrowed. The paper prospered and in September 1853 Kemp sold his interest to Fairfax for £17,500. Over the years John's boys, James and Charles, became increasingly involved in the company and it came to be known as John Fairfax & Sons.

As the city of Sydney grew, it also became one of the fiercest newspaper battlegrounds anywhere. Yet the Fairfax clan managed to maintain the *Herald*'s predominance. The first Warwick Fairfax, John's grandson, an intellectual and the truest journalist the family ever produced, presided over the company from 1930 to 1976. Facing increasing competition – most notably from Frank (father of Kerry) Packer's *Daily Telegraph* and *Australian Women's Weekly* – Fairfax became expansionist, launching a *Sunday Herald* in 1949 and the *Australian Financial Review* in 1951. Other newspaper, television, radio, and magazine interests were built up, including the 1973 acquisition of control of *Age* publisher David Syme & Co. Ltd in Melbourne.

The events that led to the door opening to Conrad Black can perhaps best be traced back to the ousting of Sir Warwick Fairfax as the group's chairman in 1976. Senior managers engineered the overthrow with the backing of Warwick's son James and of John B. Fairfax, son of Sir Warwick's brother Sir Vincent. James and John were motivated in part by the chairman's age but also by his increasing disagreeableless and autocracy. Another factor was the meddling ways of his flamboyant third wife, Lady Mary.

The complex relationship between mother and son – Lady Mary and young Warwick – would figure predominantly in the débâcle yet to come. As a member of a Polish Jewish family that emigrated to Australia in the 1920s, the former Mary Symonds was a sharp contrast to the rigid and reserved Fairfaxes. After she married Sir Warwick amid a swirl of controversy and headlines in 1959 (both had been married when they met), Mary soon became the self-styled 'Queen of Sydney Society'. Among other things, she appalled her in-laws by disregarding the family custom of leaving the Fairfax name out of the society columns.

'Sydney had never seen parties like Lady Fairfax's,' observed a profile in *Vanity Fair*, 'which featured everything from after-dinner opera recitals to ice kangaroos with caviar in their pouches. For a Freedom from Hunger Campaign fund-raiser, she staged a poolside fashion show for dogs. The invitation to a 1983 bash for the Australian Opera Trust Fund, at which the guest of honour was *Chariots of Fire* producer David Puttnam, asked guests to "Bring Your Own Candelabra". But she made her biggest splash in 1973, with the party she gave the night after the inauguration of the Sydney Opera House, inviting all the glamorous guests who'd flown in for that event, including the Queen of England. Elizabeth II didn't attend, but Imelda Marcos did, and the band struck up "Ho, Ro My Nut Brown Maiden" as she entered.'

By the time of his ousting, Sir Warwick's interest in Fairfax – some seventy-four per cent around the time he married Mary – had been diminished to twelve per cent through disbursements to other family members. James, Sir Warwick's son by his first marriage, owned about eighteen per cent. John's father and Warwick's brother, Sir Vincent, held another fourteen per cent. After the palace *coup*, James was appointed chairman.

Sir Warwick ceased speaking to James for four years, but not before telling him icily that young Warwick, then aged fifteen, had been given 'the full story, so that he would know the sort of man his brother was'.

Sir Warwick died in January 1987. James was still firmly ensconced in the chairman's office, and cousin John was his deputy. Warwick was studying for his MBA at Harvard at the time. He had not lived in Australia since 1979, and was increasingly involved with a U.S. fundamentalist Christian group. Warwick was as bland and introverted as his mother was boisterous and social. No one in the family or company save Lady Warwick had an inkling that he bore grievances against the way the Fairfax group was being managed, even though he was invited to board meetings. Nor did they realise that he was convinced the company, with the family holding 48.6 per cent of the shares, was vulnerable to an outside take-over.

James and John were surprised when Warwick phoned from Boston a month after attending Sir Warwick's funeral in Sydney and suggested that together they should purchase another 1.5 per cent of the company to gain absolute majority control. James and John did not agree. Warwick elected to do it himself, with a borrowed A$30 million. In one of the legion of ironies of the Fairfax saga, under a trust arrangement Warwick would have eventually inherited a block of shares from James and likely succeeded him as chairman. Although his eventual ownership would theoretically have been worth about half a billion dollars, Warwick had no income or ability to pay the interest on the A$30 million.

By launching a bid for Fairfax, Warwick could not only avenge his father, please his mother and replace what he considered an ineffectual management, he could stave off his own looming financial crisis. All that was required was a billion or two. Warwick found a willing adviser in Laurie Connell, an aggressive Perth merchant banker.*

Arrangements were put in place which called for, among other things, the borrowing of A$1.3 billion to buy out non-family

---

* Connell commanded an A$100 million success fee, which was subsequently contested.

shareholders, the sale of assets to repay debt, and a public sale of David Syme stock.

Late one Sunday night in August 1987, only hours before the public announcement, the family was informed of Warwick's bid. Then Warwick learned of his first big misjudgement: the notion that James, John and other family members would remain as minority shareholders after the buy-out. They had even less regard for Warwick's abilities than Warwick had for theirs. They would have to be bought out in full.

By the time world stock markets crashed on 19–20 October 1987, the family members had also cranked up Warwick's bid price, and Warwick faced a take-over cost of more than A$2 billion. There was still time to withdraw the offer, but he plunged ahead.

Three years later – a month after Warwick's meeting in Toronto with Conrad Black – the Fairfax receivership was announced. That same day, Warwick's mother called Mark Burrows, the Fairfax banks' adviser, to see if he might use his influence with the banks and others to get Warwick a junior reporter's job. 'He's really quite interested in newspapers,' Lady Mary enthused.

No job offer was forthcoming. Warwick and his American wife retreated to Chicago, and later Annapolis, Maryland, far from the familial complexities and the gleefully contemptuous media coverage. Several months after the fall of the empire, living in the bungalow he and his wife shared with their newborn son in a quiet Illinois suburb, Warwick gave a rare interview to the *Herald*'s weekend magazine, which featured such revelations as: 'This may sound ironic, but I'm not a big fan of huge debt.'

Yet another irony of Warwick's folly is that the members of the family he held in contempt were richly paid for their stock, and advisers to the company were rewarded to the tune of some A$100 million during his three years as proprietor. Warwick's personal loss was estimated at A$500 million.

James, despite the family tensions and his other interests, had been a proponent of continuing the dynasty. His plan had been to retire in 1991 (the sesquicentennial of Fairfax ownership of the *Herald*), passing the chairmanship to deputy John Fairfax who would continue to bring Warwick along until he was ready for the role. Cousin John saw things differently. He and Sir Vincent sold their shareholdings to

Warwick for A$306 million and purchased some of Fairfax's smaller publishing assets, which became the nucleus of a successful company called Rural Press.

The emotional shock of the buy-out having faded by 1993, John B. Fairfax commented thankfully one day in his office that his own children, then in college, were not bound to a sixth-generation of ownership. John reckoned that had Warwick not made his fateful bid, 'one day it probably would have been up to me to do something, because I don't think the two families would ever have got on terribly well together.' In his own quirky way, Warwick couldn't agree more: 'Once upon a time there was a dynasty,' he told the *Herald* when asked what he would someday tell his infant son of what had transpired. 'Fortunately, it's over.'

Black has certainly heard all the strange stories, but is uncharacteristically mild on the topic of Warwick Fairfax. 'I'm not one of those who heaps scorn on Warwick,' Black said. 'I found him a perfectly pleasant young man. But by the last time I saw him he no longer had anything to bring to the party.'

Black may have identified something familiar to him in Warwick, a young man driven by inner demons to launch an audacious take-over bid which he believed would somehow set things right. The only difference was that Black's take-over or Argus made him; Warwick's take-over of Fairfax broke him. And Black was there to pick up the pieces.

Not even a man with a well-developed sense of destiny like Conrad Black would have bet that within a year of his previous meeting with Warwick he would be the central character in one of the most vicious and highly politicised take-over battles that Australia had ever seen. By the time it was over, Black would have crossed swords with no less than three former prime ministers, legions of journalists, and bitter corporate rivals. 'This is one of the great institutions of Australia and one of the great newspaper companies of the English-speaking world,' Black growled after the six-month brawl for Fairfax. 'And for its fate to be settled in a spectacle of political influence-peddling like that is nothing that anybody involved in it should be proud of in my opinion.' Still, like a medieval conqueror, Black is clearly pleased with his campaigns in the Southern hemisphere. 'I always look forward to going there and I always enjoy myself when I am there,' he reflected. 'It's a fabulous country in a funny way. But it is a different culture and a faraway place and assimilating it can't be done overnight.'

Despite the recession that was battering newspapers in Britain and North America, Black was in a secure financial position to resume his global newspaper hunt. So he was ready when Kerry Packer phoned in May 1991 and said it was time to get serious about Fairfax.

Black might also have found the diversion helpful. This was a time of personal change and introspection for Black. He and his wife Joanna were in the process of separating after thirteen years together. At the same time, aged forty-seven, he had just taken to writing his memoirs, perhaps in part to take his mind off an unhappy domestic situation.

Commercially, however, these were confident times. In the year ended 31 December 1990, the *Telegraph* achieved a profit of £34.7 million on turnover of £222.1 million. Although the company's budgets would be reduced as advertising revenue fell, the *Telegraph* would prove to be more profitable than all the other quality UK dailies combined during the recession of the early 1990s.

More important to Black than profit and loss columns is cash flow – the amount of actual cash available to finance activities in a given year. In 1990 it was holding steady at £32.6 million – enough to cover interest payments on debts ten times that size. On top of that, the *Telegraph* had another £40 million in cash on hand. 'A company's cash flow is like a dictator's army,' Black once explained. 'You've got to do something with it. You can't just stand around like Franco's Guardia Civil, waiting for something to happen.'

A Fairfax bid gathered momentum amid a flurry of telephone calls and faxes over the next few weeks. Black and Packer met twice more in Packer's suite at the London Savoy. And the more Black looked at the numbers, the more he liked what he saw. During the three years ended 30 June 1991, Fairfax had incurred operating losses of almost A$600 million against financing expenditures of almost A$800 million. But beneath the crippling interest charges, board room instability, and the recession, the underlying newspaper businesses had fared very nicely. In the fiscal year 1991, the company had a pre-tax and pre-interest operating margin of 16.5 per cent, which is better than many newspapers in non-recessionary times. Black knew that Packer would be limited to a fifteen per cent ownership in the company because of cross-media ownership laws.*

Black, meanwhile, set his sights on being Fairfax's largest shareholder, with at least twenty per cent of the company.

Packer had invited another foreign partner into the deal: San Francisco-based investment bank Hellman & Friedman. The investment bank managed large pools of money and had been looking to make its first investment outside the U.S. On one level, Hellman's participation seemed superfluous. The *Telegraph* would provide the newspaper expertise and Packer would be a financial partner. The level of foreign participation allowed by the Australian government would be limited. So every bit of Hellman's involvement meant less ownership for Black. He went along with Hellman's inclusion, however, in the spirit of his discussions with Packer.

From Packer's point of view, he liked what he knew of Black but did not know him well. They agreed on politics, and they had friends in common, including Goldsmith and John Aspinall. Nevertheless, Hellman was more familiar to Packer than Black, and he liked the idea of a partner whose interest, combined with his, could give him control down the road.

Since being appointed receiver and adviser to the Fairfax banks in December 1990, Mark Burrows of Baring Brothers Burrows & Co Ltd had been laying the groundwork in Sydney for an auction of the newspaper business. Burrows's clients, ANZ Bank and Citibank, ranked first among creditors and were owned A$1.27 billion. As a result of a refinancing by Michael Milken's Drexel Burnham Lambert in January 1989, a further A$550 million in junk bonds were outstanding. Other unsecured creditors brought the total Fairfax owed to some A$1.85 billion. Burrows determined that the best plan for the banks was to keep the Fairfax group intact.

Every Australian investment house was on the prowl for a piece of the Fairfax fee bonanza. Among the canniest players was Malcolm Bligh Turnbull, a fiery, brainy former lawyer whose firm's merchant banking services had been retained by Warwick three years earlier to

---

* Packer owned the Nine Network, highest rated among the country's three commercial television networks.

elicit bids for *The Age*. Now, Turnbull & Partners was retained as the bondholders' exclusive adviser. Turnbull knew the bondholders felt deceived by some of the figures put forward by Warwick and the banks in 1989. And since they ranked behind the bank debt in seniority, there was good reason to believe that the bondholders would be left in the cold.

Turnbull reckoned he could arrange for the junk bonds to be paid at least thirty cents in the dollar in a Fairfax sale. His strategy hinged on suing the banks for having earlier misrepresented the company's financial health. Turnbull liked to say this didn't just give the bondholders a seat at the table, they were nailed to it. Without their consent, the litigation could tie the company up indefinitely. Turnbull's view was that an exclusive arrangement with the bond-holders could prove a major strategic advantage for one of the Fairfax bidders.

Initially, Burrows was not overly concerned with the bondholders. His legal advice was that the bondholders' case was not a strong one. Moreover, he could sell Fairfax's assets instead of the whole company, which would skirt the bondholders entirely. The downside of doing this was that the buyers would have to pay stamp duty and would not gain access to Fairfax's significant accumulated tax losses.

One of the first bidders Turnbull approached, Irish newspaper owner and H. J. Heinz Co. chief executive Tony O'Reilly, apparently concurred with the receiver's view and decided not to deal with the bondholders. Meanwhile, brokerage firm Ord Minnett teamed up with Turnbull to bring the bondholders into a consortium and underwrite the eventual deal (gaining Turnbull & Partners another success fee). Ord executive Neville Miles and Turnbull together sold the idea to Kerry Packer, who was an old friend and occasional client of both men.

Black and Dan Colson met Packer and his son Jamie for a luncheon in Packer's lavish suite at the Savoy in May. Ord Minnett and Turnbull & Partners put together a strategy for prospective Fairfax buyers and flew to London to present it to Packer and Black. The Ords people produced a proposal that, in the words of one of its architects, 'read like a military document' because they had researched the Canadian and knew of his interest in military history.* The first formal meetings of the full consortium took place at the Savoy on Monday, 3 June 1991, with Turnbull, Miles, and Hellman & Friedman executive Brian Powers among those attending.

Black strode in at about three p.m., some five hours into the meeting. Packer dominated the proceedings, as always, speaking in short bursts punctuated with profanities. Black, statesmanlike by comparison, was quiet and controlled, occasionally pronouncing words longer than entire Packer sentences. Whereas Black liked to surround himself with the business and political intelligentsia, Packer seemed happiest when touring the world with a posse of ex-boxers and golf pros. Black spent his waking hours in snug-fitting business attire; Packer's taste ran to baggy track suits. 'They're both very focused about what they want in business, very single-minded about getting it, and good tacticians at getting things done,' observed one person who knows both men. 'They're not as different as you'd guess. Stylistically they're different but not incompatible partners at all.'

Partnerships are not Black's style. But in this case, he could see clear advantages to joining forces with Australia's richest man. A lead investment in Fairfax would gain Hollinger even greater stature on the world stage. The Australian newspaper market was carved up neatly between Fairfax and News Corp., Rupert Murdoch's company.† Between its national broadsheet, *The Australian*, major market tabloids and smaller holdings, News accounted for sixty-two per cent of all papers in the country. Fairfax produced a further twenty per cent, but the prestige and influence of its titles considerably outstripped Murdoch's.

Under the initial proposal, the *Daily Telegraph* would take a twenty per cent interest in the company which would purchase Fairfax. The vehicle would be an Australian shelf company called Tourang. Packer would take the maximum 14.99 per cent allowed under cross-media laws, and Hellman & Friedman would take another fifteen per cent.

From Packer's standpoint, an investment of around A$180 million wasn't a huge amount to fret over. 'Okay guys, we've now done the

---

* A deal with the debenture holders, the document proposed, 'represents a unique opportunity to exclude all other potential bidders from the sale process and thereby give control of [Fairfax] without the need to become involved in either an expensive bidding duel or extensive legal proceedings'.
† The British subsidiary is News International.

deal,' Packer declared at one point. 'You go and fix it, and I'm going to go and play polo.'

Black said his participation in the bid would be handled by Colson. The Irish-blooded Montreal-born son of a police detective was no stranger to complicated deals – during a three-year stint in Hong Kong, Colson had done everything from financing duck farms in China to handling major investments in Canada for Hong Kong billionaire Li Ka-Shing. Fairfax would be his most complicated and acrimonious assignment yet.

Black invited Turnbull, Powers and the rest of the team to the *Telegraph* the day after the Savoy meeting. In his office, Black was a genial host, good cop to Colson's bad cop as the lawyer openly scoffed at Turnbull and his bondholder agreement. Colson and Turnbull had clashed during Black's 1988 bid for Melbourne's *The Age*; the Aussie's reappearance representing the bondholders on the one hand and the consortium underwriters on the other reinforced Colson's impression that he was dealing with a tireless opportunist. Neverless, no objection was raised when Turnbull added that he wanted to be the bondholders' representative on the Fairfax board once the deal was done.

Turnbull, it seemed, knew everyone in Australia's small, closely connected business community. In addition to his Fairfax work, Turnbull also had links to Packer, having worked for him as a young barrister, becoming at one point his personal legal adviser. A 1984 profile on Turnbull in *Business Review Weekly* was headlined, 'Thirty, Rich and Kerry Packer's Lawyer'. But Packer was not Turnbull's most famous client, for in 1987 Turnbull achieved near-hero status through his successful defence against the British government's prosecution of the publication of the book *Spycatcher*.

Although Black and Packer had agreed at the Savoy that the bondholders would receive A$125 million in return for the exclusivity agreement, Colson sparred with Turnbull, dismissing the figure as too high. Colson was determined to make it plain from the outset that the people who would be driving the Fairfax transaction were those who put up the money, not those trying to salvage a bad investment in junk bonds.

Tourang and its bid for Fairfax were not yet public knowledge, but Black couldn't resist dropping a few boastful hints at the Hollinger

The Rileys in Winnipeg: Conrad Black's mother Betty (née Riley) sits second from the right; his father George stands third from the left. George later wrote that he was grateful that Betty's family 'bore my callow unsophistication with benign indulgence'.

Riley family group, Christmas 1953: Conrad, aged nine, sits on the stairs, (third row back), his father to his left. Monte is standing on the stairs on the far right; Betty Black stands fourth from the left, in the second row.

The 'Boy Wonder
of Canadian Business':
Conrad Black around
the time of his
stunning takeover
of Argus Corp.

Conrad and Montegu Black at the 1987 Hollinger annual meeting.
Conrad had bought out his older brother the previous year, once
almost all of Argus had been sold off. 'He was the logical one to
carry on,' said Monte, 'and I was very happy to move on.'

Financier Hal Jackman, now Lieutenant-Governor of Ontario, kisses the hand of Conrad Black. 'It may not seem so in the press,' says Jackman of Black, 'but he's always making fun of himself and the people who are subservient to him.'

Joanna and Conrad Black noshing popcorn at the twentieth anniversary party of Toronto Sun Publishing at the SkyDome in Toronto in November 1991. Despite appearances, the Blacks were already estranged. They were divorced the following June after almost fourteen years of marriage.

At a rehearsal at his Park Lane Circle home in October 1986 for the fundraising spoof *Much Ado About Something*. In the photo, taken by his wife, Black is dressed as Caesar and joined by comedian Don Harron, who penned the script for the event.

Dan Colson (*below left*), Black's long-time legal and tactical adviser and now Chief Executive of the Telegraph group. Colson negotiated some of Black's biggest deals, including the acquisition of the Telegraph and John Fairfax. Here, he answers questions at a press conference after winning Fairfax in late 1991. Colson, says Telegraph director Rupert Hambro, is 'absolutely impossible to roll over'.

Peter White (*below*), with whom Black began in the newspaper business in 1966 at the *Eastern Townships Advertiser* – a publication White had bought for one dollar.

The directors of the *Daily Telegraph* in 1988, in the midst of the paper's
dramatic turnaround. The former proprietor Lord Hartwell – standing behind
Black, on the right – looks considerably less pleased than the new owner.
Top row: Adrian Berry, Harbourne Stephen, David Radler, David Montagu,
Lord Camrose, Lord Hartwell, Lord Rawlinson, Daniel Colson, Rupert Hambro.
Bottom row: Alan Rawcliffe, Joe Cooke, Sir Frank Rogers, Conrad Black,
Andrew Knight, Tony Hughes, Anthony Rentoul (Secretary).

The old *Daily Telegraph* offices in Fleet Street and (right) the new
ones at One Canada Square in Canary Wharf, Europe's largest office
tower.

A happy – but short-lived – triumvirate: Shortly after Hollinger outbid Robert Maxwell for the *Jerusalem Post*, new chairman David Radler (*centre*) poses with *Post* editors Erwin Frenkel (*right*) and Ari Rath. Within months, both men were gone and the traditionally liberal paper was under the control of publisher Yehuda Levy.

(*left*) Yehuda Levy, the former Israeli military colonel put in charge of the *Jerusalem Post*. He had not read the *Post* before being appointed, but Radler liked the way he bridged Israeli and North American business cultures. Levy 'proved his courageousness in the battles'.

(*right*) Hollinger president Radler, Black's implausible *alter ego* and partner for a quarter-century, throwing out the first pitch at a baseball game in Israel. Radler is based in Vancouver and Black in London, but, says Radler, 'We run a certain wavelength.'

Kerry Packer (*above left*), Australia's richest man and a one-time partner in the battle for John Fairfax. Now he is a major Fairfax shareholder and Black's chief rival for control of the country's premier newspaper chain. Black, claims Packer, 'has no right to control John Fairfax'.

Paul Desmarais (*above right*), the Canadian tycoon whose Power Corporation bought into Southam alongside Black, creating an uneasy alliance. The two men agreed to take the post of chairman on alternate years. Desmarais considers Black 'a character'.

Global media baron Rupert Murdoch, who launched a price war between his *Times* and Black's *Daily Telegraph* in September 1993 – the biggest commercial threat of Black's career. 'Don't worry about the *Telegraph*,' Murdoch told another newspaper executive. 'Leave them to me. I'll put them out of business for you.'

THE RUPERT ✦ MURDOCH

No. 61,994

HAVE THEY GOT VIEWS FOR YOU.

The Conrad Black

No. 61,240

Heir to the throne . . . in TV show . . . and escapes unscathed in aircraft scare

THE INDEPENDENT INDEPENDENT

The *Independent*'s advertising campaign in response to the price war between Black's *Daily Telegraph* and Rupert Murdoch's *Times*. Black actually looked at buying the *Independent* but pulled out when the price seemed too high.

Conrad Black and Barbara Amiel on the steps of Chelsea
Registry Office in London, where they were married on 21
July 1992. It was the beginning of a fabled power-coupling,
evoking comparisons with Henry and Clare Booth Luce.
'You couldn't think of two people with more differing
backgrounds,' observed a friend, 'and yet they really are soul
mates.'

The Blacks mingle with Margaret Thatcher at the wedding of the son of Thatcher's former senior adviser, Sir Charles Powell, in 1993. When Black and Thatcher first met in 1986 it was, says Powell, 'love at first sight – in a political sense'.

Black is inducted into the Canadian Privy Council by Queen Elizabeth, with then Prime Minister Brian Mulroney, and Governor-General Ray Hnatyshyn.

(*above*) Former U.S. president Richard Nixon attending the
Hollinger Dinner in 1992; (*below*) Henry Kissinger attending the
annual meeting in 1989. Black's attraction to luminaries may look
like shameless social-climbing, but Black claims it is just good
business. 'I'm interested in relationships that can be useful,' he says.
'I'm not interested in just trotting these people around.'

The press baron defending the future of newspapers at the World Economic Forum in Davos, Switzerland, in January 1995. Despite troublesome statistics and gloomy talk about information super-highways, on the future of print, Black contends: 'The best is yet to come.'

annual meeting at Toronto's Royal York hotel later in June. He had spoken for some years about using Hollinger's cash flow for acquisitions 'when economic conditions open up such opportunities'.

Black could also not resist noting that Bob Rae's socialist Ontario government had indirectly encouraged companies like Hollinger to seek better prospects elsewhere. 'The government of Ontario appears to believe that capitalists, including average shareholders, are omnivorous and undiscriminating predators who will greedily pursue a one per cent return on their investment or gross revenues with just as much ardour as they would forage for a ten or twenty per cent return,' Black waxed. 'The inevitable consequences of these misconceptions are that capital and talented people will avoid or flee Ontario until a more favourable climate returns.'

An investment like the one he was privately planning, would allow Hollinger 'to avoid being unduly inconvenienced by exactly the sort of absurd and punitive parochialism that is now being inflicted in Ontario'.

While in Toronto, Black was also visited in his office on 18 June by Trevor Kennedy. A one-time Fairfax journalist, for the past twenty years Kennedy had been running Packer's magazine publishing arm, Consolidated Press. Over the years, Kennedy had been close to the tycoon but by 1990 had wanted to move beyond Consolidated and Packer. They had agreed that by June 1992 – Kennedy's fiftieth birthday – he would take his leave. By the time he met Black, Kennedy had set his sights on becoming chief executive of Fairfax, and had even been lobbying the Fairfax banks.

Kennedy's ambition was encouraged by Turnbull, whom he had known a long time. In fact Kennedy had been one of Turnbull's referees for his Rhodes scholarship. Both men's links with Packer would soon prove to be a greater problem for the Tourang consortium than anticipated. Under the Australian Broadcasting Act, there was a possibility that they could be considered 'associates' of Packer. If they were, the Australian Broadcasting Tribunal could deem that Packer held *de facto* control of Tourang and so contravened the cross-media ownership rules which limited him to a passive minority position of under fifteen per cent. More importantly, if the ABT called an inquiry into the matter, Tourang might be unable to close the bid much before April 1992. Not only was that well past

Baring Brothers Burrows & Co's autumn deadline to have the sale resolved, but on 16 January Tourang's exclusive agreement with Turnbull's bondholders expired.

On the other hand, as long as Black had the lead shareholding in the consortium, there seemed to him little reason to worry about the ABT. Black liked Kennedy and put him forward for the managing director's job at Tourang, agreeing that having a respected native of Australia lined up would smooth the way politically and with the banks.

In *The Bulletin*, the news magazine published by Packer's Consolidated Press, Black gave a curious account of how the Tourang consortium came together, one that underscored that he, not Packer, was the bid's driving force. 'Kerry's involvement arose out of my seeking to hire Trevor Kennedy as the prospective managing director of the Fairfax group were we to gain control of it,' the magazine quotes him as saying. 'Since I knew Kerry, I thought this would be a gross breach of protocol if I did not ask him in advance. When I did, he said he would not stand in the way of any man's career but if I did go ahead he would like a piece of the deal. I agreed.' Black recounted a similar version to the *Financial Post*, saying of Kennedy: 'I wasn't just going to raid this guy without talking to him [Packer].'

Black's hectoring style invariably projects a mien of self-importance. Yet he's also able to see the absurdity that comes with being a magnet for attention. The sight of his face glaring out from the cover of *The Bulletin* and advertisements for it bemused Black when he arrived in Sydney in mid-July for Tourang's official launch. Kennedy whisked him, in a white Rolls-Royce, from clusters of media men and women at the airport, to Ord Minnett's Grosvenor Place offices. In the lobby, a second crowd of media people awaited Black. Showing little evidence of jet lag, he toyed with the eager crowd. How would he like to be seen in Australia, asked one reporter. 'As the Samaritanly philanthropist that I am,' Black quickly replied. 'I'm just here to help you, you know that.'

On seeing the quote in the *Herald* the next day, Hellman & Friedman's Brian Powers asked in amazement: 'Conrad, did you really say that?'

'Yes,' Black replied with a grin. 'I suppose I did get a bit carried away.'

At the thirty-fourth-floor offices of Ord Minnett, each of the board rooms is named after a stock index – All Ords, Nikkei, Hang Seng, etc. Until this was explained to him, Black was a bit miffed that one was called the Financial Times. Why couldn't they have a board room named after the *Telegraph*?

The day after Black's arrival in Australia he spent in Canberra with Kennedy, meeting briefly with prime minister Bob Hawke and treasurer John Kerin (whose responsibilities included foreign investment), and lunching with communications minister Kim Beazley at the glass-encased Carousel restaurant. Media crews peered through the windows snapping photographs while Black, Kennedy, Beazley and his adviser Patrick Walters noshed uncomfortably.

There was no question that the Fairfax prize would be the most politicised prize Black had yet pursued. The federal government had a large degree of discretion in determining the appropriate level of overseas ownership. 'I hope that my arrival,' Black told *The Bulletin*, 'will dispel the notion that I have cloven feet and pointy ears.' In reality, there were few, if any, preconceptions about Black. As he would soon discover, Packer was the lightning rod. 'It is the fellow sitting next to you who will be the problem,' Beazley noted during their meal, nodding at Kennedy. Black paused, then turned to his executive, 'Okay, Trevor, you're sacked.' The lunchers all laughed.

Black flew to Toronto for the summer, satisfied that he had played his part well. As far as the bid itself went, he wasn't thrilled with receiver Burrows's efforts to exchange confidential Fairfax information for an indication of how much Tourang would bid. In response, Black warned, via an interview with the *Financial Post*, that he was not willing to win Fairfax at any cost and would not be drawn into an all-out bidding war. 'I've lived throughout the whole of my life up until two weeks ago without even being in Australia,' Black declared. 'I could continue without ever seeing it again. Don't get me wrong, it's a very nice place.'

Still, Black was in daily contact with Colson, who was becoming a fixture in Sydney hotels, switching whenever he realised he knew the room service menu better than most of the staff. During the next twenty-two months, Colson would make nineteen punishing trips from London to Australia. To pass the time, he would try to keep up with his friend's intellectual pursuits, on one trans-Pacific flight reading a voluminous tome on nineteenth-century British Cardinal John Henry Newman, one of Black's favourite subjects, and a three-volume biography of Richard Nixon.

Black also spoke regularly with the other key players in Tourang. But he saw no pressing need to be in Australia working on the cut and thrust of the deal. Rather, he could confer with his field marshal, Colson. 'If it had been necessary for me to be there I would have gone. But I didn't see the need. You can make a study of command techniques,' Black explained. 'Someone like MacArthur did both. Some of his greatest actions were right when he was at the front himself, and equally brilliant ones were when he was hundreds of miles away.'

Even without Black, the front was getting crowded. Two other serious bidders had emerged, one local, the second another high-profile foreigner. The local group had money and was, in theory, politically attractive. Australian Independent Newspapers was a blue-chip group of Melbourne-based investors backed by major institutions and headed by former Qantas chairman Jim Leslie.

The other entry, Tony O'Reilly, was certainly a busy man when he decided to go after Fairfax. This was the year the former rugby international was paid US$75 million as chairman of H. J. Heinz, earning him the title of world's highest paid executive. While taking home US$205,000 a day for running Heinz, he also found time to purchase thirty per cent of Waterford Wedgewood, to sponsor rugby's World Cup, and to bid for Fairfax. In his native Ireland, O'Reilly also controlled the Irish Independent group, the country's largest media group, which published about sixty per cent of the country's newspapers. A profile in Black's *Sunday Telegraph* dubbed the flamboyant O'Reilly 'The Great O'Gatsby of Ireland', his country home 'Ireland's Camelot'. Although Black called O'Reilly a friend, he dismissed him as a ketchup salesman and the 'world's greatest leprechaun', a poseur who, despite his enormous income that year, lacked the means to play in Tourang's league.

On the surface, foreign ownership would be less of an obstacle for

O'Reilly's Australian Provincial Newspaper group. APN was a modest chain of thirteen regional newspapers printing about 250,000 copies daily. O'Reilly had first travelled 'down under' in 1959 while touring with the British Lions rugby team and three years later had married an Australian. They had six children, and eldest son Cameron was deputy chief executive of APN.

But the word from Colson and the other partners was that Tourang had the edge. Despite the all-Australian group's institutional backing, it was not favoured by key members of the Labour caucus for political reasons. And commercially it lacked the other bidders' record of real newspaper proprietorship.

Tourang also believed its bid was more credible than O'Reilly's. Unlike the Irish mogul's offer, it would pay all cash, no so-called 'soft equity'.* Also, Tourang had the exclusive bondholder agreement in hand. 'I was always amazed that this kind of Mickey Mouse, rinky-dink bid was taken seriously at all,' Black later mused. 'It's only a credit to O'Reilly's *showmanship* and his *panache* that anybody could attach any credence at all to that fly-by-night bid.'

The biggest factor against Tourang was the Packer connection – but seeing as Black would not have been there at all without the Australian, there was nothing he could do about that. And when it came to making Tourang's case in Canberra, Packer's renowned lobbying apparatus was in full motion.

It needed to be. Fairfax journalists and many prominent politicians were lining up against Packer's bid. Along with the legitimate political concern about media concentration, there was an undercurrent of fear that Packer saw this as payback time for journalists who had written critically about him in the past. Black and others repeatedly reassured Tourang's critics that there would be no firing squads in Fairfax newsrooms if they took control – although Black was sympathetic with Packer's antipathy towards the media.

After two-thirds of Australia's parliamentarians signed a petition against media concentration, Black opined that he too would sign such a document – indeed, his presence in Australia represented new

---

* Soft equity are shares or notes that are repaid only after a successful listing on the stock exchange at a later date.

diversity in ownership. Nonetheless, Black was rapidly recognising from afar that Packer was going to be 'heavy baggage' for Tourang's bid.

Turnbull was also a concern. As Packer's personal counsel, he had played a major role in helping him rebut the accusations of mob connections. Black believed the idea that Turnbull was an 'associate' of Packer's just because he had worked for Packer years earlier was 'getting into Kessler-Kafka-Orwell country'. Black knew that if critics could only glimpse into the inner chambers of Tourang, they'd realise just how different Turnbull's agenda had become from Packer's. Indeed, dissension within Tourang was rapidly becoming a more serious issue than either the Packer factor or even the competing bids. Egos, cultures and agendas clashed at virtually every turn.

Hellman's Brian Powers and Dan Colson, found themselves increasingly at odds with their supposed Australian allies, Turnbull and Kennedy. Powers and Colson became fast friends, spending countless hours together quaffing Diet Cokes and working on strategy.

Long Island-bred, Yale-educated Powers was a classic American investment banker, parlaying a law degree from the University of Virginia into a career on Wall Street, where he worked for James Wolfenson, a prominent Australian and close friend of Packer's. In 1986, Powers moved to Hong Kong to work for the huge Hong Kong trading company, Jardine, Matheson, and two years later was the surprise choice as Jardine's executive chairman, the first non-English taipan. Just five months later, when his wife contracted a lung disease and needed to get away from the Hong Kong climate, Powers quit Jardine and returned to investment banking in the U.S., which led to his role in the Fairfax bid.

Powers shared Colson's antipathy towards Turnbull. Now Kennedy was proving to be equally difficult, particularly for Colson. Powers and Colson were spending more and more time with Packer, and Kennedy and Turnbull seemed envious. Packer was distancing himself from his old friends. He started to suspect that Turnbull and Kennedy planned somehow to hijack Fairfax once the money was in. With just under fifteen per cent of the newspaper company, Packer would, as Black put it, be entitled to little more than a tour of the plant and a free lunch. The principals at Tourang were starting to get the uneasy feeling that Kennedy and Turnbull had their own agenda.*

In the meantime, Colson felt Kennedy wasn't pulling his weight as chief executive-in-waiting. Kennedy scoffed at the suggestion – he already knew the territory. Unlike Colson, he was not in Australia solely to work on the deal round the clock. He disliked Colson and dismissed him as a lowly functionary or company lawyer, rather than a *de facto* principal. It was a serious underestimation of Colson's place in the Black orbit. While Kennedy thought Colson 'very second eleven' – a cricket term meaning second string – Colson labelled Kennedy 'another Andrew Knight'.

'What that means I don't know,' barked Kennedy. 'I hope Andrew Knight never took him seriously either.'

Although Kennedy had worked with Packer for years and had at times been a close friend, they had grown apart. Kennedy later claimed things soured entirely when his former boss tried to pressure him to make changes at Tourang, in particular to diminish Turnbull's role. As far as Kennedy was concerned, with Black at a safe distance in London, Packer was lavishing attention on Colson and Powers in an effort to manipulate the bid. 'Kerry can be extraordinarily charming when he wants to be, and has of course a lot of toys and other objects with which to suborn people and earn their favours,' Kennedy later remarked. 'And he threw these at Colson with great abandon.'

At one point Kennedy phoned Black in London to complain about Colson. Black listened but responded with little more than a grunt of acknowledgement – his faith in Colson was unflinching. Besides, he was fielding similar calls from all the players, each griping about someone else's perceived shortcomings. 'I'd just basically be trying to be a placatory influence – not with any great success it seems,' Black later recalled. 'But I would never accept criticism of Dan Colson.'

Colson, meanwhile, was mystified that Kennedy had worked for Packer for as long as he had. Black thought Kennedy a 'good old boy' in the hard-drinking, hard-headed Aussie tradition, but believed that perhaps Fairfax needed a more 'energetic' figure in charge. Also, the *Telegraph*'s printing plant guru Alan Rawcliffe, while in Sydney to

---

* 'The idea,' says Turnbull, 'that I, as one non-executive director out of ten, would be able to exercise some Svengali-like spell over the rest of the board is laughable.'

participate in the due diligence, had observed that Kennedy was not a production man. This worried Colson, since the Sydney newspapers were in dire need of new printing presses, the cost of which would run into the hundreds of millions of dollars. By the second week of October, as the bids were being finalised, Colson and Powers had decided that Kennedy's employment contract would have to be renegotiated.

In a famous scene recounted in the Australian book *Corporate Cannibals*, Kennedy was summoned to Colson's suite at the Regent, but not before Colson had carefully hidden all potential weapons, such as a letter opener and ashtray. He told Kennedy that the partners had doubts about his suitability for the chief executive's job. His contract, and its ten million free options to buy Fairfax stock, would be scaled back; the term would now be one year instead of three. Kennedy was hit hard. It was clear Packer had not taken up his defence. After more nasty repartee with Colson, Kennedy decided to quit. The last thing he did was phone Black, with whom he had enjoyed working. Black deferred to Colson on the sacking, but diplomatically asked Kennedy if there was anything that could be done to change his mind. Kennedy said no.

The resignation coincided with the day bids were delivered to Baring Brothers Burrows. Damage control was a top priority. Kennedy threatened to hold a press conference to explain his side of the story, which elicited a settlement of half a million dollars. In return, Kennedy had to sign a confidentiality agreement and a press release that served the consortium's interests. In a neat manipulation of the media's anti-Packer stance, Tourang hid its own internal strife behind what appeared to be a capitulation to public pressure. The press release talked of 'McCarthyism' as the reason for Kennedy's exit and the difficulties he would have faced as Fairfax chief executive if his independence from Packer were subjected to continued enquiries and investigations.

Kennedy later maintained that he was 'under siege' and that agreeing to the press release was a mistake. Certainly, it was a more palatable message for all concerned than the fact that the Canadian and American orchestrating the bid had branded one of Australia's most respected media executives an incompetent.

Black trumpeted the McCarthyism angle the following week

during an interview on Australian television. Asked about rumours that Kennedy's departure was the result of clashes within Tourang, Black played them down. 'There were some abrasions between some of the personalities, but nothing unusual, nothing spectacular, nothing justifying the lurid rumours that seem to be circulating around some of the personalities there. I haven't had any problems with anyone, but then again I've been away for a while now.'

Asked if he had been as happy with Kennedy on the day he left as he was when his appointment was announced three months earlier, Black replied: 'Reasonably so. Yeah, I was happy with him. It was a loss. And it was an unfair treatment of an honest and capable man, I think. Rather a sad story.'

In any event, Kennedy's departure did little to quell anti-Packer sentiment towards Tourang. In some quarters it heightened the view that Packer was the guiding force behind Tourang. After all, if there was no problem, why the sudden departure of his mate?

On Wednesday 16 October, the report from Colson to Black was grim. Despite Kennedy's dismissal and the submission of bids to Baring Brothers, Tourang was under assault in a major way. Early that morning, journalists had gathered at major public transport junctions in Sydney to hand out leaflets prepared by the Friends of Fairfax to rally support against Tourang. (A Melbourne counterpart, *The Age* Independence Committee, separately worked towards the same objectives.) At Fairfax's offices on Sydney's Broadway, a twenty-four-hour strike had been called. At noon, hundreds of journalists and supporters began picketing the offices of Fairfax's largest creditor – ANZ bank – in Martin Place, waving placards with such slogans as 'Save us from Packer'. Brochures included a form with a message to the chief executive of ANZ warning that 'if you sell the Fairfax papers to Mr Packer, I will close my accounts with the ANZ Bank.' Over the next week, some 2,000 forms were submitted.

Colson found the whole episode surreal: 'I remember walking down the street with Powers and the so-called Friends of Fairfax were handing out leaflets on Pitt Street. This very unimpressive young man handed me this flyer, obviously not knowing who Powers and I were. "Stop Packer, Stop Black," it said.

'I said, "Who is this guy?" He obviously assumed I was an American tourist, so he started telling me how Black was this horrible right-wing fanatic interfering newspaper proprietor who was going to put an end to the editorial independence of these great newspapers – it was absolute crap. So we spent a good five minutes or so really winding the guy up, which gave us a little bit of comic relief which was in short supply at the time. We said, 'Well what's wrong with that?"' '

Adding to the affray, former prime ministers Gough Whitlam and Malcolm Fraser – sworn enemies in Australian politics during the 1970s – joined forces with a group of other former politicians to sign a petition against concentration of media ownership and to express concern about foreign ownership of print media. At one point, Fraser charged that Black was 'not a proper person to own media in Australia'. The battle was escalating, and the efforts of Whitlam and Fraser ensured that the story spilled out of the business sections and on to the front pages. The fax machines at the *Telegraph* and at 10 Toronto Street were humming with each day's clippings. The time had come, Black decided, to launch a few intercontinental verbal missiles of his own. Letters from lawyers representing Packer and Black were faxed to four Fairfax journalists responsible for one of the pamphlets handed out during the protest.

Conrad Black whistled 'Waltzing Matilda' as he descended the staircase at Brooks's club in London on the evening of 22 October 1991. He had just excused himself from the dinner and drinks that followed a *Spectator* board meeting, having agreed to a live interview with Australian journalist Jana Wendt ('the rather pulchritudinous interviewer', he wrote in his memoirs). Wendt was the host of *A Current Affair*, a top-rated news programme that aired on Packer's Channel Nine network. The Fairfax saga had become a national drama. In the Newman Street studio, Black, clad in grey suit and sporting a navy tie emblazoned with boxing kangaroos, settled into a chair behind a backdrop featuring London Bridge. The Blackspeak was unmistakable, even half a world away.

'How do you rate your chances now of taking out the Fairfax prize?' Wendt began.

'I wouldn't put it in quite such predatory terms. I think our chances are quite good. . . . I, of course would have to be *brain dead* to be unaware of the fact there's some political controversy, which I've found somewhat mystifying.'

'I know that when you were in the country you were bemused at all of the disquiet about Mr Packer's involvement,' Wendt continued. 'You are clearly aware that that feeling has intensified since you left the country. . . .'

'It has, I think, intensified, but that's perhaps a word that implies spontaneity. I think it has been amplified by certain people. What strikes me as rather *piquant* is that some of the critics of Mr Packer have conducted against him – and he will defend himself, he doesn't need me or anyone else to do that – have conducted against him an absolutely scurrilous and relentless campaign of defamation. And I think that the so-called self-conferred Friends of Fairfax will ultimately wish to ask themselves if this is really the dignified and reasonable and cool-headed manner in which the fate of these great newspapers should be determined in the national interest which has so often been invoked there.'

At the interview's conclusion, Wendt asked Black how badly he wanted Fairfax. 'It's hard to quantify. Obviously if I wasn't reasonably highly motivated I wouldn't have put up with even the inconvenience that I've been subjected to,' he replied, levelling a serious glare at the camera before him. 'They're fine papers, but I mean, can I live without it? Will I jump off the bridge behind me as I speak if I don't get it? No, of course I won't.'

Black's appearance was mere warm-up for the main event on the following evening's *A Current Affair*. Kerry Packer had agreed to give a rare interview (albeit to his own network) and to face his critics. Packer's enormous head, with droopy eyes and large ears, seemed propped atop his large frame. His expression, behind his half-glasses, was a peculiar balance between fatherly solemnity and menace.

Wendt asked Packer to respond to the charge that he was 'some kind of insidious force that is going to threaten the independence of a great Australian newspaper group'.

'Well, Jana, I have a problem answering that, because it's such a preposterous suggestion,' he began earnestly. 'And it's been put forward by so many people who should know better that I find it extraordinary. Fifteen per cent will not control John Fairfax. Under the law, all I'm allowed is fifteen per cent. I have known that from day one. I will not control Tourang, which is the company which is bidding for John Fairfax. Why the big lie? Why the suggestion I'm going to control it? I'm not going to control it.'

If he could not control it, why the interest in Fairfax? Packer, like Black, acknowledged that he was not known for making passive investments. He explained that 'for fifty years of my life, in some form or other, Fairfax has been competition to me or my family'. Over the years Fairfaxes had owned newspaper, television and magazine interests which competed with the Packer empire. 'I mean, this has been The Challenge,' Packer explained. 'The idea that I can end up buying fifteen per cent of John Fairfax, and the Fairfax family have departed from Fairfax, amused me.'

(A journalist later asked Black if Packer's reference to being amused did not infer an element of revenge. 'No, I see in that a regrettable choice of words,' Black offered. 'I think he was endeavouring to show that he was not fanatically motivated, he wasn't doing it out of vengeance, that he didn't really mean he was "amused" but that he thought it would be nice to be a shareholder. He didn't mean it as a Caligula, engaged in degenerative sadistic games, he meant it in the sense of an interesting thing to do.')

After a commercial break, Wendt and Packer were joined by three Fairfax journalists, whom Packer quickly engaged in a haughty debate over journalistic ethics and the coverage given Tourang. When the debate turned to his partnership with Black, Packer explained that the Canadian would ensure higher standards of accuracy at the papers. Tom Burton of the *Herald* asked how durable their alliance was. 'I think very durable,' Packer snapped. 'It's become apparent, hasn't it, that we are prepared to stand up and put this bid together? And after that, Conrad Black will run the thing, not me. I'm very happy for Conrad Black to run it. I think Conrad Black is a very capable newspaper person.'

'Why look overseas?' asked Burton.

'Who are you suggesting? . . . What do institutions know about running a newspaper for God's sake? Conrad Black is used to running a quality newspaper. Are you really suggesting there are better partners to do that here than him? If so, name one. If not, withdraw the question. *Who* is better than Conrad Black at running the Fairfax group?'

The following weekend, Packer was joined at Ellerston, his country retreat in the Hunter Valley, by Dan Colson and Brian Powers. The purpose of the sojourn was not to avail themselves of the magnificent property's extensive recreational facilities and fully equipped polo grounds, but to help Packer prepare for another public appearance.

Since the beginning of August, a parliamentary inquiry into the print media had been underway in Canberra to debate the issue of media concentration. It had been a side-show to the actual bidding for Fairfax until Packer's television appearance. After *A Current Affair*, Packer agreed to appear before the Print Media Inquiry on 4 November. Tossing a ball around the Ellerston 'library' – it seemed to stock as many videos as books – Colson and Powers prepared likely questions and effective answers for Packer.

In his opening statement, Packer defiantly reiterated that he would not control Fairfax under the Tourang bid, and indeed did not want to: 'Last year I suffered a major heart attack and died. I didn't die for long, but it was long enough for me. I didn't come back to control John Fairfax. I didn't come back to break the law. And I certainly didn't intentionally come back to testify before a parliamentary inquiry.' It was Packer's finest hour in the Tourang affair. He went on to intimidate the panel and deny repeatedly and forcefully that he would have any role in Fairfax other than that of a minority shareholder. In fact, he badgered, to suggest otherwise would be to call him a liar.

For his part, Black followed up his *Current Affair* appearance by granting a lengthy interview to the *Sydney Morning Herald*'s New York correspondent, John Lyons, in his Toronto office. The interview ran verbatim over several pages. This was his chance to speak out against some of the more irksome criticisms of Tourang and himself. He condemned what he saw as an orchestrated effort to thwart Tourang's bid by his rival publisher Rupert Murdoch. As it happened, Black had seen Murdoch at a dinner the night before the interview and had told him that the way his papers were carrying on wasn't doing Tourang any favours.

'It is the corporate policy of News Corp. that they would prefer not to compete with Packer and me,' Black told the Fairfax-owned

*Herald.** 'Mr Murdoch has not enjoyed competing with me in London and he would prefer to compete in Australia with people who have less background in the industry. . . . No-one has ever accused Rupert of erring on the side [of] excessive quality or independence in his newspapers, which makes all this hypocrisy and bile about them purporting to say how best to maintain the standards of the Fairfax papers almost ridiculous and unworthy of any credence at all.'

Indeed, Black noted, Murdoch, through his ownership of newspapers and satellite television in Britain, and television and newspapers in the U.S., was 'one of the greatest cross-media owners in the world'.

Black credited Murdoch and O'Reilly equally with the persisting charge that Packer would be the dominant shareholder at Fairfax. Packer would not even have a seat on the board and Black noted that it would have a majority of independent Australian directors, including the eminent Sir Zelman Cowen, a former chairman of the British Press Council, who would serve as Fairfax chairman, and Sir Laurence Street, a former chief justice of New South Wales.

'Mr Packer will not be dictating editorial judgement; he will not be muzzling reporters; he will express his views as [an] investor who put up A$70 million. He has his right to express his views in general but he will not be sitting there either figuratively or, in fact, governing the management of those papers and promoting and demoting people.

'I, for one, at the risk of sounding sanctimonious, would never be party to such a thing. If you asked me would Rupert Murdoch be party to such a thing, I would say, "Yes, Rupert's a fine fellow but he's an authoritarian publisher," and I'm being put in pillory as being some sort of virtual totalitarian intermeddler with my journalists. This is absolutely scurrilous. This myth grew and grew and like a Frankenstein monster has achieved a life of its own that lurches all around the Australian media every day. The fact is the working press of Australia are going to have to explain eventually how this happened.'

* News Corp's managing director Ken Cowley issued a statement the following day calling Black's assertion of a corporate policy on the sale of Fairfax 'completely false. There is no corporate policy. To suggest any such policy would be followed by our editors is preposterous.' He also disputed Black's interpretation of his views presented to the print media inquiry. 'I think that Mr Black must only have read press reports,' Cowley said.

Black's concern about the Fairfax media's objectivity in covering its own affairs was not diminished when Lyons began quizzing him about the various controversies which had surrounded him, such as the Ontario securities investigation a decade earlier. In a scolding tone, Black replied that if an investigation that went on for almost a year 'resulting in absolute exculpation' is 'deemed to be a blot on the ledger of somebody, then truly you people who are upholders of professional integrity in the press in Australia should engage in some agonising, and, as Kissinger would say, "prayerful" self-analysis.

'You give me some concern that this witch-hunting vocation that the Australian media has demonstrated on this issue is not entirely absent from your own thoughts.'

Back in Australia, the rifts within Tourang were deepening. Soon Powers and Colson came to the conclusion that the bid could go no further with Turnbull's involvement. They believed that the deal would not be done if Turnbull remained closely involved. Neville Miles, as head of the underwriting group, agreed with Turnbull that ousting him in the wake of Kennedy as a proposed Fairfax director would only attract more scrutiny from the regulators. Their view was that it was best to wait until Fairfax was in hand, then deal with the personality problems. Miles phoned Packer, then on a polo trip in Argentina, privately to air his concern. All Packer knew was that he wanted a piece of Fairfax and if his partners didn't want Turnbull on the board, then so be it. 'Look, I'm sitting in Argentina, I'm trying to buy fucking horses,' Packer replied. 'What do you want me to do about it?' Unlike his friend Kennedy, Turnbull would not be signing a press release citing McCarthyism; instead, he announced to the press that he had been turfed out because he was too 'independent'.*

'I explained to Black that if you want to be an assassin, you have to be prepared to have a little blood on your hands,' Turnbull later

---

* Despite Black's and Packer's claims to the contrary, Turnbull says being a Fairfax director was never that important to him. 'I was opposed to the firing of Kennedy and I was opposed to the removal of myself from the board because I believed it was not in the best interests of the deal. The reason I believed that it was not in the best interests of the deal was that in my experience, in contested deals of this kind, it is a terrible mistake to have visible signs of dissent and falling out among the ranks of a group of people that are supposedly working together.'

recalled. 'Conrad responded by saying that I didn't just want him to have blood on his hands, I wanted his fingerprints on the dagger. He was quite right actually.'

In the end, no amount of defiance or bravado could keep Kerry Packer in the bitter Fairfax contest. His involvement in Tourang ended six months after it had begun when Trevor Kennedy submitted a diary to the Australian Broadcasting Tribunal which emphasised that he reported equally to Packer and Black during the bid. It contradicted statements that Kennedy had made earlier, and although he was sued by Tourang for breaching his confidentiality agreement, Kennedy claimed his lawyer told him he had no choice but to submit the diaries when requested by the Australian Broadcast Tribunal. (He had prepared them thinking that perhaps he might write a book about the episode.) The fact that the diary he submitted was not an actual diary but a revision of some rough notes did not diminish their impact. On 26 November, ABT chairman Peter Westerway announced an inquiry into Tourang. Kennedy later said of the diary, 'Packer, in my view, had a very, very serious influence over events – probably more than what was being admitted elsewhere at the time. They were all trying to infer that really Kerry was just a bit player and a sort of passive investor in this exercise. That was the attempted charade.'

It was Tourang's worst fear. A cross-media inquiry would drag on for weeks, maybe months, certainly into the new year and past the expiry of the bondholders' agreement on 16 January. Black was incensed on other grounds too. He had not worked to achieve his position as one of the world's leading press proprietors to be labelled some sort of front for a man he didn't even know very well. 'Even my severest detractors have never accused me of being a minion,' he complained. The matter was put to rest two days later when Packer phoned Black to tell him he had had enough of the public spotlight and would withdraw from Tourang in the best interests of the bid. 'My last words to him prior to that decision were that if he wanted to fight it out, we'd fight it out with him,' recalled Black. 'He shouldn't feel any pressure from us to withdraw.' Perhaps deliberately choosing an image he knew Black would appreciate, Packer replied, 'A good general has to know when to advance and when to retreat. And in the better interests of the cause, I shall now retreat.'

Now it was just the Telegraph and Hellman & Friedman bid against Tony O'Reilly and AIN. Black regretted Packer's departure, but knew that with him out of the way Tourang's chances for success were improved. O'Reilly intensified the pressure against Black, decrying him as 'an interventionist, right-wing, pro-Thatcherite owner'. The Irish tycoon explained that Black's and his own views of running newspapers 'are quite dissimilar. Lord Thomson of Fleet was my hero. He built some of the greatest papers in the world on a totally non-interventionist basis.' Black shot back that 'we are not talking about selling snake oil, but the future of Australia's leading newspapers'.

The final Fairfax bids were submitted in early December, and Black and Colson were optimistic. Packer was no longer a concern; nor were Turnbull and Kennedy; only Tourang had a deal with the bondholders and could fully repay the banks. The final hurdle was approval from the Foreign Investment Review Board, and this seemed a no-brainer. In October, the Labour caucus had issued a policy statement limiting foreign voting equity in media companies to twenty per cent. This was the level proposed by the *Telegraph*, with Hellman holding a further fifteen per cent in non-voting shares. Once the bids had passed the Foreign Investment Review Board Burrows could make his recommendation to the receiver and the whole affair could be wrapped up before Christmas.

Although it appeared AIN was offering the most money, its bid was still considered inferior because it was not an experienced newspaper operating company, and its financing relied on a public flotation. O'Reilly's bid was also conditional, both on a share issue and approval of Australian Provincial Newspapers' shareholders. It was never far from Mark Burrows's mind that a market crash or correction could scuttle these conditional bids, just as the 1987 crash ought to have stopped Warwick Fairfax.

On the Friday before the bid deadline, Prime Minister Bob Hawke, who was fighting for his political life under a leadership challenge from Paul Keating, announced he was sacking his treasurer, John Kerin, for reasons unrelated to Fairfax. As it turned out, Kerin's last act in the portfolio would be to rule on the Fairfax acquisition. George Pooley, the executive member of the Foreign Investment Review Board, had been dealing with lawyers and executives from Tourang's and O'Reilly's camps for months. Pooley sent the FIRB's confidential recommendations to Kerin on 5 December. While reviewing the caucus resolution limiting foreign voting ownership to twenty per cent, it noted that both Tourang's and O'Reilly's bids could be blocked on the basis that control of Fairfax would fall to foreign hands. That argument, Pooley wrote, rested on the 'commercial reality' that despite complying with the numerical ownership limit, the bids were ultimately put together largely by O'Reilly and Black, 'each of whom expects to significantly influence Fairfax strategic and management policy, at least initially'. On balance, Pooley concluded that 'effective control' of Fairfax would indeed pass to foreign hands if either bid were approved.

The minute implies that in the FIRB's view, AIN was not in the game. Obviously, as the only all-Australian bidder, it did not require FIRB approval, but a serious home-grown alternative could have coloured the treasurer's thinking. In the minute, the FIRB made several questionable assumptions about AIN, including that it had 'no newspaper experience' (even though the group's proposed chief executive, Greg Taylor, was a veteran Fairfax executive, and at least two of its other proposed directors had extensive newspaper experience). It also questioned AIN's ability to close the deal. This later incensed the group, who claimed Pooley had turned down their requests to provide him with fuller information. The upshot was that to Kerin it appeared that Tourang and O'Reilly were the only legitimate bidders.

The board was split down the middle. In the minute, two of the FIRB's four members recommended that Kerin reject both Tourang and O'Reilly on the grounds that their bids would both result in foreign control. The other two, including Pooley, recommended that both bids be allowed to go forward with no objections from the government because foreign ownership issues would be 'outweighed by the benefits of foreign newspaper expertise, such as higher quality journalism and more modern technology'. The minute also concluded that a decision to approve both bids would be easier to justify, provided Kerin was satisfied they were consistent with the caucus decree. 'Whatever decision you take will be criticised,' Pooley noted.

That was a mild way of describing Conrad Black's reaction in London to the astonishing news that Kerin had rejected Tourang on the basis it was 'not in the national interest' and approved the bid by O'Reilly. Black blasted the decision as 'sleazy, venal and despicable.

'We have been the victim of sleazy political lobbying,' he told the *Herald*. 'I'm sure the Australian public are shocked and appalled by these tactics.' Black suspected that 'O'Reilly and his pimps' were behind the lobbying, knowing that Hawke had preferred O'Reilly's bid all along. 'I have been portrayed as a fanatical right-winger, an interfering meddler, and that is simply not true, not true.'

At the same time, O'Reilly was attempting to get the bondholders to defect to his bid on the assumption that the Tourang bid had come unglued. But it was still fighting for its life. Legal letters were dispatched to O'Reilly's camp warning him not to induce a contract breach with the bondholders. Meanwhile, Tourang agreed to pay the bondholders an additional A$15 million to keep them on their side.

As far as Burrows was concerned, the bonds' role all along was secondary to paying the banks and satisfying the government. In representing the banks, his strategy for selling Fairfax was to ignore the bondholders until the deal was done. Then, he would either make a deal with them or sell the assets out of Fairfax, avoiding the bondholders' claim in the process. O'Reilly was worried by Tourang's repeated statements that its bondholder agreement assured them victory, and said so to Burrows at various times over the previous months. The bid was costing him more than A$3 million, and O'Reilly did not want to be strung along just so that Burrows would have a field of bidders. O'Reilly had first raised the matter of the bondholders with Burrows in May, when the general view was that the offers for Fairfax would probably not be enough to pay the A$1.27 billion owed the banks (Black had initially spoken of a bid in the range of A$1.1 billion including the A$125 million paid to the bondholders.) 'With respect to the bondholder litigation,' Burrows wrote to O'Reilly on 22 November, 'we have always maintained that based on the advice we have received from the lawyers this could not be a factor in the receivers' decision-making process.'

Barings maintained that the bondholder agreement would not be used by Tourang to effect a 'sub-economic' deal with the banks, and that the whole basis of the bondholder litigation was questionable in the first place. But in late October, the bids actually surpassed the bank debt. 'As a consequence, the agreement may now have some value,' Burrows admitted to O'Reilly in his letter of 22 November, 'although this did not become evident until late October.'

Of course, the bondholder agreement would be of no value at all to Black if Tourang could not reformulate his bid within forty-eight hours to meet the 11 December final deadline. Colson heard that the rejection had originally been set for the deadline day itself, which would have given Tourang no chance to adjust its bid. Only the political infighting that led to Kerin's removal from the treasurer's portfolio bought them time. It was that close a call.

The bid was resubmitted, with the *Daily Telegraph*'s voting interest reduced to fifteen per cent. Hellman & Friedman's non-voting interest diminished to a mere five per cent. This brought Tourang's foreign ownership level in line with O'Reilly's bid. The new treasurer, Ralph Willis, despite being bedridden with the flu, approved the revised structure on 13 December. At three a.m. on 16 December 1991, the banks accepted Mark Burrows's recommendation that Fairfax be sold to Tourang for A$1.6 billion. Just before dawn, Colson telephoned Black to relay the news: Fairfax was his. Black wondered to his friend if it had been his 'sleazy, venal, and despicable' fusillade that had won the day. Colson didn't think so.

At eight fifteen a.m. the following day, weary from the twenty-two-hour flight but bearing a full grin, Black strode out of customs at Sydney airport, pin-stripe jacket slung over his arm, and straight into his first of several media scrums. Breakfast at the Ritz Carlton was followed by lunch at the Union Club, interspersed with meetings with institutions. Everywhere he went, camera crews and journalists pursued. Black assured them that no Fairfax journalists were earmarked for 'busting', and although the Australians were not familiar with that colloquialism, they deduced no busting must be a good thing. He added that 'contrary to wide-spread rumours, it is not a plan of Mr Colson's or myself to erect a guillotine at Broadway and move journalists through it on a random basis.' Asked at one juncture to point out the best and worst aspects of Australian media, he said that on the negative side the press seemed rather preoccupied with itself. On the plus side, the recently separated Black quipped, 'there do seem to be rather attractive women in the field.'

In his second whirlwind tour of Australia, Black could not help but be struck by all the scorched earth on the path to victory. Of the principal personalities from six months earlier – Packer, Black, Colson, Powers, Turnbull and Kennedy – only himself, Colson, and Powers remained. And for all of Powers's efforts, Hellman & Friedman's investment in Fairfax was a third of what it had hoped to take. (At the celebratory dinners, Powers was ribbed about how low his profit sharing would be for 1991.) His role in the Fairfax saga reaped other rewards, however, when the fast-talking American later joined Kerry Packer as chief executive of Consolidated Press, which was Trevor Kennedy's old job. For his troubles, Packer was given a payout from Fairfax based on whatever gains Fairfax stock would record after being taken public. Each A$1 rise in the value of the stock would be worth A$30 million to him. Black took the role of Fairfax deputy chairman and Colson continued jetting back and forth to London as Fairfax's interim chief executive while a search was conducted to find the right candidate. Still seething about Tony O'Reilly's conduct during the bid, Black damned him with faint praise on the Australian Broadcasting Corporation programme, *Four Corners*. 'A delightful man and a great talent,' Black said, his facial expression conveying no indication that he meant it. 'He just got a little carried away. I mean, to use an analogy of highway traffic, he crossed the double white line. But that's all right, he's back in the proper lane now.'

For his part, O'Reilly launched a suit in the Federal Court against several parties, including Ord Minnett, Baring Brothers Burrows and Tourang. The AIN group soon joined O'Reilly's Independent Newspapers as a co-plaintiff. O'Reilly claimed that he had been misled about the importance ultimately placed on the bondholder agreement by Burrows, and otherwise might not have wasted A$3 million on his bid. Tourang countersued, claiming it had had to increase the bondholder payment by A$15 million at the eleventh hour as a result of O'Reilly's attempts to lure them away. Such is corporate warfare: the bondholder agreement which was designed to avoid costly and lengthy litigation was now itself the object of costly and lengthy litigation.

A few months after the lawsuit began, John Fairfax Holdings (as Tourang was now called) changed its tack and decided that if the auction had indeed been rigged, it too had been a victim. While O'Reilly may have been out of pocket by a few million, Fairfax figured that it could be out by as much as A$500 million, depending on how much the three-way auction had bid up the price. A settlement was finally agreed to by all parties in May 1995, under which the banks and Barings reportedly paid A$15 million to O'Reilly and AIN.

The word in Sydney legal circles was that Black and Colson warned from the outset that under no circumstances was Fairfax to contribute a dime to O'Reilly's settlement. Indeed, after some last-minute hardball by Stephen Mulholland around the bargaining table, Fairfax received a settlement of A$2.5 million

Despite his 'no busting' promise, Black's brief visit to Australia did little to dispel the paranoia running through the Fairfax ranks about the new owner. The day after Black's arrival in Australia, Max Hastings faxed Colson a copy of a memo that had been forwarded by the *Daily Telegraph*'s foreign editor, Nigel Wade. It was an unsolicited and unflattering view of the Fairfax mastheads and their editors by an Australian acquaintance of Wade's. The fax began: 'The general view is that John Alexander, editor-in-chief of the SMH [*Sydney Morning Herald*], Max Prisk, editor, and Gerard Noonan, editor of the *Fin[ancial] Review*, are definitely the B-team: grey men for a grey time. . . .' Hastings and *Telegraph* executive editor Jeremy Deedes had met that morning with Alexander, who was passing through London. 'He was highly nervous, which I guess was predictable,' Hastings said in the memo to Colson. 'But both of us found it a little odd that he is going on from here for a holiday in Italy, when one might have thought that, if he was a serious player, he would want to get home fast, and be with his troops in their hour of need. I would, if I was in his shoes.'

As it happened, the fax machine in Colson's room was out of paper so he had the memos sent to the front desk, where a hotel worker had been paid off by Murdoch's *The Australian* to intercept and photocopy any incoming faxes. The fax from Wade was plastered on the front page of *The Australian* the next day, creating yet another furore. Colson called the police and the culprit was fired, while he and Black spent much of the following day pointing out the insignificance of the 'leaked' memos.

To the Australian public, Black emerged from the shadow of Packer as an object of immense curiosity. 'There, as in Britain, they've got this narcissistic self-obsession that extends to the owners,' he later said. 'And they attach a morbid fascination to the minutiae of the lives and existences of the owners. And I think it's a lot of nonsense. If Rupert Murdoch had haemorrhoids or something they'd want to bring out a special edition of every paper in the country to talk about it.'

As soon as the Telegraph assumed management control of John Fairfax, Black and Colson began plotting to increase the Telegraph's ownership position from fifteen per cent to twenty-five per cent. As largest shareholder, the Telegraph called the shots and had the support of the institutions that had backed their bid. But they saw it was tenuous control at best; Black had learned as much from his Argus days.

The Fairfax contest and some of Black's public comments had not endeared him to everyone in Australia's Labour Party. Still, new prime minister Paul Keating was the person who would ultimately decide whether Black could increase his interest, and Black got along with him. Black and Colson began complaining publicly and in private about how they had fifteen per cent of the stock in Fairfax but one hundred per cent of the responsibility. With less than twenty per cent, the Telegraph could not even consolidate Fairfax's earnings into its statements. Fortunately, showing the government that the Telegraph was a good corporate citizen, while generating a worthy return on the Telegraph's more than A$100 million investment in Fairfax were not incompatible goals.

The executive search for a new Fairfax CEO produced 300 prospective candidates. The Fairfax board settled on a man whom Colson had met while scouting prospects in South Africa in 1990, and whom Black had known for several years: Stephen Mulholland. The son of an Irish stonemason, Mulholland arrived at Fairfax from the post of chief executive at Times Media Ltd., one of the companies owned by gold magnate Harry Oppenheimer, which counted the *Johannesburg Star* and the *Financial Mail* among its titles. In dollar terms, Times Media was a considerably smaller company than Fairfax, but with almost three decades at Times Media in various capacities, Mulholland was precisely the sort of hard-nosed, disciplined man of action that Black felt Fairfax needed after four years of managerial limbo. A former All-American swimmer, the intense, tough-talking

Mulholland can come across as a drill sergeant (his curriculum vitae includes a stint as a private in the U.S. Army).

The appointment of a foreigner to the top job at Fairfax created another minor furore, but was mitigated by the hiring of a native Australian, Michael Hoy (who had been with Murdoch's *South China Morning Post*), to be Fairfax's deputy chief executive and editorial director. Colson, who had worked practically full-time representing Black, still ostensibly had a law practice at Stikeman Elliott in London. Now, Black finally convinced Colson to join the Telegraph full-time in the position of vice-chairman, with continuing responsibility for the Australian investment.

While no one expected job cutbacks on the massive scale that had been implemented at the *Daily Telegraph* when Black took control in 1986, Black explained in *Australian Business Monthly* that there was certainly room for reducing Fairfax's 4,340-strong work force. 'To put it in military parlance, what we need is more trigger-pullers. LBJ used to say he had more than half a million people in Vietnam but only 200,000 trigger-pullers. Fairfax may have too many support people. There are far too many slovenly work practices there. That's the encrustation of years. You can't get rid of that overnight. Steve Mulholland is an impatient man. He would like change *now*. But I think it's better done gradually through the application of constant but not brutal force, for increased efficiency.'

Sitting in his fourteenth-floor office at Fairfax's Broadway headquarters one day in early 1993, Stephen Mulholland would certainly not argue with Black's description of him as 'impatient'.

'It's a failing, something I've battled all my life,' he said. 'However, when I arrived here, I can tell you that impatience was the order of the day. There were an enormous number of things that had to be done.' In his first speech to the Fairfax troops a week after joining the company, Mulholland explained that cost-cutting and managing the company's debt-load were going to be top priorities. One Sydney employee enquired if such cost-cutting might include a reduction in Mulholland's executive salary. It would not. 'I can only say I have been seduced,' Mulholland explained. 'I like tailor-made suits and driving around in nice cars. I fly first class and all that. I'm a victim. I have been seduced by a capitalist system.' He went on: 'Well, executives just work very hard. We come in early in the morning, we leave late at night and we worry like hell. We don't sleep much and that's the sacrifice we make, in return for which we get paid great deals of money. That's the way life is. We worry about it; it is executives who get fired from jobs which they have worked all their lives and take risks to achieve. They get fired if a company does not perform, so that is the sacrifice we make. We don't see our families. We suffer, we drink too much.' Executive talent had a price, 'and included in the price is the status symbol of driving around in a luxurious motor car – it is not Russia.'

True to his word, Mulholland went through Fairfax like a cyclone in his first few months. He axed an unprofitable regional edition of the *Herald* to make annual savings of A$500,000; he stopped pressmen wrapping bundles of papers as they came off the press, saving A$1 million a year; he began selling an ad on the *Herald*'s front page, which would bring in A$1.3 million a year. But he was just trimming at the edges and sending a message of urgency to a complacent work-force. The biggest challenge would be managing Fairfax's A$700 million debt while facing capital expenditures of A$300 million which were needed to replace the ancient letter-set presses in Sydney.

Mulholland also set to work on what he considered a serious morale problem exacerbated by historic competitive animosity between the *Herald* and *The Age*. As far as he was concerned, the two papers should have been working together better, sharing costs in such areas as overseas bureaux. Before long, the head of David Syme was 'retired' and all of Fairfax's top editors were shuffled, with mixed results. One of the more successful moves was the appointment of *Sydney Morning Herald* editor-in-chief John Alexander to head the *Australian Financial Review*. He replaced Gerard Noonan, the only Fairfax editor to be sacked in the shuffle. Noonan had an inkling he was not going to fare well under the new regime when, on encountering Black, the new proprietor said to him, 'Why do women from places with unpronounceable names write to me saying you are a foaming-at-the-mouth goddamn commie?'

Was there an ideological shift to the right at the Fairfax press under its new owners? *The Age* certainly became harder-edged under new editor Alan Kohler, moving away from its traditional small-l liberal viewpoint. For example, in early 1993 the paper endorsed hardline conservative Jeff Kennett, who was elected premier of recession-ravaged Victoria. 'If you're inclined to a conspiracy theory, you could say this is part of the new Black regime,' noted Claude Forell, a columnist of forty years who retired several months after Kohler assumed the helm. 'On the other hand, it could be argued that the paper had fallen into a bit of a rut. It needed to be shaken up a bit.'

Indeed, several months later in the Federal election all but one of Fairfax's major titles endorsed Liberal Coalition leader John Hewson instead of Labour's Keating. Former Fairfax chairman James Fairfax said he could discern no problems with the company's new direction. A year into the new ownership, Chris Warren, deputy secretary of the Media, Entertainment and Arts Alliance, the union repesenting Fairfax journalists, gave a mixed assessment. While Warren acknowledged that Black's 'priorities in a lot of ways are right', there were questions about the new owner's approach. 'I get the impression', he added carefully, 'that to a certain extent there's still a lot of coming to terms with Australia and Australian society.'

Black chafed at such suggestions. 'I think that's absolute rubbish,' he said. 'We understand Australia all right. The people who say that mean that we don't understand the tradition of Australia's ostentatious lack of martyrdom to the work ethic, but we'll cope with that as best we can. . . . I don't know where they get off saying we don't know Australian traditions. Christ, I went to lunch with Keating and had a very learned discussion about the history of the New South Wales Labour Party. And we went all through Jack Lang and everything. I actually consider that I know a little bit about Australian history.'

While Mulholland's new position had its challenges, it was clear he was managing something akin to gold mines. Within a year of listing Fairfax on the Australian stock exchange at A$1 a share, the stock was trading at A$2.02 – Black's investment had grown by more than A$100 million. In the year ended 30 June 1992, Fairfax recorded earnings before depreciation, interest and tax of A$152 million on revenue of A$729 million, despite operating in the worst recession since the Great Depression. Between them, the *Herald* and *The Age* had a stranglehold on classified advertising, commanding against competition from Murdoch's tabloids more than eighty per cent of their respective markets.

Based on Fairfax's improving results and share price, Black might have expected a warmer reception when he returned to Australia for the first annual meeting of John Fairfax Holdings, held at the Sydney Opera House on 25 November 1992. But the wounds of the Fairfax contest festered. Among the 800 shareholders packed into the concert hall were Trevor Kennedy and Malcolm Turnbull. In fact, Turnbull had spearheaded a legal challenge in the Federal Court to a proposed executive option plan. The various option schemes provided for 3.5 million free options to be issued to Mulholland, two million to Hoy (who was also to receive a A$1 million interest-free housing loan), and 500,000 to Colson. What particularly rankled with Turnbull and some others was that the options were exercisable immediately at A$1 and the stock was already trading at some A$1.44. Turnbull was supported by the Australian Shareholders Association, which labelled the options 'excessive', particularly in light of Fairfax's recent history.

Turnbull had a small victory: the resolution dealing with the options was withdrawn because a technical mistake had been made in the drafting of the notice of meeting. Fairfax agreed to pay Turnbull's costs for his action. The meeting dragged on for most of the day, with Turnbull filibustering and portraying the withdrawn resolution as a moral victory for Fairfax shareholders and a public humiliation for Black. Afterwards, both men laid claim to the most applause.

Black thought it outrageous that Turnbull, who made fees totalling A$6.3 million from the deal and 'worked every side of the street in a manner which was almost Homerically dextrous', was now accusing Fairfax's new directors of being greedy. 'Malcolm is singularly implausible and bizarre as a source of that accusation,' Black said later. 'Normally I take Malcolm fairly light-heartedly. He is a fairly histrionic and picturesque character. He does a great deal of to-ing and fro-ing and every now and then gets a little out of control. It's a pity. Malcolm is a talent and an attractive man but he involves himself in these quixotries and renders himself susceptible to really serious questions about both his judgements and his efforts.'

Turnbull's opinion of Black is equally favourable. 'When he is here, he tends to give very colourful and verbose speeches to all and sundry, most of which are couched in terms that are difficult to understand. Some of the things he said just don't make sense. You sometimes wonder whether he doesn't have a sort of random word selector somewhere in his brain. Words just sort of pop out. It's a bit odd.'

Amid the slanging matches at the annual meeting, trading volume was particularly strong in Fairfax shares, and the price was going up. A rising share price is typically considered good news, but in this case Colson and Black were a bit troubled. The trades were being made through Ord Minnett, one of Packer's main brokers. Rumour had it that the big man had decided to get back into the Fairfax game on his own terms, and had not bothered to inform his former allies.

ELEVEN

Media Merger

'Why, I ask myself, does someone stay in
a wretched occupation like
journalism?' BARBARA AMIEL

The victory in Australia was bitter-sweet for Conrad Black, who returned to Canada to face the demise of his thirteen-year marriage. He and Joanna had been estranged since September when he returned to England and she remained in Toronto with their three children. But Black wanted to maintain appearances and had asked Joanna not to tell anyone of their difficulties, not even the children. To outsiders and friends, the theory grew that Joanna disliked London and was having difficulty fitting in with society there. 'She was just an appendage,' said one London friend of Conrad's.

Regardless of their locale, the Blacks had grown apart. A bright, lively woman, Joanna did not covet being a fixture on the London social circuit as her husband seemed to. Black's position as head of the *Daily Telegraph* exposed him to a fascinating array of people and events, but Joanna was not interested in establishing a salon. She wanted to spend time with their children, and estimated that they only saw Conrad for a day and a half a week, on Saturday afternoons and Sundays. Looking back over their relationship some time later, she recalled the qualities which had attracted her to the young *Duplessis* author in 1977: 'I was attracted to the *real* Conrad Black – the person that is under there,' she explained. 'When I first met him I didn't see that real person, I saw this arrogant stuffed shirt. But after a while I realised that underneath that arrogance was a wonderful, vulnerable, very shy man.'

Following their move to England two years earlier, Joanna had seen the private Black transforming more and more into his public persona. 'See, Conrad is very quotable because I think he's living in a book,' she explained. Even before Conrad decided to write his memoirs, Joanna used to think that her husband had mapped out the life story of a great man and was determined to live it. 'Conrad had written his life and he'd had it all planned out,' she said. 'And everything he spoke was quotable. Not to me – he would say "Let's get a pizza" to me – but if he were being interviewed by somebody or if he were at a dinner party with people there of interest or influence, he would be very quotable, very colourful.' Perhaps the character in the 'book' is the true Conrad Black? 'Absolutely not,' says Joanna. 'Absolutely not.'

After separation, Joanna flew over to London twice, once for a wedding and later for the October 1991 Hollinger Dinner. Held at Lord Rothschild's Spencer House, it again featured Prime Minister Margaret Thatcher as the speaker. The guests, including William F. Buckley, Lord Carrington and Henry Kissinger, milled around one of the house's grand rooms before dinner. At one point, one of the guests touched Joanna Black lightly on the arm. It was Barbara Amiel, the glamorous *Sunday Times* columnist and long-time friend of Conrad's.

'Joanna,' Amiel said in her soft manner, 'you *must* come back to England or you'll lose him.'

Joanna returned Amiel's light touch. 'Barbara,' she replied, 'he'll lose me.'

Amiel had already made her excuses, and left the dinner before Thatcher's speech in order to fulfil an engagement on the television show *Newsnight*, where she gave her thoughts on the sexual misconduct case of U.S. Supreme Court Judge Clarence Thomas.

The next month, the Blacks attended the twentieth anniversary celebration of the *Toronto Sun* newspaper at Toronto's SkyDome, where they were photographed happily chatting to each other and noshing on popcorn. But soon after this the Blacks' children were told of their parents' separation, along with some friends. Black returned to London, then flew to Palm Beach from Australia. Joanna Black flew to Palm Beach to join Conrad for Canadian senator and businessman Trevor Eyton's annual holiday party in late December.

Since October it had been painfully clear to Black that the marriage was over. Black whimsically noted later that their house in Toronto was transformed into a 'seminary'. His wife's interest in Catholicism (her father was Catholic, her mother Protestant) was renewed after their move to London. Instead of this being a shared interest, however, Black was dismayed by her preference for Westminster Cathedral over the grandeur of Brompton Oratory.

Joanna grew close to a priest she had met. He soon left the clergy and after the Blacks' divorce they married. Black uses a religious analogy of his own to describe the effect this had on him: 'For months after my wife left me, I lived like a Benedictine monk, trying to decide what to do, whether to try to save my marriage.'

When news of the breakup began to circulate, one British friend asked Joanna, 'How could you leave a man on his way up?' Another friend in Toronto was astonished that she would leave a man who will 'eat anything you put in front of him'. Of her split with Conrad, Joanna said simply, 'I didn't leave him for anybody. I left him for me.'

The dissolution of his marriage left Black deeply wounded, and for a time he was much less visible on the London salon circuit. 'I can remember Conrad often looking terminally glum and gloomy, and obviously one didn't know why at that stage,' recalled *Telegraph* editor Max Hastings. After some dark days of lonely reflection at his Highgate mansion in late autumn – interspersed with Fairfax plotting – Black decided to get on with his personal life. There were any number of attractive female acquaintances whom friends of his thought he could have dated: Marie Josée Drouin,* Cathy Ford (daughter of Gerald), Princess Firyal of Jordan among them. From reading Black's autobiography, *A Life in Progress*, it is apparent it did not take long for Barbara Amiel to be elevated from 'cordial acquaintance' status to 'the summit of my most ardent and uncompromising desires'.

Amiel had made it abundantly clear over the years that Conrad Black was her type. In 1990 she called him 'my role model'. Shortly after he acquired the *Daily Telegraph* she wrote, 'I never have noticed how he handles knotting his tie or washing behind his ears, because he handles words with such considerable skill . . . I have always been intrigued by the manifestations of Conrad Black. He understands power.' In a prescient article in the Canadian monthly *Chatelaine* entitled 'Why Women Marry Up', she observed that 'power is sexy, not simply in its own right, but because it inspires self-confidence in its

* Drouin later married New York leveraged-buyout king Henry Kravis.

owner and a shiver of subservience on the part of those who approach it'.

When Black began pursuing Amiel in mid-November, she was reportedly involved with screenwriter William Goldman, contemplating a new life in New York. She was so surprised by Black's advances that she suggested he see a psychiatrist. 'She was worried that Conrad was not in a sane frame of mind at the end of his marriage,' recalled Miriam Gross, the *Sunday Telegraph*'s literary editor and one of Amiel's closest friends. He went, at her bidding. The prognosis was that Black was quite sane.

At Conrad's request, Joanna had held off announcing their separation but now she warned that it 'wouldn't be right' for him to take up with Amiel so publicly after the recent news of the split. It would appear, she predicted, that Amiel was the cause of the breakup. But Conrad told Joanna he was 'not going to make the same mistakes with Barbara' that he had made with Joanna when he had concealed her pregnancy before they were married. 'I'm not going to keep her in a closet.'

By early January – within weeks of the Blacks' children hearing the sad news from their parents – the first reports linking the pair began to appear in the British, then Toronto press.

In mid-June, 1992, Stephen Grant, a lawyer representing Conrad Moffat Black in his motion for a divorce from Joanna Catherine Louise Black, submitted his client's affidavit to a Toronto family court judge. In it, Grant's client stated that he and Joanna had been living 'separate and apart since 15 May 1991. Since that date there has been no resumption of cohabitation between the respondent and me, nor have we reconciled our marriage. The separation was by mutual agreement. There is no possibility of reconciliation between us.'

The Blacks had attended various social events together during the previous months and had lived under the same roof at various points throughout the summer and winter of 1991. But they were not living as husband and wife. When they had sat down in May 1992 to finalise the details of their divorce, Black had first proposed that the date of separation be set at the previous September, when he had returned to London and Joanna had stayed in Toronto. She had countered that December was appropriate, because that was when their children and friends had been told. After all, she had wanted to leave him in June, but, following his wishes, had for months maintained the charade that their marriage was intact.

From Joanna Black's perspective, her husband had wanted to keep under wraps the fact that she had left him to give him time to get his personal life in order. Once he had begun seeing someone new, he could appear a man in control rather than one whose wife had left him.

When the bickering over the date of separation had begun to get heated, they agreed simply to back-date it to May 1991, and to divorce as quickly as possible.

In London, where Barbara Amiel was a weekly columnist for the *Sunday Times*, the talk was of what an exciting salon this union would create – a modern day Henry and Clare Booth Luce. The thrice-married, neo-conservative occupied a special place in British newspaper punditry. 'She looks like Gina Lollobrigida and writes like Bernard Levin – and do get it the right way round,' a friend said in 1988.

In Toronto, the angle was that journalism's *femme fatale* had snared her ultimate catch. The tabloid *Toronto Sun*, where Amiel had once been the editor, reacted to news of the dalliance by featuring Amiel as its daily Sunshine Girl – 'beauteous and brainy, right-wing and right on' – trotting out a photo of her in a skimpy red and black showgirl number with fishnet stockings that she had once donned for a fundraiser.

Although she had not lived in Canada since 1985, Amiel was still a well known personality there, through her columns for the *Sun* and *Maclean's* magazine. And before she had gone overseas she had left an indelible stamp on the city as a writer, and, briefly, as the first female editor of the *Sun*. 'Conrad and Barbara can say big words to each other,' commented Toronto socialite Catherine Nugent, 'words that Shirley/Joanna had never heard of.' Sniffed another member of the same milieu: 'They're doing this to spice up their CVs. He needs sex for his image, she needs power.'

Amiel professed she wanted to keep private matters private, but, like Black, she could not allow all the barbs to go unchallenged. 'Now, the knives are drawn,' Amiel wrote in the monthly column she penned for *Maclean's*, the Canadian news magazine. 'My marriages and even

the cup of coffee I had with a friend become "an item" in My Past. . . .
The upside of all the nasty remarks that peppered the Canadian press
about my friendship with Conrad Black is that, speaking for myself,
happiness is an elusive bluebird and all the screechings in the world
can't make its song sound any less sweet.'

Certainly she and Black shared a similar world view and sometimes
crossed paths in London journalistic and society circles. But in many
respects Black could not have found someone more unlike himself.
'You couldn't think of two people with more differing backgrounds,'
observed financier and Hollinger director Peter Munk, 'and yet they
really are soulmates.'

While Conrad Black was making his name in the realm of
corporate conquest in the late 1970s and early 1980s, Barbara Amiel
was establishing herself as a figure of comparable notoriety. In those
days, Black would send her annual holiday wishes for 'an ideologically
uplifting Christmas'. When Black held a party for Andy Warhol at the
Art Gallery of Ontario in 1981, Amiel was in attendance.*

She was a self-promotion machine who derived obvious satisfaction from rattling the Establishment, dispensing potent opinions, and
seeing her name in the papers. 'I do get tired of all these milk-sops
calling to ask me wimpy questions,' she explained to one interviewer.
'So I take a childish, perverse adolescent pleasure in telling them I like
to get laid. I love to tease – and I don't mean sexually.'

In 1980, aged thirty-nine, Amiel decided to publish her autobiography, *Confessions*. Intended as a journal of ideological self-discovery –
her upbringing was British Marxist and she had attended the
Communist World Youth Festival in Helsinki in 1962 – it was more
noted for chronicling a troubled but adventurous life in sometimes
embarrassing detail. In *Confessions* could be found the evolution of an
uneasy soul, toughened by harsh experience that also left her insecure
and vulnerable. Like Black, Amiel is a night owl. 'I've suffered from
insomnia all my life,' she once explained. 'My earliest memory as a
child of four was being sedated to sleep.'

Amiel was born into a comfortable middle-class Jewish family in
east London in 1940. Her father was a lawyer and a colonel, her

* Warhol painted a three-panelled portrait of Black, which hangs in 10 Toronto
Street.

mother a nurse. They divorced when Barbara was nine, and in 1952 her mother remarried an Anglican draftsman of lower social standing and the family emigrated to Canada. They settled in the steel town of Hamilton, Ontario, where her stepfather had a difficult time supporting the family of five.

Relations between Barbara and her mother were tense. When she was fifteen, the family moved about half an hour away to St Catharines, but Amiel remained in Hamilton. She spent the next year boarding with strangers in basements and working odd jobs in chemists, canning factories and dress shops while attending school.

After a year, Amiel had a tenuous reconciliation with her family and rejoined them in St Catharines. Shortly after, she received devastating news from England: her father had committed suicide.

Despite her hardships, Amiel is remembered by classmates in St Catharines as being erudite and worldly. She read *Punch*, listened to opera, and spent summers with relatives in England. On a bursary, Amiel enrolled at the University of Toronto in 1959 to study philosophy and English. There she met her first husband, Gary Smith, a tall, handsome political science student who hailed from the upper-crust enclave of Forest Hill. They dated for four years, but their 1963 marriage lasted less than nine months.

After university, Amiel joined the Canadian Broadcasting Corporation as a typist. She quickly ascended to script assistant and eventually to on-air interviewer. She was not a great success on television, and later deprecated herself as 'a lacquered apparition with bouffant hair, glazed smile, and detachment bordering on the unconscious often reinforced by the mandatory dosage of Elavil'. Amiel was addicted to Elavil, an anti-depressant, for seven years. She began taking pills in university to cope with stress and fatigue, and was known to pop as many as twenty painkillers a day. Her only experience with marijuana, to which she reacted badly, was in a Times Square hotel room with poet and singer Leonard Cohen.

At the age of twenty-four, while a script assistant at the CBC, Amiel had an illegal abortion. 'I believe it to be morally wrong,' she wrote. 'At the time I had my own abortion I believed it to be morally wrong.' But rather than waiting four more months for the child's birth, 'I chose murder instead.'

Amiel's second husband, George Jonas, is a poet and journalist, who wears a black motorcycle jacket and has a vehicle to match. With Jonas, Amiel co-authored her first book, *By Persons Unknown,* about an infamous contract murder taken out by a Canadian businessman on his model wife. The marriage to the Hungarian emigré lasted five years until 1979 when she left him for Sam Blyth, a travel agent thirteen years her junior. The relationship with Blyth didn't endure, but Amiel and Jonas remained close friends and Amiel considered him her ideological mentor.

One of her best-remembered journalistic endeavours was an account of a trip to Mozambique in early 1981, when she and two male companions were imprisoned for ten days for entering the country without a visa. At one point, Amiel ate her press card to avoid identification. That year, she became a columnist for the *Toronto Sun,* and then its editor.

In 1983, she met cable-television magnate David Graham, and a year later the Ottawa Valley native became her third husband. Conrad and Joanna (who was then known as Shirley) Black were among the guests who fêted the marriage at a lavish party at Toronto's Sutton Place hotel. Amiel relinquished her editorship of the *Toronto Sun* and moved to England with Graham in 1985, but the marriage was dissolved three years later. She had no children by her three marriages.

In England, Amiel pounded the pavement to find a job as a columnist. But her Canadian credentials did not immediately open any doors. One of her earliest interviews was with *Sunday Telegraph* editor Peregrine Worsthorne. 'I remember it very well because this was still in Fleet Street,' says Worsthorne. 'She was, then as now, sexy, slinky, beautifully dressed, and she was wearing some enormously sexy scent. You had to walk down the corridor in this very old building and scent, therefore, would climb. She stayed about an hour.' Worsthorne enjoyed meeting her, but did not offer her a job. Instead, Amiel was hired at *The Times.* 'At this time she was totally unknown, and I would have been taking a completely unknown Canadian journalist, who looked in a way, rather absurd in those days,' explains Worsthorne. 'She didn't look as if she would be a good columnist. She looked flighty and it was very stupid because she is very good. And by the time of course we did try and get her, she'd made a name for herself on *The Times* and was already very well paid.'

By the time she and Graham split, Amiel had established herself as one of *The Times*'s top columnists, dispensing opinions first on the women's page against feminists, gay rights, and state-financed abortions. The magazine *Tatler* dubbed her 'Wapping's own Iron Lady', and in 1988 she was runner-up in the Press Association's Best Columnist category. In 1991 she became the lead political columnist in the *Sunday Times*.

Although she later maintained the relationship was purely platonic, she was for a time linked romantically with the publisher Lord Weidenfeld. Despite her successful career, Amiel was not universally accepted by the British in-crowd. Just as she was whispered about in Toronto for her thickening Oxonian accent, in London Amiel was often treated as an outsider, neither truly a Canadian nor a Brit. And her outspoken views did not make her universally welcome. 'The fashionable intellectual world in English journalism tends to be among those on the left', noted her friend Mirian Gross. 'To be ideological is not British at all.' Joanna Black recalled running into Amiel in a shop on Sloane Street a few months after the Blacks had taken up residence in London in 1990. Amiel congratulated Joanna on how well she was doing in London and how she must have done the right thing to become so popular. 'Everybody likes you,' she recalled Amiel telling her. 'It's terrible not to be liked.'

Like Conrad Black Amiel erected a fortress around her personal life when queried by journalists, yet revealed plenty of herself in her sayings and writings. 'I so loathe the permissive promiscuous society and so long for fidelity, stability and monogamy, but it is always just out of my reach,' she lamented in *Chatelaine* magazine in 1980. 'There is a thing called discipline. I have tried to inflict it on my work. I've tried to inflict it on me. But all that emerges is self-indulgence. Really, I won't talk about my personal life because I am ashamed of it.'

In June 1992, Black had other matters besides his personal life to attend to in Toronto. For instance, chairing Hollinger's annual meeting. He took time out from revelling in the Fairfax victory to deliver another of his considered tirades against Ontario premier Bob Rae and his New Democrat government: 'Ontario has the distinction of being practically the only jurisdiction in the world except for Cuba and North Korea that officially discourages the incentive system. No serious businessman can co-exist comfortably with such a regime.'

The next evening, a red rose tucked into the lapel of his tuxedo, Black stood expectantly while a light tapping of silver against crystal silenced the dining room at the Toronto Club. Escorted by Amiel, Black was presiding over the Hollinger Dinner. This year, the chowdown's guest speaker was Richard Nixon. 'As emotionalism has subsided,' Black said of the once-disgraced president, 'he has been seen to be a profoundly and widely esteemed figure, an elder statesman. I think there has been no American political leader since Thomas Jefferson who has been in the forefront of the country's attention for so long.'

Black's views on the former president had clearly evolved (as had many people's) from a decade earlier, when Black told biographer Peter Newman that Nixon was 'sleazy, tasteless and neurotic' and 'deserves the compassion due to sick people'.

Before introducing Nixon, Black scanned the room, playfully acknowledging some of his guests. Dwayne Andreas, the fabulously successful head of Archer Daniels Midland, was introduced as 'allegedly the most politically influential businessman in the United States . . . a man who because he is in the agri-business masquerades as a bit of a hayseed'; Cardinal Emmett Carter, Black's close friend and spiritual adviser was noted as 'dressed tonight in his raiment as the ecumenical chaplain of 10 Toronto Street, as well as the ecclesiastical Toronto stringer for the *Jerusalem Post*'; Lee and Walter Annenberg were recognised for having served as ambassadors to Britain under Nixon. 'Above all else,' Black opined of Walter Annenberg, he was 'the man who sold *TV Guide* and the *Daily Racing Form* to Rupert Murdoch for one *billion* dollars more than they were worth.'

'I would like to remind you that there was life before, as there will be life after, the so-called New Democratic Party,' Black continued, introducing two former premiers, William Davis and David Peterson, and the leaders of both current opposition parties, Lyn McLeod and Michael Harris. As usual, Black saved his best lines for his old friend and favourite verbal slagging partner, Hal Jackman. Jackman had left Hollinger's board the previous year when he had become Ontario's lieutenant-governor. Noting this in the Hollinger annual report, Black had written that Jackman would be an 'invaluable source of wise counsel to a government notoriously in need of it'. Now at the dinner, Black took credit for the appointment by mischievously suggesting it was the result of Black's calling Jackman a 'useful idiot' at the previous year's annual meeting, where Jackman had sat in the front row reading the *Independent* as a prank.

'Of course, he is not my enemy, he is my friend,' Black said of Jackman, 'although I'm sure that some of us will think – as he drives up University Avenue and gives us a jaunty, vice-regal wave from his landau, on his way to give royal assent to the latest statutory stage in the *sssssodomisation* of what were the commanding heights of a flourishing economy – that with friends like Hal we don't always need enemies.'

Before beginning his lecture on international politics, Nixon took the podium and said he was impressed by his host. 'I thought I knew something about American history, but he knows far more. And it was fascinating to hear him recount speeches that he could remember – that even I have made.'

Two weeks after the Hollinger Dinner and six days after the uncontested petition was filed, Conrad and Joanna Black's divorce was granted. 'You and I wouldn't have a hope of getting [a divorce] as quickly as that,' Toronto lawyer Erica James commented in the *Globe and Mail*. Less than a month after that, on the late morning of 21 July 1992, *Daily Telegraph* editor Max Hastings waited on the steps of Chelsea registry office holding a bouquet while ignoring the taunts – 'Are those for me, love?' – of a vagrant.

Black arrived for his second wedding wearing a dark double-breasted suit, while Amiel wore a green and white dress from Place Vendôme. Black's old friend Brian Stewart, now a senior television journalist with the Canadian Broadcasting Corporation, flew to London to be his witness; Miriam Gross would be Amiel's.

Amiel had recently attended the wedding of Lord Weidenfeld to Annabel Whitestone at the same registry office, and it did not escape her that the brief ceremony contained not a hint of the grandeur one might expect of the nuptials of Conrad Black. Indeed, under section forty-five of the Marriage Act, religious references were barred from registry office ceremonies.

Two days before their wedding was set to take place, Black and Amiel chatted with the Chelsea registrar, Norman Stephens, for a routine pre-nuptial chat. Warned of the blandness of the ceremony by his bride-to-be, Black asked Stephens if he and Amiel could not produce 'a more resonant rationale for our desire to marry than "the absence of any legal impediment to do so" '. As Amiel later related in a *Sunday Times* column, Stephens looked puzzled. 'I was thinking of God,' Black explained.

'Mr Stephens looked very glum at this,' Amiel recalled, 'and repeated that any cribbing from known ecclesiastical ceremonies such as "love, honour and obey", was out, never mind God.' No one tells Conrad Black what to do, and he unleashed a flourish at the hapless civil servant about how parliament might have the right to dictate how he performs his job, but it had no business muzzling what he and his intended could say at their own marriage. To defuse the situation, Amiel pulled out some words she had written 'in perfect samizdat language' for the service and ran them by the registrar, who was satisfied they did not contravene the law. 'They were horribly pompous,' Amiel admitted of the phrases she had composed, 'all about "human beings are more than blood and flesh and city and state" and ending up with a vow to my future husband of true love in the "name of my fathers, their fathers and the faith and beliefs that have sustained us through time".'

For Black, the Marriage Act was just another obstacle to be outwitted. 'I, too, should like to add to the ceremony,' Black ventured. 'I wish to say that, were it appropriate, I would pledge what was normal in a Christian ecclesiastical marriage oath, but as that is not appropriate, I would like it recorded that the sentiments in that oath are the ones I hold.' Stephens held his ground and said this would not do.

Despite the setback, the wedding went off as planned. That night, the newly-weds celebrated by dining at exclusive Annabel's, in a private room where the walls were covered in wine bottles. The twenty-odd guests included the Duchess of York, Sarah Ferguson, Lord and Lady Weidenfeld, Lord Rothschild, Baroness Thatcher and Sir Denis Thatcher, broadcaster David Frost and former U.S. assistant secretary for national security policy, Richard Perle. In addition to Brian Stewart and his wife, Hollinger president David Radler and wife Rona flew over from Canada.

To critics of the newly-weds, the event had a 'rent-a-celebrity' quality about it. The Duchess of York was there, Conrad Black later explained, because 'I had met her a number of times when she was with her husband, but he was away at sea a lot, being in the Navy. She sometimes had me as the additional man at these dinners of hers, so to some degree I owed her.

'Secondly, it's because of her marital problems and in a completely discreet and neutral way she found the fact that I had had problems of that kind as well something of a – not exactly a shared interest but a shared experience. And I was endeavouring, when she asked me, which was not very often, to give her advice on how to avoid some of the worst horrors that would await a person in her position. I have to be a little delicate here, in saying that. I don't wish to imply that as it all turned out she did avoid them but she occasionally asked my views and I occasionally gave them. That was why I invited her. It was because she occasionally had me to dinner and so why not? . . . We just invited people that we knew and we could only invite a few so we did invite a few. And frankly we had some unattached men so we needed some unattached women.'

In the text beneath the photo of the newly-weds looking adoringly at each other on the Chelsea registry steps, the next day's *Daily Telegraph* dutifully noted that 'the couple, who have homes in London, Toronto and Palm Beach, leave today for an extended holiday and working trip in North America'. Black stopped at his home to change in preparation for the trip and found, slipped through his letter box, a couriered hand-written note from John Major wishing him and Barbara well. The first stop on the trip was New York, via Concorde, where they dined that evening at La Côte Basque with William F. Buckley, his wife Pat, and John O'Sullivan, Buckley's successor as editor of the *National Review* and a close friend of Amiel's. 'It was a very chirpy evening and they had some political disagreement at dinner,' Buckley recalled. 'Nothing deep. Decriminalising drugs. She was pro, he was not. Certainly their conversation suggested that she had by no means been satellised in the twenty-four hours they'd been married.' A few days later the pair attended another dinner and concert at the Buckleys' home, and from there they went to a Maine cottage owned by David Rockefeller, where they were joined by Black's children and Amiel bashed out her weekly column, choosing her wedding as its topic. Black had vacationed at the cottage with his former wife and their children the previous year. The cottage had no fax, let alone a television, and Black quickly discovered the price of husbandly duty as he drove around trying to find a fax machine in order to send his wife's column to his chief competitor.

Black and Amiel soon took another trip, this time to Fiji and Australia, and his friends and employees began to notice a marked difference in Black's demeanour. One noted drily that Joanna had kept Conrad's feet on the ground, certainly 'more so than his present wife'.

'They've become incredibly glamorous as a couple,' observed Miriam Gross. 'One notices when they come into a room at a party. Everyone knows that they're important including, I think, themselves.' Max Hastings, for one, noted that the gloom that had surrounded Black after his first marriage had fallen apart quickly lifted. 'Nowadays,' he said a year after the wedding, 'he's absolutely full of the joys of spring, and terribly happy. I mean, dealing with him on business things is incredibly easy. He's infinitely more relaxed, he enjoys the social rounds terrifically. I think he feels comfortable with himself and the life he's living. You know, he's just a completely different person.'

Conrad and Barbara lived at the home in Highgate for almost a year, but it was far from Amiel's lunches in the centre of town or coffees at Harvey Nichols. And, Amiel would complain to friends, there was a long walk from the house to a waiting car that could ruin one's hair. The house was put up for sale and the Blacks moved into rented digs on Chester Square with the Black feline, Max (named by his children and not after Hastings). Friends began to notice that Black was doing things that he had said he would never do, such as live in a row house, contemplate installing a tennis court at his Palm Beach home, and wear shorts. Though four years Black's senior, it was almost as if Amiel were keeping him young. 'They're intellectually very well suited,' said Gross. 'He has these obsessive interests in Napoleon or Cardinal Newman which she doesn't necessarily share, but finds amusing and funny.'

(Among Black's peculiar passions is his collection of curios, many of them kept in the basement of his Toronto home. There, in glass cases, are wooden models of battleships which he regularly buys. ['They're all from the same scale, so if you want to see what the *Bismarck* and *Hood* looked like, how they compare, you could put them on a table beside each other.'] Also in glass cases are the hats of the late Maurice Duplessis and Cardinal Leger, and, for good measure, a cardinal's chair. He also collects the autographs of famous people including those of Lincoln, Napoleon, Roosevelt, Churchill, MacArthur, and an abdication proclamation signed by Edward VIII. He is keeping an eye out for a good George Washington.)

The relationship with Amiel also aided Black in dispelling the 'grievous myth that I am in sedentary and flabby condition physically'. Though always well over 200 pounds, Black's weight can swing dramatically up and down. But 'under the influence' of Amiel, there was a new emphasis on fitness. 'We have this personal trainer and I am actually in damn good shape in muscular terms. I do a hundred push-ups twice a week – *a hundred push-ups.*' All at once? 'No, I stop once. Look, it's strenuous stuff – and I'm not a light person to be pushing up off the floor.'

Amiel also persuaded Black to update his wardrobe. Until then, most of his suits had come with his director's discount from Toronto department store Eaton's; chief tailor Ilie Dumitru would travel a few blocks to Black's office for fabric selection and fittings.

'No disrespect to my Romanian, Eatonian friend, but I think I could make a case I'm fairly well turned out now. Since I've been in England I basically have my suits made at two tailors there. You don't go wrong at Huntsman. They're not fast and they're not cheap but they're very well cut suits. Doug Hayward is the most entertaining guy as a tailor – he's very good too.' As for his wife's influence in these matters: 'She admires all fugitives from communism, but does not consider Romanian tailoring to be the best that's available.'

Several months into their marriage, the Blacks found a new home in London, on Kensington's Cottesmore Gardens, paying about £3.5 million for a four-level mansion most recently owned by fallen Australian tycoon Alan Bond. One of its most alluring features, according to its selling agent, was an 'environmental chamber', which is an upmarket sauna room that blows cold or warm winds to simulate the climate of virtually any locale. 'It's an all-round paradise and you can transport yourself to any part of the world,' said the agent. The newly-weds hired an architect, Anthony Collett Associates, to make major renovations. The property is actually two large homes joined together, and the renovations called for a new grey slate mansard roof (which met with opposition from local council members because it threatened the uniformity of the street) and a single front door. Inside, it featured a gymnasium, jacuzzi and pool, eleven bedrooms, eight bathrooms, and two lifts. The environmental chamber did not survive the many revisions the design underwent. 'I was always sceptical it would work properly,' Black said with a shrug, adding, 'It's not my style to sit there and try to simulate a South Sea island.'*

The Blacks also hired a cook and a butler, who would fly ahead to Toronto or Palm Beach to prepare for their arrival. The butler, Werner Jankowsky, had been a fixture at Toronto's Sutton Place hotel, and was one of the reasons Robin Leach ranked it one of the world's top ten hotels on the television programme *Lifestyles of the Rich and Famous*. Jankowsky had looked after his share of the rich and famous – from Liza Minnelli and Jane Fonda to Lech Walesa and King Gustav – sometimes for weeks on end. 'I had very interesting people, for example Marlon Brando,' Jankowsky recalled. 'You know, he ate at one o'clock in the morning, and things like that. Then he read Kipling to me or things like that. He needed someone to talk to in the night.'

Sutton Place's round-the-clock butler service was an advertised feature; Jankowsky lived there and slept with a beeper. However, the hotel ran into financial difficulties and was sold in 1993. A full-time butler was not part of the new owners' marketing strategy so Jankowsky left and worked for several months during the day for Toronto money managers Ira Gluskin and Gerry Sheff. Then Black, who knew Werner from his Sutton Place days, offered him a job as his personal valet. Even though both Blacks stay up late, Jankowsky says that suits him fine – the hours are a definite improvement over Sutton Place. 'I'm used to that, you know. I don't mind the hours and they always ask me "If that is not too much" to work late. Oh ya, I love my

---

* More than two years after they bought the house, it would not be ready for the Blacks to move into. Neighbours insisted the plans be scaled back, calling them a 'folie de grandeur' and 'pretentious'. Black fired off a sardonic letter saying, 'I look forward . . . to reciprocating your helpful spirit of neighbourliness.'

job here. I love working for both Blacks. And they're nice people and that's the main thing.'

In a story entitled 'Is this London's most powerful woman?', the *Evening Standard* explored the percolating theory that Amiel was a nineties version of Pamela Hartwell, the glamorous late spouse of Lord Hartwell. Less charitable comparisons were made with Yoko Ono.

Friends took up Amiel's defence. After all, she was an easy target – ambitious, brainy, successful, attractive, certainly politically incorrect. As her husband saw it, she was 'made the subject of all sorts of common tittle-tattle about her private life and how she used, allegedly, her physical attributes to advance her career [. . .] that have had no other basis than the envy extended towards an attractive, intelligent woman.'

Black appointed her to the board of the *Spectator* and *Saturday Night* magazine, and made her the head of the private Black Foundation. It was around this time that Black encountered a shakeup of the *Telegraph* newsroom that saw deputy editor Trevor Grove sacked and replaced by Simon Heffer, signalling a toughening of the paper's conservative bent. When asked by a *Maclean's* magazine scribe whether Amiel steered his guidance of the *Telegraph*, Black's eyes narrowed. 'I was aware that there was a myth that had floated around – though I thought it had died by now – that my wife was exercising some Mephistophelian influence on my relations with the editor. I can assure you none of that is true.'

It was not difficult to discern Amiel's influence on at least one article that found its way into the *Daily Telegraph* on the last day of 1992. Black had written various weighty contributions to the paper since moving to London, such as his commentary on the Canadian elections, or his review of the *Oxford Book of Canadian Military Anecdotes*. But on 31 December, the *Daily Telegraph* published what is believed to be the first contribution by a British newspaper proprietor to the fashion pages.

Before Christmas of that year, at a party organised for department heads by Max Hastings, Black had criticised the *Telegraph*'s fashion editor, Kathryn Samuels, for writing favourably about long skirts. Standing her ground, Samuels countered that Black was welcome to write an article arguing the opposing view. Black was reluctant, but another piece in his paper on 28 December which advised 'a long, slim skirt is a basic essential' was too much for him. A more autocratic proprietor might have simply had their editor replaced for insubordination, but this was not the Black approach. During a holiday in Florida, Black wrote what he described as 'a personal offensive against the efforts of the long skirt brigade to kill off the short skirt'. Black wrote that 'the frenzied efforts of the long faction to pretend that the short has been exterminated other than among the perverse, the penniless or the reactionary enemies of style is outrageous . . . It is bunk to claim that long is in, short is out and anything above the knee, as the *Daily Telegraph* wrote of the Princess of Wales, is dowdy.' The article was accompanied by photos of various women in short skirts including the princess and, as it happened, Barbara Amiel.

Black's peculiar pronouncements brought instant reaction from the fashion world. One fashion editor accused Black of 'fashion fascism', but his tirade found support from Gianni Versace, the fashion designer, who soon after the article declared that 'for us, long is over'.

In what would become an occasional rite, Amiel took up the matter in an article of her own in *The Times*, this one a month after her husband's. She explained how, on arriving for New Year's Eve in Florida – just as Black was putting the finishing touches to his article – she had discovered an erroneously packed long skirt in her luggage. 'The offending article would not roll up at the waist, as my spouse requested, nor stay tied under armpits with string and Scotch tape.'

'No one will notice,' Black told her cheerfully. 'Just wear the top and leave the skirt at home.'

This foray into fashion punditry and sexual politics was a new wrinkle. 'The London press was claiming that I was such an admirer of my wife's thighs that I wrote it for her,' he later reflected. 'Indeed, I am an admirer of my wife's thighs. I don't want to border on indelicate, but the degree to which I see my wife's thighs does not depend on what she wears.'

It remained a matter of curiosity that Black had chosen a career journalist as his bride. After all, Black is not exactly a champion of the craft. 'Many journalists and most of the more talented ones,' Black has said more than once, 'are happy to chronicle the doings and sayings of others, but a significant number, including many of the most acidulous and misanthropic are, in my experience, inexpressibly envious of many of the subjects of their attention.'

Amiel's own writings clearly hold the answer to the contradiction – her regard for the business is only a few notches higher than her husband's. In 1993, when Margaret Thatcher's memoirs were England's publishing sensation, Amiel wrote a column condemning the editor of *Harpers & Queen*, Vicki Woods, for deceptively turning a photo shoot with Thatcher into an article about her comments and actions throughout the shoot. (Woods's article, incidentally, ran in the *Spectator*, owned by Black).

Amiel wrote that Emperor Franz Joseph 'hit the nail on the head when he described journalists as *canailles*. Today that means rogues, but as I understand it he used it in the sense of scum or sewers.' Amiel did not buy Woods's explanation that although no interview had been agreed to, the idea for the article only arose after witnessing the photo shoot.

'I am a journalist myself and I think we are all made of *merde* and the craft is *merde* . . . Why, I ask myself, does someone stay in a wretched occupation like journalism? Anything other than straight news reporting often forces us to become courtiers of people we dislike or resort to little ruses even with those we admire to get our copy – a host of smarm and iffy relationships that brings me out in spots half the time. After each profile I write I vow never to play the game again. And then the vow is broken. Why?' Amiel called on one of her favourite references, Adam Smith, to provide the answer, and explained somewhat mildly that while journalists may live in the sewer, they prevent from arising 'an even worse sewer, that of star chambers and secret power-holders in high places'.

Writing in the *Evening Standard*, press critic Stephen Glover compared her argument to 'one of those brutes who go on the rampage, spraying bullets in all directions, before turning the gun upon herself'. Glover argued that just because Amiel's personal circumstances had changed, she was not justified to attack her craft. 'Now that she is rich, Mrs Conrad Black gives the impression she wants to be on the inside. She feels differently about her chosen profession, which is not all that glamorous. Perhaps she looks forward to intimate parties and grand holidays, interspersed with a little gentle charity work.'

In another column, Amiel responded that 'one of the differences between me and my sisters in the women's movement is that I do not regard my husband's money as my own. Having married very wealthy men before my current husband, I can guarantee that I parted from them leaving both their fortunes and my opinions intact.' Amiel had been called a bitch 'all my life and did not need the authority of money to be one'. Hers was the classic celebrity line that she had not changed, those around her had. 'Me, I continue to be moody, opinionated, a bit driven and all the things that rubbed people the wrong way before I met Conrad, and rubbed some the right way which was responsible for my getting a column and other jobs.

'Ultimately, I am a north London Jew who has read a bit of history. That means I know this: in a century that has seen the collapse of the Austro-Hungarian, British and Soviet empires, reversal of fortune is this rich bitch's reality; one might as well keep working and have the family's Vuitton suitcases packed.'

Fast forward to a sunny Toronto afternoon in June 1994: Conrad and Barbara Amiel Black, as she was now known, milled about with shareholders following the Hollinger annual meeting at the King Edward Hotel. It was Amiel's first annual meeting as a Hollinger director, and a reporter pointed out that she was the first true journalist to join the board.

'Mind you, you were the one who wrote they were *canailles*,' Conrad said playfully.

'Yes,' replied Amiel, 'they are *canailles*, but they're necessary, too.'

'Barbara, if I didn't think journalists were necessary I wouldn't employ them. And indeed' – he placed his arm affectionately around his wife – 'our relationship might be quite different.'

TWELVE

All Over the Map

'There was an awful lot of shilly-
shallying and foot dragging and
pusillanimous mealy-mouthed
evasiveness going on'

In the early 1990s, the worst recession since the Great Depression blanketed much of the Western world and took large swaths out of corporate profits. It was a time of introspection and retrenching in all industries. But it was a particularly unsettling time for the media business. Legendary investor Warren Buffett, with more than a billion dollars invested in media stocks, ventured that 'media business will prove considerably less marvellous than I, the industry or lenders thought would be the case only a few years ago'. Metromedia chairman John Kluge declared of the marketplace: 'It's murder out there.'

At the same time, Hollinger's interests were expanding across the globe more aggressively than ever. Black had begun to define this strategy as 'Micawberism'. This was a typical Victorian allusion, referring to Wilkins Micawber, the impractical optimist from Charles Dickens's *David Copperfield*, whose credo was that something will always turn up. And in the early 1990s a lot did. 'I've often found with Conrad that crises or big events all happen in immense clusters,' says Brian Stewart, his friend since adolescence. 'Most of the time I think he's just dying to get back to the quiet so he can get back to his books and read, but at the same time he's caught in these great dramas.'

Yet the dramas are rarely as spontaneous as they appear when first trumpeted in newspaper headlines. Nor was it a coincidence that while others were bemoaning the state of the industry, Black was on the hunt. The *Telegraph* was proving resilient to the downturn, thanks in part to its strategy of cover price increases, which meant the paper was less dependent on advertising revenue, which was tied directly to the economy.

However, parent company Hollinger's financial health was not as pristine as Black would have hoped. At year-end 1991, net debt stood at $685 million, against shareholders' equity of $348.9 million, a ratio of debt to equity which Dominion Bond Rating Service called 'too high'. But, as always, Black had a plan. The main prong was to sell shares in the Hollinger flagship, the *Daily Telegraph*, and to list it on the London Stock Exchange.* For the task he enlisted the blue-chip investment houses Cazenove and Rothschild, whose relationships with the *Telegraph* predated Black's. But the timing was not great.

Robert Maxwell had died in mysterious circumstances while yachting off the coast of the Canary Islands in November 1991. There had always been widespread doubts cast on Maxwell's character and business practices, but few conceived of the accusations of impropriety he would leave behind. Still, the *Daily Telegraph* ran a respectful obituary of the man, written by editor Max Hastings. Hastings had rung Black, who was in his Toronto office, to tell him the news. 'Well, err on the side of generosity,' Black told his editor. He did not believe in denigrating his fellow proprietors and, commented Hastings, 'I think Conrad is sometimes inclined to give the benefit of the doubt to apparently very rich men. And Conrad would sometimes say to me that while of course he knew Maxwell was a rogue, that [he didn't] share my view that he was actually a bad man.' In any case, it was also Hastings's policy to err on the side of generosity in obituaries.

Even in death, Robert Maxwell could have an effect on Black and other proprietors. As a result of the financial scandal that emerged in the months following Maxwell's drowning, and which was crowned by the revelation that more than a billion dollars of his companies' pension fund money was missing, Black was assigned a 'tycoon factor'. 'As a swashbuckling media proprietor who pops up to buy newspapers all over the globe, has a web of companies, heavy debts, a pattern of shuffling assets between his companies – and a penchant for libel litigation – Black realised comparisons between him and the Maxwell empire are inevitable,' the *Sunday Times* wrote. 'He tackles them head-on and at length.'

---

* Black had made a pledge to list the *Telegraph* when he took it over.

On the *Telegraph*'s listing, the London Stock Exchange imposed an unusual 'geographical' separation clause under which Hollinger agreed that the *Telegraph* would be Black's sole investment vehicle for the United Kingdom and Europe. Presumably, this was to ensure that Black would not invest in a competitor of the *Telegraph*, as he had, through Hollinger, with his stake in United Newspapers, owner of the Express titles. It also meant that a thirteen per cent stake Hollinger had acquired in Trinity International Holdings plc, operator of the *Liverpool Echo* and some small newspapers in Canada, had to be transferred to Telegraph plc to comply with the rule. Coolness towards the issue was not aided by the fact that existing *Telegraph* minority shareholders – Black owned eighty-three per cent of the shares at this stage and the plan was for him to hold sixty-eight per cent – received a letter from the company explaining that an 'obscure' London Stock Exchange rule governing minority shareholder approval had been 'inadvertently overlooked'. As a result, minority shareholders were unaware that loans totalling £33 million had been made by Telegraph plc to Hollinger between December 1990 and May 1992.

The 'Max Factor' and a dismal market for initial stock offerings left underwriters Rothschild and Cazenove with 10 million of the Telegraph's 13 million shares issued at 325p. It was like a birthday party where no one showed up. The share price proceeded to plummet to a low of 222p within weeks of the offering. Said one disaffected analyst: 'The reaction from institutional investors was either a big "So what" or an acutely cynical comment about Mr Black and his bandwagon.'

If the critics were to be believed, London investors were not keen on any company that relied heavily on the visions and whims of a single person. No one canvassed the thoughts of David Radler, who was once asked what would happen if a tragedy were to strike Black. 'Well, it would be lighter on the payroll,' he said with a chuckle. 'We'd lose about four club memberships. . . . Absolutely nothing would happen, okay? I mean, all of us could be on the airplane when it went down and nothing would happen. The fact is that we own 307 newspapers, so somewhere along the line there are 307 people managing this company. And, honestly, they are the ones who produce the profit. Whether it's Joe Cooke in London or Les Plummer in Port Arthur,

Texas, not one aspect of their business will be affected by the demise of the ownership.'

To Black's satisfaction, the share price of Telegraph plc – it dropped the 'Daily' from its corporate title with the listing – soon rebounded. Stock in the company Black had secured control of at a mere 50p per share six years earlier was soon trading at 370p. Black next took other measures to get his financial house in order. He raised $150 million through preferred share issues, sold his stake in United Newspapers (at a $36 million loss), and then his interest in Trinity (at a $13 million gain). In Black's view, this put the company in an excellent position to make 'an advantageous investment'.

Robert Maxwell was dead, and Rupert Murdoch had gone to Hollywood. Now, it was Conrad Black's turn to catapult even further onto the world stage.

Hollinger held exploratory discussions with representatives of South African gold magnate Henry Oppenheimer about investing in his Times Media Ltd, publisher of South Africa's largest paper, the *Sunday Times*. Those talks fizzled out, as did discussions about joining a consortium with Time Warner Inc. to launch Britain's fifth television channel. But participation in a consortium to win one of Britain's breakfast television franchises at least left the Telegraph with five per cent of Carlton Television.

While Maxwell's death had created some problems for Black, it also presented opportunities. In the UK Black had a fleeting interest in Maxwell's Mirror Group Newspapers, but it was difficult to imagine his ownership of a left-of-centre down-market tabloid going over well either at the Mergers and Monopolies Commission or, for that matter, with Black's conscience. The *Daily News* of New York was altogether a different prospect.

Maxwell had bought the *Daily News* from Tribune Co. a few months before his death, promising to invest heavily and restore the famous tabloid to its former glory. (Tribune had actually *paid* Maxwell US$60 million to take the paper, while he assumed about US$100 million in liabilities.) The *News* soon became merely the latest big-top for Maxwell's media circus.

Founded by Captain Joseph Patterson in 1919, the *News* had once boasted the highest circulation in all America. Its circulation, at

800,000 when it went into the hands of receivers, was still considerably higher than that of its competitors the *New York Post* and *New York Newsday*, but down more than 300,000 from the previous year, when it suffered a debilitating 147-day strike.

Before his death, Maxwell had managed to bring down the number of employees at the union-fortified *News* to about 2,100 from about 2,700.

Although his home in Palm Beach and ownership of American Publishing gave him a presence in America, Black loved the New York scene.* One evening in the months following Maxwell's death, Black found himself at a dinner party in London chatting with American television interviewer-of-the-stars Barbara Walters. After discussing his newspaper exploits, she suggested Black ought to speak to her friend John Veronis, an investment banker specialising in media, about buying the *Daily News*. After a call from the Telegraph, Veronis, Suhler's managing director Martin Maleska flew to London for a long meeting with Black to discuss the New York newspaper market and the *News*'s place in it.

The *News* shared one characteristic with other Black deals: it was seriously overmanned and desperately in need of a new printing plant. On the other hand, Black had no experience in the tabloid realm and had been a vocal critic of the sensationalist practices of Britain's tabloids. Nevertheless, Black became seriously interested in the paper. He vowed to make 'a good deal or no deal'. Meeting with the bankrupt paper's board of directors during a paper-plate lunch catered by the Taste Bud deli on the eighth floor of the *News*'s renowned art deco building on Forty-Second Street, Black warned editor and publisher Jim Willse, 'I have no interest in coming to New York to clasp my lips around an exhaust pipe.'

Along with Black, Hollinger president Radler considered a formal bid. An offer would fall under the American Publishing aegis, and, besides, Radler was no stranger to New York – his father and grandparents on his father's side had been born there, and as an adolescent in Montreal he used to read the *News* for its sports. Black

---

* He used to stay periodically with his first wife in the apartment kept there by Hanna Mining when Black was a Hanna director.

and Radler agreed that if they succeeded in buying the paper, they would oversee it together.

Black had spoken for some time about his desire for an American 'flagship' for American Publishing, and the *Daily News* seemed to fit the bill. Through Veronis, Radler and Black also held talks with Peter Kalikow, who had bought the *New York Post* from Rupert Murdoch in 1990 for US$37 million and had since sunk some US$80 million more into it. Kalikow was convinced that the *Post* and the *News* should merge into one operation under one roof – his. Black and Radler met him in the spring of 1992, despite the fact that Kalikow had filed for personal bankruptcy stemming from his real estate investments. They decided not to go ahead together.

Black and Radler also talked with another, more serious bidder for the *News*, Mortimer Zuckerman. Another native Montrealer, Zuckerman had made a fortune in real estate on the U.S. east coast, then ventured into publishing by buying *Atlantic Monthly* magazine and *U.S. News and World Report*. All manner of arrangements were bandied about between Black, Radler, Zuckerman and his chief publishing lieutenant, Fred Drasner. Recalled Radler, 'At one point he talked, for instance, that we would switch every year who would control the editorial page. I had a deal with him one time where we would have what's called a "negative option": You could fire anyone but you'd have to have the okay to do a hiring. In the original negotiations, I remember he said, "I'll take the editorial, you guys take production, distribution and advertising." A little later he said, "Fred Drasner, he's a real New Yorker, he may take the advertising." So we were going to be left with circulation and production. That was the kind of thing.'

It soon became clear that Zuckerman and Hollinger would be bidding against each other. Former *Post* owner Rupert Murdoch voiced a tempered vote of support for Black. 'I think Conrad would be very good for the *News*, and he'd be better still for this city,' Murdoch remarked. 'It needs a strong voice. I think it would be good all around. I just hope that the financial markets don't punish him too much, because the tabloid wars in New York are a black hole.'

On 17 August, an offer from Hollinger to invest US$75 million in the newspaper won the backing of the *News*'s board of directors and management, but the deal, which included cutting a further one-third of the paper's jobs, was contingent on coming to an agreement with its unions. There were thirteen separate union heads to deal with, but the drivers', journalists' and pressmen's unions were the most crucial. American Publishing chief financial officer David Dodd held endless discussions with the individual union leaders, while Black and Radler each met a couple of times with larger groups. At one point, Black made a presentation at the Doral Park hotel on Park Avenue, accompanied by Rupert Middleton, works manager at the Telegraph's half-owned West Ferry Road printing plant. The unions were well aware of Black's reputation as a man of the right who had slashed work-forces throughout his career. 'He spoke to that point quite persuasively,' recalled Maleska. Black's angle was: yes we've cut back jobs, but the Telegraph maintains a lot of well-paying very desirable jobs at its West Ferry operation and has even created jobs, although staffing levels of course reached nowhere near those of the old Fleet Street shop.

Black and his colleagues were not positive enough. In the end, the crucial drivers' and pressmen's unions backed Zuckerman's bid, while a third bidder gained the support of the journalists' guild. Though unwilling to raise the ante, Black was clearly agitated about yielding to Zuckerman. 'He has given the store away,' Black told the *Financial Post*. 'He has capitulated to the pressmen and the drivers.' Indeed, Black opined that Zuckerman would run the paper as a 'hobby'. Zuckerman took over the paper in October and calmly responded that as a private individual he did not have to worry about short-term profit objectives in the way a company like Hollinger did. 'We have much more of a focus on the editorial product than most people who own public companies,' he said. 'This means we have a long-term view.'

The unsuccessful bid did give Hollinger a profile in the U.S. investment community. And it showed that, unlike most latter-day New York tabloid kings, Black was not willing to win at all costs. 'The financial landscape is littered with companies which have over-reached,' Black remarked, vowing, 'We are determined never to be among them.' Besides, Black already had his sights on bigger prey.

It would be almost too easy to compare the Southams of Canada with

Britain's Berrys or Australia's Fairfaxes. But there was a sameness in the way many of the world's great print dynasties of the British empire were built in the late nineteenth and early twentieth centuries, just as there were similarities in the way many of them were crumbling by the late twentieth century.

William Southam was a hard-working twenty-three-year-old when in 1877, a decade after the British North American Act had established Canada as an independent dominion, he bought a twenty-five per cent interest in the London Free Press in London, Ontario. Southam had been born in Lachine, Quebec, where his parents, *en route* from Britain to London, Ontario, had stopped for his birth.

Ten years after buying into the Free Press, Southam put down $4,000 to buy, with partner William Carey, a controlling interest in the *Hamilton Spectator*. This produced enough profit to open print shops in Montreal and Toronto and to buy another newspaper, the *Ottawa Citizen*. Southam raised seven children, and they were increasingly involved in the expanding family business, which by 1904 included the *Citizen*, half the *Spectator* – subsequently increased to 100 per cent after Carey's death – and interests in steel mills, crushed stone and carriage works. In later years, a code of conduct was developed to govern the company: There was to be no investing outside the field of communications; no senior personnel were to serve as directors of outside firms; all employees had to steer clear of any political involvements that might impinge on the objectivity of Southam's publications.

In the first decades of the twentieth century, the company expanded westwards, buying the *Calgary Herald*, the *Edmonton Journal*, and papers in Winnipeg and Vancouver. By 1944, when a quarter of the company was sold to the public to establish value for succession duties, Southam was well established as Canada's premier national newspaper chain. When William Southam's grandson St Clair Balfour took over the company a decade later, it owned seven dailies, and over the years Balfour continued to buy major metropolitan papers and smaller trade publications in the east and west.

Balfour viewed himself as a benign caretaker. Every newspaper was run as an autonomous fiefdom by a publisher who subscribed to the family's high journalistic principles and commitment to public service. Most efforts to take advantage of the economies that a national chain of newspapers offered – for purchasing, marketing or advertising sales – were shunned as infringements on that sacred independence.

In 1975, aged sixty-four, Balfour passed the reins to Gordon Fisher, son of one of his first cousins. Fisher was less tied to the company's print roots and expanded into graphics, cable-television and broadcasting, as well as a range of databases, trade shows and electronic media.

The soaring economy of the 1980s ensured that the company continued to be profitable, and masked the waywardness of many of Southam's expansions and the full effect on some of its most lucrative markets of new tabloid competitors from Toronto Sun Publishing Corp. 'The Southam organisation has been highly principled, decent and fair,' commented long-time director Adam Zimmerman in 1990. 'I think you can argue they've done that to a fault, because they've tolerated mediocre profit performance from fine journalistic people.' Conrad Black's view of Southam was that it gave its journalists 'absolute liberty of content and virtual liberty in editorial budgets'. And over time, 'this arrangement degenerated, inexorably into soft, left journalistic pap for the readers and collapsing profits and stock price for the shareholders'.

In spring 1985, Gordon Fisher became terminally ill with liver cancer. This being the era of the corporate raider the Southam family feared its hold over the company was at risk. The once tightly held shares were dispersed among a wide group of Southams, Fishers, and Balfours, and represented considerably less than fifty per cent of the company. Until this point, nobody had seemed to care that Southam was not highly profitable, that many of its diversifications had not worked out, or that its newspaper margins were roughly half the thirty per cent that rival Thomson Corp. was squeezing out of its mostly smaller papers.

With Fisher's illness, rumours swirled that a predator was stalking rudderless Southam. The most commonly mentioned name was George Mann, an acquisitor-of-the-moment through a company called Unicorp Canada Corp. Another was Conrad Black, who had offered to take a friendly twenty-five per cent position in Southam during the spring and had been 'very politely' rebuffed by patriarch St Clair Balfour.*

Having retired as Southam chairman in April at the age of seventy-five, Balfour, whose astonishing eyebrows resemble thunderbolts shooting at angles from riveting blue eyes, was pressed back into action as executive vice-president by Fisher's illness. Although both Mann and Black were buying blocks of Southam stock – Black built a five per cent stake – both denied they intended to take a run at the company; each was merely playing the stock and waiting for someone else to make a move. On Friday 23 August 1985, rumours of a raid began to crescendo. Trading in Southam stock was particularly heavy, and much of it was through Gordon Securities, which had links to both Mann and Black. Balfour was told on good authority by one of his lawyers that a bid was set for the following Monday morning. As Black tells it, Southam was fleeing phantoms. 'I don't question Clair's sincerity,' said Black, 'but in my view all those guys were spooked. I think they were financially naïve and I think they were spooked.'

Over that August weekend, Balfour and Hugh Hallward, husband of Gordon Fisher's younger sister, arranged to meet in a Toronto hotel room with Beland Honderich, chairman of Torstar Corp. So urgent was the mood that Balfour and Hallward arrived at the hotel early, and the room had yet to be made up. Hurriedly, they straightened the bed themselves.

Balfour had high regard for Honderich and for the *Toronto Star*, Canada's largest daily newspaper, which was Torstar's main asset. The *Toronto Star*, like Southam's papers, claimed to operate under the public service principles of its founder Joseph Atkinson, although it maintained a strong Liberal Party line. Torstar was controlled by a trust composed of several families. It seemed to Balfour a most logical merger, for Torstar owned the largest broadsheet in Canada – the *Toronto Star* – and Southam had the major broadsheet daily in most

---

* Balfour and Black were not strangers to each other. Balfour had attended Black's parents' 1937 wedding in Winnipeg while working as a reporter at the *Winnipeg Tribune*. When Black began establishing Sterling Newspapers in the 1970s, Balfour put prospective sellers of small papers, including Prince Edward Island's Summerside paper the *Journal Pioneer*, in touch with him. Recalled Balfour, 'When people came to us and we didn't wish to buy them, I'd say, "There is an alternative to Thomson who I'm sure will buy it. There's Conrad Black."'

other Canadian centres: Montreal's *Gazette,* the *Ottawa Citizen,* the *Hamilton Spectator,* the *Windsor Star,* the *Calgary Herald,* the *Edmonton Journal,* even a duopoly in Vancouver, with the *Vancouver Sun* and *The Province.* But although its head office was in Toronto, Canada's largest city, the only newspaper Southam maintained there was the *Financial Times of Canada,* a national weekly of modest circulation.

Balfour had wanted to align Southam and Torstar since the early 1970s. Under the deal that was cobbled together over that August weekend, Torstar received 22.5 per cent of Southam's voting stock in return for a thirty per cent non-voting stake in Torstar. An agreement was devised that would prevent Torstar from increasing its shareholding until 1995. The Southam family agreed to consolidate its holdings into a voting trust, which bound together with Torstar's stake amounted to forty-five per cent, and effective control. 'We didn't want the newspapers to go to somebody who wasn't interested in editorial quality,' recalled Balfour – and at this stage Black's commitment to quality could be judged only on the Sterling chain. 'Call it newspaper mystique.'

Southam's share price, which had risen following all the rumours, began to fall once the agreement was announced, and some investors, such as Montreal money manager Stephen Jarislowsky, were incensed: 'It was just a way of the family saving its own ass and staying in power.'

Jarislowsky and two other investors joined with the federal competition bureau to challenge the Southam-Torstar agreement in court. Meanwhile, the Ontario Securities Commission slapped the wrists of the Southam and Torstar directors for what it saw as high-handed behaviour. The suit launched by Jarislowsky and the competition bureau led to a settlement under which Southam and Torstar agreed to dissolve their voting trust in May 1990. In theory, from that point on, the company would be vulnerable to take-over, and with a 22.5 per cent interest Torstar would have a considerable foothold from which it could take Southam over.

Despite Balfour's best intentions, Southam and Torstar cultures never meshed. Gordon Fisher's brother, John, and Hallward, who became the company's chief executive and chairman respectively after Gordon's death, did not welcome Torstar's involvement in the company's affairs (each company received three slots on the other's board). Fisher, who came to the company after nine years of running Fraser Inc., a forest-products firm in the Canadian Maritimes, was adamant that the newspapers should remain independent, which to some sounded like empty semantics aimed at preserving the Southam family's domination of the affairs of a company they no longer owned. 'Before John was there, I think the intent of the deal was that everyone would come together,' said David Galloway, Torstar's chief executive and a Southam board member for several years. 'When they brought in new management, new management said, "Torstar, stay out of the kitchen." ' A long-time Southam director says both sides were equally to blame. 'I've had a lot of experience being the majority owner or the big guy,' says the director. Both companies 'created a level of aggravation and hostility that was unnecessary and unproductive'.

The chilly relations did not matter so long as the shares first issued to Torstar at about $17 continued to rise, as they did, doubling in value by Christmas 1989. But with the recession, Southam's stock slid. Black, for his part, shrewdly sold his five per cent of Southam as the shares neared their all-time high. Then he watched the Southam-Torstar relationship from his catbird's seat.

Under the guidance of John Fisher, Southam's performance at first began to improve, then fizzled. In 1988, he sold the company's forty-seven per cent stake in cable-television and broadcast company Selkirk Communications Ltd, and later, after much nudging from Torstar, Southam's long-suffering printing operations. Southam's hotchpotch of trade publications, newsletters, trade shows and database services went through one president and restructuring after another, with little improvement to the bottom line. Coles Book Stores, Canada's largest book retailer, which Southam owned, produced respectable profits, but it was difficult for outsiders to discern any connection between a retailer and a newspaper company, save the fact that both businesses were rooted in the printed word. Meanwhile, the company's debt surpassed the value of its diminishing equity, which began to give its bankers serious jitters.

When the Southam-Torstar agreement expired in 1990, Southam's minority shareholders voted in a 'shareholder rights plan' (better known as a poison pill) for it to be made impossible for Torstar or any other shareholder to buy control of the company without bidding for all of its shares. In 1991 Southam's return on newspaper revenues had fallen from fifteen per cent in 1989 to a paltry five per cent. Southam family shareholders, many of whom relied on their Southam dividends as their primary income, were as disaffected as the minority shareholders. And Torstar's patience had run out.

Time had come to take action. Torstar was spurred on by the fact that, at about the same time, it was investing $400 million in a new printing plant for the *Toronto Star*. It also thought that it ought not to have so much of its money in newspapers, at least not in such a passive investment as Southam had turned out to be.

The divisions within the Southam 'family' factions deepened in 1992 when the board selected Bill Ardell, the tough-talking young executive who had turned around Coles and the business communications division as Southam's chief executive. He was the first of Southam's six CEOs to come from outside the clan. Bringing a reputation as a cost-cutter and turnaround specialist, Ardell's appointment was heralded as a new era for Southam. Moreover, as a sign of supposed Torstar solidarity, Galloway was named Southam's vice-chairman. Meanwhile, some members of the Southam family – which in its entirety now owned something between fifteen and eighteen per cent of the shares – approached an investment dealer to discuss the possibility of selling large blocks of their stock, perhaps to another powerful shareholder who wanted to form a counterforce to Torstar. One way or another, the alliance was coming to an end.

Paul Desmarais watched the spectacle with growing interest. As a media proprietor, the courtly, debonair financier owned Montreal daily newspaper *La Presse*, three television stations and seventeen radio stations in Montreal and Quebec. A Palm Beach neighbour of Conrad Black's, the two men shared a fascination with Southam and had discussed their respective ambitions to own it over the years. Desmarais called Black 'a character'.

Media was but a fraction of the sixty-five-year-old Desmarais' interests. From relatively humble roots, reviving his family's bus company in Sudbury, Ontario during the 1950s, Desmarais built one of Canada's most powerful business empires. In 1993 its $27 billion in assets included control of mutual fund giant Investors Group, Great-West Life Assurance Co., numerous industrial ventures in China, and half of Pargesa Holding S.A., a Geneva-based company with wide-ranging interests in European financial services, media, and industry. Over the years, Desmarais had proven himself a shrewd and agonisingly patient buyer and seller of companies. And following his latest assets sales in 1989, Desmarais was sitting on close to a billion dollars in cash.

Like Black, Desmarais believes in impeccable political connections. His son André, who oversees Power Corp's media investments, is married to Canadian Prime Minister Jean Chrétien's daughter. Like Hollinger, Desmarais has assembled an international advisory council, packed with the likes of Pierre Trudeau, Helmut Schmidt, and Sheikh Yamani. Hollinger and Power even have a couple of advisory board members in common, including fellow Palm Beach winterer Dwayne Andreas. ('They both seem to be running their businesses in a hands-on way,' Andreas says. 'I'm favourably impressed by both.')*

Torstar approached Desmarais to see if Power would be interested in joining forces for a Southam take-over. Southam stock was trading then at around $20 per share. Desmarais thought the price too high, and declined.

Torstar then held talks with Black during autumn 1991, which, according to Galloway, 'got a fair way down the road at looking at making a joint offer' for Southam. But then Torstar's board got cold feet, and the idea was put on hold. This was fine with Black, who was then putting the finishing touches on Fairfax and beginning to look at the New York tabloid.†

---

* Indeed, until Southam their paths had a way of intersecting every few years. When Black burst onto the Canadian corporate scene in 1978 through his Argus Corp. take-over, his first action was to 'bury the hatchet' with Desmarais, who had unsuccessfully tried to take over Argus three years earlier. When Black quickly began dismantling Argus and shuffling around its assets, Desmarais approvingly said it was exactly what he would have done. In 1987, Desmarais bid for Quebec newspaper group UniMedia but the company went to Hollinger.

† Black's partner Peter White was also at this time wrapping up Hollinger's first Spanish-language acquisition. For an investment of about $2 million, Hollinger purchased fifty-one per cent of *La República*, a tabloid-format paper based in San José, Costa Rica. The Central American prospect was brought to Hollinger's attention by a Florida newspaper broker who called David Radler. He turned it over to the Spanish-speaking White, who had taken on responsibilities for examining the possibilities in Latin America. White noted that most South American papers are family-owned and 'on the verge of being ripe for'

Conrad Black and Barbara Amiel could hear faint sounds of honking and cheering as they walked into the grand ballroom of the Royal York hotel, where Black was to deliver a speech to the Canadian Club of Toronto. Outside, on Front Street, a parade was in full swing marking the victory of the Toronto Blue Jays in World Series baseball. The excited pride in the Canadian champions contrasted starkly with the mood of uncertainty across the country. On this day, 26 October 1992, Canadians were voting in a referendum to ratify or reject a document known as the Charlottetown Accord, which had been approved by Prime Minister Brian Mulroney and each of Canada's ten premiers. After seemingly interminable negotiations, the accord provided a framework to bring the predominantly French province of Quebec into the Canadian constitution and finally extinguish the long-standing threat of that province's secession. The trouble was, despite the endorsements of all the leaders, national sentiment was opposed to the deal.

Black was there to shed his unique insight into the accord. He did not disappoint the packed ballroom. His first thrust was against his old foe, Ontario premier Bob Rae, who Black spat, 'seems to think that those who are interested in commerce are like scavenging animals riffling through the garbage. They may prefer a twenty per cent return on their investment to a return of two per cent, but they'll take what they can get.' Turning his attention to the accord, Black called it 'far from a solution' and described the Canadian government as 'a beached whale from whose carcass the provinces, and native people in particular, carve chunks of jurisdiction, virtually at their pleasure'.

Black laid at least partial blame for governments' pandering to special interest groups on the doorstep of the media. 'To read the press of Canada today,' said Black, 'it would be hard to avoid the conclusion that we are a society composed almost entirely of battered wives, molested children, humiliated ethnic groups, exploited workers

consolidation into larger chains. The only problem with *La República* was that its shares had to be held in a trust because foreigners were barred from owning Costa Rican media companies. Hollinger had been arguing in the country's courts that the law was unconstitutional, and in the meantime its investment in the country's second largest newspaper represented a loan to the trust which owned the paper while Hollinger managed the paper under agreement. While the vagaries of Latin American regulations represented a whole new set of legal issues, White found that the basic principles of newspapering were the same there as anywhere else.

and other groups despised for their sexual preferences or cultural attributes, all festering in a spoiling environment.' After the speech, a woman from the audience asked why Black did not enter politics to set things right. Politics, he replied, tends to be 'a contest for who can be more compassionate. And while I regard myself as a reasonably magnanimous person, I couldn't win a contest like that. I don't have the impression Canadians want me, and I'm not convinced I want them either.'

At another juncture, Black could not resist pointing out, amid all the journalists recording his utterances, that Hollinger's Quebec City daily *Le Soleil* was in the midst of an industrial dispute. 'My interest in that paper,' Black intoned with a wicked smile, 'is undimmed by the fact the journalists are momentarily on strike. But we are producing thick, informative and profitable editions, thus proving it's one of the great myths of the newspaper industry that you need journalists to produce a newspaper.'

The press of Canada was on Black's mind on this day in more ways than one. Back at his office at 10 Toronto Street, he received a phone call from David Galloway. With ScotiaMcLeod acting as adviser, intermittent talks about a joint Hollinger-Torstar bid for Southam had resumed during that autumn. Torstar's position was that it did not want to put up any new money, but it would throw its shares behind a bid and reckoned that with 22.5 per cent of Southam's stock it ought to receive a corresponding amount of the company's assets, preferably newspapers in Ontario and Alberta.

The further the talks with Hollinger progressed, the more awkward Galloway began to feel about his presence as an insider on the Southam board. Legally, he was nearing a conflict of interest position. What, for example, would happen if he knew Southam was going to issue shares or do a deal, while he was plotting his own take-over of the company from the inside? 'I need to know two things,' Galloway told Black. 'One, are you serious? And two, what's your timing? Because I'm in a bind.'

'I'm very serious,' Black replied, 'and two, I can't do it right away because I'm going to have to raise some money. We've got to wait until the spring.'

'We've got a problem then,' Galloway replied. 'I don't know what we're going to do. There is a chance that our board may suggest selling our shares so that we're not in conflict.'

Black replied quickly, 'If you want to sell your shares, I'll buy them.' Galloway said 'fine' but added that Torstar's main interest was really in getting some newspaper properties in exchange for what amounted to having ensured Southam's independence for the past seven years.

Four days later, on Friday morning, Galloway was in Caledon, about forty-five minutes north of Toronto, for a round of business golf at the Devil's Pulpit course. On the first tee, he was informed that his office had just forwarded a call. It was Conrad Black in London. 'David, I just want to reiterate what I said on the phone. I'm serious about that. If you people are interested, I just want you to know I'm very serious about that.'

Galloway told Black that he understood. The following Wednesday, Galloway laid out the situation to the Torstar board's strategic planning committee (whose members did not include any of the three appointees from Southam). In 1991 Southam had lost $153 million on revenue of $1.2 billion; it was on its way to losing another $263 million in 1992. Its quarterly dividend, which had been twenty cents in 1990, had been cut in half; by early 1993 it would be halved again. Because of its desire to diversify, the expense of the new *Toronto Star* printing plant and the fact that Black was ready and willing, the committee voted to sell. Price would not be an issue, as Torstar could only accept up to a fifteen per cent premium over the current trading price of the stock without triggering a bid for the whole company.

A full board meeting was set to ratify the sale the following Sunday. Southam CEO Bill Ardell knew something was up when he received a phone call from Beland Honderich on Friday 6 November. Honderich said that an important meeting had been scheduled for Sunday, but he couldn't tell Ardell why. Ardell was in Montreal, preparing to walk his sister down the aisle the next day. He felt uneasy about the call, and certainly the omens were not favourable: a few hours later, the church in which his sister was to be married burned to the ground.

Eighty-one-year-old St Clair Balfour sat stunned and silent at the board meeting on the afternoon of 8 November when Honderich explained that Torstar was selling its Southam shares to Black.

Balfour's thirty-year vision of a Southam-Torstar alliance officially died.

The deal, which closed in January 1993, left Hollinger as the largest shareholder in Canada's largest newspaper company, whose centre-piece was seventeen daily newspapers with a combined circulation of more than 1.5 million. The purchase price was $18.10 per share (at a time when the shares were trading at $15.38), for a total of $259 million. Black needed a bit of time to secure the financing, so Torstar agreed to provide interim financing for $189 million, to be repaid by 15 April 1993.

From the boardroom to the newsrooms, Black's arrival was viewed warily within Southam. Some vestiges of the old Southam family were alarmed that they had managed to keep Torstar at bay for so long only to see the company fall into the hands of someone they did not particularly want. Shortly after the deal was done, according to St Clair Balfour, one of his relatives dined with Senator Michael Pitfield, a Power Corp. vice-chairman. This family member expressed regret that Black had bought out the Torstar position. The next thing Balfour knew, Paul Desmarais called him up in Toronto and invited him to dinner at his home in Montreal that same evening. Desmarais promised to have Balfour home by eleven p.m.; he sent a car to pick Balfour up, and Power's jet was waiting at the airport to take him on the hour-long flight to Montreal. Another limousine ride and he reached Desmarais' Mount Royal mansion. 'Paul's got the newspa-per bug,' explained Pitfield, who attended the dinner along with Desmarais and his sons, André and Paul Jr.

Desmarais broached the subject of his buying 9.9 per cent of Southam, just under what must be disclosed under stock exchange regulations, but wanted to determine from Balfour whether enough Southam family members would vote with him to create an informal shareholder bloc. Balfour felt Desmarais was looking at Southam 'not just as a cold-blooded business proposition' and agreed to sound out some key family members. In the meantime, Desmarais had begun buying Southam shares and asked Balfour to tell any family members interested in selling shares to give him a call. The news from Balfour for Desmarais about the fractured family joining forces with Power was not encouraging. Still, Southam's share price was falling into a price range that Desmarais considered a good deal.

In the *Globe and Mail*, with which Black had certainly had his differences, editor William Thorsell penned a welcoming editorial about Black's newest acquisition. Thorsell, who, like Black, had been a columnist for *Report On Business* magazine in the 1980s, enjoyed better relations with him than previous *Globe* regimes, and the editorial reflected it. 'Businesses do best under the guidance of an informed and engaged proprietor, none more so than newspapers,' the editorial said. 'Mr Black is that rarity in Canadian capitalism, a businessman who reads. Besides his evident distaste for many journalists, he clearly loves the craft of journalism – more so than many media barons we could name. He has done much to reinvigorate the newspaper trade abroad, rescuing publications that would almost certainly have gone otherwise. We welcome his rediscovery of Canada.'

There were less favourable reviewers, such as former Royal Commission on Newspapers Chairman Tom Kent, who contended in the *Ottawa Citizen* that, 'as a multiple proprietor, he will milk many of his papers to the sacrifice of their quality and spend on some of the more important in order to bend them to his ideology'. Black rejected Kent's views as a 'pompous farrago of nonsense'.

Shortly after the Southam deal was announced, Black sat in his office at 10 Toronto Street, munching on a cheddar cheese sandwich, facing a stack of letters commending him on his recent speech to the Canadian Club and his Southam *coup*. 'I'm actually slightly *touched* by the rather generous response I seem to evoke around here,' he said. At the same time, Black was mildly fuming over a recent profile in London's *Financial Times*. His friend Hal Jackman, controlling shareholder of National Trust Company, and now lieutenant-governor of Ontario, was quoted as saying: 'The problem with Conrad is that he's always looking to the next deal.'

'Well, that's absolute crap,' Black huffed between bites of his sandwich. 'I'm not. In the meantime we manage value into what we have, but when there are opportunities there you snap them up. . . . It's all very nice to have a strategy but if you can't do the deals what use is the strategy? If I announced my strategy is to take over the *New York Times* but it's not for sale and I can't do the deal, what good is my strategy for me? You've got to go where you think there's an opening.'*

Paul Desmarais found his opening and phoned Black in early March 1993. Power, he informed Black, was putting a proposal to the Southam board to buy almost $200 million worth of equity directly out of the company's treasury.

From a corporate point of view, an investment by Desmarais could easily be justified. Southam's debt to equity levels had put it in breach of technical covenants in its loan agreements, and a cash infusion would satisfy its bankers, while giving Ardell more muscle with which to carry out his plans to cut jobs. Theoretically, a healthier Southam would also benefit its largest existing shareholder, Hollinger. Moreover, by selling shares directly out of its treasury, Southam could realise a higher price and not expend fees on brokers. Nevertheless, as far as Black was concerned, his old friend Desmarais was trying to sandbag him.

Desmarais' gentle enquiries at Southam had evolved into a clear invitation to invest from Southam directors Adam Zimmerman and Hugh Hallward. Their aim was to create a counterforce to Black. In the weeks since Black's deal, there had been much speculation that it would not be long before Black moved to tighten his hold over Southam. Both Black and his chief strategist, Dan Colson, had begun publicly to say that Southam's poison pill would not stand up to a legal challenge. And speculation was afoot that Hollinger wanted to fold some of its Canadian assets into Southam in exchange for more shares in the company. In particular there was growing dread that David Radler, the unsentimental cost-cutter, would be parachuted in as

---

* Black's comment on Jackman was, 'What did *he* do with the National Trust Company? You see, Jackman's problem is that he is very suspicious of everything that isn't very slow-moving and very deliberate, following upon his father. They've been working on a fifty-year plan, you see. . . . I mean, he's an entertaining guy but as a commentator on how to build a business he has his limitations.'

Jackman smiles at the thought of the jousting routine he and Black have had going for years. 'I like to bring him down to earth,' Jackman says, summoning one of his favourite anecdotes. 'When a Roman general defeated the Barbarians, his army would give him a triumph. And he would ride in a chariot, but behind the general they always had a slave who would be holding a wreath over the general's head, whispering in his ear, "Glory is but fleeting." So I said, "I'm the slave that holds the wreath over your head, Conrad." '

Southam's president. After all, Southam's newspaper division had 7,500 employees, and as far as anyone within Hollinger could tell, that was at least a third more than necessary.

Ardell had already laid plans to eliminate 1,300 jobs, but the refrain within Hollinger about the new Southam CEO was: 'Nice guy, don't know how much he knows about newspapers.'

Moreover, where Black was a defender of the newspaper industry's long-term prospects, Ardell painted a more pessimistic scenario. 'In most markets, we're in a stop-the-slide mode,' Ardell had said a month before Torstar sold its shares to Black. 'And if anyone's talking growth in newspapers, they're not talking reality.'

Just before Desmarais' move, concerns about Hollinger's intentions calmed down when Black and Southam chairman Ron Cliff agreed to a standstill agreement that granted Hollinger three slots on the Southam board in exchange for Hollinger agreeing not to challenge the poison pill until it came up for renewal in 1995. In order to appease its banks, Southam had also announced that it expected to be issuing new equity, but under his agreement Black was limited to taking up only his pro rata share. 'The theory that is abroad that all sorts of cheap stock is about to be shovelled out,' Black told the *Financial Post*, 'is not one that the majority of the directors agree with.'

But cheap stock was exactly what Desmarais had in mind. Under his offer, he would buy Southam stock at $13.50 per share, and underwrite a rights issue at $11.50. The overall effect would be to bump Hollinger into second-largest shareholder and force it to come up with even more money if it wanted to take its pro rata share of the new stock, which might be problematic as it hadn't yet paid for its Torstar shares.

If that were not embarrassing enough for Black, he was in the midst of a proposal to finance his Southam acquisition by re-selling a half-interest to the cash-rich Telegraph on the same terms he had paid, $18.10 per share. Even without the sudden arrival of Power, the deal was a hard sell. A circular explaining the merits of the Telegraph becoming a shareholder in Southam was due to be mailed to Telegraph shareholders on 13 March; a special meeting to vote on the matter, requiring the approval of a majority of the minority, was set for the end of March.

Black arrived in Toronto on 10 March, and learned the full details of Desmarais' proposal, which was to be voted on the following day at a Southam directors' meeting. Black was aware that before he had bought out Torstar there had been a movement to reduce the size of the eighteen-strong board by between three and five directors. He immediately began working the phones before the next day's meeting, talking to Southam directors until two in the morning Toronto time, or seven a.m. in London where his day had begun. 'We can get a better deal than this,' Black argued. 'I'm happy to have Desmarais in here, but not without an agreement with us, and not without him having an agreement with the company somewhat similar to the one we have, and not without a number of understandings between us as leading shareholders – and at a better price than this. This is a fire-sale price! It's an insult. It's an absolute shaft to the existing shareholders.'

Desmarais' proposal was defeated by a narrow margin at the board meeting the next day. 'He had managed to telephone the right directors to enlist as allies the night before, which was some feat,' recalled Adam Zimmerman. 'He got these people and he got them on side. And he got them on side because three of them were going to be dropped as directors, and he made promises to them.' Zimmerman said that Black had canvassed his views on the lie of the board after buying the Torstar shares. 'I gave him a rundown on all the people, and I told him what was going to happen,' said Zimmerman. 'Little did I think he was carefully making a list of all of us.'

Black rejects the contention that he did anything underhand. 'Those guys were scheming to throw out a bunch of directors,' he says. 'And the people they intended to throw out were either aware of their intention to throw them out or suspected that intention. I didn't refer to that intention [when I phoned them], but I did say that if they supported us on this occasion, we would not fail to remember it. And indeed that is the case.

'I'm sure from their point of view,' he says of the Southam factions that brought Desmarais in, 'they think it was unreasonable for me to do anything other than sit meekly like Torstar people did in a gilded cage being poked with sharp sticks while they mismanaged the business. But that's not quite what I had in mind.'

After Power's first proposal was rejected by the Southam board, Desmarais phoned Black. This time, they agreed they would try to work out an arrangement together and present a fresh proposal to the

Southam board. Black arrived in Palm Beach on 13 March and met Desmarais that day and the next at Desmarais' home on South Ocean Boulevard. Also present at various times were Zimmerman, Hallward and Bill Scott, a Stikeman Elliot lawyer who was handling the drafting of the legal document for Black.

On the third day, Desmarais had to leave Florida, but his son André came to Black's less ostentatious red-brick house. The resultant agreement provided for all sorts of scenarios, but at its core was designed to give Power and Hollinger virtually equal footing at Southam. Each company would have voting and board parity, and together they would be able to purchase up to forty-seven per cent of Southam during the next two years. Each company would have rights of refusal on the other's shares. Desmarais made it clear that he was a long-term player in Southam: The agreement would be good for fifteen years, so long as each side owned at least fifteen per cent of the stock. Final details were worked out over the phone; then Black descended the stairs of his Palm Beach mansion and brought out champagne. Black quickly forgave Desmarais for his sleight of hand; regardless of the motives of those who had sought Desmarais out, he decided, he and Desmarais could work well together. 'There was an awful lot of shilly-shallying and foot dragging and pusillanimous mealy-mouthed evasiveness going on,' Black reflected. 'We were generally aware of who our friends were. But you know when that cruncher vote came in March 11, they'd really lost control of things by then. That's when Desmarais concluded the only way in was to deal with me, not to deal with those guys.'

Indeed, Black and Desmarais both desired the same thing from the company – an acceptable return for shareholders derived from improved quality and efficiency at its newspapers. 'There's no problem between Desmarais and I,' said Black. 'It's a manifestation of [the Southam family's] naïvety that they actually seriously believed that they could bring him in and he would side with the authors of the nose-dive of that company over us. I mean, that's just an insane conception. They're mad.'

Under the new Power proposal championed by Black, Power invested $180 million in the company, buying almost 13 million treasury shares at $14 apiece. Combined with shares it already owned, Power now owned 18.8 per cent of Southam, roughly equal to

Hollinger's position after the dilution effect of issuing the new shares. A nagging question remained: Did control of Southam pass to Power and Hollinger without a premium being paid to shareholders? 'It was a source of discussion yes, but it wasn't viewed as being an issue,' Ardell said after the deal was announced. 'You have to recognise that they have a right of first refusal to buy the shares and it's simply a right.' As far as Black was concerned, however, the new order at Southam amounted to effective control: 'No question about that,' he said as he cheerfully told reporters in chilly Toronto that the sun was coming out over Palm Beach. 'With forty-seven per cent of the stock if you can't control a company you should join a monastery or something.' To underscore the point, in the Telegraph's 1993 annual report Black noted that the agreements among Hollinger, the Telegraph and Power 'make the three companies co-controlling shareholders although nothing approaching a control premium was paid by the three companies'.

And if Black really wanted to take over Southam, at least now the rest of the shares were in familiar hands, and Hollinger had a right of refusal on them to boot. Certainly Black's past history – with the widows of Bud McDougald and Lt-Col. Phillips in 1978 and Lords Hartwell and Camrose in 1985 – provided ample proof of his skill at using legal agreements to his best advantage. 'Taking control of Southam would be nice but it wouldn't be easy, you know,' he reflected. 'It would have been a lot of money and you would have had to contend with all their anti-take-over provisions. This way, the gates have been opened to us and both Power and ourselves have been brought within the gates. I'd rather be one of two within the gates than a sole person thundering on a closed gate.'

That situation resolved, Black needed only to pay for his Southam shares. Torstar's co-chief executive David Jolley had been quoted in the *Globe and Mail* saying that Torstar had given Hollinger time to come up with the money because its traditional sources of credit would not provide it. This infuriated Black, who maintained he had other means to pay the Torstar 'bill' if the Telegraph minority shareholders rejected the proposal to buy in. (One option, according to another Hollinger director, was that the Telegraph could have issued a special dividend, which would have provided its sixty-eight per cent owner with an instant cash boost. This would not have been appreciated in the City, however, and was not regarded as a palatable option.) A second circular for the proposed Telegraph investment in Southam – this one explaining the sudden arrival of Power on the scene – was sent to shareholders on 27 March, and the special meeting to approve the deal was put off until 13 April.

The Telegraph's independent directors, after some wrangling with adviser N. M. Rothschild & Sons Ltd, recommended the deal to shareholders, despite the wide gap between the $18.10 price Hollinger was being asked to pay, and the $14 Power had paid. In fact, other investors could still buy shares on the stock market for less than Hollinger had agreed to pay. 'We wanted to do it,' said director Rupert Hambro. 'This was the last opportunity in the English-speaking commonwealth to get into a major newspaper business which was lying on its back and could be turned around. Conrad's record on turning around newspapers is pretty strong.' To encourage investors, Black, Hambro, audit committee chairman Lord Swaythling and Dan Colson made various calls on London institutions to impress on them the merits of the deal. One of the terms of the investment even provided that the Telegraph would have the right, for a year or longer, to return its Southam shares to Hollinger at cost if the directors changed their mind. The Telegraph would also get a representative on the Southam board. In the end, the Telegraph representative turned out to be Stephen Jarislowsky, the Montreal money manager who had been a vocal critic of Southam.* Putting the pension fund-owned shares he represented behind the Hollinger and Power bloc created an absolute majority, although Jarislowsky joined on the proviso that he would be his own man when it came to voting.

A special shareholders' meeting was held at the Telegraph to approve the deal, and it passed easily, but not without a minor controversy. An article about the meeting in the *Independent* claimed that Black admitted that the Southam deal was 'in opposition to' the geographical separation clause in the prospectus of the previous year's Telegraph stock offering. In response a four-page letter from Farrer & Co., the law firm representing the Telegraph, Black, and Telegraph

---

* Jarislowsky was also a sometimes critic of Black's earlier corporate reshufflings in Canada, but the two became friends.

secretary Anthony Rentoul, was dispatched to the *Independent* editor Andreas Whittam Smith, and the article's author, Jason Nisse. The suit resulted in an apology – the second in six months from the struggling newspaper – and a settlement of £20,000, paid by the struggling newspaper to the Telegraph, Black and Rentoul.

His partnership with Desmarais caused Black to be uncharacteristically vague about his plans at Southam. 'Some of their publishers are good,' Black says, singling out Don Babick, who oversees Southam's two Vancouver papers, and Linda Hughes at the *Edmonton Journal.* 'In a company that size I'm sure they've got all the talent – or at least latent talent – they need for the senior echelons of the company. It's like the U.S. army in 1939: they had only 100,000 people in it, but amongst them were Marshall, MacArthur, Lieutenant Eisenhower, Patton. They were all there, you just had to see them and elevate them, you know. Even little guys like Ridgeway and Taylor Gavin and so on, they were all in the U.S. army; it was just a ridiculous army in terms of its size but the officer core was very talented – you've got to have someone to see the talent and bring it forward.'

At the core of Black's editorial philosophy is the belief in the proprietor model of newspapering or, put another way, his disregard for many career executives who do not have the stomach – or resources – to be owners. 'The absence of a controlling personality in a newspaper tends to encourage blandness and prolixity, as most North American chain newspapers demonstrate every day,' he says. 'Great though my admiration and liking for Roy and Ken Thomson have always been, I think their newspapers suffer from their policy of complete abstention from editorial matters. At the other extreme, such overbearing domination of editorial personnel by the chairman, such as the late Bob Maxwell, deprives newspapers of the most talented editors, who rightly decline to work in such conditions. And frequent changes of editors, as the London *Times* has endured in the Murdoch era, destabilise a newspaper. Much the best course, in my judgement, and one that is followed by many newspaper companies, including ours, is to hire editors with whom the principal shareholder is in general agreement, to minimise internal frictions.

'But the proprietor should exercise an influence, ideally to maintain standards of fair reporting and variety of opinion, but at all times to support the journalists when they are unfairly attacked, to prevent the factions of the working press from hijacking the newspaper, to order suitably abject retractions when they are required and deserved, and to help give the newspaper a personality.'

Few would dispute that Black has played all those roles and more in London. It is more difficult to envision how those principles can be applied across a nationwide chain of seventeen metropolitan newspapers, or in three major dailies half a world away in Australia.

The more newspapers Black acquires, the more frequently he is asked whether he is investing in a business with a future. The industry is filled with nervous talk and disturbing statistics about the decline of newspapers in the face of the proliferation of television and other forms of electronic media.

In the United States during the 1960s some seventy-five per cent of people read a paper every day, a figure which declined to fifty per cent by 1993 and shows no signs of reversing. The story was the same in Europe.

In Australia six (all of which were afternoon editions) of the country's thirteen mainland capital city dailies went out of business in less than a decade. In Melbourne, for example, former *Sydney Morning Herald* editor Eric Beecher noted, there were two papers selling 850,000 copies in 1993; fifteen years earlier there had been three papers selling roughly 1.4 million copies daily, and in the intervening period Melbourne's population had increased by some 500,000. 'Every sign, every indicator, every straw in the wind,' wrote Beecher, 'suggests that the business of daily newspapers is a business waiting for a replacement.'

Newspaper reading habits are formed early and here the most disconcerting statistics are found: in the U.S. in 1966 sixty per cent of 18–29-year-olds read newspapers but that figure was halved by 1991. In the United Kingdom in 1961, the average 15–35-year-old read 1.5 daily papers each day and two papers on Sunday. Over the following thirty years this declined to an average of 0.9 dailies and 1.3 Sunday papers. According to the National Readership Survey in 1992, fifty-nine per cent of British 15–24-year-olds read a daily newspaper and seventy-one per cent a Sunday paper, down from eighty-one per cent reading a daily and eighty-eight per cent a Sunday in 1974. And a study by the British Henley Centre found that young people spend 'significantly less time reading than they did in 1985 and that when they do read they are more likely to read a special interest magazine than a newspaper'.

As for older readers, the growing size of newspapers after the breaking of Fleet Street's unions – the *Daily Telegraph*, for instance, increased from, on average, 100 to 140 pages between 1981 and 1991 – suggests that although newspaper sales are down, individual newspapers are more comprehensive and people probably spend roughly the same amount of time reading them as they did a decade earlier. But the Henley Centre also found in a survey that thirty-nine per cent of readers agreed that 'It's less important to me to read a daily newspaper than it used to be'.

Technology has been regarded as the major source of the decline of newspapers. Information and entertainment can now be delivered in a faster, more vivid and targeted form over cable, satellite, computer or telephone lines. Some newspaper executives have tried to embrace this technology as the saviour of their industry, pouring considerable resources into securing a place on the 'highway' for their titles. Compared to some of his contemporaries, Black's serene views on the subject make him sound, typically, like he has just walked out of a time machine. 'Intermittently, there is fear that we are in the buggywhip business,' he admits. 'Why is it at the end of the twentieth century we are still delivering news . . . through crowded city streets on stripped tree bark? In one sense, it seems a primitive process.'

But Black believes it is 'not in the interest' of Hollinger to be on the 'cutting edge' of technology. 'We fear that over the next few years the information highway may turn out to be more like the "highways" of pioneer days – corduroy roads and mud sections with many bumps and places to get stuck.'

In the age of CNN, newspapers are struggling daily to redefine themselves as analysers and anticipators of events and consumer tastes. As Max Hastings puts it: 'Television is an unsurpassed medium of impression and a profoundly flawed medium for analysis.' Indeed, Black and others believe that the proliferation of television channels – and the hand-held remote control – will diminish the efficacy of advertising on the medium that has superseded newspapers.

But television is also a lucrative, growing industry. To be pragmatic, Hollinger and the Telegraph have examined various possibilities in the broadcast realm, such as the Channel Five bid. But in England and the United States regulations have hampered Black, either as a foreigner or as a newspaper owner, in his ability to expand. In Canada, Black exited the broadcast business in 1985 and has shown little interest in getting back since. He has periodically suggested that his next major investment will be technology-related, but so far only newspapers have enticed him to lay down his jealously guarded fortune.

After all, Hollinger's game is investing in established newspapers that have fallen on hard times. Even if the value of newspaper franchises over the long-term is declining – and there is no solid evidence to support this – Black's first rule is to pay less than market value. His second rule is to buy inefficient operations where there are costs and jobs to be pared, particularly in labour-intensive production – that is the sort of technology that excites him. Black maintains he is far from being a Luddite. By 1995, at his wife Barbara's urging, their library in London was 'wired up' so that Black (difficult though it may be to picture) could surf the burgeoning internet. 'I look like a B-52 captain or something,' says Black. 'We've got speakers and printers and screens all over one end of the room.' It was a major move for a man who, according to one reporter, once lifted up a mouse and pointed it at a computer screen as if it were a television remote-control device.

In 1994 the *Telegraph* became the first European newspaper with an internet address, and by the summer of 1995 Black claimed it was the busiest internet web site in Europe, with 20,000 entries per day.

Black is unworried by the new technology and the threat many see it posing to newspapers. 'The best is yet to come,' he maintains. 'Newspapers are still regarded as relatively unglamorous. And too many people are hung-up on raw material costs and the electronic front. I'm not saying that the newspaper won't have to evolve. What I'm saying is: one, there is one more mighty cycle of newspaper profits left, at least; and, two, the asset is what the generalists and the commentators produce. The rest is just methodology. If readers want it on a screen, they'll get it on a screen.'

Although Black makes no claim to being Ted Turner or Bill Gates, he and Hollinger president David Radler relish the prospect of a magical electronic world in which there will be no requirement for rolls of newsprint, printing presses or delivery trucks. As far as anyone can tell there will – for the foreseeable future, at least – still be a need for journalists.

THIRTEEN

Man of Letters

'Any competent writer can inflict all the
damage he wants without resorting to
defamation. I have often done it myself'

On Monday 13 September 1993, U.S. president Bill Clinton stood on
the sunny South Lawn of the White House and made history,
bringing together Palestine Liberation Organisation chief Yasser
Arafat and Israeli prime minister Yitzhak Rabin in the name of peace.
Clinton smiled and clapped. An agreement was signed. Rabin and
Arafat shook hands. Israel would now recognise the PLO and
withdraw from Gaza and the West Bank, which it had occupied
militarily since the 1967 Six Day War.

Outpourings of support came from world leaders, diplomats, and
newspaper editorial pages around the world. The *Jerusalem Post* was
not among them. In the days building up to and after the agreement,
Post executive editor David Bar-Illan was sceptical, if not outright
opposed to the settlement, and his editorials reflected this. He felt that
the proposed establishment of a Palestinian state would pose a mortal
danger to Israel. 'To recognise the PLO as the ruler of the territories is
to ensure that the Palestinian state will be, like the PLO mini-state in
Lebanon before 1982, a dictatorial terrorist state,' he warned in an
article in the *Sunday Telegraph*. His editorials in the *Jerusalem Post* noted
that it was 'difficult to ignore the deeply disturbing aspects' of the
Israel-PLO agreement, such as the fact that the PLO would be
allowed to introduce a 'large armed force, including terrorists, to
"keep order"'. Bar-Illan proposed that the agreement be put to a
referendum, and wondered 'if the architects of the Israel-PLO
agreement have made the right historic turn, or a dreadful, costly
blunder'.

After reading Bar-Illan's comments, Black decided to write an article in favour of the peace agreement for publication in the following week's *Sunday Telegraph*. He also called Bar-Illan to ask if he would publish the signed article on the *Post*'s commentary pages. Bar-Illan agreed.

'With regret,' Black wrote, 'I must dissent from the position adopted by the *Post* over the impending Israel-PLO agreement.' Black wrote that he understood 'the Arab view that Israel was created by the West out of guilt at the unspeakable barbarities inflicted on the Jews (and others) by the Nazis and the quislings who collaborated with them, and that the comparatively defenceless Arabs were made to pay for them by yielding the territory to Israel. There is some, though less than complete truth to this.'

Black agreed with Bar-Illan that Arafat and the PLO had never lived up to any agreement they had made in the past, but thought the prospect for peace was real and deserved a chance. 'Certainly the new era would be fraught with danger and would require no less vigilance and military preparedness than the past. I am not, to use the current parlance, a Polyanna, and I appreciate the anxiety as well as the hopes this agreement produces among Israelis.'

Privately, Black said he wrote the article because he thought Bar-Illan's views were too hawkish and did not reflect the views of the average Israeli. The editor's arguments were intelligent and well-reasoned, but he thought Bar-Illan was being 'cute' and criticising without offering a substitute. The *Post*, Black contended, 'could have been harmed if I hadn't written what I did, in my opinion, if it had ridden into the sunset as a cranky little paper taking a Shamir line. The fact is, the news selection was fair, the comment was chosen from a reasonable, balanced perspective; Bar-Illan's own arguments were reasoned sensibly and everyone who follows it knows that the ultimate controlling interest is in fact in favour of the agreement. So I would say we're all right.'

Two days after Black's column, the same editorial page slot featured an article on the accord by his wife Barbara Amiel – a reprint of a piece she had written for the *Sunday Times*, and which had been published on the same day as Black's column in the *Sunday Telegraph* – giving the accord tempered praise. Two days after that the *Post*'s publisher, Yehuda Levy, got in on the act and commandeered the same spot for the first time in his four years at the paper. 'I am largely responsible for turning around the paper's editorial policy. Mr Black has said he is proud of that change,' Levy began. 'As an Israeli born in Jaffa fifty-eight years ago (truly a Palestinian), I look at things differently from Mr Black who, I know, wishes Israel well and shares the hope that true peace prevails in this region. But it is the wish which is the father of the thought that often makes us blind enough to ignore some of the more disturbing elements of the situation.

'There is a basic mistake in the assumption, expressed by Mr Black, that "Israel was created by the West out of guilt" and that "the comparatively defenceless Arabs were made to pay for this". This is not only "less than complete truth", it is one of the biggest lies of the effective Arab propaganda.' Levy's editorial was soon followed by one from David Gross, the *Post*'s editor from 1990 to 1992. 'I don't need to remind Black what vast expanses separate Israel's back wall from its front. Black believes there's a "real chance" of Arafat and the PLO living up to their new agreement. He is a businessman and, as such, has taken business risks in the course of his successful career. But I'm pretty sure he wouldn't bet his bottom Canadian dollar on the chance, however "real", of a potential partner of proven cupidity and stupidity now doing the decent thing.'

Growing annoyed, Black next sent a letter to the editor for publication, saying that both Gross and Levy had misunderstood the snippets of his column they chose to take issue with. 'There is room for legitimate dissent from the Israel-PLO agreement and I had hoped that a former editor would have used more constructively than Mr Gross did the platform the owners of the *Jerusalem Post* have provided him.'

For his part, Bar-Illan thought it ironic and telling that some of the critics of the *Post*'s right wing bent under his editorship now lauded Black's interference. 'It was not only a matter of principle that publishers should not interfere with what editors do, it was that publishers who are on the right wing, or hawkish, should not interfere with what dovish editors do,' Bar-Illan noted wryly. 'The other way around is not only okay – it's to be cheered.'

Black later added, 'The fact is Bar-Illan personally moderated a bit after his exchange with me. Some of the other sentiment around there is a bit wingy, but you know it's easy for outsiders to criticise.' Bar-Illan thought it interesting that Amiel submitted her own article, 'which was very *piquante*, because her article doesn't agree with [Black] at all'. This was news to Black, who thought his wife's article had taken virtually the same line as his own – in support of the peace agreement but with misgivings. 'She was in favour of the agreement being signed. If they represent otherwise, then they're talking nonsense. It just goes to make my point that we are not dealing with people whose capacity to reason on that particular issue is entirely unimpaired. They're suffering from cabin fever.'

Being the world's most literate press tycoon, Black is less inclined than some publishers to disseminate his personal views anonymously through his newspapers. That is not to say that he will not order an article to be written – such as the time he thought the *Telegraph's* art critic wrote an 'outrageously nasty' piece about an endowment by billionaire Walter Annenberg. Black demanded an article with a kinder view be written. But often, if he has a problem with something he sees in one of his titles, readers and editors alike often learn about it directly from him in an article, a published letter, or both. In addition to such dispatches, over time Black would also be moved to write a book, on a subject with which he was especially familiar.

Saturday 18 December 1993, three p.m: In the pre-Christmas scramble at the Eaton Centre in downtown Toronto, shoppers queued in separate lines in two sections of the sprawling shopping complex. In the mall, children and their harried parents waited for a polaroid, a kind word, and a candy cane from Santa Claus. And in a corner of the menswear section at Eaton's department store, the crowd had been lured by the advertisements or the announcements over the address system promising that Conrad Black would be signing copies of his new autobiography, *A Life in Progress*.

Beside a dais amongst racks of blue jeans and corduroy shirts, a grey-haired, bespectacled announcer barked into a loudspeaker that a 'special guy' would soon arrive. 'This very special guy is, of course, Conrad Black, a special Canadian. . . . You are welcome to meet one of the world's most enormously successful financiers, *C-on-r-ad*, *B-lack*. . . . Conrad Black will not ignore you today, folks.'

Wearing a grey suit and blue tie, Black arrived his standard half an hour late. He was flanked by George Eaton, president of the retail chain on whose board Black sits. Before Black could sit down, a man in a toque bellowed out asking him whom he had supported in the recent Federal election, in which Jean Chrétien's Liberals had trounced the Progressive Conservatives with whom Black had been closely identified. 'I'm just an author, you know,' Black replied with a grin, adding that his company had supported various candidates. (In fact, Black voted for the Reform Party, the right-wing grass-roots movement led by Albertan Preston Manning.*) 'I'm astonished and grateful that so many people are here.'

Black and Eaton settled behind a table, and for ninety minutes Black patiently shook hands and signed books for all-comers who laid out $32.95. At one point, a curious teenager in a baseball cap lumbered over to a walkie-talkie-toting beige-jacketed Eaton sales-woman who was coolly monitoring the crowd. 'What does Conrad Black do, he own Eaton's or something?' he asked.

She looked at him as if he were from Mars. 'No, no, no, no, no. He's an *entrepreneur*.'

'He's just a big dude?'

'Exactly.'

For years, when Black arrived home from what he considered a particularly memorable encounter or event, he would write down or recount into a tape recorder his day's experiences. This distillation of moments, combined with his legendary memory, served him well when, in April 1991, he quietly decided to write a memoir.

It was, as it happened, a chronicle of war that compelled Black to put pen to paper. He had recently viewed the Public Broadcasting Service television series *The Civil Wars*. 'They were so good that they inspired me to do something.' Black was staying at Annenberg's house in Palm Springs, *en route* to Tokyo for a meeting of the Trilateral Commission, when he decided to procure a pad of paper. On his trans-Pacific journey to Tokyo, he pulled out his fountain pen and began writing away. No writer's block here – Black spent the even longer return flight from Tokyo to London at the same task. By the

* 'I cast the first *protest* vote of *my life*,' Black said privately. 'I couldn't take it from the old parties any more so I voted Reform despite my misgivings about it. I mean, not that I am unaware of limitations of the Reform Party, but they're the only ones saying anything sensible. I mean, half of what they say is rubbish in my opinion, but the other half is sensible.'

time he was back at his Highgate home, he had completed, in longhand, the first three chapters of his book.

Black was unsure at first whether he should publish the book. Despite his penchant for public rumination, Black has always maintained that he values his privacy and is amazed at the amount of attention he receives. One factor that influenced him was that at least one journalist had announced plans to write a book about him. Although Black wouldn't try to squelch other projects, he said, 'I didn't see why I shouldn't do it myself.' And, he added, at least it would not be 'Conrad Black *with*' some writer, like so many business autobiographies.

Black had reasons for publishing the book at the age of forty-nine: he wanted to write about the evolution of his thoughts on his native Canada, and explain why he no longer lived there; he wanted to 'set the record straight' on the various controversies that had surrounded him over the years, particularly when he was at the helm of the old Argus in the early 1980s. And he wanted to write about some of the 'obstacles' he had overcome, such as his anxiety attacks in the 1970s, so that anyone facing similar challenges might 'take some encouragement from it'.

The 522-page book was a bestseller in Canada, reportedly selling about 25,000 copies in hardcover. It was generally praised by reviewers, and nominated as Canada's business book of the year. In one review, author Peter Foster described it as 'the work of a man who rejoices in the intellectual and financial status of not giving a damn, of living a kind of Basil Fawlty wet dream in which Basil has not only won the football pools but has also swallowed a thesaurus and somehow acquired another fifty points of IQ.'

A Life in Progress was filled with anecdotes and reflections on the various luminaries whose paths Black had crossed, laced with large helpings of Napoleonic lore and de Gaullisms. Black's use of such words as 'fenestrated', 'preternaturally', and 'psephological' made for an entertaining, if heavy-duty, read. Wendy Thomas, the book's copy editor, was sent scurrying many times to various dictionaries during the course of the edit. She could not always locate the words Black used.

The author's descriptive technique was also attention-grabbing. For example: 'The demure, stylish, convent-educated young ladies of

Lima and their macho, blustery, or esoteric boyfriends or husbands were elegant and hospitable, but lived behind high walls and moved fretfully, darting through the congested streets in their unobtrusive automobiles.'

The book was perhaps most notable for the verbal napalm Black levelled at anyone who had ever crossed him, including even supposed friends such as Paul Desmarais, Brian Mulroney, and Hal Jackman. 'Why a millionaire many times over seems so angst-ridden and vindictive towards all those above and beneath him is somewhat puzzling,' commented *Financial Post* columnist Allan Fotheringham. The trick to deciphering the book, however, was to separate the 'Black humour' from the serious invective. 'Look,' a surprised Black said in response to a query about his pugnacious tone, 'I thought I was really rather positive about most people.'*

The way Jackman explains it, some of Black's most combative statements are just his idea of a good time. 'He's smarter than most of the people he deals with,' says Jackman, 'and it may not seem so in the press, but he's always making fun of himself and the people who are subservient to him.' Phil Lind, the vice-chairman of cable and media giant Rogers Communications Inc. who has known Black since primary school, agrees. 'Conrad has a tremendous sense of humour,' says Lind. 'He's always laughing, either with people or at people. There's always something going on. He doesn't project that at all. He projects pomposity and seriousness, and everything like that. I don't think that's the kind of guy he is at all. I'm sure he's serious, and I'm sure he's capable of being all of those things, but I know that he's laughing a lot more than people give him credit for.'

Some of Black's reflections in his memoir did not amuse their subjects. According to Black's long-time friend and business associate Peter White, the book 'infuriated Mulroney'. And White, who attended law school with Mulroney and served as his principal secretary for a period when Mulroney was prime minister, was caught in the middle. 'He cannot imagine why he gave Conrad the

---

* An understanding of 'Black humour' may also have helped readers of Peter Newman's 1982 biography of Black. 'Hal Jackman and I had this contest about who could put the more pompous remark into it,' Black later recalled, 'which I won with some bullshit about Nietzsche and Hegel.' Of course, Black may well have been joking about the contest too.

membership in the Privy Council, because he considers that his reaction has been ungrateful.

'I think what Conrad would prefer is that people accept his portrait as a balanced one and not emphasise the negative aspects of it,' says White, 'which of course is only human nature to do. People don't remember the good things you say about them, they remember the bad things. And Mulroney's very touchy, as is Conrad. The funny thing is that they're both similar personalities in that regard – they both have very thin skins when it comes to public criticism, and both of them have had to learn to try and thicken them. In private, I tell you, I get earfuls.'

In March 1994, Mulroney paid a visit to Black at his office in London and the two men began to patch things up. Mulroney's public stance was that he never actually read Black's book, although he was told about the references to him. 'At an appropriate time I'll have something to say myself,' said Mulroney. 'I'm going to be writing my own memoirs. Believe me, you're going to want to get a copy, as will a few other people. It's not a question of settling accounts or anything, you simply try to set the record as you see it. . . .

'You have to understand that I know things about Conrad and his state of mind and what was really going on that he hasn't told anybody, but that I will at an appropriate time. No hard feelings, that's just a fact of life. And I've learned a long time ago that, you know, memory tends to be selective.'

Allan Fotheringham complained about the way he was depicted in the book and said Black's 'imagination does run to Technicolor'.* He accused Black of taking poetic licence even with his reminiscences about his childhood idol, Montreal Canadians hockey star Maurice Richard. Black wrote in his book that it was Richard's 'implacable

---

* Black wrote about dropping off Fotheringham in an inebriated state at the Park Plaza hotel several years earlier, and watching Fotheringham collapse 'in a heap' at the feet of the doorman. At the launch party for *A Life in Progress* atop the same hotel, Fotheringham sulked in a corner and complained about the 'goddamn millionaire who libels me and I have to buy my own scotch'. Black later agreed that the cash bar furnished by his publisher Anna Porter was '*déclassé*', but said he contemplated asking Porter to throw Fotheringham out. To try to defuse the situation, Black's friend, Baton Broadcasting president Doug Bassett, bought Fotheringham a copy of Black's book, and even had it signed by the author. Black wrote, 'To Allan. Let peace break out. Conrad.' To which Fotheringham muttered, '*Peace* on you.'

determination' that impressed him most, such as the time he went through a sleeper train from Montreal to Detroit during a weekend home-and-home series, 'tearing open curtains to find, and pummel in his berth, one of his opponents'. Black also cited the time Richard leapt from behind a pillar in a New York hotel and tried to 'strangle a referee who had recently penalised him'. Fotheringham declared that if these anecdotes were true, Black had 'scooped the entire world of sport'. The passages were later shown to Maurice Richard via another journalist. The hockey legend said he did not recall the incident on the sleeper train, and did not strangle the referee, he 'only took him by the shoulders'.

Laurier LaPierre, who had taught at Upper Canada College and later advised Black on his Duplessis Master's thesis and debated with him on the radio in Montreal, was angered by Black's characterisation of him as a homosexual and 'one of the more enthusiastic flagellators' at UCC. After the book was published, LaPierre decided to deliver his own scathing reappraisal of the young Black in a letter to the *Financial Post*. While at McGill, LaPierre wrote, 'His contacts with his fellow students were limited and his arrogance and snobbery prevented him from participating in class with any degree of involvement. I was rather naïve in those days and not a good judge of character: Consequently his extreme right-wing views, his extensive homophobia, his disdain of the "common" ordinary French-Canadian, and his reverence for all things British did not point me in the right direction. I dismissed all of these as the affectations of a rather limited personality.'

LaPierre also wrote that Black invited him to lunch in the early 1980s 'at a famous restaurant where he had a permanent table. He, of course, kept me waiting as befits the lord of the manor. During the appetiser and the main course, we talked of this and of that. (I must admit to his being a good raconteur!) After the main course, he told me that he had heard rumours that I was gay . . . sorry! a homosexual. He needed me to confirm that. Spontaneously, I did. (Why? I have no idea!) Silence followed. Then he left the table and sent a waiter to tell me that he had been called away suddenly . . . leaving me in lonely splendour to order and eat dessert, consume a large and most expensive brandy, and linger over some good coffee. He had, however, been courteous enough to take care of the bill . . . up to the point of his departure.'

In his own letter to the *Financial Post*, Black apologised to LaPierre for the offence he took at the passage in the autobiography. 'Friendship and gratitude remain my attitudes to Laurier LaPierre,' Black wrote. 'An inadvertent psychological liberty, which I thought had been removed, entered into my description of him as a part-time school teacher which apparently prompts his anger and anguish.' Black said he would have the 'ambiguity' removed from further printings of the book. Black added that he did not libel LaPierre* or 'anyone else and Allan Fotheringham's attempt to portray my book as ungenerous, even to my own parents, or even generally malicious, is preposterous to any reasonable person who actually reads the book'.

Black said he had never 'harboured or expressed any hostility to homosexuals as a group' and denied that the restaurant conversation LaPierre described actually took place. 'I learned of Laurier La-Pierre's sexual orientation from the newspapers, respected his courage in making his position public and would never dream of thinking any the less of him, or anyone else, on that account.' Black concluded by saying that perhaps LaPierre and Fotheringham would both care to come to lunch with him when he was back in Canada. 'I promise neither to keep them waiting nor to leave prematurely.'

A more lighthearted but equally peculiar debate arose out of Black's writing that, while at Carleton University in Ottawa in 1964 'a theatre club of which I was the president staged a "Royal Nonsuch" adapted from Mark Twain'. Students were enticed to buy tickets to see *1001 Freudian Delights*, during which a student appeared nude, painted blue from head to toe and gyrated to a Beatles recording. When the music stopped, Black wrote, 'the curtain came down to generous applause that gradually gave way to restiveness several

---

* He added in a subsequent interview with journalist James FitzGerald, who was researching an oral history of UCC, that LaPierre's indiscriminate canings were 'not unlike the Lidice solution, when the Nazis killed all the innocent occupants of a Czech town in reprisal for the assassination of the SS Governor, J. R. Heydrich, in 1942. Actually, I don't want to be tendentious in bringing in that analogy. UCC was certainly not a Nazi institution and it's outrageous that I should say so. I am defaming it. I would wish either not to be quoted on that, or if I'm quoted, at least quote my withdrawal of it.'

minutes after the performer had fled to the showers and his co-producers had removed the till and deserted the gate.'

In Carleton's campus newspaper, *The Charlatan*, two former students, Ian Angus and Michael Maltby – the student who had danced nude – claimed that Black had had nothing to do with the staging of the event. 'Black was not, as he claims in his autobiography, "president of the club",' Ian Angus told the paper. 'He wasn't even a member. In 1965, a year later, he was involved for a short time with a different group, the New Theatre Club, which had nothing to do with *1001 Freudian Delights*.' Confusing things further, two other alumni involved in the event thought Black might have been the treasurer of the club that staged *1001 Freudian Delights*. Black said in a letter to *The Charlatan* that *1001 Freudian Delights* was indeed 'carried out under the auspices of the New Theatre Club', and that he later became the president of that club. 'While I was aware of the planning of the programme [for *1001 Freudian Delights*], it is true that I had nothing to do with its organising nor in my book did I claim to have anything to do with organising it . . . I certainly did not mean to "appropriate" either the idea or enactment of the scheme for myself and no responsible reader of my book would conclude that I attempted to do so. I am afraid, to judge from the intemperate and largely inaccurate letter that he has written to you, that that is not a category in which Ian Angus is to be found.

'My principal recollection of him is as the author of the most banal soporific poetry of that era. In particular the following stanza has struck me as so fatuous that it has been unforgettable these thirty years: "Reality is the elbow of society. Put it on the table and it is frowned upon." '

Looking back on the book's publication, Black felt he had accomplished what he had set out to in Canada. 'On the things that I wanted to set the record straight on, nobody has challenged my version,' he says, 'From Upper Canada right through Massey and Dominion Stores and that farce with the Hanna company and so on, I think I have laid to rest a number of irritating, to use Napoleon's phrase, "instances of lies agreed upon". So I think it was successful in those respects.'

Black labelled as 'myth' the gossip in publishing circles that libel lawyers had removed chunks of his 1,000-page manuscript for *A Life in Progress*, and that the book would not be published in the United Kingdom because of threats to sue the British publisher, Weidenfeld & Nicolson. Black said he was simply sick of author's tours – 'I couldn't face it' – and wanted to take a break and update the book for a British audience.

The publication of his book, in any case, underscored the fact that Black could indeed dish it out. Why then, his critics charged, could he not take it? 'The fact is I like to mix it up with people,' says Black. 'I've never minded a good verbal punch-up. I'm not trying to silence anyone and I'm not sensitive to people holding forth about my alleged shortcomings, but I draw the line at serious defamation.'

Invariably, Black's staunchest critics hail from the group he has disparaged since the age of twenty-five: the media. It is more than a love-hate relationship. His wife is a journalist, so too is his good friend Brian Stewart; so are other friends. Despite what some might think, Black says he likes most journalists, and indeed, most people he meets.

'You know, in newsrooms around Canada, Conrad is not an object of a lot of affection, although I think he's getting a bit more respect these days,' says William Thorsell, editor-in-chief of the *Globe and Mail*. 'I guess it waxes and wanes with the day's news. But he has played the role of the kind of politically incorrect critic of the media within the media world. And there's nothing that is more unpopular in newsrooms than anything that is politically incorrect.'

Black has also been accused of fomenting a 'libel chill' – a shield from media scrutiny of the affairs of wealthy individuals by the threat of costly libel actions.

'We need look no further than your own record as a journalist to know that you appreciate the cryptic comment, the blunt phrase, the pleasure of skinning a lie,' Trevor Ferguson, chairman of the Writers' Union of Canada, wrote in *Saturday Night* in 1991 in an exchange of letters debating 'libel chill'. 'It is a puzzle, therefore, that you have chosen to silence your own voice and pen in favour of the protracted, arcane speech of law courts. It is a puzzle and a shame that you have elected to silence others.'

Black agrees that he can fend for himself – and does – without the courts: 'Any competent writer or commentator can inflict all the damage he wants without resorting to defamation. I have often done it myself.'

Invariably, criticisms like Ferguson's miss the core of Black's position, which rests on the difference between defamation and fair comment, and lawsuits arise when Black's and other writers' definitions of what constitutes fair comment fail to mesh.

Black maintains that in each of the fifteen times he has either sued or threatened to sue for libel, it was only because he was being accused of dishonest or grossly unethical conduct. All he ever wants is a retraction, which, without a single case going to trial, he has received every time, often with costs and sometimes a cash settlement on top. 'It's a profit centre for me,' Black says cheerily.

In a 1988 speech, he said, 'Anyone who has witnessed, as I have, both as a media owner and employer and as a litigant, the pitiful spectacle of reckless journalists trying to defend under oath negligent or malicious libels with spurious apologia or glazed prevarication, will not soon forget the illustration of how much better the working press often is at dishing out abuse than at answering for its own conduct.'

Always with an eye on history, Black maintains his chief concern is that libels about him, if not retracted, will achieve immortality in archives and databases. Not to respond, he argues, would be tacitly to accept those errors as facts.

Black doesn't share any of his critics' view that the Canadian and British systems are weighed too heavily towards the litigant. Though usually a fan of things American, Black is not in favour of the adoption of the U.S. standard for libel under which malicious intent must be proved by the plaintiff. If such standards were imported to the U.K. or Canada, Black contends, 'it would be a retrograde step. As a publisher and an occasional columnist, but not necessarily as a subject of the media's attention, I would notionally gain from such a change, but that doesn't soften my opposition to it.'

Black points out that despite his own litigious history, as a proprietor he stands behind his journalists when they are sued. When former *Sunday Telegraph* editor Peregrine Worsthorne was sued by *Sunday Times* editor Andrew Neil for a leader he had written under the headline 'Editors as Playboys', which questioned Neil's cavorting at Tramp club with Pamella Bordes, the *Telegraph* defended the case until, after an eight-day trial, a jury awarded £1,000 in damages to

Neil and 60p – the cost of a single copy of the paper – to the *Sunday Times*. The *Telegraph*'s legal bill came to £66,000. 'Conrad took it on the chin,' recalls Worsthorne, 'and was totally uncensorious about the libel that I was guilty of having written. He wrote me a very nice letter.' Indeed, neither Black nor the *Telegraph*'s lawyer, Richard Sykes, considered the piece libellous in the first place. 'Perry went on TV for night after night afterwards,' Black notes, 'and we got at least £66,000 worth of PR out of it. It was damn good publicity for the *Sunday Telegraph*.'

Black said the fact that the litigant was the *Telegraph*'s chief rival also played a factor in his defence of the suit. 'I didn't want to grovel to another newspaper in the absence of some compelling moral reason to do so, which there would have been if Perry had said something frightful about the integrity of Andrew Neil. But he didn't. He just said that Andrew, as a national newspaper editor, shouldn't be spending time in a down-market club like Tramp. Which I thought was none of his business to say, but not something that impugned Andrew's character.

'The fact is we always protect our journalists unless we are satisfied that they actually had libelled someone and my opposition then is to minimalist apologies. We've had cases where Max Hastings has said, "Can't we fudge the apology a bit? I don't want to demoralise our people." I don't want to demoralise our people either, but as I've said to him, "If we have journalists, whose morale depends on their ability to libel people, then they've got to change their attitude or we've got to get new journalists", because people do have a right to their reputations. I didn't think that Andrew Neil's reputation was seriously impugned by Perry. I was rather surprised that it was found to be libellous at all. It was, it must be said, a minimal finding. It was a little like the famous lawsuit of Henry Ford against Colonel McCormick, where damage was judged to be six cents, the cost of a newspaper plus one cent.'

No libel writ launched by Conrad Black has ever been regarded as minimal by plaintiff or defendant. In several cases, the basis for the lawsuits were inaccuracies in the press about his earlier; Argus manœuvres. At various points in the 1980s, recalls Peter Atkinson, Black's libel lawyer, the Canadian media 'really had a hate-on for him. We used to call it "Black-bashing". It was a real concern. In that whole period from about 1984 to about 1989, and it just seemed that the press were really down on him. . . . With the Norcen investigation, the Ontario Securities Commission investigation, the police investigation, it was really a dark period of time for him. And at the same time, the press seemed to think that it was open season on Conrad Black, that they could say whatever they wanted and get away with it. It was kind of like, I thought, almost a mob mentality: "Who can outdo the next person in saying slanderous things about Conrad Black?" So that's when we had to be particularly aggressive in dealing with this nonsense.'

The first time Black sued for libel was over an article by Black biographer Peter Newman on the richest Canadians, which was published in the U.S. society magazine *Town and Country* in its November 1983 issue. Black engaged lawyers in New York to serve a demand for a retraction on *Town and Country*'s publisher, the Hearst Corporation. Because of U.S. libel laws, the letter was generally ignored. Because the magazine was published in Canada – where the laws are different and Black could argue more damage was done – Atkinson's firm, Aird & Berlis, served a demand. Recalled Atkinson, 'They very quickly responded and were quite polite about it, and published a very full clarification and apology, and really handled it quite well.' The lawyers also threatened to sue Newman, who only a year earlier had written his favourable biography of Black. 'It doesn't matter who you are. If you defame him,' declares Atkinson, 'he's going to consider his options.'

Over the years, Black has served writs on virtually all major media in Toronto – the *Globe and Mail, Toronto Star,* Canadian Press wire service and Canadian Broadcasting Corporation among them. One of Black's first major suits was filed in the Supreme Court of Ontario over an article written by *Globe and Mail* media reporter John Partridge and published in the paper, on 25 July 1987, under the headline 'Citizen Black'. The fact that Black, at the time, was a monthly columnist for the *Globe*'s *Report on Business Magazine* did not dissuade him from suing the paper for $7 million in damages, claiming that several of the article's passages were 'demeaning and scandalous', and that their publication has 'exposed him to contempt and ridicule'. The *Globe* initially contested the case vigorously, but almost two years later, after lengthy pre-trial proceedings, published a comprehensive retraction and apology.

'It's when [the press] don't set out the facts and they issue these bombastic statements about him that we tend to get concerned,' says Atkinson. 'And that's what happened in the action against John Partridge. Now John Partridge and Conrad get along just fine. Conrad answers his phone calls and he's interviewed by John Partridge from time to time. I think it's kind of amazing, but that's the sort of guy Conrad is.'

As it happened, two days before the publication of the *Globe*'s retraction on 30 June 1989, the *Toronto Star* published a lengthy feature about Black under the headline 'Black sheds his bad boy image'. Black sued the *Star*, seeking $7 million in damages. The *Star* filed a statement of defence denying Black's claims and arguing that the article fell within the parameters of fair comment. One passage in the article Black did not sue over was the assertion that 'it's been a long time since Black got himself into one of his famous tirades against the media'. The very next day, Black rendered that statement inaccurate with his famous column in the *Toronto Sun* in which he described investigative journalists as 'swarming, grunting, masses of jackals'.

The *Toronto Star* eventually settled with Black, but the statement it published to do so was not nearly as vehement as the lawsuit that elicited it. An 'agreed statement of facts' was published on page three of the first section of the paper's 27 July 1992 edition. In his suit, Black had complained about various passages describing involvements at Dominion Stores and Massey Ferguson, and his friendship with Cardinal Carter. The *Star*'s statement – which settled both that lawsuit and another Black had filed – referred only to the facts of the Dominion Stores pension withdrawal. The article was not headlined as an apology – 'Black settles libel suits with *Star*', it read – and it stated that 'The *Star* regrets any misunderstanding that may have arisen from the articles concerning Dominion's withdrawal of pension surplus.' The next page carried a short article about the settlement. It said the paper had spent more than $180,000 defending itself and that the *Star*'s editor John Honderich was 'happy' with the settlement. 'It should be obvious to our readers,' Honderich said, 'that we have not published the kind of unctuous and unreserved apology that Black has obtained from other media outlets.' In the same article, Black said he was 'only interested in setting the record straight. They've now set the record straight.'

Only in one instance has Black sued a writer whom he might have, at one time, considered a friend. In November 1990, Ron Graham published a book entitled *God's Dominion – A Sceptic's Quest*. Self-described as a personal narrative examining religious and spiritual life in Canada, the book earned Graham and his publisher, McClelland and Stewart, a libel writ from Conrad Black demanding $1.5 million in damages and an injunction barring the book from being published, sold or distributed. This lawsuit was a departure from previous Black lawsuits in that it did not stem from a business reference to Black, but a more general observation about his person. In fact, there were only two references to Black in the book's entire 452 pages.

Black and Graham, a well known political journalist and author, had known each other for some years, and had lunch together once or twice a year through most of the 1980s. Graham was a regular contributor at *Saturday Night* magazine when Black bought it, but thought Black handled the purchase insensitively. Several contributors, including Graham, decided to stop writing for the magazine. Graham encountered Black one day at the University Club in Toronto with Norman Webster, *Saturday Night*'s former owner. Black told Graham he'd heard that he'd refused to write for *Saturday Night*, which Graham confirmed. As Graham recalled the encounter, Black joked about it. John Fraser, Black's appointee as editor of *Saturday Night*, said his second-hand impression of the meeting was that 'Conrad felt humiliated by it'.

In autumn 1990, not long before the publication of Graham's book, he was invited by Fraser to what became a lengthy lunch. The editor wanted Graham to come back into the *Saturday Night* fold. Graham explained that he felt that Black's purchase of *Saturday Night* was an attempt to buy off the Canadian literary establishment, and he was not for sale. As Fraser recalled it, what seemed most to irritate Graham was that when *Saturday Night* had been sold he had phoned Black's office not once but thrice and the new owner had not returned his calls. Fraser called Black's office to arrange a meeting with the proprietor to discuss the situation and to see if they might all have lunch with a view to patching things up.

Meanwhile, Black thumbed through a copy of *God's Dominion* – and a particular passage caught his eye. 'In the midst of this book,' he recalled in a speech shortly after launching his suit, 'in a mid-paragraph Damascene lightning bolt of discontinuity, the author announces that having me as an acquaintance taught him that greed and ego add peculiarly to the sum total of human misery.'

As it turned out, the morning Fraser was set to discuss the Graham situation with Black – the proprietor had jetted into town to host a dinner for Zulu chief Mangosuthu Buthelezi at the Toronto Club – he picked up his morning newspaper and learned that Black was suing Graham. Fraser phoned Graham and deadpanned, 'How do you like that great patch-up job I've done?'

On receiving a letter of complaint from Aird & Berlis, Graham sent a letter of clarification to Atkinson, in which he regretted that Black had taken offence at the passage and noted the complaint seemed 'based upon an unfortunate misinterpretation of a few words'. Graham maintained he meant that the rich and powerful have troubles of their own – in effect the old line that money does not buy happiness. The clarification was unacceptable and on 7 November Black filed a claim in the Ontario Court (General Division). In his statement of defence, Graham again denied that he had meant the words the way Black and his lawyers read them. He added that Black had himself republished the alleged defamation in a letter to the *Globe and Mail*, 'and included his own interpretation of the words complained of, with an innuendo not intended by the defendant'; moreover, he pointed out, the newspaper had a circulation of about 331,000 whereas there were only roughly 10,000 copies of his book in print.

During the course of trying to resolve the suit without going to trial, Graham offered publicly to debate the passage in question with Black. It could be in front of a neutral judge or an audience who would vote on who was right, and the money would go to charity. Even though Graham was hamstrung by his inability actually to repeat the alleged libel in public, he felt it was a worthwhile way of airing and ending the dispute. Black did not.

The matter was concluded sixteen months and many thousands of dollars in legal bills later when McClelland and Stewart published an open letter to Black in the *Globe and Mail* co-signed by publisher and author. 'It was never our intention to cause offence to you,' it read.

'Indeed, we deeply regret that the ambiguity of the passage in question caused you offence. As leaders in Canada's writing and publishing community, we make every effort to be precise in what we write and publish. In this instance, we were not, and for that we apologise.'

Avie Bennett, Graham's publisher, felt that the wording of the apology left his company's and the author's integrity intact – and put an end to the mounting legal expenses. As far as Black was concerned, it was yet another triumph. From Black's perspective, Graham's attack on his character stemmed, at least in part, from residual anger Graham felt at not being offered the *Saturday Night* editor's job instead of Fraser. Graham denies he ever wanted the job and, in retrospect, has an equally jaundiced view of Black. 'Any respect I had for him as an intellectual or publisher or man of letters totally went, and with it my esteem for him,' Graham says. 'I always liked him and I always defended him. [But] he can flip in a minute from being very congenial and interesting and bright to being all puffed up and arrogant and cold. And I didn't like that side of him and actually felt sorry for him for having that side.'

From his vantage point in the middle of the affair, Fraser sees the suit as a 'Sicilian' tale because of its undercurrent of mutual hurt. 'The reason I think the Graham and Black thing is really intriguing,' says Fraser, 'is they both crave each other's approbation. And they both don't know how to do it. I think Ron loved the access to Conrad – a wonderful, titanic businessman figure and he was above the ordinary crowd of journalists . . . And Black, for all of the bluster on journalists, craves good journalists' approbation.'

Black prefers to cast the lawsuit as a simple matter of principle and legality. 'In effect,' recalls Black, 'what [Graham] was saying was that I had contributed sufficiently to the misery of the world that it was freakish to contemplate the fact that God had created me. I thought he was representing me as sort of a monster. His defence [was that] he meant nothing of the kind. I don't know what he meant, but he's a well experienced and at times quite competent writer, and I assume that he meant, to use a phrase from my father, "the plain simple English meaning of the words", and the plain simple meaning of the words on their face was the one that I divined from them. That was counsel's view as well.'

Black and Graham encountered each other for the first time since the lawsuit at a party in Montreal in the summer of 1993. 'I sort of gave him a merry "Hello", and put out my hand,' recalls Graham. 'He "humphed" and walked off.'

Says Black: 'That, I am afraid, is illustrative of what I was dealing with. I mean, that is a complete falsehood. I did shake hands with him. And what he would mean by walking away is that I didn't talk to him after that. But that was because other people came up, including his brother and his sister-in-law, and I talked to them for a minute. But I didn't walk away from him particularly – not that I had any great desire to speak to him, but I would never cause an incident like that, or fail to shake hands with him. That's just absolutely a completely spurious misrepresentation.'

The Graham suit was one of seven Black had simultaneously under way in 1990. After it was resolved, the author said he would not write about Black again until Ontario's libel laws were changed. He has not, and they have not been.

The last of Black's Canadian libel suits demonstrated that, as well as his name as an ethical businessman and his character, Black would jealously guard his intellectual and ideological reputation. On Monday 9 July 1990, *Globe and Mail* columnist Michael Valpy filed his regular 'Citystate' column which was, not surprisingly, devoted to Canada's latest constitutional crisis. Black had been giving his views on the subject on the CBC news programme, *The Journal*. Valpy did not approve.

Valpy had spent twenty-two years at the *Globe* in various positions. On this day, he was not in a particularly optimistic mood, as evidenced by the column's headline: 'A Myth Remains: A Nation of Losers'. The column continued in that vein, asserting that 'The millions of immigrants who have come here have done so because they were losers at home. Of course, millions more went to the United States – but to join the triumphalism of the American Revolution not the huddling together of Canadian survivors.'

Towards the end of his column, as Black recalled, Valpy turned his attention to Black and 'wrote that I was a submarine mutant oozing to the surface of Canadian society and that I was guilty of "shabby intellectual treason" '. Black was the only individual identified by name in the article, and the digression elicited a demand from

Atkinson for an immediate retraction of Valpy's statements. Indeed, it turned out that the entire premise for his attack on Black was mistaken – Valpy had misunderstood Black's point on CBC. Less than a week later, his column included the following statement:

'In a column last week, I described Conrad Black as "enthusiastically looking forward to American union". There was an implication in the column that he had voiced such enthusiasm on CBC's *The Journal.*

'According to a transcript of the interview, Mr Black said that "continentialism" has its "attractions" and that "there has always been some kind of sentiment in Canada . . . that really it was an artificial country and we'd be better off with the Americans. We could live under that scenario. It would not be the end of the world. It might be the end of the CBC, but it wouldn't be the end of civilisation in this country. But do we want that? And I suspect that, in the end, we don't." '

Wrote Valpy: 'I was wrong to suggest that Mr Black, in the interview, enthusiastically supported union with the United States. So any conclusions based on that assumption were inappropriate.'

Black was far from satisfied. Although Valpy had said that his conclusions based on the assumption that Black favoured union with the United States were 'inappropriate', there had been no apology or retraction for the actual libels. On 20 July Black filed suit for libel against Valpy and the *Globe.* Black sought $1.25 million in damages, plus costs.

On 16 August, the *Globe* filed its statement of defence, arguing that the case be dismissed and that the words in dispute were not, 'in their natural and ordinary meaning, defamatory of the plaintiff and do not bear the meaning alleged' in his claim. A 'full and fair retraction of the words complained of' had been published two months earlier; they were published without malice, and the *Globe* 'enjoyed a constitutional liberty' under the Canadian Charter of Rights and Freedoms to counter Black's public comments with those of its own commentator, Valpy.

A week later, Atkinson filed a reply rejecting the *Globe*'s defence. There was no 'full and fair' retraction, both because it did not purport to be one and because it did not address the defamatory language.

Moreover, Atkinson noted that Valpy's descriptions were 'not comment at all, but allegations of fact'.

The lawsuit was eventually settled and on 4 May 1994 the *Globe and Mail* published another retraction. It admitted that 'intemperate language' was used to characterise Black's support for a Canadian–U.S. union, but that 'In fact, Mr Black expressed no such view on *The Journal*. The *Globe and Mail* apologises to Mr Black for any unfounded inferences its readers may have drawn regarding Mr Black as a result of this publication.'

It was the last time Black sued a Canadian publication. Not one case went to trial. Is it because a retraction entails so much less expense and bother than a legal fight? *Globe and Mail* editor William Thorsell said the decision to settle both the Partridge and Valpy suits was not 'driven by economics' but by consultation with the *Globe*'s lawyers about the 'probabilities' of success in a potentially lengthy and costly court battle.

Black and Atkinson don't buy the argument that cost played a role in any of the suits. Torstar and the *Globe* are both powerful organisations; even book publisher Avie Bennett is a man of considerable wealth. Black jokes about the 'hardship cases' he has taken on. 'It's a real tear-jerker isn't it,' he says, 'the way I bullied them around?'

Says Atkinson: 'I think it's nonsense to say he has financial clout that causes them to cave in. They cave in because they cannot defend the words. I think if the *Globe and Mail* or the *Star* in particular thought they had a winner against Conrad Black, they'd take it the distance, because what would be more fun than to beat Conrad Black in court? And I constantly expect somebody to [take it the distance], but it hasn't happened yet.'

In the meantime, journalists can be assured of hearing more and more of Black's pungent opinions on the media, rankling though they may be. In the spring of 1994, flying from Palm Beach via Henry and Nancy Kissinger's wedding anniversary celebration in New York, Black arrived in Ottawa to address the Canadian Association of Journalists. He delivered his usual bombastic dissertation on the media's shortcomings, but the delivery was more tempered than in the past, a sign that his most acrimonious days of battle with the media were behind him. Afterwards, he took questions, and after the crowd had applauded him, he stayed a few minutes to sign copies of his book. 'Your speech wasn't good,' offered a ruddy-faced, blond-haired gent in a track-suit jacket, and a drink in hand. 'The questions and answers were good. I didn't understand what you were trying to say in the speech. I mean, what was your point?'

'Well,' Black, thought about it momentarily, 'it's the only speech you're going to get tonight.'

Two journalism students, Dawn and Heather according to their nametags, tentatively approached. 'Mr Black, we heard what they said about how you'll sign books if we buy them, but we're poor students and we can't afford it. So can we just ask you a question?'

'Sure.'

'Well, we want jobs. We're in journalism school and there's no jobs out there and what can we do to make sure we get jobs when we graduate?'

Black's lengthy response included a suggestion to travel to Europe – as he had done as a young man – and the advice that a journalism degree is 'better than no degree'. Studying one of the nametags, Black added that 'all work and no play makes Dawn a dull girl'. Later, as he walked out of the hall, he raised his fist towards them and bellowed, 'Don't be demoralised, girls!'

As he exited the hotel ballroom *en route* to his waiting jet at Ottawa airport, a young man – looking every bit the cocky, idealistic journalism student – came forward and pumped Black's hand. 'You know, I've never been a big fan of yours, Mr Black,' he said, looking very pleased with himself.

'Then why are you shaking my hand?'

Absolute Bunkum from A to Z

'Conrad is a wordsmith and a
romantic' PAUL KEATING

Monday 22 November 1993: Paul Keating looked annoyed, even
more annoyed than he usually appears under the expectant glare of
television lights. The Australian prime minister was in Seattle,
Washington, where he had just spent the weekend promoting his
country's trading interests at a forum of the Asia-Pacific Economic
Co-operation group. He agreed to sit for an interview with the
Australian Broadcasting Corporation, assuming it would be an
opportunity to trumpet his achievements to the voters back home.
Now what was all this nonsense about Conrad Black?

Keating told the ABC *Lateline* crew that the Black situation was 'just
an Australian sleeve issue. I mean, who cares about those things?
They are just ephemeral day-to-day things.' The real issue was that,
while leading Australia out of its worst recession since the Great
Depression, he was taking steps to ensure jobs and prosperity well into
the next century. 'This is the biggest of the big pictures and the Black
business is just not even a splash of paint on the picture.'

The Black business Keating was referring to was a ruckus over the
Canadian mogul's autobiography, *A Life in Progress*, newly published in
Australia by Random House, and including beefed up sections on his
take-over of the John Fairfax chain.

In a passage that did not appear in the book's Canadian edition,
Black wrote that Keating had pledged to 'entertain' an application
from the Telegraph to increase its shareholding from fifteen per cent
to twenty-five per cent in return for assurances of 'balanced' coverage
during the March 1993 election campaign, which the incumbent
Keating won despite being widely regarded as the underdog.

According to Black's book, in early 1992, over dinner at Kiribilli House, the prime minister's residence in Sydney, Keating had explained to him that he couldn't immediately alter the fifteen per cent foreign ownership limit imposed on the Telegraph's investment in Fairfax. Black quoted Keating saying it was 'shitty and outrageous, of course' and asking Black to 'leave him six months for matters to settle, whereupon he promised to put things right'. Black and Telegraph vice-chairman Dan Colson had met Keating again on 27 November 1992 at his Sydney office. Though he was heading into the election, Keating had 'urged' Black to apply to the Foreign Investment Review Board to allow him to increase the Telegraph's Fairfax holding to twenty-five per cent, and had said he would 'champion' the application.

'If he was re-elected and Fairfax political coverage was "balanced" he would entertain an application to go higher,' Black wrote. Opposition leader John Hewson, he added, 'already promised that if he was elected he would remove restraints on our ownership'. Keating was elected in March and several weeks later the Telegraph received permission to increase its stake to twenty-five per cent, amid protests from some journalistic and parliamentary quarters that the papers had declined in quality since Black's group had taken control. (Black added in the book that Keating 'impresses me as a more capable leader than any other current English-speaking government head, as well as a delightful companion'.) Black further claimed in a subsequent article he wrote for Fairfax's *Sydney Morning Herald* and Melbourne *Age*, that Keating had told Black he 'might be disposed to support' ownership of up to thirty-five per cent in the future.

Words are Conrad Black's currency, selected with precision and delivered with force. In expounding in his book on his Australian experiences, Black achieved something quite rare in the annals of publishing and policy: With *a single word*, he set off a massive public and political controversy, culminating in a full-blown senate inquiry that would dominate the headlines in Australia for weeks in early 1994.

The word in question – 'balanced' – was set by Black in quotation marks. He later said this was not meant to show he was quoting Keating. Rather, he explained to the senate inquiry, 'The word "balanced" was in quotes by me because that is the word that was used and that is what he meant.' Black claimed that in fact 'balanced' was his own word, a 'fair summary' which Keating 'accepted and has used since'. The prime minister made it clear, Black said, 'that he absolutely was not using the word "balanced" as a euphemism for supportive or favourable or adulatory or hostile to his enemies, or any such thing.'

Six months after the Australian election, in Seattle, the ABC interviewer pointed out to Keating that his critics were now accusing him of making sleazy backroom arrangements with the Canadian tycoon in an attempt to influence coverage from a traditionally anti-Labour Fairfax press. 'This is just simply dust in the cracks of history,' the prime minister puffed. 'Just forget about it. I mean, you are on the APEC picture; that's the picture to stay on.' As for Conrad Black's book, 'This stuff just slides to nowhere.'

When he returned to Canberra, Keating found the dust was flying. Opposition leader John Hewson, in the high-rhetoric Australian parliamentary tradition, reckoned the Black-Keating pact 'one of the most disgraceful acts in public policy in the history of this country'.

This only cranked Keating's venom up to its usual lethal levels. Although he disputed some aspects of Black's account, Keating had no difficulty relying on what the Black book said about Hewson – that he had pledged to 'remove restraints' on ownership.

Hewson, Keating raved, 'is the guilty man – the person who has made the deal that would shovel national interests to one side.'

Keating declared that he would not 'slum it' before an Opposition-led Senate 'sham' of an inquiry. But through media interviews, the prime minister explained that the only issue he raised with Black 'was the question of accuracy and reporting. He said to me in the first conversation he wanted to move the *Herald* and *The Age* towards the British broadsheet standard of accuracy. And I said to him, "This is a good thing, this needs to happen, there should be more presentation of news and less of views." '

Regardless of who had used the word or of the diarist's prerogative to put a word in quotations, Black told the inquiry, 'I hope you will take me at my word that if I had had any notion that what I wrote was going to lead to the controversy it has, I would have phrased it a bit differently.'

Outside the confines of the hearing, Black mused that he had generally intended his Australian recollections to gain attention – so as to serve his goal of increasing his ownership in Fairfax. He had hoped, by publishing his memoir in Australia, to establish himself as a 'personality', not just a faceless investor from afar who would settle for selling his investment at a 'sportsmanlike profit'. In that, there is little question he succeeded. Before long, Australian newspapers were following the unfolding story's every turn, running features with headlines such as 'What Conrad Black Said'.

Black's reaction to all the attention ranged from bemusement to incredulity. 'Rarely has such an innocent word,' Black wrote in the *Herald*, 'been the subject of such misinformed debate.' The more his critics savaged him for indiscretion, the more, in his usual enigmatic manner, he designed his public defences to give the impression that all was unfolding as part of a Black master plan.

Black was particularly astounded that anyone regarded the controversy over the memoir as an adverse development for him commercially. Although a newcomer to Australia, Black was familiar with the country's fascination with media moguls. In barely a year, he had become almost as well known and notorious a figure in Australia as in his native Canada, familiar to Cabinet ministers and taxi drivers alike. It was a stark contrast to his more reserved British persona, but Black steadfastly maintained he was not on some sort of trans-Pacific ego trip.

Reflecting on the controversy in Toronto one day in late 1993, Black ventured that perhaps the Australian publisher, Random House, had been 'a bit mischievous' in the way the crucial passage had been edited. 'But I guess it helped sales. . . .

'The fact is, it could have been better edited in Australia, but it doesn't matter.* It's not unhelpful and it's certainly not inaccurate either. Except that, frankly, Keating was a lot more encouraging than I said. I was just being discreet. Hawke and Keating, Kerin, Hewson, they all are [encouraging]. But they're going to have to say publicly what they say privately. This charade can't go on. They're just playing footsie with the foreign ownership issue.'

More pointed words encapsulated Black's feelings towards the

---

* The editor took the liberty of explaining that Maurice Richard, Black's boyhood hockey hero, was a 'basketballer'.

'elements' of the parliamentary Opposition who were leading the charges of impropriety, and the coverage it was receiving in the Murdoch papers: 'The spurious, ghoulish and malevolent coverage of this subject in some media circles makes Mr Keating's expressed concern about professional standards at Fairfax, if applied to other companies, timely and almost understated.'

In his lengthy submission to the senate inquiry, Black elaborated on the November 1992 meeting: 'Mr Keating made the point that, regardless of who won the election, he felt it would be easier for our application to be approved if no political party could reasonably accuse Fairfax of unbalanced political coverage.'

Keating himself recalled warning Black: 'If you barracked for the Opposition on the basis of your Conservative proclivities in other places, there is no way you would qualify as the owner we would like.' (He also made the flip comment, when asked by the ABC how it was that he had become the arbiter of editorial balance, 'Well, I am Prime Minister. That's how I became the judge.')

Black said the only editorial issue discussed concerned the necessity for a clear distinction between news and opinion pieces, and a desire for objective reporting. The only action Black said he took was to ask Fairfax chief executive Stephen Mulholland to ask editorial director Michael Hoy to 'request of the editors of all papers that they endorse whichever party they wished but that they ensure fair, professional and impartial coverage in the best Fairfax tradition'. Few at Fairfax could clearly recall such a grandiose edict.

Everyone from Mulholland and Hoy to the editors of the *Herald* and *Age* added their voice to the chorus, arguing that there was less interference under Black than under previous regimes. Any allegation of political favouritism rang especially hollow given that all but one of Fairfax's major titles had endorsed Hewson in the contest. Mulholland called the inquiry a 'star chamber'. Hoy called it 'dangerous' because if one or more of the papers had in fact endorsed Labor, the inquiry would have put him in a 'very difficult position' when explaining the choice. ' "Balance", broadly defined, is something for which all newspapers in the Fairfax group strive,' *Age* editor Alan Kohler noted drily.

Critics, primarily from the Opposition, persisted in sniggering that it wasn't difficult to figure out what 'balance' really meant. During one particularly fiery exchange in parliament on 24 November, the prime minister waved an old copy of the *Herald* as an example of how slanted against him election coverage had been. The front-page lead story, under the large headline 'Pork-barrel republic', covered the ALP's pre-election policy launch at a gala event. One of the sub-headlines read: '$1.1 billion in handouts . . . and a free set of steak knives, too'.

'Without a doubt,' glowered Keating while Opposition MPs feigned tears of sympathy, 'it was one of the most maliciously put together and most rancid presentations by a newspaper of any major policy speech in my time in public life.'

Meanwhile, Black continued his book tour and, despite his claims to be upholding journalistic standards at Fairfax, his candour did not boost morale among all at the newspaper company. At one stop, Black said that he didn't think Keating's criticisms about fairness within the Fairfax press were 'all wrong'. And in a Melbourne radio interview he ventured that Rupert Murdoch's *Australian* gave the election 'more attention than we did as the campaign rolled along and I thought we could have given it more coverage'. Some of the Fairfax rank and file, particularly those at the *Herald*, bristled. As far as some were concerned, the reduced coverage was, in part, a consequence of shrinking space for hard news and increasing space for so-called 'softer' features under the new owners.

Conrad Black might have had an inkling things were not going to go altogether smoothly on his Australian book tour when he first arrived in Sydney for the John Fairfax Holdings annual meeting. As 170-odd shareholders shuffled into the Sydney Convention Centre auditorium on the morning of 18 November 1993 they were handed an eight-page leaflet. An hour of impassioned argument by Michael Hoy the previous day had not convinced its authors – 'Fairfax house committees and concerned Fairfax journalists' – to halt its distribution.

For months, there had been a growing sentiment within the Fairfax ranks that the quality of some of the chain's papers – in particular the *Herald*, was slowly eroding, and that resources were being pared. As the ultimate proprietor, Black was being held responsible, and he would have none of it. 'Horsefeathers,' he said. 'That is a conspiracy between elements of the Australian Broadcasting Corporation, the

Australian and a few malcontent niches in what we might loosely describe as Sydney society. The fact is that it is a first-rate paper and the theory that the quality of it has declined is absolute bunkum from A to Z.'

Despite this friction, as far as the new proprietor was concerned, there was much to be celebrated at his second Fairfax annual meeting. Shares of John Fairfax Holdings were trading at more than A$3 on the Australian exchange, a rise of more than 200 per cent since they had been issued less than two years earlier. In the year ended 30 June 1993, Fairfax's first full year as a publicly traded entity, the company had earned A$168 million before interest and taxes, a thirty per cent increase over the previous year. Thanks to low rates, interest expense had been reduced by A$17 million and total borrowings were down to A$649 million from A$754 million. To cap a banner year, Fairfax had declared its first dividend. As far as Black was concerned, 'we should all sing off the same song sheet'.

But some journalists were definitely singing a different tune. 'Executives grow rich while their papers starve' was the main headline in the pamphlet, accompanied by a story and chart showing that three Fairfax executives had earned more than A$1 million during 1993, and a further fourteen had made between A$390,000 and A$810,000. It was pointed out that Mulholland's millionaire salary didn't include the 3.5 million A$1 shares he had received on signing with Fairfax, which were now worth more than A$7 million net. The pamphlet claimed the salaries were 'in excess of executives in companies two, three and four times the size of Fairfax', and cited numerous perceived deficiencies in practically every aspect of the editorial operation, from charges of management breaching the journalists' sacred charter of editorial independence, to declining sports and foreign coverage and budget cuts in photography and travel.

'Staff are concerned that these excessive packages are paid for out of savings made from cuts to the newspaper budgets,' shareholders read. The charge was made that journalists were routinely compromising their integrity following instructions to seek out private companies, government departments and in one case a charity to pay for their travels on assignment. (Apparently the *Herald*'s diplomatic editor flew to Angola courtesy of CARE Australia.) 'Quality newspapers such as the *Washington Post* have rules banning behaviour that is now commonplace at Fairfax.'

What commanded Black's attention most, however, was the bold headline on the back page of the leaflet: 'It's clear: Conrad's favoured child does not live in the colonies'. Black, though annoyed by the publication, could scarcely conceal his mirth. 'I have often been described as a colonial,' he later told the meeting, 'but I am now described as an exploiter of colonials and I am sure in an ineluctable way that is socio-economic progress for me.'

That 'favoured child' referred to the *Daily Telegraph* where two months earlier fifty senior Fairfax employees had spent a week studying the operation and exploring how the two organisations might share expertise and resources. This was exactly the kind of benefit that the Telegraph had promised to bring to Fairfax, yet here it was being used against him. The article cited the resultant pie-eyed report on the visit by senior *Herald* journalists as evidence that quality was indeed taken seriously at the *Telegraph*, 'while in Australia, the newspapers which make the money are being squeezed of resources more and more'.

Matthew Moore, the *Herald*'s national editor and head of its house committee, filibustered the meeting with more examples of what his group considered shrinking news coverage and journalistic integrity. Mulholland rose to refute Moore's claims, and cited a readership survey showing that the *Herald*'s readership was the highest in two decades and the Sunday *Age* – once described by Black as an 'open artery' – was improving rapidly. The company still faced capital expenditure of half a billion dollars over the next few years, Mulholland pointed out, but he assured the gathering that Fairfax's editorial budget was in line with international standards.

Moore proposed that the company appoint a director elected by the 'seriously disaffected staff' to represent its interests on the board. Another shareholder lauded the idea, adding that it seemed there was an 'imbalance of lawyers' on the board.

'Some of us, including me, are non-practising lawyers,' Black offered. 'I don't think this disqualifies us from serving. Indeed, if a few journalists wished to claim me, I think I could qualify as a journalist.'

No one picked up on Black's offer. In a more serious vein, Black defended the direction of the company and argued that there was ample evidence that, in fact, the reverse of what Moore and the journalists were complaining about was occurring. Obviously he couldn't deal with each of the individual points that had been raised, but 'I would not wish you to leave this meeting with the impression that we are systematically preventing the news from being covered'.

As for the executives' salaries, Black pointed out that given the company's increases in share price and profitability, 'I think we could make the case that we are getting value for money from these executives.' Black added that the group ought to bear in mind who gained as a result of such protests by Fairfax journalists: 'I may say, high though my regard for Mr Murdoch personally . . . it is galling to me that the chief beneficiary is the world's foremost purveyor of down-market newspapers.'

The new directors and managers had taken 'one of the great newspaper companies of the Western world out of the scandalous and degrading state of receivership' and transformed it into 'a success story that has been noted with respect and admiration whenever the newspaper is discussed anywhere in the Western world.' Yet, 'a complete outsider listening to the tenor of this meeting would imagine it a distressed company.'

Black explained that Fairfax's 1993 editorial budget was about A$120 million compared with roughly A$100 million at the *Telegraph*. (Although the *Telegraph* is only one paper, its daily sales average about one million versus some 650,000 for the various Fairfax titles combined.) To Black this proved that Fairfax was not being short-changed; to Moore and other senior Fairfax journalists it was more evidence to the contrary. And they particularly resented Black's constant references to 'the degrading state' the company had been in. From their perspective the degradation was solely Warwick's; the papers – excluding the costs of financing his misguided buy-out – had in fact remained highly profitable.

Black turned the press conference after the annual meeting around and chastised Fairfax journalists for their attacks on the new management. 'What do you people expect me to do? It's not like falling off a log. We had to clean up the shambles we found Fairfax in when we bought it. It was no tiddlywinks to get the company going again.

'Fairfax journalists should stop playing games and writing articles slagging off their own newspapers and the management and masquerading as underpaid slaves. I think it's all bunk – the journalists are not financially starved. If they are concerned about quality let them work harder and write better stories.'

Black was on the offensive to protect more than his reputation as an owner. Kerry Packer, his former ally, had steadily been buying Fairfax shares for more than a year, acquiring just under fifteen per cent of the company. It was an illustration of the perplexities of Australia's media-ownership laws that this was the same level of ownership that Packer would have had in Fairfax under his former alliance with Black. But this was very different. According to people close to Packer's broker, Ord Minnett, an agitated Colson had phoned Ord's Neville Miles a year earlier when heavy share purchases were being made through his firm. Colson had asked Miles who was behind the trading, to which Miles had reportedly said, 'We don't disclose who we're buying for.' Later, Miles asked Packer if it was okay to tell Colson he was the buyer, and Packer agreed. 'They [the Telegraph] weren't that happy,' says a source close to Ord Minnett, 'but that's life.'

A year later, it was also no secret that Packer's agents had been lobbying heavily in Canberra to have cross-media ownership rules changed so that he could retain partial control of his Channel Nine television network and increase his Fairfax stake to at least twenty-five per cent. According to one Fairfax editor, shortly before Black's arrival in Australia for his book tour, Packer had invited Stephen Mulholland to breakfast at his Bellevue Hill home, where he told him that he wanted to own as much of Fairfax as Black did and to sit on the board.

Sceptics pointed out it was not like the fickle billionaire to telegraph his moves, but the word from Packer associates was unusually consistent: while the thought of being a minority investor in Fairfax had previously 'amused' him, controlling the company had become an emotional desire. The press was abuzz with rumours that Packer was bracing to move on Fairfax. Said one of Packer's closest advisers during the summer of 1994: 'We've got A$300 million in it, at cost probably close to as much as Conrad has in it – and it's in our home town. I wouldn't think that we'll be going away.'

In the meantime, Keating denied telling Black that he might entertain the Telegraph's increasing its stake to thirty-five per cent, and brushed off Black's observation that the Labor prime minister had promoted the interests of entrepreneurs 'against the excessive appetites of the labour unions'.

'Well, that's Conrad,' Keating said to one journalist. 'Of course I did not say that. Why believe that text? I mean, Conrad is a wordsmith and romantic.' Hewson, too, suggested that Black was stretching what he had said. Black had written that during a meeting in February 1992, Hewson had 'volunteered' that his party had no objection to the Telegraph taking fifty per cent or more of Fairfax. Hewson said that all he had done was reiterate his party's view that ownership limits are not effective policy tools but that Australian owners are preferred. Keating, meanwhile, said Black had told him that, 'John Hewson has made it very clear to me that he is completely relaxed about how much of the stock we own. They don't regard foreign investment as an issue at all.' Quoting himself, as world leaders tend to do, Keating said he replied, ' "What, he will let you go to one hundred per cent?" "Yes," Black replied. "But I don't need one hundred per cent, I just need a majority of the stock." '

Despite Keating's public claims about Black's storytelling abilities, Black maintains Keating has never expressed any dissatisfaction to him about the contents of the book. Others in Canberra were less charitable about a person who, despite ready access to the influential élite, seemingly didn't recognise the difference between a private and a public discussion with a world leader. 'All I can say is he shows a complete ignorance of Australian politics,' sniffed Senator Graham Richardson, the powerful Labor strategist. 'I think he's ensured that the Opposition couldn't ever allow him to get above twenty-five per cent.' Echoing earlier sentiments from outgoing treasurer John Dawkins, he added: 'There's no way in the world we'll let him get above twenty-five per cent.'

'Australia is run by the right wing of the Australian Labor Party,' explained one prominent Fairfax columnist, 'and they do all their deals with big business behind closed doors. For him to discuss the conversations he had with Keating was rather like one of the junior cardinals at the Vatican coming out and giving an interview with a tabloid newspaper about the Pope having a love child. He just doesn't understand the rules. You do these deals and they're never supposed to see the light of day.'

'There is much more disapproval,' agreed the chief executive of one major Australian company, 'that Conrad would talk about private conversations than the fact they took place – which is a bit of a comment on Australia.'

'*What* is controversial about that?' Black wondered as he reviewed the debated sentence from his book over and over again. '*What* is indiscreet about that? "Balanced" I put in quotes not to make a mockery of the word, but to emphasise that that was the word – not supportive or partisan or partial. And "entertain" means consider and the only point I was making is he would not be automatically opposed to it. Now, where anyone gets off by saying that that's an indiscretion I don't know.'

Incredibly, this was not the first time that a single word recollected by Black had set off a row in the hyper-sensitive area of foreign ownership of media in Australia. In April 1993, after the government had granted the Telegraph approval to increase its stake to twenty-five per cent, Black had told ABC radio that as federal treasurer during the 1991 bidding for Fairfax, John Kerin had told him 'that foreign ownership concerns below thirty-five per cent were, and I quote him, "piffle" '.

Black said the comment was made during a visit to Kerin and Hawke in July 1991, and had been the basis for much of Black's subsequent ire that following December when Kerin had rejected Tourang's first offer, which included thirty-five per cent foreign equity between the Telegraph and U.S. investment bank Hellman & Friedman. 'Pifflegate' was as bizarre as it was brief. 'We did not use the word "piffle" either singularly or in unison,' declared Kerin. 'I do not use the word "piffle" in my normal conversation, although it may be a word Mr Black finds attractive.' Whether or not that particular word was used, Trevor Kennedy, who was also present at the meeting, and is no great fan of Black's after being ousted as Fairfax's CEO-in-waiting, agrees that Kerin did give the unmistakable impression that thirty-five per cent was an acceptable level. The "piffle" affair concluded when a *Herald* scribe seeking a rebuttal of Kerin's claims from Black was told sternly by his secretary in London:

'Mr Black prefers to impute inaccurate recollection rather than mendacity.'

When Black had first arrived in Australia for the launch of his Fairfax bid in July 1991, he had been bemused at seeing his own face glaring out from the cover of the Packer-owned weekly news magazine *The Bulletin*. It was a well-timed, positive piece designed to draw attention to the fact that the unknown foreigner, Black, not his then-partner Packer, would be calling the shots at Fairfax. Soon after Black appeared at the senate inquiry which began on 4 February 1994, he was again featured on the cover of *The Bulletin*, but this time the treatment was far from sympathetic. Under the headline 'Loose lips and lost chances', the article by Nick Richardson began: 'Conrad Black has a monumental problem. Nothing he can do now will undo the injury he has inflicted upon himself and his hopes to lock up control of Fairfax, the fattest and juiciest publishing empire in Australia.'

This, of course, was far from the way Black saw it. 'The whole thing is so absurd it's a little hard to take it seriously,' Black observed of the inquiry. 'We're not at risk in it. Neither is anybody else, by the way – other than the Opposition for making fools of themselves.' To him, the inquiry presented a glittering forum from where he could push forward his case for increasing his ownership. After all, Black maintained, in mid-1991 he had been given clear indications that the government would allow foreign ownership of up to thirty-five per cent in the newspaper chain. This was why he had been unimpressed when in April 1993 the Telegraph had been given permission to buy up to twenty-five per cent of Fairfax but at the same time treasurer John Dawkins had concluded his press release with the emphatic statement: 'The government will not countenance any further increases in the permitted level of foreign involvement in mass circulation newspapers.'

In his submission to the inquiry, Black noted that Australia's oft-stated desire to become more integrated with the Asia-Pacific economy and encourage foreign investment were 'not easily reconcilable with the irrational fear in some political quarters of levels of foreign media ownership that would not in most jurisdictions be considered worrisome'.

Of course, the crux of this debate had less to do with the global economy than it did with the hulking shadow of Kerry Packer. Assuming his cross-media ownership difficulties were dispensed with, under Australian take-over rules, once Packer acquired twenty per cent of Fairfax he would have to make an offer to all shareholders. Packer could then make a low-ball bid – his speciality – or maybe propose a merger involving stock in his magazine group, Australian Consolidated Press.*

If a proposed Consolidated Press merger with Fairfax were rejected, Packer could still proceed with a creeping take-over of the company at the permitted rate of three per cent every six months. If Packer or anyone else made such a move, Black was counting on the government to grant him the flexibility to mount an effective defence or counter-offer. He had not come this far to become, as Black argued in his submission, 'a corporate fatted calf awaiting the convenience of a local predator'.

The government, he submitted, 'must decide whether they would rather have Fairfax possibly controlled by Mr Packer, or provided with internationally experienced and professional newspaper management and input from the Telegraph. And they must decide whether they wish to see virtually the entire media of Australia controlled by Mr Packer and Mr Murdoch, prominent American as he has become.'

Amid the spectacle of the proceedings Black was privately mulling over his options: if he could not go to thirty-five per cent within a reasonable period of time, he would 'hype the stock and sell', taking a huge capital gain that, thanks to the Telegraph's interest being held through a Netherlands Antilles company, would be tax-free. Indeed, Black's inability to increase his ownership in Fairfax was holding him back from applying some of the financial engineering techniques he had perfected during his Argus days. He had considered a reverse

* With visions of a multi-media company encompassing newspapers, television and magazines, Packer had pursued a similar tactic in 1986 when he had proposed to merge his Consolidated Press with the newspaper group Herald and Weekly Times. The proposal was rejected and soon after Murdoch acquired the Herald and Weekly Times group, eliminating one of the country's three powerful newspaper chains and giving his News Corp. more than sixty per cent of the market.

take-over of the Telegraph using Fairfax – with Hollinger selling its interest in the Telegraph for shares in Fairfax – as a way of shoring up his control over the Australian company without expending capital. Similarly, Black noted the Telegraph could jointly acquire new businesses in partnership with Fairfax – particularly in Asia, a natural move for the Australian company – if its ownership were more secure. With real control, Black could even combine the cash flows of his far-flung newspaper holdings in Australia, Britain and North America to acquire much larger newspaper properties, in particular a large, prestigious daily in the United States.*

Black made his appearance at the Senate Select Committee on Certain Aspects of Foreign Ownership Decisions in Relation to the Print Media on 21 April 1994. At precisely 2.01 p.m. Black strode into the Jubilee Room at Sydney's New South Wales Parliament House and accepted an invitation to make a few opening remarks – speaking until 2.51 p.m. without notes. He was accompanied by his wife, Barbara, who told him she would wear her 'best Mo Dean outfit' (a reference to Maureen, wife of disgraced Nixon counsel John Dean, who had gazed admiringly at her husband throughout his testimony during the Watergate hearings). Despite the press's portrayal of Black and Packer as titans clashing over who would control Fairfax, the Blacks were invited to dinner with Packer and his wife Ros at their Bellevue Hill home.

By the time Black made his appearance before the committee, he had reviewed all thirty-four written submissions and fifty-one testimonies of previous witnesses. The most extreme claimed that the Fairfax take-over was part of an international conspiracy to plunge the world in a 'dark age', linked to attempts to destroy the global monetary system. Black was more concerned with less bizarre and potentially more damaging theories.

Malcolm Turnbull was certainly one witness with whom Black had his differences. When asked by the inquiry to give his view on Black's depictions of his dealings with Keating and Hewson, Turnbull said, 'Black is a man who is an extraordinary egoist. I think that is fairly

---

* Black had used the combined power of Hollinger and the Telegraph in a similar way when in 1993 he had split the acquisition of 18.7 per cent of Southam between the two companies.

obvious. Truthfully, I do not believe his word can be trusted on matters where his own involvement is concerned. His book is full of misrepresentations and he, in my experience of him, has almost no regard for telling the truth.' Black responded that such 'allegations emanating from him are, to say the least, bizarre.'

Veteran media executive Trevor Kennedy proved a helpful witness for Black – especially as he had no reason to support Black – telling the hearing he did not think any deals had been made with the government. 'He is an urbane character,' Kennedy opined of Black at the hearing. 'He is not unintelligent. Although for a smart bloke, he has done some pretty stupid things. If he had not opened his big mouth, none of us would be here.'

The nastiest stoush (Australian for dust-up) in which Black found himself was with Bob Hawke, the former prime minister. Hawke's role in the Fairfax sale had been minor, as he had met Black only once, in July 1991, shortly before being ousted as Labor leader and replaced by Keating. Unhappy with Black's portrayal of him in *A Life in Progress*, Hawke kicked off his testimony to the inquiry by declaring: 'At the obvious risk of disadvantaging myself at the hands of Mr Black, who has made it quite clear that he thinks proprietorship gives him the right to determine the policies of his papers . . . the simple fact is that Conrad Black has the habit of distorting events through the prism of his own self-interest.'

Hawke claimed that Black had inaccurately recalled that their only encounter had taken place in Kerin's office. In his book, Black concluded from the meeting that 'it was obvious that Hawke and Kerin were not reliable'.

Hawke said the meeting in fact took place in his own office. 'It's a bit rich . . . for this media mogul to say that Hawke and Kerin are not reliable,' Hawke said. 'He gets wrong where the meeting was held and then asks to be believed in terms of this self-serving version of what happened.'

As far as Hawke's own version went, 'I found it a rather boring meeting. I was at the outset not particularly impressed with Mr Black, who regarded it as relevant and necessary to tell me he was not Jewish. He came having said he owned the *Jerusalem Post*. . . . It didn't create a very favourable impression upon me that someone has to make that statement.'

When Black had his chance to respond to the inquiry, he levelled a torrential verbal barrage on the former prime minister. Black and his associates were particularly unhappy because Hawke's comments had been reported in newspapers around the world, at a time when two of Hollinger's other subsidiaries, UniMedia Inc. in Quebec and American Publishing Co., were attempting to raise money in the public markets. Accusations from a former world leader that Black was a liar did not aid the cause.

None of the points raised by Hawke was too minute for debate. Black told the inquiry that the references Hawke relied on – articles in *The Age* and *Herald* – to prove that Black did not know in whose office they had met, were in fact published on different dates from those Hawke had recalled. 'I was never under the illusion we were meeting anywhere but the prime minister's office,' he said. 'Indeed, it would have required a person of extraordinarily low intelligence not to realise where we were meeting.' Black laid the blame for the erroneous placement on the normally diligent Fairfax scribe who had written the article, and spat 'it is extremely irritating for a man who has held the great office that he has to attempt to magnify an episode derived entirely from his sloppy research.' On this particular point, the senate committee concluded in its report that 'both witnesses were dogmatic and even pedantic in arguing that theirs was the more accurate recollection of what happened, particularly at the July meeting. Both witnesses endeavoured to damage the credibility of the other by reference to matters of fine, but irrelevant, detail.'

Black was understandably even more outraged by Hawke's recollection of his pointing out that he is not Jewish; Black interpreted that as Hawke suggesting Black was anti-Semitic, although one could conceive that the fact that the *Jerusalem Post* is owned by a gentile could be relevant in a discussion about foreign ownership policies in other nations. Black recalled only a discussion on foreign ownership in which he mentioned that Hollinger owned the *Post*, and says he never pointed out that he is not Jewish. In responding to Hawke, Black noted that he has several prominent Jewish people on his boards including Sir Zelman Cowen, Fairfax's chairman, Lord Rothschild, Henry Kissinger, James Goldsmith, even Hollinger president David Radler. 'My principal business associate, and the chief operating officer of our company, is Jewish. My wife, who is here today, is

Jewish. For me to be represented in this way by Mr Hawke is absolutely scandalous and reprehensible.

'I think,' Black continued, 'that his words constituted a degradation of every office that he has held and to the committee. If he had any sense of shame, he should exercise it on this occasion.'

Black offhandedly added that Hawke, 'despite being unimpressed with me at our meeting, saw fit to ask my colleague Mr Colson some months ago whether we would anonymously hire him and pay him US$50,000 to be, and I quote, "our eyes and ears in Canberra, to keep an eye on the successor". We did not accept the offer.'

'I have my detractors,' Black later added, 'and they are exceedingly vocal at times but they do not accuse me of lying and they do not, I might add, accuse me of being in any sense racially or religiously bigoted either, as Bob was kind enough to suggest.'

At this, Hawke, who had read Black's comments in newspapers while in Hong Kong, flew home and demanded to reappear before the inquiry the next day. He called Black's depiction of his statement about being Jewish a 'grotesque distortion' of what he had said. 'How can what I actually said possibly, by any stretch of imagination – even one as fervid as Mr Black seems to be possessed of – begin to found the proposition that I am accusing him of racial or religious bigotry?' To Hawke, Black's performance was further evidence that 'he simply cannot be relied upon'. Hawke said what offended him about Black pointing out he is not Jewish was the notion that it would matter. 'I regard it as an insult that someone regards me as thinking it to be relevant whether they are or are not Jewish or are or are not Catholic.'

As for his purported offer to be a consultant for Black, Hawke said it was Colson who had raised the idea with him at Sydney's Ritz-Carlton, where Colson stayed while in town and where Hawke was living at the time. Hawke said Colson told him his people were interested in an analysis of the political field, and that he would raise the matter in London and get back to Hawke.

'I did not hear anything more from him,' Hawke recalled. 'I made no approach to them. That was the context of what happened. Out of that . . . we get this preposterous statement from Conrad Black, which has led to this sort of stuff, that I have asked for $50,000 to spy on the prime minister. What do you make of a man who does that?'

Black called Hawke's performance 'pathetic'. 'What possesses Bob Hawke to carry on in this asinine fashion I don't know,' Black mused to two reporters from the *Sydney Morning Herald*. 'But I would have thought just the dignity of being ex-prime minister would require him to behave with a little more decorum.'

While he was outwardly defiant and visibly enjoying the joust, Black and particularly Colson were concerned that the sideshow with Hawke was starting to deflect from their main objectives in speaking at the inquiry: to quash any suspicions of a deal with Keating, and to lay the groundwork for increasing the Telegraph's ownership in Fairfax. While Black eagerly volunteered to take part in a television debate with Hawke, he also asked Fairfax's Mulholland quietly to approach the former prime minister with a proposal to end the matter by agreeing to disagree. Hawke agreed. Black personally drafted a large portion of the resulting statement, which was issued on 26 April 1994. 'The recent public disagreement between Conrad Black and Bob Hawke has been concluded,' it read, 'with the acceptance by both of them of the principle that people can sincerely have differing recollections of past meetings. This principle applies to their only conversation in July 1991, and to Mr Hawke's discussion with Mr Black's associate, Mr Colson, in 1993, about a possible corporate relationship between them. All reciprocal allegations of untruthfulness are withdrawn. All disparaging reflections over the venue of the 1991 meeting, over Mr Hawke's professional activities subsequent to his retirement as prime minister, and over Mr Black's motives in raising Israeli matters with Mr Hawke in the 1991 meeting, are also reciprocally withdrawn.

'Mr Hawke intended no suggestion or implication that Mr Black had any anti-Semitic attitudes and Mr Hawke repeats his assertion to the senate committee that he had no reason to believe this to be the case. As mentioned above it is agreed that it is possible for people to have different recollections of conversations and with regard to the discussion between Mr Colson and Mr Hawke, Mr Black accepts Mr Hawke's integrity and the sincerity of Mr Hawke's statement of his recollection. For his part, Mr Hawke also accepts Mr Black's integrity.

'Mr Black withdraws the statement in Sunday's *Sun-Herald* concerning the term "official greeter" and Mr Hawke having retainers with foreign companies to spy on his successor. With these misunderstandings removed, both men profess a reasonable regard and absence of ill-will for the other.'

Given the ruthlessness of the slagging that had led up to the statement, the senators hearing the inquiry were not persuaded by the sudden about-face, concluding the recantations 'were simply an exercise in media damage control rather than a genuine change of heart'. And if the statement could not be taken seriously, what of the two men's testimony?

As far as Black was concerned, the highlight of the affair was when his wife was interviewed on Australian television and said Hawke's performance made a convincing argument in favour of public flogging. 'I thought that was a scream,' Black said later.

The committee's first report into the affair was released in June 1994. The Opposition majority accepted Black's claim that he was given a 'positive indication' from Kerin and Hawke that the Telegraph could own up to thirty-five per cent of Fairfax. The committee also concluded that Keating had indeed been attempting, albeit in vain, to influence coverage of the 1993 election in the Fairfax press through his discussions with Black. It was a victory for Black, though not a complete one. According to the report: 'Black's writings and interviews, however much he subsequently sought to disguise the nakedness of the arrangement, made it clear that he was willing to trade at least a promise of proprietorial intervention to enhance his prospects of increased foreign ownership in the Fairfax empire.' The report also took exception to Black's observations on Australia's foreign ownership policies, calling his views 'indignant and conde-scending'. And, as in some quarters of Fairfax, Black's assertions that he had played a part in the resuscitation of an industry virtually bankrupted by nationals offended the committee. 'The suggestion that a major portion of the Australian print media industry was crying out to be rescued from insolvency by a foreign white knight,' it wrote, 'is a misleading and romantic attempt to disguise the purely commercial nature of the deal. This is a dangerous and inaccurate view of the situation.' As far as Black was concerned: 'It was not foreigners who put your entire media industry into the tank, you had dinky di Australians to thank for that.'

The four Labor senators on the committee of nine authored a dissenting report. Perhaps its most useful finding was that the inquiry

was 'a pointless and expensive exercise in deliberately misunderstanding the trivia of public life at the taxpayers' expense'. The Labor
report also noted that the way Black turned his meetings with world
leaders into narrative prose in his book gave his tale continuity but
'established a false sense of causality to events'. Indeed, a separate
inquiry might have been commissioned to examine why Black's book
– and a single word within it's 500-plus pages – had been taken so
seriously in the first place. As Gerard Henderson, executive director
of the Sydney Institute noted, 'Relevant chapters of *A Life in Progress*
have been critically examined in much the same way as scholars pore
over the Dead Sea Scrolls.' The master media manipulator had
conquered a new medium.

By autumn 1994, Black was confident of his Australian prospects.
But his travails seemed to have left him a bit sensitive on the subject.
When a Canadian reporter left him a message in London seeking
comment on a report out of Sydney that he was stepping down as
deputy chairman of Fairfax, Black, as he sometimes does, left a
lengthy reply on the reporter's telephone voice mail. 'I don't know
how you can possibly have such inexhaustible sources of misinforma-
tion and how you could credulously even ask me if I was retiring as
deputy chairman of Fairfax,' he thundered. 'I am afraid people are
playing tricks on you. It is an absolutely preposterous suggestion and
indeed things have never gone as smoothly at Fairfax as they are now.
Our *de facto* control of the company is not an issue and I expect our
permitted shareholding to increase during 1995.' Scant minutes later,
the reporter phoned Black back and found him in a much less
bombastic state. Black explained quietly that he may indeed have
agreed to give up the title of deputy chairman, and forgotten about it.
It was a non-executive title which never meant anything anyway. He
would remain on the board, and his effective control of Fairfax would
be unaltered. Warming up to the subject, the *Daily Telegraph* executive
chairman declared, 'The one thing I've learned from Deng Xiaoping
is that title does not matter.'

FIFTEEN

The Price of Success

'I like my opposition to be run by
competent people. *You don't get unnecessary
price wars*' RUPERT MURDOCH

In public, Conrad Black's sometimes brooding appearance and
hawkish nature can give the impression that he is not an entirely
happy man. He was once taken aback when a television interviewer,
Charlotte Corbeil, asked him why someone so successful did not
appear more cheerful.

'How do I look? Do I look gloomy?' he asked her.

'No,' she replied, 'you sort of look a bit blasé.'

'Now look here, Charlotte, you're going too far here now. I can't
apologise for my appearance or my mannerisms. I tell you that I am
an optimist and you'll just have to take my word for it.'

Indeed, since his marriage to Barbara Amiel, Black says he has
never been happier – and the feeling, by all accounts, is mutual.
Continuing to work as a weekly columnist for the *Sunday Times* while
married, however, was 'very hard' for Amiel. Her friend Miriam
Gross explained that 'in the sort of life she now leads with Conrad,
dinners here and staff problems there' it was difficult to maintain a
career.

The marriage meant adjustments professionally. After all, Amiel
worked for the *Telegraph*'s chief competitor, Rupert Murdoch's *Sunday
Times*. 'Since my marriage, I have no longer attended editorial
conferences, or known what the lead story of the *Sunday Times* will be
each week,' Amiel explained early in 1993. 'My one organising
principle has always been to work from home – that way I stay away
from office politics. Equally, if there are staff changes at the *Sunday* or
Daily Telegraph, I learn about them through the papers or friends. And
then I pummel him.' Apparently the arrangement suits her husband

just fine. 'It is not cutthroat,' Amiel said. 'As far as he's concerned, he's just got a dotty wife bashing away at the computer upstairs who occasionally comes down looking frantic – he doesn't think, when he brings me a cup of tea, that he's helping the *Sunday Times.*'

Murdoch is one person towards whom Conrad Black, regardless of his wife's employment, has normally been respectful, even reverential. 'He's sort of a funny guy,' says Black. 'He's very friendly and affable on a social basis, but as a competitor he's a real brass-knuckles type.' From inheriting a single newspaper in Adelaide, Australia, Murdoch has methodically launched and gobbled up media properties around the world. His News Corporation is now the largest media enterprise in the world controlled by an individual. In England, through subsidiary News International, it includes five national newspapers – *The Times, Sunday Times, Sun, News of the World* and *Today* – and the satellite television service BSkyB; in the United States it controls the Twentieth Century Fox movie studio and Fox television network, New York *Post* and a huge newspaper insert business; in Asia, it owns the Star TV satellite service; and in Australia, in addition to newspapers accounting for sixty per cent of the country's circulation, Murdoch has an interest in the Channel Seven television network and a new pay-television consortium.

Black's regard for Murdoch, however, does not mean he tries to emulate him. 'I don't see him as ever having tried to do the same sort of thing we're trying to do,' Black explains. 'You see, he was never a big quality newspaper owner. He had *The Times* and the *Sunday Times* and he produced *The Australian** basically as a hobbyhorse, as far as I could see, but his big effort in newspapers was in down-market tabloids. That's his speciality, whether it's Australia, the U.S. or Britain. And we aren't in that field. The fact is it's a much more vulnerable part of the market to electronic media than the quality areas.

'Of course he's a direct competitor with the *Telegraph* and he's sort of a slight competitor with *The Australian*, but that's all. We've got another concept here. I'm not saying it's better than his – it isn't.'

And Black concedes that Murdoch is more of a gambler than he is. 'He's a plunger by nature, you know, both financially and otherwise,

---

* Murdoch's national Sydney-based broadsheet.

and he falls in love with places and industries . . . He's much more peripatetic and much more courageous than I am. I wouldn't roll the dice like that. As a friend of mine in New York says, "He's the only guy I know who'll bet a billion dollars of borrowed money to make a point." Well, I admire it in a way but I don't do that.'

For his part, Murdoch professes to be similarly impressed by Black. In an autumn 1992 interview in his New York office, he said, 'I'm a great admirer of his. He's done a superb job in London. He's got a great opportunity in Australia, although he's limited to fifteen per cent, which is ridiculous.' Of course, Black was later allowed to increase his ownership of Fairfax to twenty-five per cent, but Murdoch predicted that if Black were kept below true control at Fairfax, one day 'someone will come and take it away from him'. And this, Murdoch contended, would not be good. 'I like my opposition to be run by competent people,' he maintained. '*You don't get unnecessary price wars.*'

A more recent encounter with Murdoch was recounted by Sir David English, head of Lord Rothermere's Associated Newspapers, publisher of the *Daily Mail*. English ran into Murdoch in the autumn of 1993, and Murdoch asked if Associated were interested in buying the *Independent*, which was floundering and seeking new capital. English explained that he no longer considered the *Express*, a mid-market tabloid like the *Mail*, as the *Mail's* 'major rival'. Rather, the *Mail* was going after the *Telegraph*. Although English reckoned that a reinvigorated *Independent* could usefully divert the *Telegraph*, he felt the cost of making the *Independent* viable would be 'vast'.

'Much more than vast,' Murdoch replied. 'And I'll tell you why.' He then proceeded to tell English of plans to drop the *Times's* cover price. 'Don't worry about the *Telegraph*,' Murdoch said. 'Leave them to me. I'll put them out of business for you.'

In September 1993, when News International reduced *The Times's* cover price to 30p from 45p, it was selling 356,000 copies per day, versus about 1.1 million for the *Daily Telegraph*, which retailed at 48p. Murdoch's public rationale for the move was that the price of British newspapers had increased at twice the rate of inflation; the price of *The Times* had gone up by eighty per cent since 1987, inflation by 40.7 per cent. However, Murdoch was also concerned that *The Times* should reverse the gnawing decline in its circulation: it had sold 6.4 per cent fewer copies in July 1993 than in July 1992.*

Not surprisingly, Black did not buy Murdoch's inflation theory. 'While it is entertaining to see Rupert masquerading as the Robin Hood of the media – the frugal consumer's friend – it is scarcely believable,' he told the *Observer*. He added: 'It does not frighten us and we will not be lowering our price.'

Cover price increases were a major ingredient in the success of all British newspapers, and the *Telegraph* in particular, in the post-Fleet Street years. Without union constraints, papers could add more pages, sections and colour, and charge more for their product. 'The argument that newspaper price increases have been excessive is easily refuted,' Black wrote in the *Telegraph* a few days after Murdoch's move, in the first column to feature a photo of the proprietor. 'Many more pages and improvements in content and production techniques have been proportionately greater than cover price increases. Circulation losses have been generally due to a decline in multiple newspaper purchase as most titles have become more comprehensive.'

Although the average circulation of national daily newspapers declined in the United Kingdom from 14.9 million copies in 1982 to 13.7 million in 1991, the quality daily segment had actually risen by fourteen per cent, largely as a result of the launch of the *Independent* in 1986. But during the same 1982 to 1991 period, estimated gross circulation revenue of quality daily newspapers increased by 135 per cent – thanks to steady cover price increases.

When Black first invested in the ailing paper in 1985, its cover price was 23p compared to *The Times*'s 25p. Once he had replaced Lord Hartwell at the *Telegraph*'s helm, one of Black's first strategic decisions was to insist that as the market leader, the *Telegraph* ought also to be the price leader, selling at a price at least equal to *The Times*'s. A succession of *Daily Telegraph* price increases followed.† And with the successful move to make the Saturday *Telegraph* that day's dominant paper, its

---

* By comparison, the *Telegraph* and *Guardian* circulations were relatively unscathed, down 0.2 per cent. Only the struggling *Independent* was faring worse, down 10.4 per cent. And it had neither Murdoch's gambler's instincts nor his deep pockets.

† The last price increase for the *Daily Telegraph* was in February 1993, from 45p to 48p.

cover price rose 160 per cent between 1985 and 1992, from 23p to 60p. The *Sunday Telegraph*, meanwhile, doubled its price to 70 pence.

By 1993, the *Telegraph* boasted one of the industry's highest ratios of circulation revenue to advertising, with circulation accounting for about forty-five per cent. This was a key factor in the paper's ability to prosper during the recession, when the advertising market suffered and therefore a big reason why Black was expanding his interests at a time when other publishers had stumbled.

Within Murdoch's organisation, the *Telegraph*'s pricing strategy was being analysed in a different light. Murdoch thought back to the 1920s, when *The Times* had a circulation of 200,000 compared with the *Telegraph*'s 100,000, and both sold for two pennies a copy. Then, on 1 December 1930, the proprietor of the *Telegraph*, Lord Camrose, had audaciously dropped the price of the *Daily Telegraph* to one penny, taking up his predecessor Lord Burnham's vow to make the *Telegraph* 'the largest, best and cheapest newspaper in the world'.

Competitors sniffed that a serious paper could not sell for the same price as the tabloids. But *Telegraph* sales doubled to 200,000 in January 1930, and settled into a steady climb towards a million copies per day from which the paper would never look back. Camrose 'took the quality premium away from the price', Murdoch later explained. 'He was allowed to get away with that for fifty years and establish total domination of the quality market. We are in the business of taking that back.'

Those within Canary Wharf could not deny the shared logic behind Murdoch's and Camrose's tactics, but took solace in the notion that the newspaper business – and its consumers – had become much more sophisticated since Camrose's day. In editorial positioning, the *Telegraph* and *Times* were not dramatically different – both were quality, Conservative papers – but *The Times* was less consistent than Black's *Telegraph*, and over the years had been through several editors and related 'repositionings' both up- and down-market. By comparison, the *Telegraph* was 'big, rich and serene'. As Simon Midgley described it in the *Independent on Sunday*, 'The *Telegraph* usually cuts the figure of a Queen Mary among national daily newspapers; opulently fitted out, carrying more passengers, displacing more water and maintaining a higher profile than any of its rivals.'

Indeed, the *Telegraph* was precisely the sort of big, established target that Murdoch seemed most to enjoy toppling. One of his key advisers at News International was executive chairman Andrew Knight, who had captained the *Telegraph* as its chief executive during the first three years of Hollinger's ownership, until his resignation and bitter falling out with Black in 1989. After the price cut, critics railed that *The Times*'s real aim was to eliminate the struggling *Independent*, which Knight denied. '*The Times* is the natural competitor of the *Telegraph*,' Knight, a lithe bespectacled figure in grey flannels, grey sleeveless sweater, crisp shirt and burgundy tie, explained shortly after the price cut. 'If people want to go on concentrating on what impact it will have on the *Independent*, by all means let them. But the real debate is between us and the *Telegraph* over a ten-year period.'

One thing Knight and the strategists at News predicted when they lowered *The Times*'s price was that Black would not respond by cutting the *Telegraph*'s price immediately. In their view, Black was a financier first, a newspaperman second – they believed he would not jeopardise his cash flow or share price unless he absolutely had to.

Black did indeed stand his ground, through not for the reasons Murdoch and 'his numerous spear carriers and boot-lickers' (as Black called them) gave. No stranger to things historical or military, Black reasoned it would be better to let the enemy expend resources for as long as possible while the *Telegraph* solidified its financial position. Moreover, like many newspaper executives, Black did not believe cover price was the factor determining why readers selected their papers. 'They'll hang in for a while, but I don't think they'll get anywhere,' he said after the first month of *The Times*'s price cut. 'You've got two directly competing theories here. I mean, Murdoch's theory is "don't overestimate the intelligence of the reader, keep going down-market and keep it cheap". And our view is "people will pay for quality" – so we'll see who wins.'

Three months after the price cut, there was still little evidence that *The Times*'s manœuvre was having an effect on the *Telegraph*; thanks in part to a bolstered promotional budget, the *Telegraph*'s sales were down only 1.9 per cent and remained at slightly above one million. But *The Times* was gaining ground, having increased circulation by twenty-four per cent from 359,000 to 439,000 in December. 'The scary thing is if they fired the editor and got a serious editor at *The Times*, and put out a quality product and kept the price low, then we really would have to respond,' Black said. 'But they could give *The Times* away and it still wouldn't affect us. It's not a very good paper. They've got a good sketch writer. Bernard Levin still has his moments. They've got a good economics writer, who we use on Sunday, Kolansky, the leaders are coherent, the letters are strong, the rest of it is horseshit. You know, the *Telegraph* has magnificent news judgement, splendid stories of various human interest categories from the salacious through to the relatively wholesome, stronger features in everything except fashion, I would say. Very good sports, better City, and it's a paper of *integrity*. I mean *The Times* has become another shlocky Murdoch tout-sheet . . . It's a magic carpet for all his vendettas. It just doesn't have any integrity. Particularly in a sophisticated country like that. I mean, God knows the English have tiresome traits at times, but you can't bullshit them. The broadsheet readers in Britain are a very sophisticated, intelligent, literate readership, and you can't bullshit them. They know crap when they see it, and they don't like it.'

One effect of *The Times* price cut was that by year-end 1993, the *Independent* was in serious trouble. The paper was born in 1986 largely out of the ambitions of three former *Daily Telegraph* journalists who dreamed of a proprietor-free newspaper. But by this juncture, the *Independent*'s circulation was just over 300,000, the *Independent on Sunday* about 350,000. Despite the papers' reputations for quality journalism, these were not considered sustainable levels, and in the year ended 30 September 1993, the newspapers' parent Newspaper Publishing plc, lost £423,000 on revenues of £81.4 million. With bank lines expiring at the end of March 1994 and Spanish and Italian shareholders scrambling to preserve some of their much-diminished investment, the company was seeking a new backer. Black phoned Andreas Whittam Smith, Newspaper Publishing's vice-chairman and one of its co-founders, and expressed an interest in helping out. Whittam Smith made no mention of the fact that his papers had paid Black some £40,000 in libel settlements over the previous eighteen months. For his part, Black sensed a delicious irony unfolding. 'It finally, belatedly, dawned on Murdoch's lackeys that the price war they started has not hurt at all the serious competitors,' Black noted at the time. 'And as I predicted in that piece I wrote in the *Telegraph* in early September, the effect is to drive the *Independent* into stronger hands financially, whether they're United, Associated or us, the *Independent* would be in stronger hands, and what does that do for Murdoch?'

Telegraph vice-chairman Dan Colson studied the prospects for buying the *Independent*. Colson discovered much chaos and animosity between the Italian shareholder *La República* and Spain's *El País* newspaper, and the English directors of the paper. The Italian and Spanish shareholders would speak to each other, but not to the British.

La República and *El País*, which owned thirty-eight per cent, wanted the Telegraph to buy out the minority shareholders and run the paper. The British directors wanted the Telegraph to buy new shares out of the company's treasury which would put much-needed money into the company but nothing into the pockets of the Italians and Spanish, diluting their shareholdings in the process. The way Colson and Black conceived the deal, the Telegraph would preserve the paper's editorial independence but assume responsibility for all business functions, from administration to circulation, advertising sales and printing. Colson thought the plan would be acceptable to the Mergers and Monopolies Commission. 'As far as the MMC is concerned, if you can demonstrate that the thing is in serious financial jeopardy – which it clearly is – than I think we'll be all right.' In the end, the bidding, led by Mirror Group newspapers, went beyond what the Telegraph thought the paper was worth, and Black pulled out. 'We're not interested in buying properties as properties. We're interested in buying opportunities. If the price takes the opportunity away, something else comes our way.'

Black and the other top executives within Hollinger could be equally unsentimental when it came to properties they already owned. And when a publication within Hollinger demanded special attention, David Radler was usually not far behind.

'The well has run dry, gentlemen,' Radler's voice rang through the conference room and he tapped the table lightly for effect. 'The well has run dry.'

Those listening silently round the table at *Saturday Night* on this day in October 1993 included Jack Boultbee, Hollinger's vice-president of finance and president of Saturday Night Magazine Inc., Jeff Shearer, the magazine's publisher, Alan Gottlieb, Saturday Night's vice-chairman, Michael De Pencier, whose Key Publishers own five per cent of the magazine, and John Fraser, its editor. Radler need not have said anything – Hollinger's Vancouver-based president had not set foot in the magazine's offices since the company bought it in 1987, and his mere presence at the monthly executive committee meeting in Toronto was a clear sign that things were not going well and were going to have to change. 'Conrad calls him "The Refrigerator", chuckled Fraser. 'You know: "Don't try to talk to him – he's cold and solid." '

During each of the first three years Black owned *Saturday Night*, Fraser maintained the magazine's ties to the Canadian literary establishment and brought in many awards. But its losses continued to increase. Peter White, Jack Boultbee, and Allan Gottlieb each acted as the magazine's publisher, but after a while Fraser began to realise a full-time executive with magazine experience would have helped (he himself was a newspaper person). Speaking to journalists after one Hollinger annual meeting, Black described the losses as a 'pinprick', which comforted Fraser, but not greatly. After a while he feared Black was losing patience with the magazine, and indeed at one point Toronto financier Christopher Ondaatje had approached Black about buying it, and had looked seriously at its books. 'It just happened to coincide with my dawning realisation that I had to get my act together,' Fraser recalled.

In 1990, Fraser and Shearer, a former Telemedia publisher who was brought in as a consultant by De Pencier, put together a plan to increase its circulation of 110,000 fourfold by inserting it for free in some 320,000 copies of the *Globe and Mail* and certain Southam dailies, while maintaining a paid circulation of some 80,000. The move attracted a great deal of attention in the magazine world, along with Fraser's repositioning of the magazine away from its more literary roots and toward a glitzier, *Vanity Fair*-like feel. In the first full year of the plan, 1992, although the costs of producing the magazine were much higher, its losses were halved. 'Jack Kent Cooke, where are you now?' Black boasted in reference to the one-time Canadian mogul who had owned the magazine in the 1960s. But in increasing the size of the magazine, Fraser had exposed it much more to the effects of the economy and Canada's fickle advertising market. A downturn in advertising would be felt much more acutely.

After a similarly promising start to 1993, the magazine's advertising took, in Fraser's words, 'a precipitous, frightening dive'. Since the circulation of the magazine was now predetermined and largely unpaid for, the editor's goal was to increase the readership of the magazine so that the advertising rates could be increased to the point where it made money. Readership – the number of people who actually read each issue rather than just receive it – at that stage was, according to the Print Measurement Bureau, about 540,000. Under the model developed by Fraser and Shearer, the magazine would need a readership of 750,000 in order to increase its rates to the point where it would be profitable. By autumn 1993 the magazine was haemorrhaging badly, and Black participated by telephone in the September executive committee meetings. The fourth quarter projections forecast more bad news. Recalled Black, 'I said that we couldn't agree to the budget and we simply had to reduce the loss a lot further than that. Or I would take radical measures.'

The following month, the radical measure walked through the door and began picking apart the budget. The magazine was *en route* to losing a little over a million dollars in 1993 and Radler demanded a break-even budget. Fraser went down six editorial pages, which saved $400,000 a year alone on print costs; the insertion deal with Southam was renegotiated, and Fraser's legendary kill fees (amounts paid to writers for articles that, for various reasons, never appear in print) were curtailed drastically. Twice, a budget was submitted, and twice Radler sent it back, until a feasible break-even target was set. 'Radler offered all kinds of practical help in addition to his General Bull-Moose performance,' said Fraser. 'It was a very necessary enema.' Having completed nearly six years as editor and with his fiftieth birthday approaching, Fraser had considered leaving *Saturday Night* earlier in the year, but decided that he could not leave because he had not proven that the magazine as he had shaped it could be profitable. Then the magazine had a surprisingly strong December 1993 issue, and there were signs that the Radler-inspired measures were paying off. Fraser decided the time was right to go out on a positive note and told Black he would retire as soon as a replacement was named. 'There was a certain amount of me being fed up,' he said. 'There was also altruism. I mean, they were onto my tricks, too. I couldn't charm my way out of it.' Fraser was surprised when Black, whom he'd felt had lost interest in the magazine in recent years, took an avid interest along with Gottlieb in selecting the new editor, eventually settling on Albertan Ken Whyte, one of the magazine's top editors, and a talented columnist with a noticeable right-wing political bent.

When Fraser's seven-year relationship with Hollinger ended in mid-1994, he was awarded a 'bonus' on leaving his job – normally something accorded someone who is fired – but Black insisted the payment was given for precisely the opposite reasons. 'The fact is *Saturday Night* should be very close to break-even this year, and that wouldn't have been possible without that distribution arrangement that enabled us to raise our rates and really go after advertising seriously,' says Black. 'John worked like a beaver to get that. It's far outside the normal ambit of an editor's job. He deserves great credit for it and there was never the slightest idea of his being pushed at all.' The admiration is mutual. 'Conrad, in fact, has been the best proprietor this stupid old magazine's ever had,' says Fraser, who thinks that anyone other than Black would be lauded for preserving the literary institution. 'And he certainly hasn't liked everything I've done and I've certainly heard about it, but in a very forthright, straight manner. And when he really couldn't stand it, he'd write a letter bitching about it, and we'd print it.' One Hollinger director, on hearing of Fraser's departure, flashed a smirk and suggested another motive behind the parting of ways: 'I think he told that story about Conrad stealing exams at UCC one time too many.'

In the quarter-century that Black and Radler had been together, Radler had been cast in the role of the fixer who relishes the art of the deal just for its own sake. In addition to overseeing his side of the publishing interests, Radler is also in charge of Western Dominion, the former Black family company that now trades on the Vancouver Stock Exchange and is the operator of Slumber Lodge Motels in Western Canada and several Jessop's jewellery stores in Southern California.* A workout at *Saturday Night* was just a minor diversion

---

* One of the few signs of Hollinger's ascension in Radler's office are the 'three levels' of coffee service: every day, java is served in brown Lily mugs which hold disposable white plastic cups; the next level up is the '*Jerusalem Post* freebie china'; there is another set, says Radler, even 'better than the *Post*', and brought out only for visits from luminaries.

for Radler. In late 1993 and early 1994, his chief preoccupation was putting the finishing touches on Hollinger's deal to buy the *Chicago Sun-Times*.

The eighth-largest daily newspaper in the United States began operations as a morning paper in 1950 when Marshall Field III, member of the legendary department store family, bought the *Chicago Daily Times* and merged it with his *Chicago Sun*. The Field family owned the paper for almost twenty-two years, until it was sold, in 1984, to Rupert Murdoch. The two years Murdoch owned the paper are remembered without fondness by most Chicago journalists, who watched as the mid-market paper took a turn down-market and ploughed resources into classic Murdoch reader contests like 'Wingo'. In 1986, when the Federal Communications Commission forced Murdoch to choose between owning the paper or a TV station in the same market, he chose the latter. An investor group which included New York investment bankers Adler & Shaykin bought the paper and soon expanded its operations by acquiring sixty-three weekly and bi-weekly papers distributed in the Chicago suburbs.

Several months after buying the paper, *Sun-Times* chairman Leonard Shaykin was invited to lunch at the Four Seasons in New York with Conrad Black, new owner of the *Daily Telegraph*. Black explained who he was and that he was trying to build a global newspaper group. Shaykin explained that Adler & Shaykin were financial buyers, not operators. 'If you ever decide you want to sell, give me a call,' Black told him. 'That's a telephone call you will get,' Shaykin replied.

Shaykin phoned Black in 1991, tracking him down in New York in the midst of Black's pursuit of the *Daily News*. 'You're buying the wrong paper!' Shaykin joked, and they again went to lunch. 'After you lose your enamour of the *Daily News*,' Shaykin told him, 'come back and let's talk.' Around the same time, one of Radler's newspaper connections suggested the time was right to buy the *Sun-Times*, and that he should contact Sam McKeel, its publisher. Radler was flying from Vancouver to meet Hollinger's jet in Chicago for one of his periodic whirlwind tours of American Publishing newspapers. He and McKeel agreed to meet at the Butler Aviation Terminal at Chicago's O'Hare Airport.

The remote location and clandestine atmosphere seemed to

suggest to Radler that his tip-off was accurate. 'We were in this kind of nondescript boardroom, thirty miles from the centre of Chicago,' recalled Radler. 'And McKeel said, "The *Sun-Times* is not for sale." 'And all I could think was "What the hell are you doing in this stinking board room thirty miles from the centre of Chicago?" '

Radler received his answer, but it took two more years of lunches and phone calls – usually about baseball – with McKeel and Shaykin.

With a circulation of 523,000 in 1993, the *Sun-Times* boasted the largest sales in the city of Chicago; the problem was that the mighty *Chicago Tribune*, with a circulation of 697,000, was the preferred paper in the suburbs, where most people lived. The *Tribune* commanded seventy per cent of the advertising market. A major challenge facing the *Sun-Times* was the fact that the population of the city was declining, and the paper's circulation with it – between September 1991 and 1994, circulation was down 3.6 per cent during the week and eleven per cent on Sundays.

Moreover, as a leveraged buyout under the Shaykin group, the *Sun-Times* had lacked the resources to invest in the paper when the economy had worsened in the early 1990s. With heavy financing costs, *Sun-Times*'s management was always strapped for resources, and Adler & Shaykin were not about to put more equity into the business. In fact, the fund that bought the paper was being wound down in 1993 – and the *Sun-Times* was one of two assets left to be sold.

But Shaykin and Radler could not agree on price and the deal was stalled. At the same time, Shaykin did not want to hold a full-fledged auction for the paper. For one thing, he wanted to sell to a committed newspaper owner who would slug it out with the *Tribune*. Second, he felt newspapers were 'delicate things' and having prospective bidders trapsing through the newsroom kicking the tyres would be best avoided. 'Conrad was the logical buyer and the perfect buyer,' says Shaykin. 'He knew that, I knew that, Radler knew that. All we really had to deal with was the timing of the issue and the appropriate price.'

In autumn of 1993, some of the smaller banks in the *Sun-Times*'s syndicate became nervous about their exposure to the paper and offered to sell their debt at a discount to newspaper and financial buyers they thought might be interested – including Hollinger. Black and Radler declined to buy any of the debt, but the fact it was being offered signalled declining confidence in the company. Shaykin brought his asking price down from US$240 million into Hollinger's range. After all, argued Radler, if the banks are selling out at a discount, why should Hollinger pay full price? Over drinks at the Four Seasons on Michigan Avenue, the basics of the deal were agreed on. Radler keeps the cocktail napkin it was written on.

In December 1993, American Publishing bought the *Chicago Sun-Times* group of papers for US$180 million. The *Sun-Times* added a weighty new dimension to the American Publishing group. Until its purchase, the largest title was the Texas *Port Arthur News* with a daily circulation of 23,900.

Black now owned a major American newspaper. It was also a tabloid and traditionally Democratic in its editorial bent. It had film reviewer Roger Ebert to the *Tribune*'s Gene Siskel. Black was quick to point out that, in contrast to its Murdoch days, it was a fairly sober mid-market paper. And rather than being a 'second' paper in the market, there was so little overlap between it and the *Tribune* that he reckoned the papers were actually quasi-monopolies.

There was also plenty of room for operational improvement in the *Sun-Times*: in 1993, it generated US$136 million in revenues, but only US$2.6 million in operating income – a mere two per cent margin. With 2,200 employees, it would take a long time for Radler to count the chairs. Nevertheless, American set aside US$10 million for voluntary redundancies when it took control. Among the first people to leave were four vice-presidents and the company's treasurer and then, in July, publisher and chief executive Sam McKeel. As far as Radler was concerned, the resignations were a predictable result of a new owner coming in and proclaiming that the results the company had been achieving were no longer good enough. 'Then there's the style thing,' says Radler. 'Some of my American Publishing executives are a little *rough* around the edges, okay? I mean, they come from a background of entrepreneurship, okay? They don't have the style or the presence – presence isn't the word, there's probably too much presence – that these kind of people are used to.'

Within six months of buying the paper, Radler had taken an apartment in Chicago and was doing things like cutting the coloured advertisements out of the *Tribune* that he reckoned the *Sun-Times* could get if only it had decent presses capable of proper colour. Twenty of the group's bi-weekly papers were printed by a contractor, and Radler visualised major cost savings by bringing them in-house.

In December the company bought a nearby community paper with a circulation of 60,000, the *Daily Southtown*, from Pulitzer Publishing. The *Southtown* included a modern printing facility with long-term contracts for the *New York Times*, *USA Today*, and the *Wall Street Journal*. Analysts hailed the purchase for not only bolstering the *Sun-Times* group's regional presence against the *Tribune* but laying the groundwork for a new printing facility.

Black first visited the *Sun-Times* five months after its purchase, sporting cufflinks with Franklin Delano Roosevelt's head on them – his way of allaying fears the paper's Democratic bent was in jeopardy. He sat in on an editorial conference and met senior department heads. 'For such an architecturally well-endowed city, it really is a terribly humdrum building, isn't it?' Black observed of the offices. 'I wouldn't say it's ugly. It's just sort of pedestrian.'

By 1995 American Publishing, which had not existed nine years earlier, ranked as the twelfth-largest chain in the U.S. based on circulation, and second-largest when measured by the number of newspapers operated. With no sign of the price war abating in England, the stage was slowly being set for Black to shift more and more of his interests to America.

Despite Black's early contention that Murdoch's misguided price-cutting gambit would soon be called off, it continued. And when, after nine months, Black decided to cut the *Telegraph*'s price by 18p to match *The Times*'s 30p, critics wondered whether Black had made a serious tactical blunder. Indeed, if the *Telegraph* had matched *The Times*'s price cut immediately, would the price war have been over before it began? Given that Murdoch countered the *Telegraph*'s price cut nine months later by cutting his price again, to 20p, probably not. And during the intervening period, Black busily raised money in the debt markets and laid plans to issue stock to the public in Hollinger's American and Quebec subsidiaries. 'From my perspective, he's been very fair and very rational,' observed Lauren Fine, media analyst at Merrill Lynch in New York. 'Arguably, he held on as long as he could to make no price cut.'

Hollinger raised $121 million through a debenture issue linked to the price of its Southam stock, and another US$144 million through an issue of notes. There was also Hollinger's contentious sale of Telegraph stock. The public issue of American Publishing shares brought in another US$98 million and accomplished an important strategic objective for Black. Unlike many Canadian companies controlled by individuals, Hollinger has only one class of voting stock, and all shareholders are treated equally. Black owns about half the company indirectly, which means any issue of new equity to the public would dilute his control – unless he put in more money to maintain his stake. For the American Publishing share issue it was decided that Class A stock would have one vote per share and be listed on the NASDAQ exchange, whereas Class B shares – all of which would be retained by Hollinger – would have ten votes per share. As a result, at the end of the issue, Hollinger owned sixty-seven per cent of the company's equity, but ninety-five per cent of its votes. It could now issue much more Class A stock without jeopardising its control over American. For Black, the financial engineering possibilities of this structure were virtually limitless.*

Despite the turmoil of the lowering of the *Telegraph*'s cover price, and Murdoch's response, the British newspaper business settled into an uneasy calm. Despite Black's predictions, the mid-market tabloids, the *Daily Mail* and *Daily Express*, did not join in the price war. 'If you produce good newspapers, you don't need to cut the price,' claimed Lord Rothermere. 'It's always easier to cut your prices than to get them up again.'

With the 10p – or fifty per cent – differential between the two papers, average *Telegraph* Monday to Saturday circulation remained above one million, and the *Telegraph* maintained a margin of about 450,000 copies more than *The Times*. Both newspapers claimed higher advertising revenues offset reduced circulation sales. *The Times*

---

* Another piece of the puzzle involved buying out most of the remainder of Lord Hartwell's stock. Hartwell and his family, whom Black had displaced as the *Telegraph*'s proprietor almost a decade earlier, still owned almost eight million Telegraph shares, representing close to six per cent. For three months, Colson negotiated with Hartwell, often visiting him in his office until he finally secured an agreement to acquire seven million shares at 450p. Some of the scenarios Black had in mind would involve the approval of three-quarters of the Telegraph's minority shareholders. Hartwell's six per cent could have gone a long way towards making up the 10.7 per cent of shareholders needed to scuttle Black's plans.

increased its advertising rates by fifteen per cent to reflect its higher reader base, which the *Telegraph* claimed consisted largely of elderly readers on fixed incomes who are not appealing to advertisers. The *Telegraph*, meanwhile played up the fact that its lower price attracted more of the elusive younger readers.

But the effect of the price war on the *Telegraph*'s financial statements was undeniable – a £23.5 million reduction in circulation revenue in 1994. Throughout autumn 1994, the Telegraph's shares continued to trade well down on their pre-cover price cut levels. In October, with Telegraph stock at around 305p, the company began buying its own shares back, something a company is permitted to do at the rate of five per cent per year. Despite the controversy surrounding Hollinger's sale in May, before the price cut, of nine per cent of its Telegraph holdings at 587p, Black was not going to miss a chance to buy back shares on the cheap, regardless of what people thought. The controversial May sale of nine per cent had raised about $150 million; the October purchase of five per cent was expected to cost about $50 million. 'We're basically buying dimes for nickels,' Black said. 'What's wrong with that?'

Black had been saying for years that Hollinger's share price did not reflect the value of its assets; indeed, before the *Telegraph* price cut the market value of Hollinger was at times lower than the net value of Hollinger's stake in the *Daily Telegraph* alone. Taking American Publishing public, Black argued, the group's true value would be set by the market and reflected in Hollinger's share price. There would be no more 'Black Factor'.

Now, however, due to the price war, circumstances had changed and Black vowed to do the reverse: if the Telegraph share price remained depressed, he would take it private.

On 25 August 1994 Conrad Black turned fifty. He spent a quiet evening with his wife, in part because Amiel had recently undergone surgery. Black reflected that he was now 'too old to be called a "whiz kid", but too young to get any respect'. Ostensibly because of her need to take time off for surgery and a desire to do other things, Amiel had also given up her regular column in the *Sunday Times*. Friends said it must have been difficult for her to continue working for Murdoch given the hostilities between *The Times* and *Telegraph* (especially since she was now a Hollinger director), but this was denied by all involved.

At the World Economic Forum in Davos, Switzerland, on 31 January 1995, both Black and Murdoch delivered speeches on the future of the media. Afterwards, in an impromptu joint interview with journalists from *Bloomberg Business News* and the *Globe and Mail*, the ever-cordial rivals ventured that their price war might be cut short by a new factor: rising newsprint prices.

At any rate, having Black and Murdoch in the same place made for an amusing exchange. 'Would you please,' Black turned to Murdoch, 'assure these people that our personal relations are good?' 'Excellent,' Murdoch concurred. 'Never been better, always been very good.'

When one of the reporters asked Murdoch what the price war had cost him, he replied, 'It's achieved a doubling of the circulation. We think it's the cheapest thing we've ever done.'

'Rupert,' Black interjected, 'if you were implying that you've had no real cost in this, you'd be pulling your leg a bit.'

Murdoch cheerfully argued that *The Times* was worth considerably more as an asset with a 600,000 circulation than it was with 350,000. And editorially, Murdoch noted of Black, 'We are trying to emulate him.'

When asked how *The Times* was performing financially, Murdoch said, 'We are a very profitable business. We are going to make well over £130 million this year.'

'Rupert,' Black again interrupted, 'broken out [i.e. without the Sunday paper], *The Times* itself isn't profitable.'

You have to look at the profitability of the paper over seven days, Murdoch replied, not just the Sunday and the weekdays separately. 'You've got to put your seven days together, and then we're fine,' said Murdoch. 'You're fine and we're fine,' agreed Black. 'What are you asking us questions for? Go and ask the *Independent*.' With that, the tycoons rejoined their wives and left.

Despite the public chumminess, Murdoch's five per cent stake in Fairfax was cast in the media as an assault on Black's exposed flank. Indeed, between the impact of the price war on the Telegraph profits and the spectacular financial performance at Fairfax, Black's 24.8 per cent interest in the Australian company accounted for fifty-four per cent of the Telegraph's pre-tax 1994 profits.

At Davos, Murdoch blithely claimed that he owned Fairfax shares because they are a good investment and added he might like to own up to ten per cent. 'I'd rather buy shares in a company that's well run and makes lots of money,' he said, 'than leave it to some money manager in a bank.' Black returned the compliment: 'I'd rather have a shareholder like you than an imbecile institution.'

The mutual admiration was a bit much for Kerry Packer. Reading Murdoch's comments in the Sydney papers infuriated him. Packer was limited by Australia's cross-media ownership laws from owning more than fifteen per cent of Fairfax. Now his long-time rival Murdoch, who had relinquished his Australian citizenship to become an American, and who already owned Australian newspapers – and had recently outmanœuvred Packer for the rights to launch a cable pay-television venture – was talking about buying more of Fairfax. Packer could also no longer let pass without comment the angling by Black, another foreigner, for thirty-five per cent of Fairfax. In his first public interview since the Fairfax battle four years earlier, Packer took his case to the television screens of the nation via an interview on his network's television programme *A Current Affair*. Black 'has no right to control John Fairfax', Packer told the television programme. 'This law is designed to stop him controlling Fairfax. This plea that he be allowed to increase his stake is a completely fallacious argument. The law says you may not have more than fifteen per cent. Why is he entitled to have any more?'

At the same time, Packer set out to challenge the laws that said he could not control more than fifteen per cent of Fairfax. He increased his stake in Fairfax beyond this threshold to around seventeen per cent, and presented the Australian Broadcasting Authority* with evidence to prove that the rules designed to prevent a television owner from controlling a newspaper did not apply to him. As long as Packer owned less than Black, he reasoned, how could he possibly be considered to have control?

Finally, Packer admitted what had been unspoken for so long: 'We would like to be able to take a controlling interest in it [Fairfax].' A

* Successor to the Australian Broadcasting Tribunal.

shudder went through the Australian media world when it heard that Packer was now so intent on getting the chain that he had given up his beloved polo. 'This is open warfare,' declared Dan Colson. 'It's nothing to do with personalities.'

In May 1995, Packer proved his point. The ABA found no evidence that he was pulling the strings in the Fairfax boardroom, and accepted that he had acted within the bounds of the Broadcasting Services Act by buying 17.2 per cent of the company, even though it exceeded the cross-media limit. Where Packer would go from here was anyone's guess. As Ivor Ries noted in the *Australian Financial Review*, 'Packer can be expected to go on buying Fairfax shares until the referee blows the whistle.' The only thing to hold him back was that once he reached twenty per cent, another Australian law would limit him to buying only a further three per cent of Fairfax every six months.

In disregarding the fifteen per cent law Packer came into public conflict with Paul Keating, and a couple of months later the whistle was blown by Canberra. The Australian Cabinet proposed new cross-media rules which barred Packer from owning more than fifteen per cent of Fairfax. It just so happened that Colson was in Australia on one of his regular visits, stepping up the lobbying for the Telegraph to increase its interest in Fairfax to thirty-five per cent. Black and Colson believed that Keating's public dust-up with Packer nicely complemented their argument that diversity of ownership – theirs in particular – had proven to be a positive for the country's media. But once again Keating was heading into an election and may have preferred to defer the matter to avoid any more controversy over Fairfax's ownership.

For some time, Conrad and Barbara Amiel Black had been looking at apartments in New York City, and finally settled in December 1994 on an east-side co-op on Park Avenue at 66th Street. The price was US$3 million, which, together with 'customary transaction costs and expenses and needed capital improvements and furnishings', would be paid by American Publishing. Black would be able to use the apartment rent-free. The reason for the purchase, according to American Publishing documents, was 'to facilitate the rendering of management and advisory services' and 'to enhance the business interests of the corporation with the financial community, the newspaper industry and otherwise'. While Hollinger executives might have thought they were doing the right thing by being up-front about disclosing the purchases rather than renting out fancy hotel suites which shareholders would never hear about, the apartment purchase – and a similar $1 million apartment for Radler's use in Chicago – were the focus of snarky articles in *Forbes* and *Business Week*.

Along with hiring a decorator for the new pad, Black's first move was to execute a master plan he had hatched in February 1995. Under it, American Publishing would acquire one hundred per cent of the Telegraph plc and Hollinger's nineteen per cent stake in Southam. The deal would take the Telegraph private – as Black had warned he would do if the City kept punishing his share price – and cloak the effect of the price war on the paper by merging it into a bigger entity. It would also increase Black's profile in the world's financial capital, and combine his publishing interests in a vehicle which he could expand without fear of diluting his voting control.

Even before the proposed shift of Black's power base from London to the United States, he and his wife had been spending more and more of their time in Manhattan. Despite the cut and thrust of the price war in London, it seemed to some of his friends that Black was growing restless, even bored. 'No, not a bit,' said Black. 'In my position I move around not exactly according to what municipality I most like the public parks in, the theatres or the skyline. I go where my essential economic interests lead. I like London and I like New York. So I'll be a good deal in both of them.' Another theory was that Black was growing disenchanted with the political scene, particularly with the prospect of a Labour government and the Tory *Telegraph* being an Opposition paper. 'That's all a load of bullshit. God knows where that nonsense comes from. In the first place, it is well known that we've been highly critical of the government here. In the second place, my relations with the leader of the Opposition are perfectly cordial. In the third place, I never particularly care who the government is anyway, unless it's some completely oppressive regime.*. . . You don't pack up and leave like a dung beetle moving from one place to another. If

---

* Black even appeared to mellow towards his old adversary, Ontario premier Bob Rae. To the surprise of some present, Rae was among the guests at a dinner at Black's home honouring political philosopher Isaiah Berlin in November 1994. As Black predicted, Rae's socialists were defeated in 1995.

you're the head of an international company you might choose to have residences in more than one of the countries that you do business in. And that's all I'm doing.'

Two days before announcing the reorganisation, Black spent much of his evening at home in London, attending the Fairfax board meeting in Australia via telephone, and the following night he spent even longer running through the reorganisation with associates and advisers in Chicago and Toronto. At one point, Black's wife Barbara said, 'You always have a military analogy for what you're doing. What is it now?'

'Aha!' Conrad replied, 'I will show you.'

Recounted Black: 'So I got out General Fuller's life of Julius Caesar and I opened it to a map of the Battle of Alesia. This was in the suppression of the revolt of the Gauls, you see, and Caesar chased his enemies into this town and laid siege to them. But then a much larger enemy force came and laid siege to him. So you had two lines, a line of *circumvallation* and a line of *contravallation*, and I said, "There he was – he was between those two lines. He was keeping the inner group in and the outer group out, but it was making for an awful lot of fighting all the time."

'She said, "Did he win?"

'I said, "Oh yes, he won."

'So that's my little analogy. I was thinking about it. It always struck me as the most astonishing military map I had ever seen, along with its description of Caesar himself charging around in his red cape for weeks on end. He'd be in the east and he'd be in the west. . . . I'm joking. I'm not saying I'm in that kind of position. It's just that there's a lot going on at once.'

Being Black

'What the hell am I paid for? I've got to
do something for a living'

On a typical London morning at around one or two a.m., Conrad
Black turns out his bedside lamp and goes to sleep, usually after
reading his couriered copy of the coming day's *Daily Telegraph*. Black
dreams about 'exceedingly mundane things'. He has read Freud's first
book on the interpretation of dreams, and used to try to record them
as best he could when he woke up, to try to make sense out of them.
'For the most part they just are snippets of things that are really
happening, with somewhat fantastic flourishes to them,' he found.
Sometimes, like many people, he has slightly unpleasant flashbacks
that he is back in university taking exams. 'I remember Churchill
writing, "They seem distant and unimportant to us now, but few
things are more terrifying to us at the time."'

After seven or eight hours, Black awakens, but does not always leap
out of bed; often he gets on the telephone immediately, absorbing the
latest matters of import at one or another of Hollinger's papers
scattered across three continents. Once dressed, fed – raisin bran
cereal is the Black breakfast of champions – and installed via
limousine in his fifteenth-floor proprietor's office at 1 Canada Square
in Canary Wharf, Black is surrounded by paintings of battleships and
a couple of cruise liners. There is a photo of Queen Elizabeth II
reading the *Telegraph*. On a wall beside his desk is a painting of
Napoleon in a battlefield setting. Nearby is another painting, of
Admiral Nelson. 'You see there's Napoleon after Waterloo and
behind him is Nelson before Trafalgar,' notes Black. 'Napoleon lost
and survived and Nelson won and died.' What significance can be

read into that? 'Seen from a certain perspective, he who seems to win loses, and vice versa.'

A side table in front of the couch is piled high with various newspapers; on the coffee table fashioned around a metal plate from old *Telegraph* printing presses are more stacks of publications from around the world: Polish magazines and Italian newspapers, the *Jerusalem Post*, the *Financial Post*.

Black says that when he is in his office he spends most of his time thinking. Three men he has spent a lot of time thinking about are Rupert Murdoch, Kerry Packer, and Paul Desmarais. By 1995 it was clear that the progress of Hollinger would depend on how Black handled these three tycoons, each with ambitions at least equal to his and financial means far outstripping Hollinger's. 'In an ideal world maybe I would have no peer,' says Black. 'I'd own everything I wanted to own and there wouldn't be anyone else to have the effrontery to have a different view or a different interest. But that's not the way the world works, so you've got to deal with who's there. You could do worse with people to deal with. It creates issues, but, you know, what the hell am I paid for? I've got to do something for a living.'

At Southam, Black professes that everything has gone smoothly since Desmarais' Power Corp. invested alongside him in 1993. The following year, Black and Desmarais appointed themselves co-chairmen, and at the 1995 annual meeting the agreement limiting both men from owning no more than forty-seven per cent of Canada's largest newspaper company expired. On Black's prompting, Southam sold Coles Book Stores, and the Southam executive suite has seen several senior executives come and go. But the company's newspaper profits have not improved as quickly as any shareholder would have liked, and rising newsprint prices have added new pressures to the bottom line. Assuming the chairmanship in May 1995 (he and Desmarais agreed to rotate the post), Black vowed that more change was on the way. But despite all the talk of their shared goals, those close to Black say privately that it is merely a matter of time before one side buys the other out. Some at Hollinger believe Desmarais would sell should Southam stock rise into the $18–$20 range. Those closer to Desmarais say that he and his family intend to play a greater role in running Southam than perhaps Black had envisioned. Others on Bay Street, Toronto's financial centre, are betting that Black, frustrated by the arrangement, will sell out to Desmarais and pour his resources into other acquisitions.

In Australia, Black appears, more than ever before, poised to sell out of Fairfax if he is not allowed by the government to increase his ownership in the company. Privately, he has not excluded the possibility of working out some sort of deal with Packer, either. 'The tergiversations of the last year have indicated that the present situation is inherently unstable and cannot continue indefinitely,' he wrote in Hollinger's 1994 annual report. 'At present market prices, making no allowance for block premiums, we have an unrealised gain of over $250 million on our Fairfax investment.'

In London, the price war between the *Telegraph* and *The Times* has become a fact of newspapering life. Black does not take the Murdoch threat lightly, but he believes the worst is over. In early July 1995, *The Times* raised its cover price 5p, to 25p, citing a fifty per cent rise in the cost of newsprint. The *Telegraph* followed suit, nudging its price up 5p to 35p.

Black maintained the *Telegraph* had 'won the price war in England'. The victory, to Black, was clear, because, with a 10p differential between the papers, Murdoch was no longer closing the circulation gap. Murdoch could also claim a partial victory – his *Times*, which had been losing readers two years earlier, had almost doubled its circulation, and surpassed both the *Guardian* and the *Independent* by a considerable margin. He had taken *The Times* from being a marginal competitor to within striking distance of the *Telegraph*. As in all wars, it can also be concluded there were no winners, at least commercially. The *Telegraph* made less money and *The Times* lost more. Only the readers were winners, because newspapers were cheaper for the first time in years.

Black looks on the bright side of the price war: two years into it, 'we took a tremendous uptick in the demographic desirability of our reader, and *The Times* was adding the eighty-year-old captains in Bournemouth who used to write to me in droves if their paper arrived ten minutes late. I told Murdoch, "They're good people. Now you can get their letters. You're welcome to them".'

While he does not want to sound 'triumphant or overconfident', Black believes the biggest commercial threat to his newspaper empire has been arrested. 'The conventional wisdom of a year ago was that *The Times* would eventually surpass the *Telegraph*, and you couldn't set foot outdoors without hearing it,' he says. 'Through the fall and into the new year we had the deep pockets argument, war of attrition – the side with greater manpower and reserves would win. That gradually petered out in the spring. And I made the point – when Rupert said at his annual meeting he's going to keep the pressure on – "he's the one whose newspaper is losing money in that market, not ours. So he's holding his own feet to the fire, not mine." The fact is, the losses that they were running were quite material. Yes, it's a big company and it makes life a lot easier if you can round up *chumps* in the telephone business to pour *billions* into your treasury to buy passive share-holdings,* but the fact is he is an eminently rational man. He's very bold and he's very tenacious but he's rational. He's not interested in throwing money out of the windows.'

Murdoch intimates claim that *The Times*'s pricing strategy is henceforth to sell for less than the *Telegraph*, just as the *Telegraph* was cheaper than *The Times* for decades before Black bought it. They continue to hold the view that, over time, an improving editorial product and lower price will make it an appealing alternative for *Telegraph* readers. *He who seems to win loses, and vice versa.*

Black and his associates are counting on improving results from other acquisitions, such as the *Chicago Sun-Times*, to compensate for the pressure on the *Telegraph*. And with Black increasingly residing in New York, it is only a matter of time before another large American acquisition joins the Hollinger fold.

His plan to take the Telegraph private was called off in May 1995, three months after it was announced. A committee of independent Telegraph directors led by Lord Swaythling voted against endorsing the offer Hollinger was willing to make, which was around 450p. The first public sign that the deal was not going to happen came through an interview Black granted, in which he said the offer would be 'nowhere near' the 500p figure being circulated by some stock analysts. Swaythling told the *Financial Times* he was 'extremely surprised and not a little annoyed' to read of Black's price proposal

* American long-distance company MCI Communications Corp. invested US$2 billion in News Corp. for a minority shareholding in 1995.

through the media – there had not yet been a formal offer. 'The press,' agreed an unnamed fund manager who obviously was not familiar with Black, 'is no place to make an opening shot.' There is nothing to prevent him from trying to take the *Telegraph* private again in the future, as a straight offer to shareholders will not require board consent, just the approval of ninety per cent of the shareholders.

A 1994 profile of Black in *Time Magazine* described him as a billionaire, but nobody checked with him. 'In French francs, yes,' he quips when asked about this, 'but in Canadian or American dollars or pounds, no.' The worth of his roughly fifty per cent shareholding in Hollinger,* is close to $300 million. As Hollinger's chairman and chief executive, he draws a salary of more than $2 million, plus stock options, and the dividends he earns on his shares, making him one of Canada's highest-paid executives. 'I have run up a profit every year for a great many years,' Black adds, indicating that his worth is considerably beyond the value of his stock. And he has other means, such as Ravelston's investments in Western Dominion, the pet company of David Radler. Black deals in large sums, to be sure, yet his fortune does not place him among the world's or even Canada's most monied individuals. 'That is a perfectly legitimate question I often put myself,' Black reflects, for ever amazed by the attention he receives. 'I mean, I'm a well-to-do person but there are lots of wealthier people around.'

Financier and Hollinger director Peter Munk suggests Black might find an answer close to home. 'He does seem to lead a lifestyle that would match people who belong to the international world of the heavyweight financiers – which he's not,' says financier Munk. 'As long as I have known him, he seems to be attracting attention. He does not particularly seem to mind it: he does drive around in one of the finest old Rolls-Royces in England. You can be Rupert Murdoch and drive around in a black Ford.'

In fact, Black owns about a dozen cars. They include the 1954 Rolls in which he has been sighted in London, the simple blue Cadillac of recent vintage in which he is transported while in Toronto, George

* Held through his 67.5 per cent interest in Ravelston Corp.

Black's 1967 Cadillac limousine ('14,000 miles, nice car, about twenty-two feet'), and his personal favourite, his father's 1955 Packard.

Sometimes, it is difficult to distinguish Black the person and Black the caricature. When he appeared on the BBC radio programme *Desert Island Discs*, on which guests are invited to play songs they would choose if confined to a desert island, Black's eclectic selections included Beethoven's Emperor piano concerto, Paul Robeson's version of 'Londonderry Air', the Mormon Tabernacle Choir's rendition of 'The Battle Hymn of the Republic', and General Douglas MacArthur's 1951 farewell address to the United States Congress.

Charlotte Corbeil, the television interviewer, asked Black what he wants as his epitaph. Just his name and dates, he replied. 'Oh come on,' Corbeil said with mock disappointment, having expected something more grand, given Black's fascination with historical figures and world leaders. Black explained that in fact the more exalted a person, the less is written on their tombstone: Charles de Gaulle just has his name and dates, Winston Churchill has the same, Otto von Bismarck has only his last name, and Napoleon Bonaparte has only the letter 'N' with no dates at all. 'By those criteria,' Black intoned, 'I suppose I should aspire to have an absolutely *blank* tombstone, because I'd be so well known, no explanation would be necessary.'

Such proclamations notwithstanding, Black contends he has been falsely typecast by the media 'as a sort of blustering, Henry VIII, predatory tycoon. That's essentially bullshit. To the extent that I'm that, that's a very small extent.' He is the first to admit that not all his public pronouncements should be taken at face value. 'Most of what goes on is a bit of a game,' he says. 'You've got to enjoy the game.'

Being Black means living life on a massive scale, yet having an aversion to faddish things and prevailing values. This can perhaps be explained by Black's view that rampant consumerism is the dark side of capitalism, and partly responsible for a decline in conservative values. 'When I noted in 1976 at Christmastime that Walter Cronkite's newscast was sponsored in part by an electric denture-cleaning device, I had a profound conviction that his economic trajectory simply could not continue,' Black recalled. 'It was, I think, more this compulsive and garish aspect of capitalism – consumerism in its most vulgar form – that disillusioned so many. Another problem, it seemed to me, was that materialism had come to appear singularly unheroic. "The Stock Exchange," as Schumpeter remarked, "is a poor substitute for the Holy Grail." For these reasons, socialism attracted and held the allegiance of most intellectuals for more than a century.

'Because intellectuals do dominate the power of the word, the conservative philosophy of capitalists, until recently, made a very poor showing in the history of ideas. Businessmen largely have been unable or unwilling to defend themselves with words; and even when they tried, they long tended to bellow ultra-right clichés like wounded dinosaurs, much to the amusement of the intellectual left.'

It is not difficult to conclude that Black views himself at the forefront of a movement to reverse this trend. As do others. 'I find his views are engaging and engagingly expressed,' says William F. Buckley, who sits on Black's international advisory board. 'I knew Maxwell a little bit, the Hearsts, the *New York Times* people. I don't think any of them are as emphatic in their political inclinations as Conrad is. He's moderately, not obtrusively, but moderately messianic about conservatives, which suits me fine.'

'I think he's first and foremost an intellectual,' says Peter White. 'Ninety per cent of his pursuits are intellectual pursuits – even his interest in baseball. But he recognises that success in business brings great advantages in life, not the least of which are monetary. And that the newspaper business is a wonderful vehicle for meeting almost anybody in the world that he wants – particularly when you're the owner of the *Daily Telegraph*.'

'He always has been attracted to people of fame,' says Munk, 'which may not be the way you would run a business or I would run a business; it's the way he runs a business, and it works for him.' Black asserts that if he hadn't known Andrew Knight through the Bilderberg Meetings, he never would have pursued the *Daily Telegraph*; if he hadn't known Henry Kissinger, he would not have got out of Norcen just as oil prices were heading south; if he hadn't known Sir James Goldsmith, he would not have been at dinner that fateful night when he and Kerry Packer first met and laid plans to bid for Fairfax.

'I don't spend all my time just chatting with people, shmoozing,' Black contends, 'but it is important to have contacts who are well placed just to keep in touch with them. If you're trying to build a business to find out what's available, what's going on, it's important. That's what I'm interested in.'

At times, Black has seemed like a human steamroller, trampling rules, foes, and conventions that have blocked his path. He adamantly refuses to be told what to do, even growing indignant at the sight of an outstretched seatbelt, friends say. On the subject of Conrad Black, most people's views are as strong as his own. Those who admire him do so precisely because he is someone who does exactly what he wants in life. Those who do not, find him infuriating and surprisingly thin-skinned.

That his style and views do not make him universally popular is okay by Black – he has always been suspicious of overly popular people. The historical figures that fascinate him are often autocratic, frequently beleaguered, usually misunderstood – Duplessis, de Gaulle, Napoleon, Nixon. 'I'm not interested in popularity, I just don't want to be synonymous with something that is a magnet for public hatred,' Black explains. 'And I think I've achieved what I wanted to achieve. I did what I had to do. There were stages in the course that led to a good deal of negative publicity. Some of it was a naturally negative interpretation of what I was doing in a manner that was fair, debatable but fair. Some of it was ideological opponents sticking the knife in. Some of it was just the Canadian spirit of envy and spitefulness. But I weathered that.'

Black's long-term plans remain as unpredictable as ever. He says he would like to go on buying newspapers indefinitely, and probably will expand into other media at some point. It is not surprising he is happy to let others blaze the trail onto the information highway. When they stumble, Black will swoop – just as he does with newspapers. In July 1995, Hollinger bought nineteen small newspapers from Thomson Corp., among them the first papers bought by Roy Thomson. The following week, Hollinger bought another twelve papers from Thomson in the U.S. The multibillion dollar Thomson Corp. had decided to focus on bigger assets, particularly electronic databases, and papers such as the *Guelph Mercury*, *Peterborough Examiner*, *Corbin Times-Tribune* and *Oswego Palladium-Times* no longer had a place in the company. Meeting publishers from the Canadian papers in Barrie, Ontario, an hour north of Toronto, Black felt a tinge of nostalgia for his younger newspapering days, when much of what he learned was from Thomson executives.

As perhaps the archetype newspaper proprietor for the next millennium, Black speaks of gathering and packaging information and entertainment in an appealing way for readers, not of the 'public service' and 'social obligation' that the founders of the publications he commands once embraced. 'There's a terrible amount of self-righteous claptrap about a sacred trust,' he says. 'If the small guy's guardian is the media, then the small guy is in bigger trouble than I thought.'

Like his father, by the age of fifty Black had all the money he or his family could ever need. Like the young Conrad, eighteen-year-old Jonathan Black has had a turbulent scholastic career – complete with expulsion – but is now progressing well at an exclusive school in California. 'They're absolute clones,' says his former wife Joanna of son and father. For his part, Black has tried to stay close to Jonathan, Alana and James despite usually being separated by distance, but professes to have no dynastic ambitions. 'These kids should do what they want,' he says. 'If they're interested in my business, they're welcome. But if they're not they're under no pressue whatsoever to take an interest in it.'

For Black, a quest that may have been fuelled by a sense of destiny coupled with a craving for the approbation of his deceased father has moved far beyond earlier motivations. 'He's on a roll,' says Joanna Black. 'He doesn't know how to stop. In a way, not being in the scene any more, I say "Well why should he stop?" It's not my life. He keeps going on. He's a success. He's doing well in business and he seems to enjoy the social whirligig and knowing important people.'

Hal Jackman also believes Black will continue buying newspapers. 'It's just what he gets off on,' says Jackman. 'It's expanding, it's like collecting books, toy soldiers, anything. Once you stop collecting, you will effectively lose interest in your collection. Curators will tell you that if you collect art and you stop buying art, then within five years you'll give away your collection. You'll lose interest. You wanted to get one of everything. The danger of course is that you over-extend yourself.'

This, in Black's view, is not a problem. He has certainly seen corporate implosions from close range: his friend from Laval

University, Jonathan Birk, lost control of the famed jewellery retailer Henry Birk's & Sons; and former Hollinger directors include fallen real estate tycoons Paul Reichmann and Robert Campeau. Despite the pace of deals and the appearance that Hollinger is poised to take over any newspaper in the world at any given time, Black contends that he will not jeopardise what he has built. 'If you want to be rich, you've got to do it once,' he says, suggesting that the several million dollars he inherited from his father in 1976 does not fit his definition of 'rich'. 'In essence I did it twice, but I would never do it again. Never. Absolutely not. Never bet more than you can afford to lose. No matter how enticing the prize is, don't do it. Don't bet the company.'

The goal is invincibility, if not immortality. Until it is achieved, as surely as there are millions of people reading Hollinger newspapers today, Conrad Black will be fighting to own the final word.

Acknowledgements

Although this book is unauthorised in the literal sense, the first thanks must go to Conrad Black, whose conversations with me were an integral and appreciated ingredient of my research.

From the conception of this project, Daniel Colson, Black's long-time legal adviser and now vice-chairman and chief executive of Telegraph plc, was encouraging of a book chronicling the incredible transformation of Hollinger. Within Hollinger, president David Radler and director Peter White were very generous with their time and insights. Thanks also are due to vice-president of finance Jack Boultbee.

Colson's assistant, Jane Martin, was always helpful, as was Black's London assistant Rosemary Millar. At 10 Toronto Street, Black's inscrutable long-time assistant, Joan Avirovic, was a great help right up to her retirement in autumn 1994.

Two key people who declined to be interviewed were Black's wife, Barbara Amiel Black, and brother Montegu. Amiel Black said that as long as she is a journalist she has decided to be the one doing the interviewing, not the other way around, and had nothing 'economical' to add to the story in any case. Monte Black conveyed after some months through an assistant that he was not 'comfortable' getting involved with such a project, and later reiterated his decision in person.

At the *Financial Post*, I am grateful to Maryanne McNellis, David Bailey, and Douglas Knight for giving me the latitude to complete this project. While at the *Post*, Michael Babad was especially helpful, encouraging and wise. Thanks also are due to Theresa Butcher and the *Financial Post* library staff for their assistance and excellence. The libraries of John Fairfax, the *Daily Telegraph, Financial Times* of London, *Toronto Sun* and *Jerusalem Post* were all valuable resources.

Although book-writing is a solitary exercise, many people on three continents provided input or support that helped bring this book to fruition. Some agreed to be interviewed on condition of anonymity, and thus cannot be thanked individually. Among those who can be, and in this group I include colleagues who helped in other ways, I would like to acknowledge: Suzanne Altman, Bill Ardell, Peter Atkinson, St Clair Balfour, Sarah Band, David Bar-Illan, Adrian Berry, Patricia Best, Joanna Black MacDonald, Brome County Historical Society, Glen Burge, Mark Burrows, Dixon Chant, Charlie, Ronald Cliff, Joe Cooke, Crosbie Cotton, J. Douglas Creighton, Alan Deans, Jeremy Deedes, Michael De Pencier, Norman Elder, James Fairfax, John B. Fairfax, Lee Falvey of Crescent Hotel, Sydney, Douglas Fisher, James FitzGerald, Robert Fleury, Allan Fotheringham, John Fraser, David Galloway, Richard Gilbert, Marianne Godwin, Hirsch Goodman, Ron Graham, Rupert Hambro, Lord Hartwell, Max Hastings, George Hayhurst, David Horovitz, Jaimie Hubbard, Charles Ind, the Hon. H. N. R. Jackman, Stephen Jarislowsky, Trevor Kennedy, Ed Klein, Andrew Knight, Laurier LaPierre, Deborah Lamb, Gilbert Lavoie, Alfred Leblanc, Yehuda Levy, Philip Lind, John Macfarlane, Linda McQuaig, Rod McQueen, Charles Moore, Peter Munk, Peter Newman, Robert Normand, Leon Pearce and the Australian High Commission in Ottawa, Stephen Petherbridge, Sir Charles Powell, David Ramsay, Ari Rath, Eric Reguly, Ronald Riley, Sir Frank Rogers, Ted Rogers, Richard Rohmer, Gary Ross, Sir Evelyn de Rothschild, Andrea Roy, Jean Roy, Stephen Salmon at the National Archives of Canada, Leonard Shaykin, Hanan Sher, Chris Silvester, Bernard Simon, Clayton Sinclair, Donna Soble Kaufmann, Brian Stewart, Arthur Ochs Sulzberger Sr, Lord Swaythling, Charles Taylor, Kenneth Thomson, William Thorsell, Malcolm Turnbull, Mike Urlocker, Araminta Wordsworth, Sir Peregrine Worsthorne, Norman Webster, Jennifer Wells, and Adam Zimmerman.

For specific materials, I am grateful to Duff Hart-Davis for furnishing his 1986 interview with Conrad Black; to Ian Austen for shipping from Ottawa boxes of documents relating to the Norcen investigations; and to Ann Shortell for excavating her basement to dig out some useful materials. Ann, with Anne Kingston, must also be thanked for providing invaluable comments on the manuscript and for their great friendship. Similarly, thanks to Colleen Ryan for her help with the Australian sections and to Brian Rogers in Toronto and Mishcon De Reya in London who added wisdom.

For friendship and support, I would like to acknowledge Gayle MacDonald, Tycho Manson, Andrew McCreath, Glen Watson and Brian Stock. Elizabeth Webster was an unfaltering voice of encouragement and enthusiasm from the project's inception to completion.

My agent Dean Cooke, with whom this idea originated over a chance meeting in a coffee shop, must be thanked for championing it; thanks also to his skilled Curtis Brown affiliates Peter Robinson in London and Tim Curnow in Sydney. At Reed Canada, managing director Susan Jasper and publisher Oliver Salzmann brought energy and talent to the project; thanks also to Jennifer Byrne and Adrian Collette at Heinemann Australia. At Michelin House in London, thanks to Victoria Hipps and to my editor and Heinemann publisher Tom Weldon, with whom I felt a shared vision of what this book should be from our first meeting.

The final thanks must go to Natasha Bacigalupo for everything, to my brother Eugene for his brilliant business insights, and to my parents Alex and Suzanne Siklos for teaching me courage and spurring me on over the course of this journey.

New York,
July 1995

Notes and Sources

Abbreviations

ALIP Conrad Black, *A Life in Progress*, Key Porter Books, Toronto, 1993.

CB Conrad Black, author interview

DC Daniel Colson, author interview

DR David Radler, author interview

MB Montegu Black, divorce testimony

PW Peter White, author interview

Introduction

p. 3 'Conrad became for a while': PW.

4 'I think he has a Byzantine side': Stephen Jarislowsky, interview with the author.

Prologue   War

p. 7–10 Black at National Club: Author present.

8 'Conrad is the master opportunist': PW.

9 'He's a student of history': Ken Thomson, interview with the author.

9 'extravagant failure': CB.

11 decision to cut price of *Daily Telegraph*: DC, CB, author correspondence with Max Hastings.

11 'We should do it': CB.

11 'may well prove to be the most dynamic press couple': George

Weidenfeld, *Remembering My Good Friends*, p. 461, HarperCollins, London, 1994.

12 'Murdoch is a Darwinian': CB.

12 'If *The Times* wants to cut': CB.

12 [Footnote] 'Around £6.00': Author present.

12 'the first time in recent memory that Cazenove had voluntarily resigned': *Financial Times*, 1 July 1994.

12 'an orgy of self-righteous English hypocrisy': CB.

13 'The credibility of the management is somewhat suspect': *Maclean's*, 1 August 1994.

13 'He has pissed off the Establishment': *Ibid.*

13 'You can't make war and peace': *Financial Times*, 25 June 1994.

1 Early days

p. 15 'Small children, dogs, fish': George Black Jr, interview with Maurice Hecht, 1973, E. P. Taylor Archives.

16 'He has tried his hand at most sports': *Saturday Night*, 26 March 1955.

16 meeting Prince of Wales: *Winnipeg Tribune*, 13 October 1924.

17 'seven financially lean': George Black Jr, foreword to C. S. Riley's memoirs, published by his family.

17 growth of Winnipeg: J. Castell Hopkins, *The Canadian Annual Review of Public Affairs, 1912*, pp. 70–80, Annual Review Publishing Co. Ltd, Toronto, 1912.

17 'a big "untrue" ': George Black Jr, interview with Maurice Hecht, 1973, E. P. Taylor Archives.

18 'bore my callow unsophistication': *Ibid.*

18 'standing in a trench looking like an idiot': *Ibid.*

18 'a hopeless bunch of ghouls': *Ibid.*

19 'goddamned liars': *Ibid.*

19 'buy some steaks': *Ibid.*

19 'come to Toronto and work with me': *Ibid.*

20 formation of Argus: *Financial Post*, 24 November 1945.

21 'there was beer, blood and broken glass': George Black Jr, interview with Maurice Hecht, 1973, E. P. Taylor Archives.

21 'I've fired so many people': *Ibid.*

21 'Since I was dealing with Machiavellian opponents': *Ibid.*

22 'too many policies and decisions were being made at head

office': Richard Rohmer, *E. P. Taylor: The Biography of Edward Plunket Taylor*, p. 205, McClelland and Stewart, Toronto, 1978.

20–2 'I am opposed philosophically': Section on Canadian Breweries sourced from author interviews with CBL colleagues, Maurice Hecht interview with George Black Jr, newspaper clippings, company documents and Richard Rohmer's *E. P. Taylor*.

22   'I find the phone works just as well': *Globe and Mail*, 7 October 1958.

22   'He astounded himself by shooting a sixty-seven': Ian Dowie, interview with the author.

23   'If you can't turn around and snarl at these guys': George Black Jr, interview with Maurice Hecht, 1973, E. P. Taylor Archives.

23   E. P. Taylor on George Black Jr's abilities: E. P. Taylor, interview with Maurice Hecht, 1973, E. P. Taylor Archives.

24   'I did the best I could, Eddie': George Black Jr, *ibid.*

24   'I have all the money I'll ever need': *Ibid.*

24   'Certainly there was a good chance for Conrad to become a total dilettante': George Hayhurst, interview with the author.

25   'Mostly we played with the slot machine': *Ibid.*

25   'His father was a bit distant': *Ibid.*

26   'I don't think it does any harm': George Black Jr, interview with Maurice Hecht, 1973, E. P. Taylor Archives.

26   'To Conrad this was torment': Brian Stewart, interview with the author.

26   [Footnote] 'He had an extraordinary affection for his mother': Sarah Band, interview with the author.

27   'accumulated life savings of $60': Conrad Black, address to Harvard Business School Club of Toronto, 16 September 1992.

27   'I was young and reasonably credulous': *Ibid.*

27   '[Campbell] had come to the house': Joanna Black, interview with the author.

27   'I was very young': CB.

27   'That's the only time we've ever played toy soldiers': Hal Jackman, interview with the author.

28   '[rushing] home early from school to watch the McCarthy

hearings': Conrad Black, address to Harvard Business School Club of Toronto, 16 September 1992.

28 'It was an unbelievably great speech by FDR': Brian Stewart, interview with the author.

28 'His father had an outstanding memory': *Ibid.*

29 'Where do you think North Carolina comes': George Black Jr, interview with Maurice Hecht, 1973, E. P. Taylor Archives.

29 'You always had to be careful what you said to Conrad': *Toronto Star*, 17 June 1978.

29 'I know he rarely, if ever, did any work': George Hayhurst, interview with the author.

30 'gauleiters': John Fraser, *Telling Tales*, pp. 75–83, Collins, Toronto, 1987.

30 'This place is a concentration camp': CB.

30 unattributed UCC colleagues on Black: Author interviews.

30 'All those who, by their docility or obsequiousness, legitimised the excesses of the school's penal system': ALIP, pp. 11–12.

31 'a systematic campaign of harassment and clerical sabotage': *Ibid.*

31 'a lot of money for a fourteen-year-old': *Ibid.*

31 'I was not seeking attention': CB.

32 'Those who had been among the most eager to purchase were suddenly transformed into the Knights of New Jerusalem': John Fraser, *Telling Tales*, pp. 82–3, Collins, Toronto, 1987.

32 'I am neither proud nor ashamed of what happened': ALIP , pp. 14–16.

32 'I was fourteen years old at the time': 'The Fight for Fairfax', *Four Corners*, Australian Broadcasting Corp., 16 March 1992.

32 'I concluded the courses were more interesting if I took general arts': CB.

33 'Diefenbaker's government was in a minority position': Conrad Black, speech to Carleton University convocation, Ottawa, 8 June 1989.

33 'He's extraordinarily hard working and an extremely shy person': *Toronto Star*, 15 December 1979.

33 'Paul Martin was very very ponderous': PW.

34 George Black's health: CB.

34 'Conrad was the apple of his father's eye': PW.

35 'discussing the world, where Rommel went wrong': Brian Stewart, interview with the author.

35 'He had just read the book *Citizen Hearst*': *Ibid.*

35 'Conrad clearly had a mystical love of America': *Ibid.*

36 'Conrad has always been impressed by the impressive': *Ibid.*

36 'Social unrest had become severe': Conrad Black, address to Harvard Business School Club of Toronto, 16 September 1992.

37 'He was really wondering what he would do with his life': Brian Stewart, interview with the author.

37 'It was more like, "What do I do between now and when my destiny is fulfilled" ': PW.

2 Coming of Age

p. 38 history of *Eastern Townships Advertiser*: PW.

39 'bucolic redoubt': Conrad Black, *Duplessis,* p. 172, McClelland and Stewart, Toronto, 1977.

39 'He was a young kid who drove too quickly': Maureen Johnston-Main, interview with the author.

39 'Conrad, what the hell do you care what all these people think': Brian Stewart, interview with the author.

40 'He was always very curious and anxious to know what people thought of him': PW.

40 'We used to regularly have long boozy dinners': DC.

41–2 purchase of *Sherbrooke Record*: DR, PW, Ivan Saunders, interviews with the author.

42 inherited at least $200,000: CB. According to court documents, Black inherited money from his grandparents which was held in trust by his father until he reached the age of twenty-five, in 1969. In 1964, the value of the trust was $468,050. Black did not recall seeing any of that money, and notes it was mainly in illiquid private company stock and therefore of debatable value.

42 'Conrad was crapping in his pants': DR.

43 'great mentors for somebody who was starting out in the business': Crosbie Cotton, interview with the author.

43 'downward payroll adjustment': Irwin Ross, 'The Boy Wonder of Canadian Business', *Fortune*, 29 July 1979.

43 'a certain playfulness': Lew Harris, interview with the author.

44 'I used to go get a dictionary': Crosbie Cotton, interview with the author.

44 'scutcheon': Words from *Duplessis* (McClelland and Stewart, Toronto, 1977), which Black was writing at the time.

45 'I announced myself to the marine guard in the lobby': Philip Marchand, 'Rich, young powerful and heir to Bud McDougald's throne . . . meet Conrad Black', *Toronto Life* August 1977.

45 'the highlight of my sporadic career as a journalist': ALIP, p. 65.

45 'less coverage, more wires': Charles Bury, interview with the author.

46 'Of course, the personal lives of journalists were never any of my business': Conrad Black, speech to Canadian Association of Journalists, Ottawa, 8 April 1994.

47 'an avid devourer of bulky legal and theological tomes': *Duplessis*, p. 660, McClelland and Stewart, Toronto, 1977.

47 'a gentleman could allow himself almost no informality': *Ibid.*, pp. 664–5.

47 'decried as dictatorship and corruption': *Ibid.*, p. 679.

47 'I can remember vividly going to visit Conrad': DC.

47 'He would come to the country and we would say, ' Remove your tie Conrad, for god's sake" ': Laurier LaPierre, interview with the author.

47 'It would be unjust to omit all reference to Duplessis' personal manner of government': *Duplessis*, p. 218, McClelland and Stewart, Toronto, 1977.

48 'Without attempting a psychoanalysis, this condition can have psychological consequences': *Ibid.*, p. 685.

48 'gratuitously insulting': CB.

48 'I have no idea why he's so upset': Philip Marchand, 'Rich, young, powerful and heir to Bud McDougald's throne . . . meet Conrad Black', *Toronto Life*, August 1977.

48 'Remember those old games with the Montreal Canadiens where you'd have seventeen seconds left and a bench-clearing brawl?': *Ibid.*

49 'You know, Conrad, I appreciate this very much, but it's over 1,000 pages': Douglas Creighton, interview with the author.

49   'We didn't suddenly sit down one day and decide we would become media tycoons': *Toronto Star*, 17 June 1978.

50   'We used to tell the bank': DR.

51   Cranbrook airplane crash coverage: Peter Newman, *The Establishment Man*, p. 54, McClelland and Stewart, Toronto, 1982.

51   'There's a lot of things about them that anybody in the field of journalism wouldn't be too thrilled about': *Financial Post*, 14 November 1992.

51   'Radler told us he wrote some editorials': Canadian Royal Commission on Newspapers, p. 94, 1 July 1981.

52   'The English community here': ALIP, p. 136–7.

52   'no degrees, but several attempts': MB.

53   'this kamikaze raid': Philip Marchand, 'Rich, young, powerful and heir to Bud McDougald's throne . . . meet Conrad Black', *Toronto Life*, August 1977.

54   'He was happy enough': CB.

54   'came the unnerving crack': ALIP, pp. 169–70.

54   'He was getting a bit incoherent': CB.

55   'I never heard him say that': CB.

55   'The physical symptoms': ALIP, p. 52.

3   Boy Wonder

p. 56   Draper Dobie phone instructions: Joanna Black, interview with the author.

56   'Doesn't she *know* who I am?': *Ibid.*

57   'ample experience': ALIP, p. 108.

57   'as if encased in cement': Laurier LaPierre, interview with the author.

57   'The curious sense he projects': Philip Marchand, 'Rich, young, powerful and heir to Bud McDougald's throne . . . meet Conrad Black', *Toronto Life*, August 1977.

59   He sliced his hand while carving a turkey: Douglas Creighton, author interview.

59   'a tired group of entries': *Financial Post*, 29 May 1989.

61   'bring him along exceedingly slowly': *The Canadian Establishment. Part 1: 10 Toronto Street*, Canadian Broadcasting Corporation, first broadcast in 1980.

61 'We were happy to co-operate': *Ibid.*

61 'We are running this company': ALIP, p. 195.

61 'McDougald was a real divide-and-conquer kind of guy': *Ibid.*

61 'You're rushing your fences': *The Canadian Establishment. Part 1: 10 Toronto Street,* Canadian Broadcasting Corporation, first broadcast in 1980.

62 'Well, I need hardly tell you that was music to our ears': MB.

62 'Knowing something of the propensity of elderly ladies': Conrad Black, James Gillies Alumni Lecture, Toronto, 18 June 1991.

62 'Bide your time': Rod McQueen, 'The Young Lion: How Conrad Black Made Argus His Own', *Maclean's,* 26 June 1978.

63 'To achieve a little more recognition': *Saturday Night,* October 1980.

64 'enthusiastic urging': Rod McQueen, 'The Young Lion: How Conrad Black Made Argus His Own', *Maclean's,* 26 June 1978.

64 'When the inevitable publicity ensued': Conrad Black, James Gillies Alumni Lecture, Toronto, 18 June 1991.

64 'I agree with everything': *Globe and Mail,* 15 June 1978.

65 'There is no doubt that these ladies were aware': *Ibid.*

65 'If Bud McDougald were here': Dixon Chant, interview with the author.

65 'On the day that Conrad heard about the ladies' ploy': *Canadian Lawyer,* September 1980.

66 'If it came to a crisis': *Ibid.*

66 'We're talking about business': Hal Jackman, interview with the author.

67 'I'm sorry to have to keep bringing this up': Brian Stewart, interview with the author.

67 'the new Mrs Black has never entertained on a large scale': *Toronto Star,* 18 June 1991.

68 'When they phoned my mother-in-law': CB.

68 'That's fine, quite right': CB.

68 'I'm a man of the people': Rod McQueen, 'The Young Lion: How Conrad Black Made Argus His Own', *Maclean's,* 26 June 1978.

68 'We had a very difficult time': Mariellen Black, divorce proceedings transcripts.

69 'I really don't understand': *Ibid.*
69 'Well, it's a monopoly game': MB.
69 'was startled that this amount of money had been borrowed': *Ibid.*
70 'seriously disquieted': Conrad Black, James Gillies Alumni Lecture, Toronto, 18 June 1991.
70 'asset upgrade': *Ibid.*
70 'my brother and I had known Argus all our lives': *Ibid.*
70 'I was slightly miffed': CB.
70 'The price was a price': MB.
71 'We had to . . . eliminate those companies': MB.
71 'It was a revealing encounter': *Wall Street Journal*, 8 November 1994.
71 'a wild bowdlerisation': *Ibid.*
72 'There is mounting evidence the company is turning round': *Globe and Mail*, 30 December 1978.
73 'I am amazed by the number of so-called financial experts' Gillian MacKay, 'Massey faces the grim reaper', *Maclean's*, 22 September 1980.
73 Rice on Black's workload ratio: Peter Cook, *Massey at the Brink* p. 239, Collins, Toronto, 1981.
73 'Herb Gray's remark to us': Dixon Chant, interview with the author.
74 'I was not prepared to tolerate': Conrad Black, *Financial Times of Canada*, 6 October 1980.
74 'as surprising and controversial': Peter Cook, *Massey at the Brink*, p. 258, Collins, Toronto, 1981.
74 'For a self-appointed spokesman': *Ibid.*, p. 259.
74 'the sort of irresponsible, self-serving action': *Toronto Star*, October 9 1980.
75 'What then possessed the editors': *Toronto Star*, October 11 1980.
75 'For the record, (not that the *Sun* is a newspaper of record . . .)': *Toronto Sun*, 14 October 1980.
76 'the base': DR.
76 [Footnote] 'The major item': MB.
76 'You've got to take these opportunities': CB.
77 'I understand you're negotiating': David Hayes, *Power and*

Influence: The Globe and Mail *and the News Revolution,* p. 160, Key Porter Books, Toronto, 1992.

77   'Well, I'm not against this': CB.

77   'We will have to do something about this': Richard J. Doyle, *Hurly-Burly, A Time at the* Globe, p. 421, Macmillan, Toronto, 1990.

78   'He's just getting rich': *Financial* Post, 23 March 1985.

79   organisation charts: Jack Boultbee, interview with the author.

4 Blacklash

Most of the events surrounding Norcen's investment in Hanna Mining are sourced from court transcripts and examinations for discovery in the ensuing court case. Black's deposition took place on 10 April 1982 in Palm Beach. The trial began five days later in Cleveland.

84   'Palm Beach isn't everyone's cup of tea': Peter Newman, *The Establishment Man,* p. 202, McClelland and Stewart, Toronto, 1982.

84   'a fierce litigious and regulatory firefight': Conrad Black, James Gillies Alumni Lecture, Toronto, 18 June 1991.

89   'Z family': Decision of Judge Manos, 11 June 1982, p. 19.

92   'Our thought was that we had a real good shot to negotiate something': CB.

93   'It was the adventures of King Pyrrhus': *Ibid.*

95   'strained and unpersuasive': Decision of Judge Manos, 11 June 1982, p. 39.

95   consent decree with SEC: *Globe and Mail,* 2 July 1982.

96   'I never had any fears how it was gong to end up': Peter Newman, *The Establishment Man,* p. 257, McClelland and Stewart, Toronto, 1982.

96   'Conrad was astounded, I think, at the strength and the force and the viciousness of the response': PW.

98   Conrad Black's visit to Roy McMurtry: Linda McQuaig and Ian Austen, 'The Law and Conrad Black', *Maclean's,* 21 February 1983; plus tapes of McQuaig and Austen's interviews with Black and McMurtry.

99   'in such a way as to make it look like we're routinely regarded as criminals': Conrad Black, interview with Linda McQuaig.

99   Brian Johnston on warrants: Interview with the author.

100 'I have always got along well with him': ALIP, p. 299.

100 'I can guarantee you that any suggestion that my conduct was anything other than friendly': Brian Mulroney, interview with the author.

100 'I'm willing to take up the cudgels for those less able to defend themselves than I': *Globe and Mail*, 25 December 1982.

101 'fairly aggressive': Roy McMurtry, interview with Linda McQuaig and Ian Austen.

102 'a lot of police were going round saying I'm in your pocket': *Globe and Mail*, 25 December 1982.

102 'Isn't that *tragic*': Conrad Black, interview with Linda McQuaig and Ian Austen.

102 'I find this not only highly unusual, bizarre, peculiar': Linda McQuaig and Ian Austen, 'The Law and Conrad Black', *Maclean's*, 21 February 1983.

103 'And that's exactly what happened. And so [Conrad] brought the whole bloody thing on himself': Hal Jackman, interview with the author.

103 cockroach anecdote: John Fraser, 'Basic Black', *Saturday Night*, July 1994. Fraser confirmed in an interview with the author that the man referred to as 'R' in the magazine was Roy McMurtry.

104 'He was as wounded over that whole affair as anyone could possibly be': Peter Atkinson, interview with the author.

104 his wife would assure him that his reaction was normal: Joanna Black, interview with the author.

104 'not unusual at all': Ian Austen and Linda McQuaig, 'Power in High Places', *Maclean's*, 25 April 1983.

105 'We have been completely exonerated': *Ibid.*

105 'I suppose I overreacted a bit, but it's very tiresome': CB.

106 'He's not keen on the spotlight, but he loves the big life': Sarah Band, interview with the author.

106 'Monte is an extraordinarily capable person': *Ibid.*

107 'already in steep decline': Conrad Black, 'Black's Arts', *Report on Business*, July 1987.

108 'It was a dry rot': Dixon Chant, interview with the author.

108 'As other chains tried new ways of marketing, Dominion lost

touch': *Maclean's*, 18 February 1985.

108 'become a relatively soft competitor': *Toronto Star*, 14 February 1985.

108 'your company represents the basic cause of Dominion's decline': *Toronto Star*, 1 May 1985.

109 'Conrad Black has created nothing': *Maclean's*, 25 February 1985.

109 'We had all kinds of people who lost their jobs': *Toronto Star*, 28 June 1989.

109 'was run by an inbred, furtive, overconfident and, in some cases, disingenuous management': *Report on Business,* July 1987.

109 'In commerce, as in matters of mundane physiology and probably journalism too, enemas are sometimes necessary': *Report on Business*, February 1986.

109 withdrawals of funds in 1986: *Financial Times of Canada*, 28 April 1986.

110 'Dominion's managers saw the pension funds as a source of succour': Judgement of Justices Reid, Montgomery and Ewaschuk, p. 10, 18 August 1986.

111 'In my opinion, the commission failed in its duty of fairness': *Ibid.*, p. 32.

111 'I have a question for the Premier': Legislative Assembly of Ontario, *Hansard*, pp. 3477, 27 January 1986.

111 'a symbol of swinish, socialist demagoguery': *Toronto Sun*, 30 January 1986.

111 'I never said that anything that Mr Black has done was illegal': *Ibid.*

112 'We had $30 million in produce stolen': *Globe and Mail*, 29 January 1986.

112 'I recommended that a scythe be taken through the ranks of the low-lives at the warehouse': ALIP, p. 326.

112 'But now everything at the commission is dated BC or AD': *Financial Post*, 23 March 1987.

113 'virtually synonymous': Ann Finlayson, *Whose Money Is It Anyway? The Showdown on Pensions*, pp. 116–17, Viking, Toronto, 1988.

113 result of lawsuit against Finlayson: *Globe and Mail*, 2 August

1990.

113   'You know, I think I've only met him once in my life': Bob Rae quoted by Hal Jackman, interview with the author.

5 *The House Black Bought*

p. 114   New Year's Eve 1984/5: Peter Atkinson, Joanna Black, interviews with the author.

115   'I am just trying to do my job': *Report on Business*, April 1985.

115   'It was showtime': Peter Atkinson, interview with the author.

115   'The end of the line was coming': MB.

116   'As far as I was concerned the thing was over': *Ibid.*

116   'Conrad and I put in money each year': *Ibid.*

117   Arrowwood meeting: CB; Andrew Knight, interview with the author; Conrad Black, interview with Duff Hart-Davis.

117   'one more fiery little armagnac': Andrew Knight, interview with the author.

119   'Send me the stuff': *Ibid.*

119   The reference to Thomas Riley's owning part of the *Telegraph* comes from *The Memoirs of Robert Thomas Riley*, published privately in 1947. No reference to Riley's involvement is found in the published histories of the newspaper, but under commercial structures of the day his interest may have been as small as one sixty-fourth. The best histories of the paper are Lord Burnham's *Peterborough Court: The story of the* Daily Telegraph, Cassell & Co., London, 1955; Duff Hart-Davis's *The House the Berrys Built*, Hodder and Stoughton, London, 1990; and H. R. Fox Bourne's *English Newspapers, Chapters in the History of Journalism, Vol. II*, Russell and Russell, New York, 1966, first published in 1887. Other sources for the history of the *Telegraph* are *Sunday Times*, 15 December 1985 and *Financial Times*, 14 December 1985.

121   'embarked on such a hazardous course': Conrad Black, interview with Duff Hart-Davis.

122   newspaper circulations: Private placement document.

122   the paper [*Daily Telegraph*] had the most elderly readership profile in Fleet Street: David Goodhart, *Eddy Shah and the Newspaper Revolution*, Coronet Books, London, 1986.

124 'I told him to stay away from it': John Tory, interview with the author.

124 'I've never heard of him': Lord Hartwell, interview with the author.

124 'They were making hay or something': Rupert Hambro, interview with the author.

125 'The trouble was I introduced myself but I had his deaf ear': Rupert Hambro, interview with the author.

125 Section on airport meeting based on Duff Hart-Davis's interview with Conrad Black and on author interviews with Daniel Colson, Conrad Black, Andrew Knight, Evelyn de Rothschild, Rupert Hambro and Lord Hartwell.

125 Impression Hugh Lawson made on Black: John Fraser, 'The Taking of the Telegraph', *Report on Business*, May 1986.

126 'I don't think we can resist': Conrad Black interview with Duff Hart-Davis.

126 'all he had to worry about was which pocket it was coming from': Lord Hartwell, interview with the author.

126 'I didn't think it meant very much': *Ibid.*

127 'Lie down until the feeling passes': DC.

127 'Good man, Conrad Ritblat': *Sunday Times*, 15 December 1985.

128 'I'd gone all through all that instant baptism with the media': CB.

129 'I have generally been disappointed by the lack of integrity and serious analysis in British (and most foreign) reporting of American affairs': *Spectator*, 10 August 1985.

129 *Economist* dinner: Andrew Knight, Frank Rogers, interviews with the author; Frank Rogers quoted in Duff Hart-Davis, *The House the Berrys Built*, p. 309, Hodder and Stoughton, London, 1990.

131 'I was told I could wait for several weeks and I was referred to *The Times*': *Financial Times*, 18 November 1989.

131 'Many of us felt we should sue': Rupert Hambro, interview with the author.

132 'I didn't get the advice': *The Oldie*, 16 October 1992.

132 'handed the Berry family's balls to Conrad Black on a silver

salver': Duff Hart-Davis, *The House the Berrys Built*, p. 307, Hodder and Stoughton, London, 1990.

132   'He's not actually against the Berry family': Rupert Hambro, interview with the author.

133   'our kind of people': Lord Hartwell, interview with the author.

133   15 November meeting with Hartwell: DC.

135   'I told the then – Governor afterwards': Lord Swaythling, interview with the author.

137   'No ordinary medic is going to touch Lord Hartwell': John Fraser, *Report on Business*, May 1986.

137   'What exactly is it you want my brother to do?': DC.

138   'Also, I pointed out that this was a totally new deal – again!': *Ibid.*

139   'screaming match': DC, Nicholas Berry interview with the author.

141   'I do not know him very well': *Daily Telegraph*, 14 December 1985.

142   'Why are you doing this?': Lord Hartwell, interview with the author.

142   'The trouble is that we are a family with no other outside financial interests': *Daily Telegraph*, 14 December 1985.

142   'The British as a matter of course have concentrated so heavily on questions of ritual': *Toronto Star*, 24 December 1985.

6   *Waking the Giant, Drowning the Kittens*

p. 143   Black's house: The house was featured anonymously in *Architectural Digest*, April 1988. Although the article did not identify Black by name, it was not hard to recognise the 'power to be reckoned with in Canada' who owns 'a major London daily'.

143   'As Thierry was finishing up here, he was just starting to work on the Statue of Liberty restoration': *Ibid.*

144   'I'm not a great sportsman': *Ibid.*

144   Worsthorne lunch with Andrew Knight: Peregrine Worsthorne, interview with the author.

144   'Perhaps because of all the excitement surrounding this happy event': Peregrine Worsthorne, *Tricks of Memory*, pp. 245–6,

Weidenfeld and Nicholson, London, 1993, and interview with the author.

145 'thinking very seriously about some *coup* being possible': Max Hastings, interview with the author.

145 'Ah, yes, HMS *Warspite* entering Narvik': *Ibid.*

145 'except for the proprietor's almost obsessional preoccupation': Peregrine Worsthorne, *Tricks of Memory*, pp. 245–6, Weidenfeld and Nicholson, London, 1993.

146 'I think he was probably anxious to show': Peregrine Worsthorne, interview with the author.

147 'another publicity-seeking, self-promoting Commonwealth person': Conrad Black, interview with Duff Hart-Davis.

147 'not just a materialistic caricature': *Ibid.*

147 'They said when I had been in newspapers long enough': *Financial Times*, 22 February 1992.

148 'most important single thing': Andrew Knight, interview with the author.

148 'He quite rightly sees that Dan's better': Rupert Hambro, interview with the author.

149 'In our opinion, we have no doubt that we control the company': DC.

150 'I am still editor-in-chief': Author interviews with Lord Hartwell, Lord Swaythling, Adrian Berry, DC.

150 'I suppose if I'd had any guts, I ought to have resigned': Lord Hartwell, interview with the author.

151 'I think it has worked out for the best': *The Oldie*, 16 October 1992.

151 Shah's early triumph: Charles Wintour, *The Rise and Fall of Fleet Street*, pp. 253–5, Hutchinson, London, 1989.

152 'This is not the year of Eddy Shah': Andrew Knight, interview with the author.

152 'draconian': Conrad Black, James Gillies Alumni Lecture, Toronto, 18 June 1991.

152 showdown at Wapping: William Shawcross, *Murdoch*, pp. 270–5, Simon and Schuster, New York, 1993.

153 'It's a terrible bore to put barbed-wire fence around the office': Adrian Berry, interview with the author.

153 'There wasn't the will': Joe Cooke, interview with the author.

153 'It sounds amazing but that was an original concept at the time': Andrew Knight, interview with the author.

153 'distant ogre in Canada': *Ibid.*

154 'a man of considerable intelligence': *Evening Standard*, 29 January 1986.

154 Joe Cooke's plans for new plant: Author interviews with Joe Cooke, Max Hastings, Andrew Knight, Jeremy Deedes, and Adrian Berry; Conrad Black, *Financial Times*, 22 February 1992.

155 'Not quite all': Adrian Berry, interview with the author.

157 'Love at first sight': Charles Powell, interview with the author.

157 'It became evident [. . .] that Conrad knew far more about the history of the Tory party': Andrew Knight, interview with the author.

157 'The revolution you have wrought': Conrad Black, speech to the Canadian Club, London, 1 July 1987.

158 'Although the *Daily Telegraph* always would be and should be a Conservative newspaper': Max Hastings, interview with the author.

158 'a bad call': *Ibid.*

158 'seriously fallacious analyses': CB.

158 'good at drowning the kittens': Max Hastings, interview with the author.

159 'One morning after I became editor, I came up to my office and I found a tramp sleeping outside the door': *Ibid.*

159 'I got in the car with him, and he said, "You'd better have a look at the staff salary list" ': Jeremy Deedes, interview with the author.

160 'The primary brief was to introduce budgeting': *Ibid.*

160 'Well, you've sacked lots of other people': Max Hastings, interview with the author.

160 'Given Conrad's devotion': *Ibid.*

160 'You have to defend your editor': CB.

160 Readership profile: National Readership Survey.

161 'This consisted of a good, informative newspaper': Conrad Black, James Gillies Alumni Lecture, Toronto, 18 June 1991.

162 'expanding funnel': *Ibid.*

7 Citizen Black

p. 163 'Jesus this could be embarrassing': 'Much Ado About Something'. Research by Ann Shortell. A fuller version of the event is presented in Ann Shortell and Patricia Best's *The Brass Ring*, pp. 202–4, Random House, Toronto, 1988.

165 'We needed just a bit of time': Dixon Chant, interview with the author.

165 'get these guys of my back and I'll clean it up': CB.

165 'You can't trust these banks once they decide there is a problem': *Ibid.*

165 talks with *Toronto Sun*: CB, Douglas Creighton, interview with the author.

166 'Arthur, count the chairs': Jennifer Wells, 'Paper Chaser', *Report on Business*, August 1994.

166 'Where are you guys going?': DR.

167 'I remember one day I was walking up Granville Street and suddenly I felt faint': *Ibid.*

168 'I know what he thinks and he knows exactly what I think': *Ibid.*

170 'Success is defied by the public': John Lekich, 'At the office', *Equity*, March 1994.

170 'in rust we trust': Conrad Black, James Gillies Alumni Lecture, Toronto, 18 June 1991.

171 'Even allowing for a discount for the problems inherent in doing business in Quebec': *Ibid.*

172 '[Duplessis] had nothing against Protestantism': Conrad Black, *Duplessis*, p. 679, McClelland and Stewart, Toronto, 1977.

172 'and so his [Duplessis'] segregation in his own mind between the terrestrial world': CB.

172 'Those who find trendy and undignified the Anglican tendency': *Spectator*, 26 February 1994.

172 'Ah, but would I be invited?': Ron Graham, *God's Dominion*, p. 134, McClelland and Stewart, Toronto, 1990.

174 'There was a hitch because the initial agreement had been drafted loosely': Norman Webster, interview with the author.

174 'When I arrived at Toronto Street I was inspected by a

secretary and a security guard': Robert Fulford, *Best Seat in the House*, pp. 245–53, Collins Publishers, Toronto, 1988.

176   'an extremely uncommon millionaire': *Ibid.*

176   'He was talking about the role of the monarch and the executive': John Fraser, interview with the author.

177   'What, that faggot?': James Fleming, *Circles of Power*, p. 311, Doubleday Canada, 1991; John Fraser, interview with the author.

177   'If it was a very hostile article could we try to make it less hostile?': Conrad Black, speech to Canadian Association of Journalists, Ottawa, 8 April 1994.

178   'basically to say "nothing can be done" as politely as we could': *Ibid.*

179   'He brought a sinister reputation': Charles Moore, interview with the author.

180   'In recent weeks, the *Spectator* has published an error-riddled cover piece on the Reichmanns': *Spectator*, 12 October 1991.

180   'From my observation of you, I would say that you knew at least as much about the American presidency as you do about the delicious world of Canadian real estate': *Guardian*, 7 December 1992.

181   'The thing basically lost its way': DC.

181   'We have effectively approached several situations with a view to moving slightly ahead of the conventional wisdom': Conrad Black, Hollinger annual meeting, 7 June 1988.

183   'my greatest pleasure beyond the satisfaction of basic appetites': *Financial Times*, 17 August 1987.

185   [Footnote] 'We all sat in the cabinet room': CB.

185   'The *Telegraph* was not always a strong ally to the sort of Conservative government that Mrs Thatcher was running': Charles Powell, interview with the author.

185   'you can't buy what's not on offer': DR.

185   St Clair Balfour's rejection of Conrad Black as white knight: St Clair Balfour, interview with the author.

187   'What he managed to do, I think, is turn a weakness to a strength': CB.

187   'The man is a walking *Roget's*': *Globe and Mail*, 15 July 1989.

188   'Instead of being an enjoyable pastime to share with my son,

the Toronto team is an object lesson [. . .] on the evils of defeatism, selfishness and cowardice': *Financial Post*, 4 September 1990.

188 'With passing years, the bishops have become more trendy, biased, misleading and desperate for attention': *Report on Business*, October 1987.

189 'I hold no ill-will or grievance against the fact that she won the magazine award ahead of me': CB.

189 'usually resolve themselves into a rational assumption that irrational psychopaths will respond to what would impress rational people': *Report on Business*, November 1985.

189 [Footnote] 'Conrad thinks hanging is too good for them': DC.

190 'reduction of liberty of expression': *Financial Post*, 19 January 1989.

8 Uprising

p. 192 'The aim of this paper': *Jerusalem Post*, sixtieth anniversary supplement, 6 May 1992.

193 'You're going to send the Italian guy to Rome': *Financial Post*, 14 November 1992.

193 David Radler's meeting Arye Mekel, 1988: DR, Arye Mekel, interview with the author.

194 Yehuda Levy phones David Radler about the *Jerusalem Post*: DR, Yehuda Levy, interview with the author.

194 'a certain irony after being at High Mass': DC.

195 'they thought it was a typo': Ari Rath, interview with the author.

196 'It wasn't that our bid was higher than it should have been': *Jerusalem Post*, 30 March 1990.

196 'This part of the world is most historically prone to discussions of conspiracies': *Ibid.*

196 'I consider Bob to be the main author of those wild rumours': *Ibid.*

196 'I was standing in the lobby': DC.

197 'They have a responsibility to be aware of what they're publishing and to influence it': *Jerusalem Post*, 28 April 1989.

198 'Somebody said to me, "He's just the kind of guy who will leave us alone . . ." ': Hanan Sher, interview with the author.

198   'He proved his courageousness in the battles': DR.

198   'The whole spirit of the operation [. . .] was like a big kibbutz':
Yehuda Levy, interview with the author.

199   'Let's not play games': *Jerusalem Post*, 30 March 1990.

199   'I knew it was over': *Independent*, 4 January 1991.

199   'I smell a rat': *Ibid.*

199   'You're stabbing me in the back': Yehuda Levy, interview
with the author.

200   'Ari, if anything is happening, I can talk to Black': Ari Rath,
interview with the author.

200   'And a similar such thing is taking place with regard to Ari
Rath': *Ibid.*

201   'Yasser Arafat could never dream of a better propaganda
tool': Yehuda Levy, interview with the author.

202   'I believe that you cannot call a terrorist who kills children and
women a gunman': *Ibid.*

202   Hami Shalev story: Contained in Justice Elisheva Barak's
verdict in the District Labor Court, Jerusalem, 5 May 1993.

202   'In sustaining its independent editorial views': *Jerusalem Post*,
30 November 1989.

203   'What, are you kidding me?': Yehuda Levy, interview with the
author.

204   'The changes that have been instituted have not been
introduced as quietly as we would have hoped': 1989
Hollinger Annual Report, p. 15.

204   'I was there three years as a major in Israeli uniform': Yehuda
Levy, interview with the author.

205   'I'm not against freelancing': *Ibid.*

205   'The *Jerusalem Post* will not be a mouthpiece of any party':
Jewish Chronicle, 16 February 1990.

206   'To sustain the *Jerusalem Post*, to which they had given so
much': Letter to *Jewish Chronicle*, dated 23 February 1990.

207   'I was sympathetic to Joanna's complaints, but they weren't
true': DR.

207   'My meeting with Black impressed me': David Bar-Illan,
interview with the author.

207   'Generally speaking, I knew we were standing more or less

with the same views on the most important issues': Yehuda Levy, interview with the author.

208 'They wanted results': *Ibid.*

208 'This is not a left-right bullshit thing': DR.

208 'If you call it Judea': David Bar-Illan, interview with the author.

208 'My own inclination, for what it is worth and you're not likely to read it in the *Jerusalem Post*, is that Gaza should be abandoned': Conrad Black, speech to Canadian Friends of Hebrew University, Toronto, 9 December 1990.

209 'It's not just a job': David Horovitz, interview with the author.

209 'Conrad Black is a professional': Hirsh Goodman, interview with the author.

210 'Has the *Post* been a headache?': DR.

9 The Proprietor

p. 211 'one of the most important and successful presidents and one of the most formidable political leaders in U.S. history': *Daily Telegraph*, 3 February 1991.

211 'Black once said that he was prepared to let his editors have a completely free hand': Alexander Chancellor quoted in Nicholas Garland, *Not Many Dead: Journal of a Year in Fleet Street*, pp. 109–10, Hutchinson, London, 1991.

213 'As a Canadian, I wish I could sit here, hand over heart, and tell you otherwise': *Canadian Business*, November 1991.

213 'Did you realise that anyone who owns the *Telegraph* has access to anyone in the world?': *Financial Post*, 9 May 1988.

213 'Where does Richard Nixon live? Or where was he from?': PW.

213 'He loves the atmosphere over there': *Ibid.*

213 'He charmed an enormous number of people in this country': Rupert Hambro, interview with the author.

213 'I think he's gained enormous respect': Max Hastings, interview with the author.

214 'The fact is, if you don't stay reasonably dynamic, things stagnate: *Quaynotes*, September 1989.

215 'He's very remote': Charles Moore, interview with the author.

216 'Our first job is to bolster strength': *Independent*, 29 March 1989.

216 'Black quite rightly worried about what the consequence was for the Sunday': Andrew Knight, interview with the author.

217 'You never knew quite where you were with Andrew': Rupert Hambro, interview with the author.

217 'didn't really work out': Andrew Knight, interview with the author.

217 'probably the most significant wrong-turn': Max Hastings, interview with the author.

217 'run over by a bus': *Sunday Correspondent*, 14 January 1990.

217 'I actually think I ought to step aside': Andrew Knight, interview with the author.

217 'We have created a kingdom': *Financial Times*, 18 November 1989.

218 'That may be good for him, but what about he quality of the two newspapers?': *Financial Times*, 11 October 1989.

218 'a rather picturesque illustration': Conrad Black, speech to Canadian Association of Journalists, Ottawa, 8 April 1994.

218 'I brought my hobnailed jackboot down on the necks of our journalists': *Ibid.*

218 Black claimed Knight had only three days earlier denied the latest rumours: ALIP, pp. 407–8.

218 'I think he could smell the money': DC.

219 'If you lose one of your best managers it is bound to make a difference': *Sunday Correspondent*, 14 January 1990.

219 exchange of letters: *The Times*, 8 January 1990.

223 'I advised you again and again to execute your departure without harm to your reputation': *Observer*, 14 January 1990.

224 'deluged with so many calls and notes of outrage at your conduct': *Ibid.*

224 'The constant smiler with the knife': *Sunday Telegraph*, 7 January 1990.

224 'become chief apologist for somebody whose newspapers are daily doing things that I for one couldn't be party to': Max Hastings, interview with the author.

225 'Shortly after that, my twins were born prematurely and they nearly died': Charles Moore, interview with the author.

226 'Charles was very funny about Bill's dinner at Downing

Street': Nicholas Garland, *Not Many Dead: Journal of a Year in Fleet Street*, p. 164, Hutchinson, London, 1991.

226 'I approved hiring him back from the *Independent*': CB.

226 'Unlike, let's say, Rupert or unlike a lot of tycoons, Conrad loves to play': Max Hastings, interview with the author.

226 'I think the best way to describe it is he's not Rupert Murdoch, he's not Vere Rothermere': Evelyn de Rothschild, interview with the author.

227 'His [Napoleon's] talents as a military commander': CB.

227 'The proprietor of the *Daily Telegraph* would like to go on the record to say that he does certainly *not* own Napoleon's penis': Francis Wheen, interview with the author.

228 'I couldn't and can't stand that man': Lord Hartwell, interview with the author.

228 'Jimmy assured me [that article] had nothing to do with him': CB.

228 'I don't think non-executive directors are all the shout': Lord Hartwell, interview with the author.

228 'a sort of *Almanach de Gotha* of the international right': Alexander Ross, *Canadian Business*, November 1991.

229 [Footnote] Nixon, 'if he were younger': CB.

229 'Conrad's role to some extent is to ingratiate himself in certain circles': DR.

229 'They're almost too rich, when you put those ten or twelve people in a room': William F. Buckley Jr, interview with the author.

230 'It was an experience for me, second to none': Peter Munk, interview with the author.

230 'Frankly, a lot of the use of these boards is to load them up with important people who can be helpful to you': CB.

230 'The newspaper industry in London has long attracted proprietors of immense ego': *Saturday Night*, December 1992.

231 '[Beaverbrook] will always remain a model of the panache': *Ibid.*

231 Joanna Black's change of first name: Joanna Black, interview with the author.

233 'Our cash flow is almost entirely available for acquisitions':

Conrad Black, James Gillies Alumni Lecture, Toronto, 18 June 1991.

10   *Australia's Newest Press Baron*

p. 234   Warwick Fairfax's meeting with Conrad Black: Interviews with participants.

235   'It didn't seem to appeal to us as an attractive financial opportunity': Ken Thomson, interview with the author.

235   'I would be a little bit leerier than Mr Black about acquiring papers overseas': Arthur Sulzberger Sr, interview with the author.

236   'This Fairfax company is unbelievable': Andrew Knight, interview with the author.

236   'Andrew, I find it hard enough to get on the airplane to come to London': *Ibid.*

236   'In the end we took the bait but not the hook': DC.

236   Conrad Black met Kerry Packer at Sir James Goldsmith's home: ALIP, pp. 433–4.

237   Fairfax history: A fuller history of the company can be found in Gavin Souter's *Heralds and Angels* (Penguin Books Australia, 1992), in his earlier volume *Company of Heralds* (Melbourne University Press, Carlton, 1981), and in John Fitzgerald Fairfax's, *The Story of John Fairfax* (J. Fairfax and Sons, Sydney), published in 1941 to mark the company's centenary.

238   'Sydney had never seen parties like Lady Fairfax's': Bob Colacello, 'Publish and Perish', *Vanity Fair*, April 1991.

239   '[given] the full story, so that he would know the sort of man his brother was': James Fairfax, *My Regards to Broadway*, p. 101, Angus and Robertson, Pymble, 1991.

240   'He's really quite interested in newspapers': Mark Burrows, interview with the author.

240   'This may sound ironic, but I'm not a big fan of huge debt': John Lyons, 'Once There Was a Dynasty', *Good Weekend*, 2 November 1991.

240   James Fairfax's plans to prepare Warwick Fairfax for the chairmanship of the family company: James Fairfax, *My Regards to Broadway*, p. 351, Angus and Robertson, Pymble, 1991.

241 'one day it probably would have been up to me to do something': John Fairfax, interview with the author.

241 'Once upon a time there was a dynasty': John Lyons, 'Once There Was a Dynasty', *Good Weekend*, 2 November 1991.

241 'I'm not one of those who heaps scorn on Warwick': CB.

241 'This is one of the great institutions of Australia': *Four Corners*, Australian Broadcasting Corp., 16 March 1992.

242 'I always look forward to going there [Australia]': CB.

242 'A company's cash flow is like a dictator's army': *Quaynotes* September 1989.

242 Sources for section on Fairfax's bankruptcy include newspaper clippings, Tourang documents, author interviews with Mark Burrows and others involved.

244 the bondholders would be left in the cold: Malcolm Turnbull, interview with the author.

246 Daniel Colson was determined to make it plain to Malcolm Turnbull that it would be the people who put up the money and not the bondholders who would be driving the Fairfax transaction: Colleen Ryan and Glen Burge, *Corporate Cannibals*, p. 143, William Heinemann Australia, 1992.

247 'when economic conditions open up such opportunities': Conrad Black, speech to 1991 Hollinger annual meeting.

247 'The government of Ontario appears to believe that capitalists, including average shareholders, are omnivorous': *Ibid.*

247 Conrad Black meeting with Trevor Kennedy, 18 June 1991: Trevor Kennedy, interview with the author.

248 'Kerry's involvement arose out of my seeking to hire Trevor Kennedy': *The Bulletin*, 23 July 1991.

248 'I wasn't just going to raid this guy without talking to him': *Financial Post*, 1 August 1991.

248 'As the Samaritanly philanthropist that I am': *Sydney Morning Herald*, 18 July 1991.

249 'Conrad, did you really say that?': Colleen Ryan and Glen Burge, *Corporate Cannibals*, p. 202, William Heinemann Australia, 1992.

249 'I hope that my arrival will dispel the notion that I have cloven feet and pointy ears': *The Bulletin*, 23 July 1991.

249 'It is the fellow sitting next to you who will be the problem':

Colleen Ryan and Glen Burge, *Corporate Cannibals*, p. 204, William Heinemann Australia, 1992.

249 'I've lived throughout my whole life up until two weeks ago without even being in Australia': *Financial Post*, 1 August 1991.

250 'If it had been necessary for me to be there I would have gone': CB.

250 'The Great O'Gatsby of Ireland': *Sunday Telegraph*, 9 February 1992.

251 'I was always amazed that this kind of Mickey Mouse, rinky-dink bid was taken seriously at all': *Four Corners*, Australian Broadcasting Corp., 16 March 1992.

252 'heavy baggage': *Sydney Morning Herald*, 2 November 1992.

252 'getting into Kessler-Kafka-Orwell country': *Ibid.*

252 Brian Powers's background: *Sydney Morning Herald*, 1 May 1993.

253 [Footnote] 'The idea that I, as one non-executive director out of ten, would be able to exercise some Svengali-like spell': Malcolm Turnbull, interview with the author.

253 'very second eleven': Trevor Kennedy, interview with the author.

253 'another Andrew Knight': *Ibid.*

253 'Kerry can be extraordinarily charming when he wants to be': *Ibid.*

253 'I'd just basically be trying to be a placatory influence': CB.

254 'under siege': Trevor Kennedy, interview with the author.

255 Black trumpeted the McCarthyism angle: *A Current Affair*, Nine Network, 22 October 1991.

255 Protest at ANZ Bank: Colleen Ryan and Glen Burge, *Corporate Cannibals*, p. 284, William Heinemann Australia, 1992.

255 'I remember walking down the street': DC.

256 Black whistling 'Waltzing Matilda': Nicholas Coleridge, *Paper Tigers*, p. 337, William Heinemann Ltd, London, 1993.

256 Conrad Black interview with Jana Wendt: *A Current Affair*, Nine Network, 22 October 1991.

257 Kerry Packer interview with Jana Wendt: *A Current Affair*, Nine Network, 23 October 1991.

258 'No, I see in that a regrettable choice of words': *Sydney Morning Herald*, 2 November 1991.

260 'Mr Murdoch has not enjoyed competing with me in London:
Ibid.

260 [Footnote] 'completely false. There is no corporate policy':
The Australian, 4 November 1991.

261 [Footnote] 'I was opposed to the firing of Kennedy': Malcolm
Turnbull, interview with the author.

261 'I explained to Black that if you want to be an assassin you
have to be prepared to have a little blood on your hands': *Four
Corners*, Australian Broadcasting Corp., 16 March 1992.

262 'Packer, in my view, had a very, very serious influence over
events': Trevor Kennedy, interview with the author.

262 'My last words to him prior to that decision': *A Current Affair*,
Nine Network, 29 November 1991.

262 'He shouldn't feel any pressure from us': *Four Corners*,
Australian Broadcasting Corp., 16 March 1992.

262 'A good general has to know when to advance and when to
retreat: (Black quoting Packer.) *Ibid.*

263 'an interventionist, right-wing, pro-Thatcher owner': *The Age*,
28 November 1991.

263 'endearing element of charlatanism': *Australian Financial
Review*, 2 December 1991.

264 'Whatever decision you take': Minutes of the Foreign Investment Review Board, 5 December 1991.

265 'sleazy, venal and despicable': *Sydney Morning Herald*, 12
December 1991.

265 'With respect to the bondholder litigation': Letter from Mark
Burrows to Tony O'Reilly, 22 November 1991.

266 'sleazy, venal and despicable' fusillade: Colleen Ryan and
Glen Burge, *Corporate Cannibals*, p. 432, William Heinemann
Australia, 1992.

266 'contrary to wide-spread rumours': Canadian Press, 17
December 1991.

266 'there do seem to be rather attractive women in the field':
Financial Post, 17 April 1993.

267 'A delightful man and a great talent': *Four Corners*, Australian
Broadcasting Corp., 16 March 1992.

268 'There, as in Britain, they've got this narcissistic self-obsession
that extends to the owners': CB.

270 'To put it in military parlance, what we need is more trigger-pullers': Bruce Stannard, 'Paper Profits', *Australian Business Monthly*, January 1993.

270 'It's a failing, something I've battled all my life': *Financial Post*, 17 April 1993.

270 'I can only say I have been seduced': *The Australian*, 2 October 1992.

271 'Why do women from places with unpronounceable names': *Telegraph-Mirror*, 17 February 1994.

272 'If you're inclined to a conspiracy theory': *Financial Post*, 17 April 1993.

272 '[Black's] priorities in a lot of ways are right': *Ibid*.

272 'I think that's absolute rubbish. We understand Australia all right': CB.

273 'Malcolm is singularly implausible and bizarre as a source of that accusation': *Australian Business Monthly*, January 1993.

273 'When he is here, he tends to give very colourful and verbose speeches to all and sundry': Malcolm Turnbull, interview with the author.

11   Media Merger

p. 275 'I was attracted to the *real* Conrad Black': Joanna Black, interview with the author.

276 'Joanna, you *must* come back to England or you'll lose him': *Ibid*.

277 'For months after my wife left me': *Maclean's*, 2 August 1992.

277 'I didn't leave him for anybody. I left him for me': Joanna Black, interview with the author.

277 'I can remember Conrad often looking terminally glum': Max Hastings, interview with the author.

277 'the summit of my most ardent and uncompromising desires': ALIP, p. 463.

277 'power is sexy': Barbara Amiel, 'Why Women Marry Up', *Chatelaine*, May 1986.

278 'She was worried that Conrad was not in a sane frame of mind': Miriam Gross, interview with the author.

278 'not going to make the same mistakes with Barbara': Joanna Black, interview with the author.

279 'She looks like Gina Lollabrigida and writes like Bernard Levin': *Evening Standard*, 10 May 1988.

279 'Conrad and Barbara can say big words to each other': Rosemary Sexton, *Glitter Girls*, p. 182, Macmillan Canada, 1992.

279 'They're doing this to spice up their CVs': *Ibid.*

279 'Now, the knives are drawn': *Maclean's*, 27 January 1992.

280 'You couldn't think of two people with two differing backgrounds': Peter Munk, interview with the author.

280 'ideologically uplifting Christmas': Peter Newman, *The Establishment Man*, p. 268, McClelland and Stewart, Toronto, 1982.

280 'I do get tired of all these milk-sops calling to ask me wimpy questions': Judith Timson, 'Barbara Amiel, Nothing Succeeds Like Excess', *Chatelaine*, June 1980.

280 'I've suffered from insomnia all my life': Jean Sonmor, *The Little Paper That Grew*, p. 216, Toronto Sun Publishing, Toronto, 1993.

281 'a lacquered apparition with bouffant hair': Barbara Amiel, *Confessions*, p. 74, Macmillan, Canada, 1980.

281 'I believe it to be morally wrong': *Ibid.* p. 144.

282 'I remember it very well because this was still in Fleet Street': Peregrine Worsthorne, interview with the author.

283 'To be ideological is not British at all': Miriam Gross, interview with the author.

283 'Everybody likes you': Joanna Black, interview with the author.

283 'I so loathe the permissive promiscuous society': Judith Timson, 'Barbara Amiel, Nothing Succeeds Like Excess', *Chatelaine*, June 1980.

284 'sleazy, tasteless and neurotic': Peter Newman, *The Establishment Man*, p. 191, McClelland and Stewart, Toronto, 1982.

284 1992 Hollinger Dinner: Tape of event.

286 'a more resonant rationale for our desire to marry': The column also ran in the *Toronto Sun*, 9 August 1992.

287 'I had met her [the Duchess of York] a number of times': Conrad Black, interview with Patricia Best.

288 'It was a very chirpy evening': Edward Klein, 'Black Mischief', *Vanity Fair*, p. 283, November 1992.

288 trying to find a fax machine: Conrad Black, interview with Patricia Best.

288 'They've become incredibly glamorous as a couple': Miriam Gross, interview with the author.

288 'Nowadays, he's . . . full of the joys of spring': Max Hastings, interview with the author.

289 'They're intellectually very well suited': Miriam Gross, interview with the author.

289 'grievous myth that I am in sedentary and flabby condition': CB.

289 'No disrespect to my Romanian, Eatonian friend': *Ibid.*

290 'It's an all-round paradise': *Evening Standard*, 9 December 1992.

290 'I was always sceptical it would work properly': CB.

290 'I had very interesting people, for example Marlon Brando': Werner Jankowsky, interview with the author.

291 'I'm used to that, you know': *Ibid.*

291 'Is this London's most powerful woman?': *Evening Standard*, 21 October 1992.

291 'made the subject of all sorts of common tittle-tattle': *Newsworld*, Canadian Broadcasting Corp., 14 November 1993.

291 'I was aware that there was a myth': *Maclean's*, 1 August 1994.

292 'The offending article would not roll up at the waist': *Sunday Times*, 31 January 1993.

292 'The London press was claiming that I was such an admirer of my wife's thighs': Jane Nicholls, 'The Black File', *Who Weekly*, 13 December 1993.

292 'Many journalists and most of the more talented ones': Conrad Black, speech to Canadian Association of Journalists, Ottawa, 8 April 1994.

293 'hit the nail on the head when he described journalists as *canailles*': *Sunday Times*, 17 October 1993.

293 'Now that she is rich, Mrs Conrad Black gives the impression she wants to be on the inside': *Evening Standard*, 20 October 1993.

294 'one of the differences between me and my sisters in the women's movement': *Sunday Times*, 7 November 1993.

294 'Mind you, you were the one who wrote they were *canailles*': Author present.

12 *All Over the Map*

p. 295 'media businesses will prove considerably less marvellous': *Forbes*, 1 August 1991.

295 'It's murder out there': *Ibid.*

295 'I've often found with Conrad that crises or big events all happen in immense clusters': Brian Stewart, interview with the author.

296 'I think Conrad is sometimes inclined to give the benefit of the doubt to apparently very rich men': Max Hastings, interview with the author.

297 'The reaction from institutional investors': *Sunday Times*, 5 July 1992.

297 'Well, it would be lighter on the payroll': DR.

299 Martin Maleska flew to London for a long meeting with Black: Martin Maleska, interview with the author.

299 'I have no interest in coming to New York to clasp my lips around an exhaust pipe': Edward Klein, 'Black Mischief', *Vanity Fair*, November 1992.

300 'At one point he talked, for instance, that we would switch every year who would control the editorial page': DR.

300 'I think Conrad would be very good for the *News*': Rupert Murdoch, interview with the author.

301 Black's angle was: Yes, we've cut back jobs: Martin Maleska, interview with the author.

301 'He has given the store away': CB.

301 'We have much more of a focus on the editorial product': Mort Zuckerman, interview with the author.

301ff Southam History: *A Century of Southam*, Southam Press Ltd, 1977.

303 'The Southam organisation has been highly principled, decent and fair': *Financial Times of Canada*, 14 May 1990.

303 'absolute liberty of content and virtual liberty in editorial budgets': Conrad Black, speech to Canadian Association of Journalists, Ottawa, 8 April 1994.

304 'very politely' rebuffed: CB, St Clair Balfour, interview with the author.

304 'I don't question Clair's sincerity': CB.

305 'We didn't want the newspapers to go to somebody who

wasn't interested in editorial quality': *Financial Times of Canada*, 14 May 1990.

305 'It was just a way of the family saving its own ass': Stephen Jarislowsky, interview with the author.

306 'Before John was there, I think the intent of the deal was that everyone would come together': David Galloway, interview with the author.

308 'They both seem to be running their businesses in a hands-on way': *Financial Post*, 28 May 1994.

308 'got a fair way down the road at looking at making a joint offer': David Galloway, interview with the author.

310 'I need to know two things': *Ibid.*

311 'David, I just want to reiterate what I said on the phone': *Ibid.*

312 'Paul's got the newspaper bug': St Clair Balfour, interview with the author.

312 'not just as a cold-blooded business proposition': *Ibid.*

313 'as a multiple proprietor, he will milk many of his papers to the sacrifice of their quality': *Ottawa Citizen*, 4 March 1993.

313 'pompous farrago of nonsense': *Ibid.*

313 'I'm actually slightly *touched* by the rather generous response I seem to evoke': CB.

315 'In most markets, we're in a stop-the-slide mode': News Inc., January 1993.

315 'The theory is abroad that all sorts of cheap stock is about to be shovelled out': *Financial Post*, 2 March 1993.

316 He immediately began working the phones: ALIP, p. 500.

316 'He had managed to telephone the right directors to enlist as allies the night before': Adam Zimmerman, interview with the author.

316 'I gave him a rundown on all the people': *Ibid.*

316 'Those guys were scheming to throw out a bunch of directors': CB.

317 'There was an awful lot of shilly-shallying': *Ibid.*

317 'There's no problem between Desmarais and I': *Ibid.*

318 'It was a source of discussion': Bill Ardell, interview with the author.

318 'With forty-seven per cent of the stock': *Financial Post*, 20 March 1993.

318 'Taking control of Southam would be nice': *Financial Post*, 25 March 1993.

319 'We wanted to do it': Rupert Hambro, interview with the author.

320 'Some of their publishers are good': CB.

320 'The absence of a controlling personality in a newspaper': Conrad Black, speech to Canadian Association of Journalists, Ottawa, 8 April 1994.

321 'Every sign, every indicator': *Australian Financial Review*, 27 April 1993.

321 'Significantly less time reading': Media Futures 1993, Henley Centre.

322 'Intermittently, there is fear that we are in the buggywhip business': CB.

322 'We fear that over the next few years the information highway may turn out to be more like the "highways" of pioneer days': 1993 Hollinger annual report.

323 'I look like a B-52 captain': CB

323 'The best is yet to come': *Ibid.*

13   Man of Letters

p. 326 'With regret, I must dissent from the position adopted by the *Post*': *Jerusalem Post*, 10 September 1993.

326 '[The *Post*] could have been harmed if I hadn't written what I did': CB.

327 'It was not only a matter of principle that publishers should not interfere': David Bar-Illan, interview with the author.

327 'The fact is Bar-Illan personally moderated a bit after his exchange with me': CB.

328 'which was very *piquante*': David Bar-Illan, interview with the author.

328 'She was in favour of the agreement being signed': CB.

329 [Footnote] 'I cast the first *protest* vote of *my life*': *Ibid.*

329 'They were so good that they inspired me to do something': *Ibid.*

330 'I didn't see why I shouldn't do it myself': *Ibid.*

330 'set the record straight': *Ibid.*

330 'the work of a man who rejoices in the intellectual and

financial status of not giving a damn': *Canadian Business*, November 1993.

330 Wendy Thomas could not always locate the words Black used: letter sent to *Morningside*, Canadian Broadcasting Corp.

330 'The demure, stylish, convent-educated young ladies of Lima': ALIP, p. 55.

331 'Look, I thought I was really rather positive about most people': CB.

331 [Footnote] 'Hal Jackman and I had this contest about who could put the more pompous remark into it': CB.

331 'He's smarter than most of the people he deals with': Hal Jackman, interview with the author.

331 'Conrad has a tremendous sense of humour': Phil Lind, interview with the author.

331 'infuriated Mulroney': PW.

331 'He cannot imagine why he gave Conrad the membership in the Privy Council': *Ibid.*

332 'I'm going to be writing my own memoirs': Brian Mulroney, interview with the author.

332 [Footnote] 'To Allan, Let peace break out. Conrad': Allan Fotheringham, interview with the author.

333 'only took him by the shoulders': Author correspondence with Jean A. Roy, agent of Maurice Richard, 30 March 1994.

333 'His contacts with his fellow students were limited': letter to *Financial Post*, 2 November 1993.

333 'Friendship and gratitude remain my attitudes to Laurier LaPierre': letter to *Financial Post*, dated 15 November 1993.

334 'the curtain came down to generous applause': ALIP, p. 32.

335 'Black was not, as he claims in his autobiography, "president of the club" ': letter to *The Charlatan*, dated 13 January 1994.

335 'While I was aware of the planning of the programme': *The Charlatan*, 11 January 1994.

335 'On the things that I wanted to set the record straight on': CB.

336 'The fact is I like to mix it up with people': *Morningside*, Canadian Broadcasting Corp., 29 October 1993.

336 'You know, in newsrooms around Canada, Conrad is not an object of a lot of affection': William Thorsell, interview with the author.

336 'We need look no further than your own record as a journalist': *Saturday Night*, May 1991.

336 'Any competent writer or commentator can inflict all the damage he wants': Conrad Black, speech to Canadian Association of Journalists, Ottawa, 8 April 1994.

337 'It's a profit centre for me': CB.

337 'Anyone who has witnessed, as I have': *Ibid.*

337 'it would be a retrograde step': Conrad Black, speech to Canadian Association of Journalists, Ottawa, 8 April 1994.

337 'Conrad took it on the chin': Peregrine Worsthorne, interview with the author.

338 'Perry went on TV for night after night afterwards': CB.

338 'I didn't want to grovel to another newspaper': *Ibid.*

338 'really had a hate-on for him': Peter Atkinson, interview with the author.

339 'They very quickly responded': *Ibid.*

339 'It's when [the press] don't set out the facts': *Ibid.*

341 'Conrad felt humiliated': John Fraser, interview with the author.

341 'In the midst of this book': Conrad Black, speech to Canadian Friends of the Hebrew University of Jerusalem, Toronto, 9 December 1990.

341 'How do you like that great patch-up job I've done': John Fraser, interview with the author.

342 'Any respect I had for him as an intellectual': Ron Graham, interview with the author.

342 'The reason I think the Graham and Black thing is really intriguing': John Fraser, interview with the author.

343 'In effect what [Graham] was saying': CB.

343 'I sort of gave him a merry "Hello" ': Ron Graham, interview with the author.

343 'That, I am afraid, is illustrative of what I was dealing with': CB.

344 'wrote that I was a submarine mutant': Conrad Black, speech to Canadian Friends of the Hebrew University of Jerusalem, Toronto, 9 December 1990.

345 'driven by economics': William Thorsell, interview with the author.

346   'It's a real tear-jerker, isn't it?': CB.

346   'I think it's nonsense to say he has financial clout that causes them to cave in': Peter Atkinson, interview with the author.

14   Absolute Bunkum from A to Z

The principal sources for this chapter include uncorrected proofs of *Hansard* reports from the Senate Select Committee on Certain Aspects of Foreign Ownership Decisions in Relation to the Print Media.

p. 348   'just an Australian sleeve issue': *Lateline*, Australian Broadcasting Corp., 22 November 1993.

348–9   Conrad Black's descriptions of Paul Keating and John Hewson: Conrad Black, *A Life in Progress*, pp. 453–4, Random House Australia, 1993.

349   'might be disposed to support': *Sydney Morning Herald*, 26 November 1993.

349   'The word "balanced" was in quotes by me': *Hansard*, pp. 646, 650.

350   '[Hewson] is the guilty man – the person who has made the deal that would shovel national interests to one side': *Sydney Morning Herald*, 26 November 1993.

350   'was the question of accuracy and reporting': *Lateline*, Australian Broadcasting Corp., 29 November 1993.

350   'I hope you will take me at my word': *Hansard*, p. 685.

351   establish himself as a 'personality': CB.

351   'What Conrad Black Said': *Sydney Morning Herald*, 22 April 1993.

351   'The fact is, it could have been better edited in Australia': CB.

352   'The spurious, ghoulish and malevolent coverage': *Sydney Morning Herald*, 26 November 1993.

352   'Mr Keating made the point that': Conrad Black, submission to senate inquiry, 20 January 1994.

352   'Well, I am Prime Minister': *The Australian*, 25 June 1993.

352   'very difficult position': *Ibid.*, p. 195.

353   'Without a doubt it was one of the most maliciously put together': *Sydney Morning Herald*, 25 November 1993.

353   'more attention than we did': *The Australian*, 20 November 1993.

353   'That is a conspiracy between elements of the Australian

Broadcasting Corporation': *The Bulletin*, 30 November 1993.

355 'I have often been described as a colonial': Transcript of John Fairfax Holdings annual meeting, 18 November 1993.

356 'What do you people expect me to do?': *The Australian*, 19 November 1993.

358 'against the excessive appetites of the labour unions': Conrad Black, *A Life In Progress*, p. 448, Random House Australia, 1993.

358 'Well, that's Conrad': *Sydney Morning Herald*, 30 November 1993.

358 'John Hewson has made it very clear': *Lateline*, Australian Broadcasting Corp., 29 November 1993.

358 'All I can say is that he shows a complete ignorance of Australian politics': *The Australian*, 29 November 1993.

359 '*What* is controversial about that?': CB.

359 'that foreign ownership concerns below thirty-five per cent': *PM*, Australian Broadcasting Corp. Radio, 21 April 1993.

359 Trevor Kennedy . . . agrees that Kerin did give the unmistakable impression: Trevor Kennedy, interview with the author.

360 'Mr Black prefers to impute inaccurate recollection rather than mendacity': *Sydney Morning Herald*, 24 April 1993.

360 'Conrad Black has a monumental problem': *The Bulletin*, 10 May 1994.

360 'The whole thing is so absurd': CB.

360 'The government will not countenance': Treasury press release, 20 April 1993.

361 'a corporate fatted calf': Conrad Black, submission to senate inquiry, 20 January 1994.

362 part of an international conspiracy to plunge the world into a 'dark age': Submission to senate inquiry by Citizens Electoral Councils of Australia, 27 April 1994.

362 'Black is a man who is an extraordinary egoist': *Hansard*, p. 137.

363 'As everyone who knows him is aware': *Ibid.*, p. 657.

363 'He is an urbane character': *Ibid.*, p. 163.

363 'At the obvious risk of disadvantaging myself at the hands of Mr Black': *Ibid.*, p. 523.

365 '[Hawke] despite being unimpressed with me at our meeting':

Ibid., p. 656.

365 'he simply cannot be relied upon': *Ibid.*, p. 746.

365 'I did not hear anything more from him': *Ibid.*, p. 748.

366 'What possesses Bob Hawke to carry on in this asinine fashion': *Sydney Morning Herald*, 23 April 1994.

367 'simply an exercise in media damage control': Report of the Senate Select Committee on Certain Aspects of Foreign Ownership Decisions in Relation to the Print Media, June 1994.

367 'I thought that was a scream': CB.

367 'Black's writings and interviews, however much he subsequently sought to disguise the nakedness of the arrangement': Report of the Senate Select Committee on Certain Aspects of Foreign Ownership Decisions in Relation to the Print Media, June 1994.

368 'Relevant chapters of *A Life in Progress*': *Sydney Morning Herald*, 30 November 1993.

368 'The one thing I've learned from Deng Xiaoping': CB.

15   The Price of Success

p. 369 'How do I look?': *Political Memoirs*, produced by MCTV, first broadcast 5 December 1993.

369 'in the sort of life she now leads with Conrad': Miriam Gross, interview with the author.

369 'Since my marriage, I have no longer attended editorial conferences': Catherine Ostler, 'Sleeping with the Enemy', *Tatler*, February 1993.

370 'He's sort of a funny guy': CB.

370 'He's a plunger by nature': *Ibid.*

371 'I'm a great admirer of his': Rupert Murdoch, interview with the author.

371 'someone will come and take it away from him': *Ibid.*

371 'Much more than vast': *Spectator*, 23 October 1993.

372 'The argument that newspaper price increases have been excessive': *Daily Telegraph*, 8 September 1993.

373 'took the quality premium away from the price': *Financial Times*, 6 January 1995.

373 'The *Telegraph* usually cuts the figure of a Queen Mary among

national daily newspapers': *Independent on Sunday*, 26 June 1994.

374 'If people want to go on concentrating on what impact it will have on the *Independent*': Andrew Knight, interview with the author.

374 'his numerous spear-carriers': CB.

374 'They'll hang in for a while, but I don't think they'll get anywhere': *Ibid.*

374 'The scary thing is if they fired the editor': *Ibid.*

375 'It, finally, belatedly, dawned on Murdoch's lackeys': *Ibid.*

376 'As far as the MMC is concerned': DC.

376 'We're not interested in buying properties as properties': CB.

376 'The well has run dry': CB, John Fraser, interview with the author.

377 'Conrad calls him "The Refrigerator" ': John Fraser, interview with the author.

378 'I said that we couldn't agree to the budget': CB.

378 'It was a very necessary enema': John Fraser, interview with the author.

379 'The fact is *Saturday Night* should be very close to break-even this year': CB.

379 'Conrad, in fact, has been the best proprietor': John Fraser, interview with the author.

380 'That's a telephone call you will get': Leonard Shaykin, interview with the author.

380 'After you lose your enamour of the *Daily News*': *Ibid.*

380 'We were in this kind of nondescript boardroom': DR.

381 'Conrad was the logical buyer': Leonard Shaykin, interview with the author.

382 'Then there's the style thing': DR.

383 'For such an architecturally well-endowed city': *Chicago Tribune*, 18 September 1994.

383 'From my perspective, he's been very fair and very rational': Lauren Fine, interview with the author.

384 'If you produce good newspapers, you don't need to cut the price': *Financial Times*, 6 January 1995.

385 'We're basically buying dimes for nickels': *Financial Post*, February 23 1995.

385 'too old to be called a "whiz kid' ': CB.

385 Conrad Black and Rupert Murdoch at Davos: Tape of interview by Joanne Gray, *Bloomberg Business News*.

387 'no right to control John Fairfax': *A Current Affair*, Nine Network, quoted in *The Australian*, 17 February 1995.

387 'It's nothing to do with personalities': DC.

389 'In my position I move around': CB.

389 'You always have a military analogy for what you're doing': *Ibid.*

Epilogue   Being Black

p. 391 'exceedingly mundane things': CB.

391 'For the most part they are just snippets of things': *Ibid.*

391 'You see, there's Napoleon after Waterloo': *Ibid.*

392 'In an ideal world maybe I would have no peer': *Ibid.*

394 'We got millions and millions of pounds': *Ibid.*

395 'The press is no place to make an opening shot': *Financial Times*, 2 May 1995.

396 'That's a perfectly legitimate question I often put myself': CB.

396 'He does seem to lead a lifestyle': Peter Munk, interview with the author.

396 'By those criteria, I suppose I should aspire to have an absolutely *blank* tombstone': *Political Memoirs*, produced by MCTV, first broadcast 5 December 1993.

397 'Most of what goes on is a bit of a game': CB.

397 'The Stock Exchange is a poor substitute for the Holy Grail': Conrad Black, speech to Harvard Business School Club of Toronto, 16 September 1992.

397 'I find his views are engaging': William F. Buckley, interview with the author.

397 'I think he's first and foremost an intellectual': Peter White, interview with the author.

398 'I don't spend all my time just chatting with people': CB.

398 'I'm not interested in popularity': *Ibid.*

399 'There's a terrible amount of self-righteous claptrap': *Chicago Tribune*, 18 September 1994.

399 'These kids should do what they want': CB.

400 'He's on a roll': Joanna Black, interview with the author.

400 'It's just what he gets off on': Hal Jackman, interview with the author.

400 'If you want to be rich, you've got to do it once': CB.

Select Bibliography

Amiel, Barbara, *Confessions*, Macmillan of Canada, 1980.

Barry, Paul, *The Rise and Rise of Kerry Packer*, Bantam (Australia), 1993.

Best, Patricia and Shortell, Ann, *The Brass Ring*, Random House, Toronto, 1988.

Black, Conrad, *Duplessis*, McClelland and Stewart, Toronto, 1977.

Black, Conrad, *A Life in Progress*, Key Porter Books, Toronto, 1993.

Burnham, Lord, *Peterborough Court: The story of the* Daily Telegraph, Cassell & Co, London, 1955.

Chisholm, Anne and Davie, Michael, *Beaverbrook, A Life*, Hutchinson, London, 1992.

Coleridge, Nicholas, *Paper Tigers*, William Heinemann Ltd, London, 1993.

Cook, Peter, *Massey at the Brink*, Collins, Toronto, 1981.

Fairfax, James, *My Regards to Broadway*, Angus and Robertson, Pymble, Australia, 1991.

Fraser, John, *Telling Tales*, Collins, Toronto, 1986.

Garland, Nicholas, *Not Many Dead: Journal of a Year in Fleet Street*, Hutchinson, London, 1990.

Goodhart, David and Wintour, Patrick, *Eddie Shah and the Newspaper Revolution*, Coronet Books, London, 1986.

Hart-Davis, Duff, *The House The Berrys Built*, Stoddart, Toronto, 1990.

Hayes, David, *Power and Influence*, Key Porter Books, Toronto, 1992.

Leapman, Michael, *Treacherous Estate*, Hodder and Stoughton, London, 1992.

Martin, Roderick, *New Technology and Industrial Relations in Fleet Street*, Clarendon Press, London, 1981.

Newman, Peter C., *The Establishment Man*, McClelland and Stewart, Toronto, 1982.

Riley, C. S., memoir published by family, 1971.

Rohmer, Richard, *E. P. Taylor: The biography of Edward Plunket Taylor*, McClelland and Stewart, Toronto, 1978.

Ryan, Colleen and Burge, Glen, *Corporate Cannibals*, William Heinemann Australia, 1992.

Shawcross, William, *Murdoch*, Simon and Schuster, New York, 1992.

Snoddy, Raymond, *The Good, The Bad, and The Unacceptable*, Faber and Faber, London, 1992.

Sonmor, Jean, *The Little Paper That Grew*, Toronto Sun Publishing, Toronto, 1993.

Souter, Gavin, *Heralds and Angels: the House of Fairfax 1841–1992*, Penguin Books Australia, 1992.

Wintour, Charles, *The Rise and Fall of Fleet Street*, Hutchinson, London, 1989.

Worsthorne, Peregrine, *Tricks of Memory*, Weidenfeld & Nicolson, London 1993.

Copyright Acknowledgements

Thanks are due to the following for permission to reproduce photographs: Front cover: © Patrick Fordham; page 2 *top* and *bottom*: © Brian Willer; page 3 *top*: Peter Bregg © *Maclean's*; page 3 *bottom*: Lynn Farrell © *Financial Post*; page 4 *top*: © Joanna Black; page 4 *bottom left*: Popperfoto; page 4 *bottom right*: © Brian Willer; page 5 *top*: Paul Armiger © The Daily Telegraph plc 1988; page 5 *bottom left*: Popperfoto; page 5 *bottom right*: Press Association; page 6 *top*: Dan Landau © *Jerusalem Post*; page 6 *bottom left*: Kobi Kalmanovitch © *Jerusalem Post*; page 6 *bottom right*: Nitsan Shorer © *Jerusalem Post*; page 7 *top left*: Popperfoto; page 7 *top right*: C. Morris © *Financial Post*; page 7 *bottom*: Press Association; page 8: courtesy of the *Independent* and Saatchi & Saatchi Advertising Ltd; page 9: The Associated Press Ltd; page 10 *top*: Hugo Burnand © *Tatler*, The Condé Nast Publications Ltd; page 10 *bottom* and page 11 *top*: Peter Bregg © *Maclean's*; page 11 *bottom*: Brian Condron © *Financial Post*; page 12: Popperfoto.

The author is grateful for permission to quote extracts from *A Life in Progress* by Conrad Black, published by Key Porter Books Limited, Toronto, Ontario. Copyright © 1993. And by Random House Australia, 1993.

The photographs on page 1 *top* and *bottom* are taken from *C.S. Riley* by Conrad Stephenson Riley, Toronto, 1971.

Every effort has been made to trace holders of copyright. If any inadvertent omissions have occurred, the publishers will be glad to rectify them in future editions.

Index